Reconstructing Spain

**Published by the Cañada Blanch
Centre for Contemporary Spanish Studies
in conjunction with Routledge / Taylor & Francis**

1   Francisco J. Romero Salvadó, *Spain 1914–1918: Between War and Revolution.*
2   David Wingeate Pike, *Spaniards in the Holocaust: Mauthausen, the Horror on the Danube.*
3   Herbert Rutledge Southworth, *Conspiracy and the Spanish Civil War: The Brainwashing of Francisco Franco.*
4   Angel Smith (editor), *Red Barcelona: Social Protest and Labour Mobilization in the Twentieth Century.*
5   Angela Jackson, *British Women and the Spanish Civil War.*
6   Kathleen Richmond, *Women and Spanish Fascism: The Women's Section of the Falange, 1934–1959.*
7   Chris Ealham, *Class, Culture and Conflict in Barcelona, 1898–1937.*
8   Julián Casanova, *Anarchism, the Republic and Civil War in Spain, 1931–1939.*
9   Montserrat Guibernau, *Catalan Nationalism: Francoism, Transition and Democracy.*
10 Richard Baxell, *British Volunteers in the Spanish Civil War: The British Battalion in the International Brigades, 1936–1939.*
11 Hilari Raguer, *The Catholic Church and the Spanish Civil War.*
12 Richard Wigg, *Churchill and Spain: The Survival of the Franco Regime, 1940–45.*
13 Nicholas Coni, *Medicine and the Spanish Civil War.*
14 Diego Muro, *Ethnicity and Violence: The Case of Radical Basque Nationalism.*
15 Francisco J. Romero Salvadó, *Spain's Revolutionary Crisis, 1917–1923.*
16 Peter Anderson, *The Francoist Military Trials: Terror and Complicity, 1939–1945.*

What are the roots that clutch, what branches grow
Out of this stony rubbish?

T.S. Eliot, *The Waste Land*

Reconstructing Spain
Cultural Heritage and Memory after Civil War

Dacia Viejo-Rose

sussex
ACADEMIC
PRESS
Brighton • Chicago • Toronto

Cañada Blanch Centre
for Contemporary
Spanish Studies

2 4 6 8 10 9 7 5 3

First published 2011 in hardcover, reprinted in paperback 2014 in Great Britain by
SUSSEX ACADEMIC PRESS
PO Box 139
Eastbourne BN24 9BP

and in the United States of America by
SUSSEX ACADEMIC PRESS
Independent Publishers Group
814 North Franklin Street, Chicago, IL 60610

and in Canada by
SUSSEX ACADEMIC PRESS (CANADA)
8000 Bathurst Street, Unit 1, PO Box 30010, Vaughan, Ontario L4J 0C6

British Library Cataloguing in Publication Data
A CIP catalogue record for this book is available from the British Library.

Library of Congress Cataloging-in-Publication Data
Viejo-Rose, Dacia.
   Reconstructing Spain : cultural heritage and memory after civil war / Dacia Viejo-Rose.
      p.   cm.
   Includes bibliographical references and index.
   ISBN 978-1-84519-435-2 (h/c : alk. paper)
   ISBN 978-1-84519-629-5 (p/b : alk. paper)
   1. Spain—Cultural policy—History—20th century. 2. Cultural property—Government policy—Spain—History—20th century. 3. Cultural property—Protection—Spain—History—20th century. 4. Spain—History—Civil War, 1936–1939—Influence. I. Title.
   DP23.V54   2011
   363.6'90946–dc22

                                                                            2010041530

Typeset and designed by Sussex Academic Press, Brighton & Eastbourne.
Printed by TJ International, Padstow, Cornwall.
This book is printed on acid-free paper.

Contents

List of Figures, Tables, and Text Boxes

Sources for all reproduced material are given *in situ* in the text. Many of the unsourced illustrations are the author's personal photographs. CP indicates that the figure is also reproduced in the colour plate section, after page 98.

Figures

Tables

Text Boxes

Acknowledgements

Among the most positive experiences of the research project here presented have been the numerous persons that I encountered who were extremely supportive and generous with their time and thoughts. For their encouragement and for sharing their insights at the early stage of my research I am grateful to José Álvarez Junco, Paloma Fernández Aguilar, Carlos Sambricio, and Alison Sinclair. Ángel Llorente Hernández was exceptionally generous sharing material from his own research, especially on monuments to the fallen, indicating further contacts and archives to explore.

For assistance in accessing their archives, locating and copying documents, I thank the librarians and archivists at the following institutions in Spain: Biblioteca Nacional de España (Madrid), Colegio Oficial de Arquitectos de Madrid, Archivo General de la Administración (Alcalá de Henares), Archivo Histórico Nacional (Madrid), Archivo General de la Guerra Civil Española (Salamanca), Casa de Velázquez (Madrid), Centro de Investigaciones Sociológicas (Madrid), Bibliotecas de la Universidad Complutense (Madrid), Consejería de Medio Ambiente y Ordenación del Territorio (Madrid), and the Archivo Regional de Madrid. In particular I thank Mayte Ríos Reviejo of the maps section of the Biblioteca Nacional for the interest she showed in my research – often hunting down documents on her own initiative – and Yela Carreira Delgado for allowing me to use the library of the faculty of Geografía e Historía at Madrid's Universidad Complutense during my period of fieldwork. At the Consejo Superior de Investigaciones Científicas (Madrid) Carmen Ortíz, Cristina Sánchez-Carretero, and Miguel Cabañas Bravo generously shared their thoughts and experience. Jordi Carulla kindly allowed me to use some images from his marvellous collection of publicity and propaganda posters from Spain and Catalonia. The psychiatrist Enrique González Duro generously greeted me in his home and not only shared with me his thoughts on the psychological aspects of the regime and its impact on Spanish society but also gave me copies of his books. For sharing their personal memories and insights I would like to thank Tony Lyons, Pedro Caba Martín, Julia Estévez Plaza, and Carmen Negrín.

For my research in Gernika I am indebted to the warm reception I received from María Oianguren Idígoras, Director of Gernika Gogoratuz, and for her guidance on people to contact. Both she, Ana Teresa Núñez of the Archive of the Bombing at the Gernika Peace Museum, and Iratxe Momoitio, Director of the Museum helped me find my way through their collections. Juan Gutiérrez was also a great help recounting the stories and histories of peace work in Gernika and offering me a guided tour of Gernika's hidden landscape, with its emotional triggers and points of dissonance. Luis Iriondo kindly met with me during the 70th anniversary of the bombing, when he was much sought after as a spokesperson for the survivors, and shared his memories of Gernika before and after the war. At the *Ayuntamiento* of Gernika Arantza Sarduy helped me locate documents about the monuments of Gernika and the Director of *Kultur Etxea*, Ricardo Abaunza, provided me with important insights into the current monument-scape of Gernika and generously gave me publications from his office shelves. In Gernika I would also like to warmly thank José Ángel Etxaniz Ortúñez (Txato) who through e-mails and long conversations shared with me his enthusiasm and experience as well as the work he has been doing over the years as a member of the local history association Gernikazarra. An unexpectedly rich source of information was Nieves Aguirre Nabea at the Hotel Gernika who lent me books, referred me to television and radio programs and shared the stories and memories of post-war Gernika that she had heard from her parents, aunts and uncles. Throughout my stays in the town Gernikans were generous in sharing their personal insights and memories, including bus drivers, hotel receptionists, and tourist office personnel.

At Cambridge I am indebted foremost to Marie Louise Stig Sørensen for her guidance, gentle critiques and steady encouragement. This research project was profoundly interdisciplinary in nature and I am grateful to Brendan Simms, Mary Jacobus and Charles Jones for their feedback, interest and support, especially their firm backing of the Cambridge Post-Conflict and Post-Crisis Group. In London I would like to thank Paul Preston at the London School of Economics for inviting me to present part of my work at a seminar organized by the Cañada Blanch Centre for Contemporary Spanish Studies and for sending me references to relevant publications.

For my research I received much appreciated financial support from the Cambridge European Trust, Trend Fund, Dorothy Garrod Fund and Clare Hall for research and fieldwork. Clare Hall became a supportive work environment thanks to interest shown by Bobbie Wells, Rosemary Luff, by visiting fellows Professors Josep Pico and José M. González García, and by the good-cheer and friendly banter of the porters and kitchen staff. The Centre for Research in the Arts, Social Sciences and Humanities (CRASSH) at the University of Cambridge also proved to be an invaluable hub where stimulating conversations and practical support for various cross-disciplinary initiatives was always to be found. Part of the research and all of the writing up stages of this book were carried out as part of my work on the four-year research project "Cultural Heritage and the Reconstruction of Identities after Conflict" (CRIC: www.cric.arch.cam.ac.uk) which is funded through a EU Seventh Framework Funding Scheme (call identifier: FP7-SSH-2007-1, project number 217411). This research project began in 2008 and will continue until 2012 during which time period the findings will be published. The final stages of turning this research into a book were carried out while I was a College Research Associate at Jesus College, Cambridge. I would like to thank my colleagues on the CRIC project as well as the Fellows of Jesus College for all of the inspiring discussions that we shared and for the challenging questions that they put to me.

The PhD process can resemble the trials of a decathlon ending in a marathon as a test of endurance but also for the necessary moments of solitude. This run was made infinitely more endurable and rewarding by those colleagues and friends who shared the journey in various ways: Elizabeth Mills, Rosa Poetes, Sylvia Karastathi, Charlotte Andrews, Kristen Eglinton, Kara Blackmore, Paola Filippucci, Maja Petrovic-Šteger, Uta Staiger, Mathilde Allair, Andreja Fajgelj, Valerie Teller and Antonio Molina-Vázquez. I am also thankful for the help of José Velázquez, Elena Pérez Álvaro and Hannah Merron who sent me their photographs of various monuments and memorials. The one fellow traveler on this road without whose constant enthusiasm and encouragement as well as significant practical help, lengthy conversations, editing, and occasional robust pushes, this book would certainly be the worse has been Benjamin Morris.

Finally, I would like to thank my two steady guides throughout this project. Isadora Rose for sharing her substantial expertise in carrying out research in Spain; her guidance through the maze of Spanish archives was for me the equivalent of Ariadne's ball of string helping me find my way and making the process far smoother, swifter, and more amenable than it otherwise would have been. Eugenio Viejo was an equally valuable guide in helping me begin to unravel the complexities of Spain's difficult twentieth century. As well as guides both likewise acted as research assistants, editors, and most importantly of all unwavering cheerleaders throughout. Thank you.

Any mistakes in this work are only my own; that of value is dedicated to the memory of Manuel de la Escalera, Tony Lyons, Carlos Calisto Martínez, Frances Estévez Plaza, to an anonymous Bosnian man who reminded me of my own heritage, and to all those on whose shoulders it fell to fight the 'good fight' of the post-war.

Cambridge, 8 August 2010

Author's Preface

The seeds for this study were sown in the summer of 2002 while I was working at the Cultural Policies for Development Unit in UNESCO. After spending much of the previous year attending meetings and reading project reports concerning UNESCO's involvement in the Dayton Agreements for the former Yugoslavia[1] – in particular the organization's involvement in the reconstruction of cultural heritage in Bosnia and Herzegovina – I decided to travel to Serbia, Bosnia and Herzegovina.

The projects created at UNESCO expressed confidence that by rebuilding and restoring heritage, especially the more symbolic sites, a restoration of the former society, repeatedly described as one of harmonious multiculturalism, could be achieved. Yet there seemed to be an underlying contradiction. While I had come to appreciate the potential of cultural heritage to bring communities together through examining other projects, in this war it had been used as part of a battle cry, the wartime discourse being laden with conflicting claims about the past. If this was the case, how could rebuilding these contentious sites, previously utilized to signify the threat of the enemy, be drawn on to reconcile communities?

The purpose of my journey in June 2002 was to see for myself the role that culture, heritage and the arts were playing in the reconstruction. Throughout my time there I spoke with museum professionals, consulted with personnel from international organizations involved in cultural projects, and discussed issues with members of the local population collaborating with these professionals. I also had many informal conversations with young people in Mostar, Sarajevo and Belgrade and was able to attend a number of ceremonies inaugurating reconstruction projects. The observations and conversations from this trip helped me to see more clearly the vast chasm that existed between the discursive aims set out by reconstruction projects and the on-site realities. For example, the reconstruction of the Mostar Bridge did not seem to be reconstructing, by extension, the links of trust and communication between the town's communities. Indeed, seven years on Mostar remained a divided city with segregated schooling, two football teams (Zrinjski supported by Croats and Velež supported mostly by Bosniaks),[2] and two universities (Sveučilište u Mostaru and Džemal Bijedić) in a city with an estimated population of 128,448. Not only were the Bosniak and Croat communities not integrating but the Serb community had not returned.[3] Furthermore, the circumstances of the bridge's destruction – by Croatian troops during the war – and the context of the reconstruction – by the international community – had added further symbolic dimensions to the site.

These observations gave rise to some questions: How had the meaning of heritage sites been transformed by the war? Could they now relay antagonistic rather than reconciliatory messages? How could these new meanings be acknowledged, understood, and addressed in the reconstruction process? What memories was the reconstruction cementing? Are the timeframes that guide reconstruction projects compatible with the periods of time that individuals and communities need to mourn and rebuild? On my return to UNESCO, I spoke with a number of colleagues directly involved in these projects and expressed my doubts: in the best case scenario their projects were not achieving what they set out to do, in the worst case they might be producing the opposite effect. The responses I received all coincided in acknowledging the absence of a body of research for professionals to turn to when developing policies and projects in this type of work.

These questions led me to embark on postgraduate research. From 2002 to 2003 I studied with Professor Patrick Boylan at City University, London. My research focused on Bosnia and examined the potential of cultural heritage as a mediating tool in post-conflict reconstruction processes. The conclusions of this work proposed consultative and participatory project designs that incorporated multiple interpretations of heritage sites. A concern that remained, however, was what I perceived as the potential for cultural heritage to be an instrument in prolonging violence, particularly in the case of internal or civil wars. This bore implications for the reconstruction process as well as for societal reconciliation in the middle and longterm. Further questions about changes in the use and valuation of heritage over time were also raised during a collaboration with the French NGO Patrimoine Sans Frontières in Voskopojë, Albania. These issues led to the investigation at hand. In order to observe the evolution of a reconstruction process through time and to see how what was once presented as common heritage is reinterpreted, I chose a historical case study and a civil war.

The experience of researching Bosnia had shown me that conflicts and their aftermaths are so complex that it would be preferable to study a case where the language and culture were familiar to me. I dedicated my first round of fieldwork to Spain and discovered that the national archives contained important materials that had not been thoroughly studied. Reading through the documents also confirmed how important it was to have a profound knowledge of the language in order to be able to read between the lines, appreciate the significance of subtexts and the choice of words, and glean what was *not* being said. For this reason I decided to adopt a case study approach, focusing on Spain as a case study from which to draw empirical material and contribute to understanding reconstruction as a multifaceted process with far-reaching consequences.

At this stage, new research questions had emerged: What are the motivations of those who rebuild cultural heritage in the wake of civil wars? What do they seek to achieve and how? Are these aims ever successfully reached? How does it affect the feeling (*zeitgeist*), memory and identity associated with a place in the medium and long term?

The objective partisan

In 1938 George Orwell wrote in the *Times Literary Supplement* that "everyone that writes about the Spanish War writes as a partisan"[4] (in Rankin 2007: 5). One of the challenges throughout this research has been to question my own acquired knowledge. Often, I have had to second-guess myself in order to ascertain how much of what I 'knew' was borne out by ascertainable facts and how much was itself the product of myth-making and inherited 'memory'. Having left Spain as a child in 1979, much of this acquired knowledge was gleaned from conversations with my father, his friends, and from listening in on their discussions over the years. Among these friends were people who had spent up to 20 years in Franco's jails as political prisoners. At the same time as this legacy posed a challenge to me, it also convinced me that a form of group consciousness, memory or experience is transmitted from one generation to the next, and has powerful formative effects on younger generations, shaping their views of past and present and their expectations for the future. The methodological issue here is reflexivity, in particular reflexive ethnography (Aull Davies 2008; Alvesson and Skoldberg 2000). I have tried to balance my position thorough archival work and analysis; I can only hope that my unavoidably partisan stance has not impeded me from untangling the complex process of reconstruction of Spain's cultural heritage, the meanings and memories that were woven together in the process but has added richness to the assessment.

The process of dismantling and contesting my own acquired knowledge has allowed me to appreciate how effectively a collective 'memory' or understanding of past events can be constructed and transmitted. As an example, when I decided to focus on the case of Gernika, I did so 'knowing' that the town had been bombed by the German Condor Legion under Franco's orders and that it had been the first bombing of civilians. Throughout the research I learned that Italian planes also took part in the bombing, that there is no proof that a direct order was given by Franco – though he was ultimately responsible as head of the Nationalist government and army – and that it was not the first aerial bombing of civilians. Constantly, I was revising my own assumptions and revisiting the myths that I had accepted as fact.

However, I am also an 'outsider' to Spain; having left only four years after Franco's death – and despite annual summer visits and two years, 1997–99, when I returned to live in Madrid. This long-distance relationship with Spain means that I did not live through the political transition nor the worst years of ETA's (Euzkadi Ta Askatasuna/Basque Country and Liberty) terrorism – and the government's counter-terrorism. In the Basque Country I was doubly an outsider, both from Spain and from the Basque Country. This also meant that the degree to which the threat of violence affects everyday life in the region came as a shock during my fieldwork there: the *Ertzaintza* (Basque police) walking the streets of San Sebastian (Donostia) heavily armed and wearing black ski masks; the convoy of civil guards that pulled the Madrid–Bilbao bus over on the highway and paced the aisle of the bus, weapons hanging from their shoulders, demanding to see the identity papers of every young man.

Notes on language and translation

As far as possible I have worked with the original texts in Spanish and translated them into English myself. I have translated as literally as possible in an attempt to convey the tone of what is being said. The use of language during the Franco period – in public documents, publications and speeches – was particular, elaborated with long sentences full of flourishes and twists. The translations try to convey this, occasionally sacrificing syntax, in order to put across the tone of the rhetoric. In approaching my translations in this way I wish to convey the density of a discourse, with its many layers of meaning and subtext communicated through particular turns of phrase and choice of words. If the reader can begin to intuit these layers then perhaps the odd English of the translations will be justified.

Another language issue that came up is the difference between English, Castilian and Basque spellings of place names. I decided to prioritize English spellings and when these do not exist I have used the local spelling. The most difficult decision involved the various spellings of the town of Gernika (Basque), Guernica (English and Castilian) and Guernika (a combination of the two that occasionally crops up).[5] In the end, I decided to use the Basque spelling to refer to the town and the English/Castilian spelling to refer to Picasso's painting. There was no political motivation behind this choice, only a desire to clearly distinguish between the town and the painting. However, in citing other texts, the spelling that appears in the original has been maintained.

The idea of researching Spain first took root on a summer morning in Sarajevo when, waiting for a press conference to begin, an elderly man sat down next to me and handed me a piece of paper from a stack he was distributing. To my surprise, this flier was a call to remember the International Brigades that had fought in Spain and a request for funds to publish a book on the subject. It turned out that this Bosnian man had been a *brigadista* and before the press conference began we were able to exchange a few enthusiastic words in Spanish. Thus, the Spanish Civil War found me in Bosnia and there I thought it might not be a bad idea to tend to my own garden before poking around in those of others.

Images used on the cover

FRONT: Visit to Gernika of Moreno Torrres, Director General of *Regiones Devastadas* (España, Ministerio de Cultura, Archivo General de la Administración, F/04246); ceremony to the 'Glorious Fallen' in Madrid's Complutense University, 1941 (España, Ministerio de Cultura, Archivo General de la Administración, 1941, F/04087, detail). BACK: "All to Reconstruct Spain!", unsigned Spanish postwar poster produced by the *Servicio Nacional de Propaganda*, printed by Gráficas Laborde y Labayen, Tolosa Guipuzcoa, 1939–1942 (Ministerio de Cultura, Centro Documental de la Memoria Histórica, PS-CARTELES, 1975); cover of the second issue of the magazine *Reconstrucción* from May 1940.

The Cañada Blanch Centre for Contemporary Spanish Studies

In the 1960s, the most important initiative in the cultural and academic relations between Spain and the United Kingdom was launched by a Valencian fruit importer in London. The creation by Vicente Cañada Blanch of the Anglo-Spanish Cultural Foundation has subsequently benefited large numbers of Spanish and British scholars at various levels. Thanks to the generosity of Vicente Cañada Blanch, thousands of Spanish schoolchildren have been educated at the secondary school in West London that bears his name. At the same time, many British and Spanish university students have benefited from the exchange scholarships which fostered cultural and scientific exchanges between the two countries. Some of the most important historical, artistic and literary work on Spanish topics to be produced in Great Britain was initially made possible by Cañada Blanch scholarships.

Vicente Cañada Blanch was, by inclination, a conservative. When his Foundation was created, the Franco regime was still in the plenitude of its power. Nevertheless, the keynote of the Foundation's activities was always a complete open-mindedness on political issues. This was reflected in the diversity of research projects supported by the Foundation, many of which, in Francoist Spain, would have been regarded as subversive. When the Dictator died, Don Vicente was in his seventy-fifth year. In the two decades following the death of the Dictator, although apparently indestructible, Don Vicente was obliged to husband his energies. Increasingly, the work of the Foundation was carried forward by Miguel Dols whose tireless and imaginative work in London was matched in Spain by that of José María Coll Comín. They were united in the Foundation's spirit of open-minded commitment to fostering research of high quality in pursuit of better Anglo-Spanish cultural relations. Throughout the 1990s, thanks to them, the role of the Foundation grew considerably.

In 1994, in collaboration with the London School of Economics, the Foundation established the Príncipe de Asturias Chair of Contemporary Spanish History and the Cañada Blanch Centre for Contemporary Spanish Studies. It is the particular task of the Cañada Blanch Centre to promote the understanding of twentieth-century Spain through research and teaching of contemporary Spanish history, politics, economy, sociology and culture. The Centre possesses a valuable library and archival centre for specialists in contemporary Spain. This work is carried on through the publications of the doctoral and post-doctoral researchers at the Centre itself and through the many seminars and lectures held at the London School of Economics. While the seminars are the province of the researchers, the lecture cycles have been the forum in which Spanish politicians have been able to address audiences in the United Kingdom.

Since 1998, the Cañada Blanch Centre has published a substantial number of books in collaboration with several different publishers on the subject of contemporary Spanish history and politics. A fruitful partnership with Sussex Academic Press began in 2004 with the publication of Christina Palomares's fascinating work on the origins of the Partido Popular in Spain, *The Quest for Survival after Franco: Moderate Francoism and the Slow Journey to the Polls, 1964–1977*. This was followed in 2007 by Soledad Fox's deeply moving biography of one of the most intriguing women of 1930s Spain, *Constancia de la Mora in War and Exile: International Voice for the Spanish Republic* and Isabelle Rohr's path-breaking study of anti-Semitism in Spain, *The Spanish Right and the Jews, 1898–1945: Antisemitism and Opportunism*; 2008 saw the publication of a revised edition of Richard Wigg's penetrating study of Anglo-Spanish relations during the Second World War, *Churchill and Spain: The Survival of the Franco Regime, 1940–1945* together with *Triumph at Midnight of the Century: A Critical Biography of Arturo Barea*, Michael Eaude's fascinating revaluation of the great Spanish author of *The Forging of a Rebel*.

Our collaboration in 2009 was inaugurated by Gareth Stockey's incisive account of another crucial element in Anglo-Spanish relations, *Gibraltar: A Dagger in the Spine of Spain*. We were especially proud that it was continued by the most distinguished American historian of the Spanish Civil War, Gabriel Jackson. His pioneering work *The Spanish Republic and the Civil War* first published in 1965 and still in print quickly became a classic. The Sussex Academic Press/Cañada Blanch series was greatly privileged to be associated with Professor Jackson's biography of the great Republican war leader, Juan Negrín.

Our publications in 2010 were inaugurated by the fascinating study by Ramon Tremosa i Balcells of the economic future of Catalonia and of the role being played in that future by the region's ports. They were continued with *Catholicism, War and the Foundation of Francoism: The Juventud de Acción Popular in Spain, 1931–1939* by Sid Lowe. This dealt with one of the least known elements on the road to civil war in Spain. The mass Catholic youth movement, the Juventud de Acción Popular, contributed to the polarization of politics within the Second Republic. After the right-wing defeat in the elections of February 1936, a large proportion of its militants went over to the overtly fascist Falange. They played a crucial role in the Falangist militias, both in frontline fighting and in rearguard repression.

This year, 2011, promises to take the series to new heights. Two remarkable and complementary works, Olivia Muñoz Rojas, *Ashes and Granite: Destruction and Reconstruction in the Spanish Civil War and its Aftermath* and Dacia Viejo-Rose, *Reconstructing Spain: Cultural Heritage and Memory after Civil War*, have opened up an entirely new dimension of the study of the early Franco regime and its internal conflicts. They are to be followed by Richard Purkiss's *The Valencian Anarchist Movement, 1918–1936: Democracy, Trade Unions and Political Violence in Spain*; and David Wingeate Pike's *France Divided: The French and the Civil War in Spain*.

Preface by Series Editor Paul Preston

Dacia Viejo-Rose has produced not only an utterly original piece of work that throws unexpected light on the Spanish Civil War and the ensuing Franco dictatorship but also carries broad implications about the role played by cultural heritage in post-conflict reconstruction. Despite the large number of international and civil wars in the last hundred years, there are few works to match this one on the nature of the relationship between conflict and both pre-war and post-war cultural heritage. Dr Viejo-Rose's book is a source of insights into how cultural heritage, a highly symbolic domain, has immense power as a tool in the destruction or construction of memory and therefore of identity. It is used during wars and in their aftermaths first as a target for destruction of sites considered precious to the enemy and then as a weapon in propaganda battles and reconstruction projects. Accordingly, cultural heritage can play a role both in the justification of the prolongation of violence and as a contribution to the process of reconciliation.

The main thrust of the book is the process of reconstruction carried out by the Francoist dictatorship. Much of the destruction that needed to be remedied had been the consequence of the bombing and artillery barrages of the victorious military rebels. Nevertheless, a shattered Spain was attributed by the dictatorship to the destructive instincts of the defeated Republicans. Reconstruction could be used as a propaganda device to smear the vanquished because the regime had control over popular memory through its totalitarian grip on the media and the education system, on public memorials and commemorations as well as the monopoly of choices about what to preserve, rebuild or neglect. The choice of sites for reconstruction was such as to emphasise the Republican role in the destruction.

In its exploration of these issues, *Reconstructing Spain* is startlingly original. Its multi-disciplinary approach allows it analyse various elements of the reconstruction pursued by the Franco dictatorship both in physical and architectural terms as well as through more obviously 'cultural' devices, such as the rewriting of history and the demonization of the defeated. The book not only examines the material destruction of cultural heritage during the civil war but also the equally significant violence of the rhetoric and propaganda campaigns that constructed stereo-types of the Republicans as sub-human criminals. This was consol-idated after the war through the re-writing of historical narratives in order to create a definition of 'true' Spanish heritage that excluded the so-called 'anti-Spain' of the progressive Republic. This 'reconstruction' process continued the violence against the defeated by its endless reiteration that only half of the nation, the victorious half, had any right to, or even continuity with, 'real' Spanish culture, history or values. In this sense, the process of reconstruction carried out by the Franco regime spurned reconciliation and was aimed at the consolidation of the division of Spaniards into victors and vanquished.

Dr Viejo-Rose's analysis is carried via an examination of the rebuilding of historically significant sites and the contemporaneous and subsequent political and ideological exploitation thereof. Several sites subjected to near total destruction, such as Brunete near Madrid, Belchite in Aragón, both destroyed in battle, and the Alcázar of Toledo, destroyed by the Republican siege, are perceptively analysed as is the great symbol of the dictator's triumphalism, the Valle de los Caídos, his gigantic mausoleum at Cuelgamuros near El Escorial. In all of these examples, the wartime violence was cemented into the post-war reconstruction and, in the case of the Valle de los Caídos, in its construction by Republican prisoners used as slave labour. The central example used is the Basque town of Guernica which was annihilated by German bombing raids on 26 April 1937. As a site of huge symbolic importance for the Basque people, Guernica provides a fruitful case for tracing the underlying premises of the Francoist reconstruction process. Dr Viejo-Rose makes an especially subtle analysis of the contradiction between the regime's desire to stamp its image on the rebuilt town and its awareness of the need to show some respect for local architectural traditions.

The book explains the reconstruction of the Franco dictatorship with a wealth of fascinating examples. It is adequately placed in the context of a useful account of pre-1936 cultural heritage and the impact of the Spanish Civil War on Spain's cultural heritage. The impact of this policy is examined in two subsequent periods – the transition to democracy that followed the death of Franco in November 1975 and the period of the early twenty-first century when 'the recovery of historical memory' became a burning and controversial issue in Spanish politics.

The primary sources for this research are impressively wide and varied, ranging from architectural drawings and plans, photographs, paintings, maps, memorials, monuments, built landscapes, cartoons, contemporary news-reels, movies and documentaries, to contemporary newspapers, journals, magazines, project plans, tourist information brochures. The two most thoroughly mined sources are the magazine *Reconstrucción* (*Reconstruction*) and previously unexplored archives of the Franco regime's main reconstruction body the *Dirección General de Regiones Devastadas* (General Directorate for Devastated Regions). The wider secondary reading is very considerable. Dr Viejo-Rose's analysis throughout is sophisticated and nuanced.

The abiding achievement of this remarkably original work is to throw light upon the aftermath of the Spanish Civil War and the Franco dictatorship by showing the long-term destructive effects of both on Spanish cultural heritage. It shows how physical destruction and reconstruction are processes that are part of attempts to remodel history and identity. Although primarily concerned with Spain, both the methodology and the conclusions are widely applicable to the aftermaths of other international and civil wars.

London School of Economics
April 2011

"Cultural heritage in its many different expressions and manifestations, from sites and monuments, through museums and collections to the intangible and oral heritage, has become an increasingly important part of contested identities over recent decades, and in many countries is now seen as a key element of national and regional identities . . . This book is an important and original contribution to a field that is of considerable importance and continuing present-day relevance."

Patrick Boylan,
Professor Emeritus of Heritage Policy and Management,
City University of London

1 Cultural Heritage and Post-Conflict Reconstruction

Purpose, Theory, and Method

Ultimately, the central line of questioning of this volume seeks to understand what role cultural heritage plays in post-conflict reconstruction, whether as a motor for the prolongation of violence or as a resource for building reconciliation. At the beginning there were three points of departure. First, that in order to understand post-conflict reconstruction – the selection of sites and their significance – it is necessary to look back to see how those sites were used during the war and how this use was interpreted then and in the aftermath. The importance of understanding this is that the meaning and symbolism associated with sites can change dramatically as a result of violent conflict and it is precisely in this changed context that reconstruction is carried out. Secondly, in the aftermath of civil wars and contrary to what the word implies, post-conflict *reconstruction* is not always about the restoration of what was there before. This is the case partly because the conflict changes social, urban and power structures and transforms the meaning of places, and partly because of the frequent desire by incumbent leaders to make their mark on the emergent landscape to reflect the new status quo or dominant ideology and to shape memory. Finally, the way that cultural heritage, as a symbolic element, is rebuilt and reincorporated – or not – into the national discourse of a society in the aftermath of civil war has long-term effects, but not necessarily those intended by the authors of the reconstruction.

The research presented here set out to test these premises and discover how they unfolded. It was driven by two main goals: first, to understand the post-conflict reconstruction process in terms of cultural heritage; second, to identify how this process evolves in the medium term and the impact it has on a society's ability to achieve a successful form of reconciliation in the aftermath of civil war. To do this, the study examines the processes of selection, value change and exclusionary dynamics of the reconstruction and the responses it elicits. This research project aspires to inform future reconstruction policy and practice. Its aim demands the question: What kind of impacts will reconstruction interventions have on the future development of the societies in which they have been carried out?

The stories that a society tells itself about its past are constantly woven together, and periodically revised, to meet the changing needs of the present. These narratives, whether presented as myth, memory or history, are often grounded in material heritage: objects and architecture that act as both tangible 'proof' of the stories and as evocative sign-posts, reminders of a common past. Knowledge of these narratives and understanding the codes that the objects stand for contribute to the creation of a landscape, simultaneously physical and symbolic, that nourishes a sense of group identity and cohesion, situating the group within space and time. Individuals, politicians and communities must constantly make choices concerning what remnants of the past to preserve and what to eliminate in the name of development. These decisions both reflect attitudes and support narratives of history and belonging that in turn shape attitudes.

At the most general level the aim of this research is to explore and contribute to our understanding of the relationship between cultural heritage, power and society. In order to do this it is especially revealing to closely examine a context in which circumstances converge to make these links explicit. What makes periods of conflict and acute crisis valuable for study is that they render regularly occurring dynamics more visible (Hoffman and Oliver-Smith 1999: 11). A line from a play by German playwright Hanns Johst (1933, Act 1, Scene 1) often paraphrased as "when I hear the word 'culture', I reach for my gun", can be turned on its head to "when I hear a gun, I reach for my culture".[1] Periods of crisis within societies, whether economic or political, often call into question the very character of the society: the behaviour, attitudes and values of its constituents. As Keane writes:

> *As a rule, crises are times during which the living do battle for*
> *the hearts, minds and souls of the dead. They are also times in*
> *which controversies erupt about the prevailing definitions of how*
> *to understand the past in relation to the present. The belief that*
> *history is simply history tends to be undermined during crisis*
> *periods, as is the belief in the neutrality of methods of accounting*
> *for the past.*
>
> (Keane 1988: 204)

What we can learn about heritage during these periods can help to bring to light the multiple readings of sites. Hodder argues:

> *. . . changing meanings through time [of material culture] are*
> *often involved in antagonistic relations between groups. Past and*
> *present meanings are continuously being contested and*
> *reinterpreted as part of social and political strategies. Such*
> *conflict over material meanings is of particular interest to*

> *qualitative research in that it expresses and focuses alternative*
> *views and interests.*
>
> (Hodder 2000: 398)

By redefining the parameters that demarcate a society, moments of crisis can provoke changes in how the past is valued, and what moments of history are to be highlighted; this inevitably affects choices about what material manifestations of the past are to be safeguarded. An example of this occurred after the 7th of July 2005 bombings in London when David Lammy, then Minister of Culture, called for the need to revise notions of British identity and cultural heritage so that they should be more inclusive and reflect the make-up of British citizenry in the twenty-first-century (Lammy, 24 October 2005).

While revisionist reactions are common to moments of political transition, economic crisis, and natural disasters, as well as wars between countries, in cases of civil war these reactions become particularly explicit. The tectonic plates of a society, the very basis on which it lies, shift, dealing a traumatic blow to its foundations and shaking everything that rests on them. As in other forms of war, propaganda often draws on historical symbols and myths to rally people to one side or another, and as new symbols emerge and old ones are reinterpreted the symbolic landscape is transformed. However, during civil wars, the symbols become appropriated by the different factions to create an 'us' and 'them' within communities such that family members and neighbours frequently fight on opposite sides. Furthermore, internal and civil wars have become the most pronounced form of armed conflict today;[2] thirty-two such wars were underway in 2006 and the trend shows few signs of ebbing (Armitage 2008). One general characteristic of this type of conflicts is that they are part of a cumulative process; experience is refracted through history and memory with past tensions and grievances revived, reinterpreted and projected into the future. Another characteristic is that they are recurrent, and this threat of recurrence plays a decisive role in how their aftermaths are approached (Armitage 2008). In terms of cultural heritage this type of war is relevant because each side seeks to silence and delegitimize the other; as a result mutually exclusive visions of cultural heritage can develop. These conflicts also draw heavily on notions of collective memory and identity, with the warring parties characterizing themselves as legitimate heirs and defenders of 'authentic' heritage and traditions. This propagandistic use of heritage can profoundly transform group narratives of belonging.

In the aftermath of civil war, the transformed landscape and narratives of belonging become part of the blueprint for reconstruction projects.[3] A symbolic landscape can be built that prolongs the violence of the war into the post-conflict period, planting antagonistic symbols of difference that continue to provoke fear and hatred and operate against reconciliation. Thus, the reconstruction of cultural heritage can be fundamental in determining whether antagonistic narratives remain ingrained in society, planting a potential time-bomb for future conflicts. Between 1989 and 1999 all fourteen of the major peace-building operations launched were in countries that had just been through civil wars (Paris 2004: preface). The international community has become increasingly involved in the post-conflict reconstruction of cultural heritage – in places such as Cambodia, the former Yugoslavia, Afghanistan, and Timor-Leste. These trends have lent a sense of urgency for the need to acknowledge and better understand the role of cultural heritage in abating conflict and building peace. In the absence of this awareness, the risk is that in the rebuilding a symbolic landscape will be created that carries the elements of fear, hatred and division of the conflict into the 'peace'. In order to better understand the relationship between cultural heritage and the creation of meaning and memory in society this study focuses on the process of reconstruction (Figure 1.1).

Deconstructing the reconstruction process

The word 'reconstruction' is misleading for while in a post-war or post-disaster scenario it can be motivated by desires to restore and remake a place exactly, it can also seek to re-imagine place, constructing a new vision that reflects changed power structures – economic, ideological and political – or simply to modernize and improve infrastructure. Most often, the reconstruction of a country will be driven by several of these motivators. In order to break down the process into some of its constituent parts,

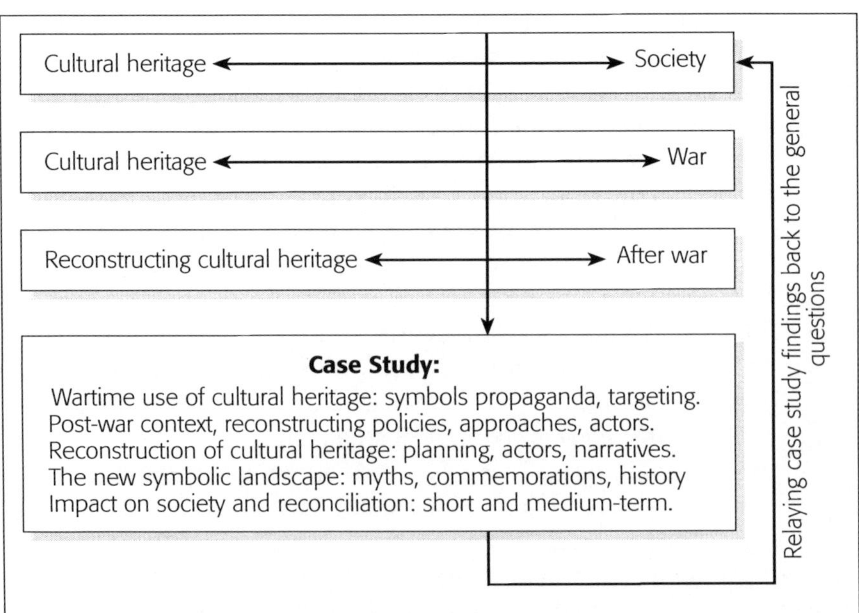

1.1 Narrowing the focus of the research.

it is useful to distinguish between rebuilding and reconstructing for the purposes of this study. *Rebuilding* will refer to the technical, administrative, functional, and physical part of the process, *reconstructing* will refer to an endeavor that works to re-image a community on the levels at which political rhetoric, public ceremony, commemorations, education, history writing and the media intersect.

All of these levels at which reconstruction functions bear consequences which this research seeks to investigate. One of the possible consequences of reconstruction is that it can take the form of symbolic violence (Bourdieu 1984, 2000) or cultural violence (Galtung 1990, 1996) continuing the war by other means. As Galtung indicated, "the study of cultural violence highlights the way in which the act of direct violence and the fact of structural violence arc legitimized and thus rendered acceptable in society" (Galtung 1990: 292). By imposing a constructed grand narrative (Lyotard 1983) that is presented as 'normal', no room is left for alternatives which are either silenced or delegitimized. As the official, public memory of the conflict is constructed, so other memories go 'underground' or into exile. In the following chapters an attempt is made to reveal how the grand narrative is woven into post-conflict reconstructions and what happens to alternative narratives in the process.

Locating the field

Post-conflict scenarios are so multifaceted that they can be approached from the perspective of many disciplines. Developing a holistic vision involves a process that resembles that of making a collage. First the relevant work in each discipline is identified and then the relations between them, how they inform one another, are analyzed and put together to form a new image. Overlap exists between the disciplines that can be both useful and at times confusing. For example, in the humanities the dynamics and mechanisms of memory have been the focus of study for psychologists, historians, social anthropologists, philosophers, and sociologists. The discoveries and theories developed by each of these disciplines help to understand how social memory is constructed, the interaction between individual and public memory and the process by which traumatic experience is remembered, to note but a few areas. In what follows, areas of research and analysis from various disciplines have been identified to inform this one line of enquiry into the role of cultural heritage in a post-conflict reconstruction process.

The literature that has been drawn on brings together historical, political, anthropological, sociological and legal approaches to the analysis of both material culture and post-conflict situations. The literature on cultural heritage has informed this work with respect to signifying practices, approaches to the representation of the past and the links between material heritage and the building of group belonging. The vast majority of work on conflict and cultural heritage has, until recently, drawn primarily on examples from the First and Second World Wars, focusing on destruction, looting, protection attempts, the material remains of war and on exploring the technical and legal aspects of conservation and return.[4] This tendency changed in the mid-1990s due mainly to two factors: an evolution in thinking about cultural heritage and the wars in the former Yugoslavia.

Changes in the appreciation of cultural heritage on an international level can be observed by looking at a selection of normative instruments developed for its protection. Initially, these focused primarily on the materiality of sites and objects: Athens Charter for the Restoration of Historic Monuments (1931), Convention for the Protection of Cultural Property in the Event of Armed Conflict (1954, known as the 'Hague Convention'), International Charter for the Conservation and Restoration of Monuments and Sites (1964), Convention on the Means of Prohibiting and Preventing the Illicit Import, Export and Transfer of Ownership of Cultural Property (1970), and the Convention for the Protection of the World's Cultural and Natural Heritage (1972).[5] In the mid-1970s this began to change as a number of countries called for the recognition of other forms of heritage: folklore, oral traditions and expressions, performing arts, traditional craftsmanship and know-how. The increasing awareness of the immaterial qualities of heritage led to the UNESCO Convention for the Safeguarding of the Intangible Cultural Heritage (2003). Efforts to define and develop ways to safeguard this form of heritage made more visible a dichotomy between the tangible and the intangible dimensions that lay at the centre of heritage.

The wars that marked the breakdown of Yugoslavia (1991–1995)[6] had a significant impact on awareness of the role of culture in conflict and its aftermath, both because of the deliberate targeting of cultural heritage and the cultural and ethnic overtones of the war-time discourse. One of the direct consequences was the elaboration in 1999 of the Second Protocol of the Hague Convention of 1954 which clarified categories and strengthened the original text by including mechanisms with which to supervise its enforcement. It was in the 1990s that the influential peace theorist Johan Galtung introduced a new category to his typology of violence: cultural violence.[7] International involvement in negotiating an end to hostilities and in peace-keeping activities also instigated a wave of interest in reconstruction and the place of culture in that process (Barakat, Calame and Charlesworth 1998; Layton 2001; Barakat 2004). To a large extent, this work has focused on trying to minimize the impact of armed conflict on cultural heritage, evaluating the role of museums and cultural institutions in preserving and protecting physical heritage in these situations, and developing programmes to raise awareness and valorization of heritage. Even this type of work is still exceptional, however, and most research dedicated to rebuilding post-conflict societies largely overlooks cultural issues; including attempts at holistic approaches such as those developed by the World Bank (World Bank 1998) in which there were merely token references to culture until very recently. When culture *is* considered in the reconstruction and peace-building literature, it is in the broadest sense of the word, with little or no attention paid to material culture.[8]

Reconstructing cultural heritage: meaning and memory

The influential work directed by Pierre Nora published in the seven volumes of *Les Lieux de Mémoire* (Nora 1984–1992, English language edition Kritzman 1996, 1997) – which has been translated as either sites, places or realms of memory – has been fundamental to understanding how a building, historical figure, song, or color can become an evocative national symbol, acting as a trigger for a set of emotions and memory narratives. Nora defines a *lieu de mémoire* as "any significant entity, whether material or nonmaterial in nature, which by dint of the human will or the work of time has become a symbolic element of the memorial heritage of any community" (Nora 1996: preface, xvii). He has dissected these signifiers in France, analyzing their role in the construction of a national sense of identity. In his analysis, these iconic sites provide a codified interpretation of the past expressed in terms of national identity and belonging. Writing about how he selected the sites of memory, Nora explains the desire to find the symbolic reality and memory that sustained these sites, beyond their historical significance:

> *It was no longer enough simply to select objects; instead those*
> *objects would have to be constructed: In each case one would*
> *have to look beyond the historical reality to discover the symbolic*
> *reality and recover the memory that it sustained.*
>
> (Nora 1996: preface, xvii)

An important distinction in thinking about post-conflict attempts to interfere with the symbolic reality of sites and construct new monuments is the element of intentionality. Alois Riegl distinguished between intentional monuments, created with the purpose of keeping a particular event "alive in the minds of future generations" (Riegl 1903/1982: 21), and unintentional monuments that derive their meaning from how they come to be perceived. Similarly, though with a different emphasis, Nora distinguishes between what he terms 'dominant' and 'dominated' sites (Nora 1989: 23, 1996: 19). 'Dominant' sites are those in which a symbolic and memorial intention is inscribed in the object itself: national flags and triumphal arcs are examples of dominant symbols. The 'dominated' sites are those that through a series of unintentional circumstances are transformed into durable symbols. What remains to be seen is how these different sites – intentional or unintentional, dominant or dominated – fared in the reconstruction of Spain in the immediate and medium term.

In order to further understand the form that heritage sites take and how the meaning and memory that they communicate changes, it is useful to combine Roland Barthes' deconstruction of myths (1973), Pierre Nora's *lieux* (1984), and Anderson's (1991) notion of the collective imagining of communities. The working understanding of cultural heritage used throughout this book focuses less on its quality as a good or product and far more on its essence as a social and symbolic construction, a sign and identifier for an amalgamate of meanings. As Stig Sørensen has clearly set out:

> *Objects not only have immediate meaning, they also act as memory caches, as containers of emotions. They represent, in an apparently timeless form, values, symbolic meaning and created associations. They bridge generations and create contacts in a unique manner between that which was, which is and which will be.*
>
> (Stig Sørensen 1996: 24–25)

A number of researchers have analyzed how meaning is derived from material culture – Miller, Rowlands and Tilley (1989), Hodder (1987, 1991, 2000), Buchli (2002), Miller (2005), Henare, Holbraad and Wastell (2007). Hodder (2000: 397) identifies two types of material symbolism, the representational and the evocative, indicating that they are not mutually exclusive and often work together. Both material culture and its related meanings or 'readings' have to be studied in the context in which they were produced, used, neglected, destroyed, reused or revived. In a post-conflict scenario, this theoretical approach is useful in that it makes visible how objects and sites take on new symbolism. Doing this allows us to identify various interpretations and how they change. It is through association and practice that material culture derives the meaning that transforms it into a symbol (Hodder 2000: 396). Symbols are objects invested with abstract meaning that come to represent something else, even if the meaning evoked is not the same for different people. They are used in lieu of description to evoke ideas or emotions. As Hodder indicates: "practice, evocation and representation interpenetrate and feed off each other in many if not all areas of life" (2000: 397). National flags, for instance, take on very different meanings, whether raised at an Olympics ceremony, draped over the coffin of a soldier, or planted on a disputed territory. The same object used in the three instances retains a common reference, yet the association, gesture and performance in each case provokes a different reading and set of emotions. Thus, gesture and performance can also be read as texts that transmit and create symbolic meaning (Ricoeur 1971). This book will examine how in post-conflict reconstruction scenarios, parades, commemorative events and inaugurations add an essential dimension, looking at their capacity to imprint meaning, moving through a landscape that in turn acts as a stage setting.

Cultural heritage is intrinsically political and symbolic, as such it gets drawn on in attempts to construct a sense of historical continuity or public memory which contribute to the definition of an 'imagined community' (Anderson 1991). It can also serve a mnemonic purpose: memory triggers in the landscape associated to particular historic events. The contemporary study of memory as a social phenomenon has evolved from the work of Halbwachs (1925) – who understood collective memory to be socially mediated and more than the sum of individual memories – to explore its relation to history (Bloch 1998), forgetting (Augé 2004), or both (Ricoeur 2000). The association between memory and material heritage is long-standing: in the 1920s, for instance, Aby Warburg saw the visual symbol as being imprinted with and preserving a traumatic memory. The landscape of visual symbols thus became, for him, an archive which he intended to demonstrate through the creation of a *Mnemosyne* Atlas (Gombrich 1970: 283–306).

The branches of memory research that most directly inform post-conflict reconstruction work are those studies that look at the memory of collective experiences of traumatic events and those that focus on the material representation of memory (for work on the material forms of memory see Huyssen 1995, 2003; Sebald 2003; Bevan 2006; Jones 2007; Moore and Whelan 2007). These two branches come together in the memorialization of traumatic events (Rowlands 1996; Caruth 1996; Ball, Crewe and Spitzer 1999; Alexander *et al.* 2004; Edkins 2003; McNally 2003). Much of the work on this subject has focused on the First and Second World Wars and the Holocaust in particular (Young 1993; Saunders 2004; Winter 1995; Gillis 1994; Ashplant, Dawson and Roper 2000). Three important edited volumes that, although drawing heavily on the World Wars, move beyond it, are Winter and Sivan (1999) on the encoding of grief and the trauma of war; Deák, Gross and Judt (2000) which examines justice, retribution and the appropriation of memory; and Müller (2002) which examines the power-memory nexus. Studies about memory have also looked at other types of traumatic events: natural disasters (Morris 2011); terrorist attacks (Sturken 2007); periods of political transition or economic collapse; prolonged periods of trauma and injustice such as Apartheid or the military dictatorships in Chile and Argentina (Antze and Lambeck 1996; Das *et al.* 2000; Jelin and Langland 2003), in an attempt to discern the paths of memory across communities and generations and to understand practices of memorialization.

Central to the concept of a *lieu de mémoire* is how memory becomes transformed from a nebulous substance to something concrete. There is no consensus on how this happens, nor whether it is actually memory that becomes contained in these objects and sites or rather a set of associations to a determined historical narrative. Michel de Certeau (1984: 87) argued that memory is everywhere, not localizable, but when fixed to an object it begins to decay. Certainly, war memorials are highly selective in terms of what they portray as worthy of being remembered (Rowlands 2001; King 2001). In the process of concretizing and communicating memory, values, protagonists, and plots are woven into a seemingly straightforward and linear narrative. Understanding the physical manifestation or locus of something as elusive as memory is not an easy task:

> . . . *it is clear that the relationship between objects and memory is less straightforward than Western thinking has been in the habit of assuming. We cannot take it for granted that artefacts act as the agents of collective memory, nor can they be relied upon to prolong it.*
>
> (Forty and Küchler 2001: 7)

Another aspect of memory still open to debate is whether or not the concept of 'collective memory' is actually a useful analytic tool or rather confuses the issue. While the idea of collective memory might obfuscate the multiple aspects and dynamics of the phenomenon that it seeks to encapsulate, there is a need nonetheless to formulate a way of thinking about the realm that lies in between individual memory and history. Only then is it possible to examine that form of memory that individuals appropriate by drawing on a pool of communal experiences, thereby constructing a memory of experiences that they have not lived through personally. This is the form of memory that national identity draws on and which is constructed through listening: to the memories of family members, friends, and public figures; to the historical narratives presented for popular consumption via the arts, media, ceremonies and memorials; and through national educational curricula. Foucault (1974) argued that a form of popular memory is constructed largely by the radio, television and cinema which show, and shape, how particular events are to be remembered. This becomes relevant in post-conflict scenarios when attempts are made to mould a public memory, censoring parts of it and highlighting others, to force one interpretation of events into becoming the official version of a remembered past. One of the points of this research therefore is to examine the tension between the attempt to impose a public account of events and the resistance offered by other memories.

As will be seen in later chapters, the term 'historic memory' has recently become omnipresent in public discourse in Spain, but not without being criticized by many for blurring the distinction between memory and history and in the process unhelpfully objectifying one and relativizing the other. What is often overlooked is the affective, emotional element of memory, as Santos Juliá points out:

> *Historic memory is made up of narratives constructed with the purpose of reinforcing an affective link between the person or group that does the remembering and past events that have some significance for life in the present.*
>
> (Juliá 2006)

The focus in this study is on how during a period of reconstruction attempts are made to shape public memory through the memorial forms, sites, references and public rituals. Notwithstanding the difficulties of studying the social dynamics of memory, this type of work is on the rise (Huyssen 1995; Antze and Lambeck 1996). For instance, the importance of memory in processes of political transition has lately become the subject of research with studies based in Germany, Spain, Portugal, Russia, Argentina, Chile, South Africa, Rwanda, Japan, Cambodia and China, among others.[9] The broad range of case studies suggests that a transversal look at reconstruction practices across these regions would be fruitful.

The making of meaning and memory is central to much heritage work – sites are given the heritage label because they are outstanding representations of a moment of human history, creativity, industry, know-how, world-view or belief system – and in the post-conflict context they come together in many ways. The areas of intersection that will recur throughout this study are those of landscape, the politics of space, and performance.

From landscape to heritage-scape

> *Much more than a transparent window through which reality may be unproblematically viewed, the cultural landscape is now conceived of as an emblematic site of representation, a locus of both power and resistance, and a key element in the heritage process.*
>
> (Moore and Whelan 2007: introduction, x)

In researching the material for this book and trying to create an overall picture of the reconstruction process and its impact, the idea of landscape or more specifically of '-scape' kept recurring. Gradually landscape metamorphosed into memory-scape, memorial-scape, symbol-scape, meaning-scape, and eventually heritage-scape.[10] Underlying this struggle with the language was an attempt to think about those invisible but nonetheless real and internalized, mental cartographies that each individual and community has of its surroundings. A useful concept to understanding the impact that these 'scapes' can have is the French term *l'imaginaire collectif*, which does not refer to a pure figment of the imagination but rather to something that is imagined, a shared point of reference, as in Anderson's 'imagined community' (1991). For Anderson it refers to how a community or landscape too large for any individual to have ever seen and known in its entirety can nonetheless exist notionally in their imagination. This landscape is not empty, but peopled with stories and characters; as Malraux suggests, even when a nation "does not create imaginary characters", it nonetheless "creates an imaginary representation of characters" (1947: 14). This concept is useful in analysing post-conflict reconstruction as the attempt to re-represent this imagined community and its 'scapes'. In studying the Spanish reconstruction one of the points of interest is how re-interpreted heritage sites were used as landmarks, coordinates that were meant to serve as guides by which to interpret the post-war landscape that people moved in while mapping out a newly reformulated imagined community. Writing about religion, Halbwachs (1992: 119) reflects that collective memory "does not preserve the past but reconstructs it with the aid of the material traces, rites, texts, and traditions left behind by the past" and, he adds, with the aid of factors in the present. These traces become landmarks in the physical and imagined heritage-scape, acting as prompts for specific narratives to be 'recalled'. The most explicit way in which this is done is through the construction of memorials and their strategic placement. The resulting memorial-scape constructs a narrative about those people and events worthy of being publicly commemorated.

Heritage-scape is here used to refer to the panorama that results from the selection and designation of specific sites.[11] This panorama can change over time more or less drastically. For example, the iconoclasm that took place during the French Revolution (involving the destruction of effigies, monuments, and material culture related to the monarchy) radically changed the heritage-scape of Paris. A less drastic period that was nonetheless transformative in France was that of the cultural policies introduced by Jack Lang when as Minister of Culture (1981–86, 1988–92) he promoted the idea that cartoons (*bandes dessinées*) and circus arts could be considered 'high arts' and *patrimoine*. Both of these moments in France transformed the heritage-scape by changing what was valued. Similar changes have occurred throughout Europe as industrial vestiges have been salvaged, restored, and labelled as heritage. In these re-evaluations of places we witness an evolution in the meanings with which places are imbued, how they are understood, valuated, and moved through, their historical associations and aesthetic appreciations.

The politics of space and performance

A further layer of meaning is added to the heritage-scape by how people use the space, move through it and interact with it. The specific ways in which spaces become imbued with meaning was developed in Lefebvre's (1974) work on the production of space.[12] In the post-conflict context, the construction of places and spaces provides the stage-setting in which the reconfigured nation or community can be performed. A common denominator to post-conflict scenarios is the abundance of ceremonial acts, parades, commemorations and inaugurations. They offer a vehicle for a new regime to convey its vision of the past and of what is to be remembered;[13] these performances move through the ruins and sites of reconstruction, implanting them with new codes and specific meanings transmitted through gesture, dress, and rhetoric. The impact of rites and rituals, as Geertz (1973: 112–113, 131) has indicated, has a significance that reaches far beyond the moment of their enactment for it serves to mark both the territory in which they take place and the 'imagined' landscape.

Central to the construction of physical and social space and the performances that contribute to demarcating these spaces and imbuing them with meaning are the twin forces of ideology and propaganda. As Hodder has argued, material culture is active (Hodder 1989, 2000) in the sense that it creates meaning, having not only a material but a social and ideological impact. The same can be said for sites of memory: "Indeed, a 'realm of memory' is a polyreferential entity that can draw on a multiplicity of cultural myths that are appropriate for different ideological or political purposes" (Kritzman in Nora 1996: foreword, *x*). Furthermore, contestation can be inscribed in a landscape through direct interventions such as vandalism or graffiti, or through the construction of alternatives with competing narratives.

In the case of Spain it will be important to consider how ideology shaped the reconstruction, from the choice of decorative details to ambitious town plans; how it supplied the subtexts and meta-narratives on which the reconstruction project rested; and how competing aspects of the ideology and its contradictions became visually manifest throughout the reconstruction. The analysis furthermore will detail how the image of the reconstruction presented through the regime's propaganda compares with that which emerges from people's experiences and memories.

Research Methods

> *The qualitative researcher as bricoleur or maker of quilts uses the*
> *aesthetic and material tools of his or her craft, deploying*
> *whatever strategies, methods, or empirical materials are at hand.*
> *If new tools or techniques have to be invented, or pieced together,*
> *then the researcher will do this.*
>
> (Denzin and Lincoln 2000: 4–5)

The methodological approaches and analytic tools used for this research project were the result of *bricolage* work, a term developed by Lévi-

Strauss (1966: 17) to refer to an approach by which a researcher draws on a variety of theoretical tools and methods to investigate a subject. This also reflects an attempt to analyze culture without falling into the 'escape' strategies that Geertz signaled:

> *There are a number of ways to escape this – turning culture into folklore and collecting it, turning it into traits and counting it, turning it into institutions and classifying it, turning it into structures and toying with it. But they are escapes.*
>
> (Geertz 1973: 29)

Research methods were determined by the material available in and on Spain, the questions being asked and how the answers to these evolved. Only through using a variety of materials was it possible to identify – and even more so interrogate – the multiple dimensions of the reconstruction when it came to heritage, and in particular how it contributed to creating and assigning meaning.

While the first temptation was to do a comparative analysis of several conflicts and their ensuing reconstruction, in the end the case study approach was chosen as the research strategy that would more readily enable the use of multiple methods of enquiry (Stake 1995). The case study approach is particularly well suited to the study of processes and contexts over a period of time and establishing cause and effect within them. This makes it appropriate for the present research. The Spanish example was thus an interpretative case study. It was also instrumental, since a pragmatic aim of the research was to see what Spain could reveal about the trends and dynamics of reconstruction processes that could be useful in analyzing other cases.

Heritage work, both theoretical and practical, addresses concepts such as memory and identity which can be teased apart and whose threads can be used to spin eloquent texts yet it is important to ground heritage work in a solid base of evidence. The work requires a considerable amount of observation and contextualization that relies heavily on description, relating the who, what, when, and where of an event, indentifying trends and making connections before moving to the level of analysis. In conveying the results of this research, a narrative of the reconstruction was largely pieced together through documentary material and the fieldwork carried out in Gernika. Much of the text that follows tries to elucidate the significance of reconstruction and the webs of meaning spun by it. Although thick description[14] was not used per se – neither field-notes nor detailed accounts of conversations and observations are included in the text – it was nonetheless a useful tool for thinking about the deeper context of the reconstruction and the multiple layers at which it occurred. The classic example used to explain thick description is the distinction between an eye twitch and a wink (Geertz 1973:

6): while they both look the same to an outsider, the latter is replete with potential significance depending on the context and socially established code in which it is employed. In this study it was used to decode certain acts of reconstruction in order to understand their significance beyond the physical action of rebuilding.

Description is of course not free of interpretation; in the process of selection it was necessary to decide what was relevant – the unavoidable dilemma of the researcher's 'voice' introduced in the Prologue. It has been argued that when a researcher's personal experience encroaches on the research, in a reflexive and open manner, it can add a rich layer of reflexivity to the study (Aull Davies 2008; Alvesson and Skoldberg 2000). Certainly in the present research there was a deliberate alternation between periods of field-work in Spain and periods away; this was especially important because of the tense political situation and memory battles that went on in Spain during the period of research between 2005 and 2008 and which focused precisely on the civil war and Franco periods.

The primary sources for this research comprised visual material and written documents. The visual material consisted of architecture, architectural drawings and plans, photographs, paintings, maps, memorials, monuments, built landscapes, cartoons, contemporary news-reels, movies and documentaries. The written material also drew on contemporary newspapers, journals, magazines, project plans, reports produced by the regime's reconstruction institutions, opinion polls, speeches and accounts of contemporaries collected from autobiographical writings and novels. Some material bridged both the visual and the written, such as tourist information brochures, publicity and propaganda material including flyers, postcards and posters.

By far the richest sources of material – visual and textual – were the magazine *Reconstrucción* (*Reconstruction*) and the archives of urban and architectural projects of the regime's main reconstruction body the *Dirección General de Regiones Devastadas* (General Directorate for Devastated Regions). While the first was easy to access and has been well trawled by students and researchers, the latter constitutes a vast source of fascinating material that has been underused, partly because the archaic cataloguing system employed makes it difficult to handle. This archive is currently housed in the *Archivo General de la Administración* (AGA, General Archive of the Administration in Alcalá de Henares, where all Ministerial archives are sent once they are no longer in use) and contains reconstruction projects, maps, layouts, designs, photographs, correspondence, budgets, propaganda material and newspaper articles from all over Spain relating to the reconstruction. At the AGA it was also possible to consult documents from the Spanish Falange concerning reconstruction and housing plans. In Madrid, the *Colegio Oficial de Arquitectos de Madrid* (COAM, Official College of Architects of Madrid) has a very useful collection of materials, including the magazines

Reconstrucción and *Revista Nacional de Arquitectura* (RNA, National Architecture Magazine), and monographs on the key architects involved in the reconstruction.

The *Filmoteca Nacional* (National Film Archive, Madrid) was indispensable for viewing contemporary newsreels, documentaries and fictional films, which supplied an animated vision of the period and, more importantly, made it possible to see how spaces of the reconstruction – ruins, construction projects, inaugurations, and memorials – were used and performed in. For historic documents there is the *Archivo Histórico Nacional* (National Historic Archive, Madrid), where the document *Causa General* (General Cause, discussed in Chapter 4) was consulted as well as documents relating to Picasso's painting *Guernica*, and the *Archivo General de la Guerra Civil* (General Archive of the Civil War, Salamanca) for pamphlets and propaganda material produced during the war, particularly that relating to the bombing of Gernika. Two other Madrid-based libraries used were the *Biblioteca Nacional de España* (BNE, National Library of Spain), where the cartography, photography and news archives were particularly fruitful, and the *Centro de Investigaciones Sociológicas* (CIS, Centre for Sociological Research), where opinion polls and questionnaires carried out since the latter part of the Franco period can be consulted. Additional archives consulted in Madrid were those of the *Consejería de Medio Ambiente y Ordenación del Territorio* (Council for Environment and Urban Planning), the *Archivo Regional de Madrid* (Madrid Regional Archive) and the libraries of the National Museum of Modern Art Reina Sofía and the Complutense University.

For the part of the research focused on Gernika, local archives were used in the Basque Country. The main archives consulted in Gernika were those of *Gernika Gogoratuz* ("Gernika Remembers" in Basque) and the *Gernika Peace Museum Foundation*. *Gernika Gogoratuz* has an archive dedicated to literature about peace-building, conflict resolution and mediation in general as well as a specific archive of material concerning the survivors of the bombing – accounts of their memories and oral histories. Due to their active involvement in the commemorative events related to the bombing, especially the fiftieth and sixtieth anniversaries, and their relations with Germany, they also have an important collection of material on these events. The *Gernika Peace Museum* has an archive dedicated to the bombing of the town, including copies of a large quantity of material from the George L. Steer Archive and the Southworth Archive. They also have a newspaper archive dedicated to Gernika in which can be found collections of articles from the past 20 years on the Tree of Gernika, changes to the names of streets in the town, attitudes toward Picasso's painting and the evolution of the museum's focus. The other archive used in Gernika was the municipal one housed in the Town Hall; this was particularly helpful for documenting the discussions leading to monuments and memorials being erected in the town since 1975.

Finally, in Artea, a small town south of Gernika, the archive and museum of Basque nationalism are housed. These institutions are supported by the Sabino Arana Foundation and the *Partido Nacionalista Vasco* (EAJ-PNV, Basque Nationalist Party). The museum's collections include Basque passports issued during the Republic, bus/train tickets written in Basque, handkerchiefs and banners embroidered with the Basque flag and kept secretly during the Franco period. The archive contains an extensive newspaper collection and houses the papers of the Basque government in exile. It was possible to read the letters, speeches and communiqués of the exiled government, including the communiqués made by the Basque President in exile on important occasions, such as the anniversary of the Gernika bombing.

In going through this material, the primary focus was to pull out references to historical events and personages, cultural heritage, reconstruction activities, monuments and memorials, commemorative activities, and values to see how the reconstruction was creating and assigning meaning. The apparent eclecticism of this array of materials was essential to identify those patterns of the reconstruction that permeated many aspects of life. This approach builds on the visual discourse analysis suggested by Rose (2001: 140) that seeks to study the image, in the context of a social construction of difference and authority. The data that this research works with is not only the archival material itself but how it and the stories of reconstruction that it tells connect to one another, relate to what was implemented in practice, and incite longer term reactions.

The research process alternated between the underlying research questions and the material, at once trying to see whether the developing categories and arguments were supported by the information found while at the same time letting the material suggest ideas and theories that had not been there from the start of the research. The first questions that needed to be answered were practical ones about who, what, where and when, swiftly followed by questions about their policies and goals. These questions in turn gave rise to new ones about how the rebuilding was actually carried out and how it was experienced by Spaniards. At each of these levels of questioning, it was necessary to turn to different sources and types of documents, from the correspondence between administrators to ideological pronouncements, and from propaganda publications to autobiographical writings.

Early temptations to quantify the number of reconstruction projects and the amount of money spent on them quickly fell to the wayside, partly due to the disparity between the intentions set out and what was actually accomplished. More importantly, however, was the fact that while trying to get the 'facts straight' it became apparent that part of war-making consists of weaving thick layers of propaganda and misinformation. Thus, not only are the 'facts' concealed, but a conglomerate of myths, interpretations, symbols and anecdotes is constructed that then shapes individual and collective imaginings of events. It was in these interpretations that clues were to be found about the impact of the war on the Spanish heritage-scape.

This approach also provided the freedom to address the fact that countless narratives are constructed about events, particularly ones that become highly symbolic. These narratives that often contradict one another and change according to circumstance, were the key to understanding the possibilities for reconciliation. This does not lessen the importance of determining the facts of a situation and piecing together evidence-based accounts of historical events, especially in cases when propaganda shrouded reality for decades. However, in the realm of heritage, narratives of the past, their representations, interpretations, and myths are also the facts: data to be interpreted.

While no systematic discourse analysis has been used here, the process of dissecting the heritage landscape created in the reconstruction has had intimations of a discourse analysis being applied to visual material (Rose 2001). Applying this method has meant identifying certain patterns, motifs, and symbols that recur in the reconstruction to see how they were being used to construct a narrative about the country's past, and the values by which the present should be guided. Relying on images as sources of meaning can be tricky, as Hall has remarked with regard to interpreting images:

> *Since there is no law which can guarantee that things will have 'one, true meaning', or that meaning won't change over time, work in this area is bound to be interpretative (. . .) The best way to settle such 'contested' readings is to look again at the concrete example and try to justify one's 'reading' in detail in relation to the actual practices and forms of signification used and what meaning they seem to be producing.*
>
> (Hall 1997: 9)

Thus, the practices and forms of signification used in the post-conflict reconstruction of heritage in Spain were analyzed through close readings of project documents, correspondence, speeches and articles from the period. The filmed material – news-reels, propaganda footage, and movies – was also studied to see the performance of rituals and inaugurations in these spaces and to get a sense of how people moved and lived within them.

The concept of discourse, as developed by Foucault (1972), is interesting for the present piece of research for his insight into how language can shape attitudes and behaviour, thereby producing our sense of self and our understanding of the world. Awareness of the interrelation between language, power, the creation of knowledge and action is essential when trying to understand how post-conflict reconstruction functions. Discourse analysis is used here to discover the practices of institutions and to study how they use images and texts to construct accounts of Spain and Spanishness. The flipside of a discourse of power is a discourse of resistance that counters it; this too is a useful concept when studying responses to the reconstruction, particularly in Gernika and the Basque Country.

Discourse analysis, even when applied to images and institutions, was not sufficient on its own however, it was also necessary to unearth the dominant codes and reference systems that run under the surface of visual or verbal signs. Following Geertz's understanding of culture as a 'web of significance', the attempt to discover the construction of meaning in post-conflict scenarios lead to the use of semiotic analysis.

> *The concept of culture I espouse [. . .] is essentially a semiotic*
> *one. Believing, with Max Weber, that man is an animal*
> *suspended in webs of significance he himself has spun, I take*
> *culture to be those webs, and the analysis of it to be therefore not*
> *an experimental science in search of law but an interpretative*
> *science in search of meaning.*
>
> (Geertz 1973: 5)

For this purpose, semiotics, as applied by Barthes in his essay "Myth Today" published in *Mythologies* (1972), were useful for analyzing how signs communicate meaning. Barthes took the categories and structures developed by Saussure's semiotics and applied them to composite signs to reveal further layers in the transmission of meaning, namely how public myths are constructed. An example of this would trace the evolution of the bull from animal to word to symbol of Spain (Figure 1.2). The interest of semiotic analysis is that it addresses how signs are 'read'. It emphasizes that, more than reflections of their social contexts, images and constructed spaces have an impact on that context, shaping knowledge, attitudes, and behaviour. The way that it is being used here is to show how heritage sites, or a building reconstructed in a particular style, act on their public at discursive levels, creating meaning and influencing behavior. The research centers on the material practices and rhetorical strategies developed around cultural heritage in post-civil war Spain and the Franco regime's reconstruction programme. Cultural heritage sites serve here as 'second-order signs' (Barthes 1973: 114–117), as they are caught up in a system of representation; this system is then transformed by a conflict that adds new meaning.

More interactive methods of gathering information were also used, namely informal conversations and participant observation carried out mainly in Gernika. The bulk of this work was carried out during the activities and commemorative events during the last week of April 2007 to

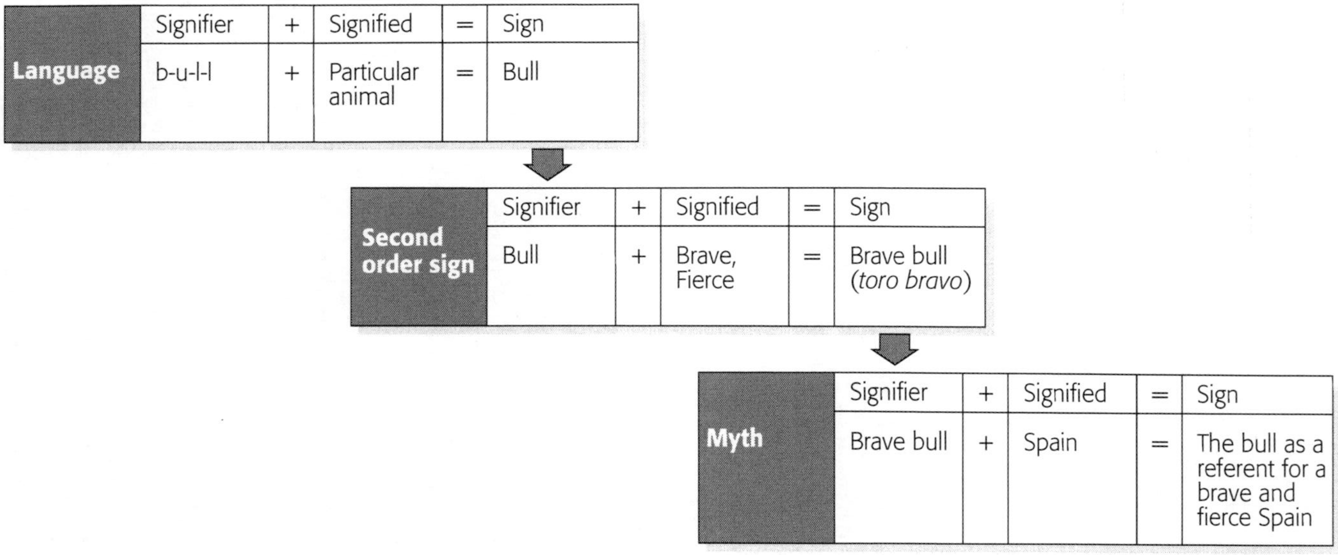

Language	Signifier	+	Signified	=	Sign
	b-u-l-l	+	Particular animal	=	Bull

Second order sign	Signifier	+	Signified	=	Sign
	Bull	+	Brave, Fierce	=	Brave bull (*toro bravo*)

Myth	Signifier	+	Signified	=	Sign
	Brave bull	+	Spain	=	The bull as a referent for a brave and fierce Spain

At the first level of language letters are assigned to signify an object, the level of second order signs shows how the word, now a sign for the object, acquires a further layer of significance when certain values are associated to it, in this case bravery and ferocity. At the level of myth, the sign, imbued with further connotations is associated with another sign, in this case Spain.

1.2 Example of Barthes' model for the creation of contemporary myths.

mark the 70th anniversary of the bombing.[16] All through that week it was possible to sit in on a number of interviews with survivors of the bombing and to view video footage of interviews carried out in the 1990s by Professor Cava Mesa (1996) – often with the same people. The lines of inquiry invariably focused on memories of the event, and after hearing the same individuals recount the same memories repeatedly it became apparent that it might be more interesting to focus questioning on the aftermath of the bombing during the Franco period. While probing in informal conversations and asking about the reconstruction period, it became clear that memories of this period had not been as often repeated or rehearsed; responses were emotionally complex because they implied revealing personal relations with the Franco regime and its local author-ities. Gernika is a small community, and while the population today is 16,171 (INE 2007), the part of the population who still have a direct memory of the bombing and immediate post-war – or 'inherited' one from family members that experienced it – is far smaller. Given the circumstances, participant observation and informal interviewing methods were used during various public acts and ceremonies, by watch-ing how people interacted with one another and within the various spaces created for the anniversary.

Throughout the fieldwork in Gernika, informal, often spontaneous, conversations, as well as several extended discussions with the past and current staff of *Gernika Gogoratuz*, served to fill gaps that could not be filled through documents; to indicate further lines of questioning and to reveal additional layers of meaning, memory and conflict. Informal inter-views were also carried out with heritage professionals, architects, academics, psychologists and people who had lived through the early post-war period in Madrid.

Structure of the Volume

In this chapter, the purpose and central lines of questioning have been laid out together with the theoretical and methodological framework used to pursue them. The following Chapter 2 will begin by setting out a histori-cal context for the interrelation of cultural heritage and conflict in Spain, its links to regional identities and evolving ideas about conservation. The chapter will then address the first point of departure – that to understand the post-conflict heritage-scape it is necessary to look at how heritage was used during the war. It will explore how heritage was drawn on in the political and ideological discourse in the lead up to the war, and then examine how heritage was interpreted, protected, targeted, destroyed, and created during the conflict and in war propaganda. Chapters 3 and 4 will deal with the nature of the reconstruction project, its motivations and dynamics. First, the overall picture for reconstruction in Spain, its agents, rhetoric and main trends will be discussed and then the particular case of Gernika will be focused in order to gain more detailed insight. Chapter 5 will address the medium-term consequences, the responses and revisions to the image of Spain constructed during the post-war period. To achieve this, two leaps forward will be taken to the political Transition of the late 1970s and to the early 2000s. Finally, Chapter 6 will bring together the evolution of trends, cycles, and changes observed. By identifying these dynamics and indicating theoretical and analytic tools for the study of heritage in post-conflict scenarios, the ultimate aim is to inform future research, policy and interventions in this terrain.

Such analysis seeks to capture a discursively complex set of practices that make up the reconstruction and in which heritage sites are claimed, rebuilt, restored or represented in various ways as signs of historical narratives, political legitimacy and national identity. The particular focus will be on the construction of a new physical landscape, the reinterpretation of history that accompanies it, the attempt to inscribe memory into this landscape, and the new symbolic–affective landscape that results. By looking at particularly emblematic heritage sites, it is possible to trace the evolution of their symbolism, their reinterpretation and manipulation in accordance with social realities and political interests.

Throughout the publication text boxes have been used to provide illustrative examples of what is being said in the central text. This format was chosen in order not to interrupt the central narrative with detailed descriptions of particular sites, while providing important supportive material to the central argument.

Before continuing, a clarification is perhaps in order. This research does not assume that monuments, buildings and paintings ought to be placed before human safety in the heat of a conflict nor in its aftermath. However, it does take the stance that in post-conflict scenarios in which poverty and social injustice are commonly high, deliberately amputating a community from part of its heritage contributes to the poverty, injustice and exacerbates feelings of mistrust and insecurity. The disastrous consequences of armed conflict on the socio-cultural development of a society include the realm of cultural heritage, but this aspect has been understudied. On the one hand, individuals and communities call for the protection of their cultural heritage, tangible evidence of their past and their culture. On the other hand, while this evidence can be interpreted to enhance mutual understanding, it can also be manipulated to fuel conflict. Developing a better understanding of the links and mutual influence of conflict, cultural heritage and identity on one another is central if we are to develop mechanisms for safeguarding cultural heritage, or to prevent it from becoming a weapon in the name of partisan claims.

2 Spain: Background and Context

*No other war in recent times, with the possible exception of
Vietnam, aroused such intense emotion, such deep commitment,
such violent partisanship as the Civil War in Spain.*

(Knightley 1975: 192)

The reconstruction of Spain in the aftermath of the 1936–1939 war is an instrumental case for developing a theoretical and analytic framework of post-conflict reconstruction. This case exemplifies a politically driven reconstruction and its motivations. Spain also offers a 70-year time span allowing for analysis that reaches far beyond the moment of initial rebuilding. By examining the reconstruction as a series of stages it is possible to demonstrate the long-term implications of such a project. This long-term gaze is all the more important for there is no consensus on when the postwar period – *la posguerra* – ended,[1] given that some aspects of the post-Civil War reconstruction of Spain were still going on in 2008.

The nearly 40 years of autocratic rule that followed the war translated into a period of continuity and unchecked power for the Franco regime to embody an ideology and promote a new image of the nation in the reconstruction of its cities and towns. This ideology – despite its fragmentation and internal contradictions – entailed an attempt to control all messages relating to national identity, history, symbols and myths leading to an unusually rich opportunity for research and critique. Furthermore, the 70-year period covering the end of the war in 1939, Franco's death in 1975 and up until today is one that includes several cycles of deconstruction and reconstruction of Spain's national image and identity.

The Spanish Transition constitutes a further cycle of politically motivated reconstruction accompanied by another re-visioning of the nation which is being contested today, as the 'amnesty pacts' agreed to then are now revisited. This temporal dimension was a key element in determining the choice of Spain as a case study, as it provides a long enough period in which to trace the dynamics of reconstruction as an evolving process, rather than a fixed end, as well as two different forms of civil conflict – civil war and dictatorship.

Despite its particularities, Spain is analogous to other more recent post-conflict periods. Spain's political transition in the late 1970s was hailed as a model of peaceful transition from totalitarianism to democracy.[2] Yet the Transition was not as complete as some proponents of the idea have argued: the current battles over memory in Spain are revealing its shortcomings. Examining a political transition in terms of reconstruction will be useful for understanding revisionist histories and memory battles that have taken place in other regions such as the former Yugoslavia and Soviet bloc. This retrospective glance is especially interesting in light of initiatives taken by the Spanish government under Rodríguez Zapatero's leadership to recover what it has termed the 'historic memory' of the Civil War and the Franco period – a further phase, it will be argued, in the post-conflict reconstruction of Spain.[3] This makes the present study timely, as Spain is currently witnessing an attempt to create the possibilities for another re-writing of its recent past. Though the initiative has been criticized for opening old wounds and inciting the re-emergence of the 'two Spains', perhaps it is only in 2006 that Spain entered the final stage of its *posguerra*.

While several libraries could be filled with material written on the Spanish Civil War and the ensuing Franco regime, comparatively little work has been done on the actual reconstruction of the war-devastated country. Yet, it is in the reconstruction of Spain that the process of rewriting the country's history, shaping its memory and redefining its system of values becomes explicit. Extant research has largely focused on the architectural, economic and political aspects of reconstruction (Sambricio 1977; Domènech 1978; Ureña 1979; MOPU exh.cat. 1987). More recent studies have been carried out at the regional level, often complementing or resulting in exhibitions (Quadra-Salcedo 2001; Centellas Salamero et al. 2006; Marín Muñoz 2007; Cinca Yago et al. 2008). A recent volume, publishing the papers presented at a conference on the topic, makes a valuable contribution addressing the conservation of cultural heritage during the period 1936–1958 (Casar Pinazo and Esteban Chapapría 2008).

Many elements of the Spanish Civil War recurred in later twentieth-century conflicts: the active participation of artists and intellectuals, third party intervention in a civil conflict, the importance of the visual media including newborn photojournalism, the impact of international public opinion, and the involvement of international organizations in trying to mediate the conflict such as the League of Nations and the International Committee of the Red Cross.[4]

Unlike in more recent conflicts, when the Spanish war ended international organizations did not become involved in the reconstruction, nor was there a summit in which the terms of the peace were arbitrated by third parties. Furthermore, the outbreak of the Second World War only a few months later meant that international attention moved swiftly away from Spain. The regime was not entirely isolated or immune to international pressures, though, and during the Second World War, the ideologues and architects of both Nazi Germany and Fascist Italy influenced reconstruction plans for Spain. Indeed the Italian connection affected cultural heritage, as officials with cultural responsibilities in Franco's government prioritized Spain's Roman period (Tarrats and Sada

2002: 38–39). However, as of 1944, when it seemed that the Axis powers would lose the war, the focus turned inward and sources of inspiration for the reconstruction were sought in Spanish history, folkloric traditions, arts and crafts (Ortíz 1999). This period lasted until 1952, when a rapprochement with the United States re-opened Spain to international influences.

In terms of international normative instruments regarding cultural heritage, while there had been some initiatives on the subject of cultural heritage, its wartime protection[5] and post-war restoration,[6] no substantial international normative instruments came into effect until after 1945. Undoubtedly, international organizations and legal instruments concerning cultural heritage have had a large impact on reconstruction activities in more recent conflicts most notably in the wars of the 1990s in the former Yugoslavia. Studying these conflicts would not, however, offer enough temporal scope to allow us to see the possible medium and long-term outcomes and impacts of reconstruction. Notwithstanding the context specific differences of civil wars, cultural heritage is often a cornerstone of ensuing reconstruction processes, used to both unify and divide, to bring stability or, to draw on Clausewitz's dictum, to continue the 'war by other means'.[7]

This outline of the reasons for choosing Spain for this study can be concluded with an observation made during a first bout of fieldwork and which determined the final decision. One morning in the summer of 2006, on Madrid's *Calle Genova*, the glass façade of a bank near the headquarters of the *Partido Popular* (Popular Party) was plastered with posters of the Spanish Falange. The slogan on the posters read: *Hay otra memoria . . . Orgullosos de nuestra historia* – "There is another memory . . . Proud of our history". Equally significant, was the accompanying image. The use of a photograph of a Republican militia firing squad aiming at the monument of the *Sagrado Corazón de Jesús* (Sacred Heart of Jesus) at the *Cerro de los Ángeles* (Figures 2.1 and 2.2) which was one of the most emblematic images to come out of the Spanish Civil War together with Robert Capa's falling militiaman and Picasso's *Guernica*. This image of a symbolic site being deliberately targeted, alongside the revival of the propaganda war in which it had been a protagonist, together with the confrontational slogan, reflected a sense of urgency about the need to better understand these relationships.

This study argues *ab initio* that the nature of the reconstruction of cultural heritage sites, their interpretation and their subsequent impact on the national imagination, can only be understood in terms of how these sites fared during the war.[8] The remainder of this chapter provides a context for the development of heritage and conflict in nineteenth-century Spain then outlines the role that heritage played during the civil war, in order to provide the grounds for subsequent chapters that address its reinterpretation and reconstruction.

2.1 Republican militia aiming at the monument of the Sacred Heart of Jesus at the *Cerro de los Ángeles* during the war, 1936. (España. Ministerio de Cultura, Archivo General de la Administración, Sig.F01418.)

Cultural heritage, conflict, and identity in Spain in the run up to 1936

. . . a society is formed not simply constituted by a mass of individuals who compose it, by the territory they occupy, by the things they use and the actions they perform, but above all by the idea it has about itself. To be sure, it hesitates about the way it ought to see itself: it feels pulled in different directions. When these conflicts break out, however, they do not take place between the ideal and the real but between different ideals, between the ideal of yesterday and the ideal of today, between that backed by the authority of tradition and that which is only beginning to gain favour.

(Durkheim 1912, in Pickering 1975: 151–152)

Two events in nineteenth-century Spain proved to be key determinants in both the Spanish conceptualization and valuation of cultural heritage and the elaboration of the national myths that played pivotal roles in the Civil War. The first was the war of 1808–1814 against the Napoleonic invasion of Spain. This war, known nationally as the *Guerra de la Independencia* (War of Independence), spurred a period of patriotic fervour and inaugurated a century of instability plagued by conflicts that included revolutions and wars of succession.[9] The second event was the so-called *Desastre* of 1898, the loss of the last fragments of the Spanish Empire – Cuba, the Philippines and Puerto Rico – and the call for a national *regeneración* that it provoked leading to national debates around the very idea of Spain. It

2.2 Posters in Madrid's *Calle Génova* in July 2006 using the same image superimposed with the Spanish Falangist symbol of a yoke and arrows.

is not mere coincidence that both of these crisis periods, linked as they were to drives in nation building and a heightened sense of nationalism, coincided with a new valorisation of cultural heritage. As a collection of material vestiges of a national past, heritage was a fecund source of 'evidence' providing symbols supporting emergent ideas of the nation and its defining myths (Díaz-Andreu and Champion 1996).

In his *Mater Dolorosa*, Álvarez Junco (2005) writes about the development of Spanish nationalism in the nineteenth century, exploring how the War of Independence spurred an episode of patriotism that went hand in hand with a retrospective look to find the roots of Spanishness. While the study of the past was not a nineteenth-century innovation in Spain, it was only after the French Revolution that, according to Díaz-Andreu (2000: 38), the past became a political instrument. The War of Independence, which spurred a form of national pride and patriotism, also saw the devastation of cultural heritage throughout Spain. Gaya Nuño argues that: "The map of monumental Spain suffered its first grave mutilation on the occasion of the War of Independence" (Gaya Nuño 1961: 16). Churches, monasteries, convents, palaces and other important secular constructions throughout Spain were destroyed, and moveable heritage (especially paintings) was pillaged by both the Napoleonic armies and other troops in their invasions. Royal, private and ecclesiastical collections were sacked of their artistic treasures, which shortly afterwards began to appear in Paris and London auction houses (Rose 1983, 2009).

The next disaster for the preservation of Spain's cultural heritage came in the shape of reform, namely various *desamortizaciones* (confiscations). The *Cortes de Cádiz* began the process in 1812 and it was continued in various thrusts in 1836, 1855 and 1858 with the confiscation and nationalization of assets that had previously been considered inalienable properties of the Church or Crown. These assets came in a variety of forms, from large terrains encompassing parks and hunting grounds, to buildings such as palaces and monasteries including their contents: vast collections of paintings, statuary, tapestries, furniture, gold and silver pieces, in sum what today would be deemed cultural property. The lands, buildings and collections became the property of the state to be reused, redistributed or sold; the revenue from sales was used to fund large public works such as the construction of Spanish railroads.

While the Napoleonic wars and disentailment laws contributed to the destruction, damage and looting of both moveable and immovable heritage throughout Spain, they also led to a revalorization of its importance and to attempts at safeguarding it. In 1844 the *Comisiones de monumentos* (Provincial Monuments Commissions) were created and given the mission of producing inventories of monuments and movable heritage as well as denouncing any damage or destruction (Hernández Hernández 2002: 94). The commissions were generally divided into: libraries and archives; fine arts; and archaeology and architecture (Navarrete Martínez 2001). They continued to develop their work on inventories and conservation reports throughout the remainder of the nineteenth century.

Another outcome of the *desamortización* was the creation of many provincial museums with collections formed of the confiscated objects. Legislation regulating cultural heritage also evolved, as the *desamortización* spurred the creation of a special category called *Patrimonio Nacional* (National Heritage) which refers exclusively to those assets of which the Crown, Church or State were proprietors.[10] During the nineteenth century Spain also saw a national version of the debate that pitted followers of Eugene Viollet-le-Duc against those of John Ruskin,[11] respectively for and against interventionist forms of conservation (Hernández Hernandez 2002: 278–286).

One of the first laws to be passed in Spain concerning cultural heritage was the 1911 law regulating archaeological excavations at a moment when archaeological studies had reached a peak. This law was further developed in 1926 with the *real-decreto-ley de Protección y Conservación de la Riqueza Artística* (Royal decree on the protection and conservation of artistic wealth) and in the same year the IV International Archaeology Congress was held in Barcelona (Hernández Hernández 2002: 153–155).

From its very start in 1931, the Second Republic began to develop legal instruments for the protection of cultural heritage as part of an effort to boost the cultural and educational level of Spaniards and to develop instruments for the organization and promotion of the arts and

Box 2.1   Numancia

The turn to particularly symbolic sites of the past to develop grand narratives in Spain is exemplified in the historiography of Numancia. The Iberian city of Numancia was renowned for having fought off various waves of Roman forces, starting in 153 BC, but it was the circumstances surrounding its downfall that lead to its legend. After a prolonged siege by Scipio in 133 B.C., the population of Numancia, refusing to surrender, is said to have committed collective suicide. The

2.3   Monuments in Numancia.

presence of several illustrious writers in Scipio's entourage – the poet Gaius Lucilius and the Greek historian Polybius (Hermenegildo 1994: 16) – meant that the story of Numancia was transmitted through history inspiring poems and plays, and eventually taking on mythical dimensions.

The archaeological site of Numancia thus became the tangible expression of a myth of national identity, a source of patriotic pride, and a symbol of the heroism and self-sacrifice of 'real' Spaniards when fighting off foreign invaders. Its legend was taken up by Cervantes in his play *La destrucción de Numancia*, written *c.*1585 (Hermenegildo 1994: 11–12). The legend of Numancia was heavily drawn on again in the aftermath of the Napoleonic wars. In 1842 a first monument to the Numantine Heroes was begun. In 1853 an attempt was made to identify the precise site of Numancia. From 1861 to 1867 the first official archaeological expeditions were carried out through the initiative of the *Real Academia de la Historia*. In 1882 part of the site of Numancia was declared a National Monument, and in 1886 a second small commemorative monument was built on the site.

Then in 1904, in the wake of the downfall and disgrace that had resulted from the defeat of the Spanish navy by the United States and the consequent loss of the last colonies, a senator from Soria launched an initiative to construct a third monument on the site; the project was approved and the monument inaugurated a year later (1905) by King Alfonso XIII.[12] Not only did Numancia make a forceful re-appearance in the national rhetoric, there was also a resurgence of celebrations and monuments to *Don Quijote* and *El Cid*. All three were taken up as symbols of a strong *Patria* at a moment plagued with defeatism and self-doubt (Jimeno and Torre 1997: 475).

Numancia came to be so intertwined with the symbol of the self-sacrifice and heroic resistance of the native Iberians against foreign invaders that it became a signifier for 'authentic' Spaniards (Barthes 1973). The myth and legend took on lives of their own, independent of the original event that inspired them and having little connection to the material, archaeological, site of the event.

Jimeno and Torre (1997: 480) point out in their study of Numancia, that the mismatch between the reality of a place and the expectations generated by its related myths helps explain why the study of the site has had little continuity and has been largely spurred by commemorative moments.[13] Nevertheless, interest in Numancia did not evaporate. Numancia has become such an integral part of the Spanish imaginary that it has given rise to a popular expression: *esfuerzo numantino* – numantiane effort – which refers to a considerable effort that involves pain or sacrifice.

education. This sense of urgency regarding heritage followed a period in which international art dealers had been negotiating the unregulated exportation of Spanish heritage. Entire palaces, castles and cloisters were dismantled and sold to foreigners who then rebuilt them abroad as in the case of the *patio* of the Vélez-Blanco Castle installed in the Metropolitan Museum of Art in New York,[14] or the monastery of Sacramenia rebuilt in Miami.[15] In response to this situation, the Republic issued decrees in 1931 against the sale and exportation of goods of artistic or historic value, declaring 897 sites of national heritage – a vast number considering that between 1844 and 1931 fewer than 400 sites had been thus recognized. These various developments were summarized in a law of December 1931 outlawing the *enajenación* – alienation – of goods of artistic, archaeological or historic value or those 100 years old or more. The draft *Ley de Protección del Tesoro Artístico Nacional* (Law for the Protection of the National Artistic Treasure) was approved by the *Cortes* on 13 May 1933. This legislation which built on that of 1926 was advanced for the time, as it set out that the public had the right to enjoy works of art and culture from the past (Hernández Hernández 2002: 8). Despite later additions and modifications, this progressive law of 1933 would be the last major normative instrument dedicated to cultural heritage in Spain until the 1985 law of *Patrimonio Histórico Español*.

The idea of Spain: *Las dos Españas*

> *Two Spains, Sirs, are caught in an incessant fight: a dead and*
> *hollow Spain riddled with wormwood and a new Spain,*
> *industrious, aspiring that tends towards life and all is arranged*
> *so that the former triumphs over this one.*
>
> (Ortega y Gasset 1914)[16]

The idea that there are two Spains, with irreconcilable visions of the country and its destiny, was often repeated throughout the Franco period and came to have a significant hold on the Spanish political imagination. The idea arose after Spain's loss of the last fragments of its Empire in the nineteenth century. Opposed in this debate were conservatives and liberals, represented by intellectuals known as the *Generación del '98* (Generation of 1898). Both sides acknowledged that Spain was undergoing a crisis but claimed different diagnosis for its causes, and hence opposing visions of how the country should be run and what its future should be. This discussion led to a revision of Spanish history, values and traditions from their very origins with conservative intellectuals calling for the need to *replantearse España* –rethink Spain – and calling for a 'regeneration of Spain' (i.e. Menéndez Pelayo after 1898).

The conservative vision represented by Menéndez Pelayo (1856–1912), Donoso Cortés (1809–1853) and Ramiro de Maetzu (1875–1936) was of a traditionalist Spain united around ideas of 'hispanicity' and founded on the reign of the Catholic Kings (1469–1504) and the *Reconquista (722–1492)*. Their writings on the history of Spain were appropriated in the 1930s by traditionalists and used to root these writers and their visions of Spain as key symbols.[17] The liberal vision represented by such figures as Ginér de los Ríos (1839–1915), José Ortega y Gasset (1883–1955), Américo Castro (1885–1972), Salvador de Madariaga (1886–1978), and Claudio Sánchez Albornoz (1893–1984) blamed the institutions of the Monarchy, Church and Inquisition for repressing the country's advance into modernity[18] (Juliá 2004: 51–55). Finally, intellectuals of neither side, such as Miguel de Unamuno (1864–1936), offered different visions based on ideologies shaped by more cosmopolitan, *casticista* (parochial) or religious stances. All did justice to Bourdieu's (1984, 1986) definition of intellectuals as being specialists in handling symbolic goods.

At the turn of the century, the failure to arrive at a consensus on the definition and common destiny of Spain and to build a cohesive form of nationalism encouraged peripheral nationalisms to develop, especially in Catalonia and the Basque Country. These regional nationalisms crystallized further in the early twentieth century in the form of the Catalan *Lliga Regionalista*, the *Solidaridad Catalana,* and the creation of the *Mancomunidad de Cataluña* (a form of regional government), and the *Partido Nationalista Vasco* (PNV, Basque Nationalist Party) formed by Sabino Arana, ideologue of Basque nationalism and creator of many of its symbols. As historiographers of Spanish archaeology have pointed out (Díaz-Andreu 1997, 2000) it is no coincidence that the greatest advances in archaeology during the first decades of the twentieth century came from Catalonia and the Basque Country. In both cases the work, led by Pere Bosch Gimpera and José Miguel de Barandiarán respectively, focused on dating the presence of human inhabitants of these lands to prehistoric times, thereby demonstrating their antiquity and cultural distinctiveness (Fusi Aizpurúa 1990: 132). This work was adopted by nationalists in both regions as evidence of their distinctiveness from the rest of Spain, stimulating a look to the past and to heritage as a means of redefining the present and providing guidelines for the future.

The above brief glimpse at the evolving appreciation of cultural heritage in nineteenth- and early twentieth-century Spain reveals that it was stimulated by a series of wars and crises, thereby linking it with notions of 'Spanishness' that were in confrontation at the beginning of the twentieth century. Now we turn to the Spanish Civil War of 1936–1939 and its impact on cultural heritage.

The Spanish Civil War and its symbols

*The reality of the war is but rhetoric, torrents of rhetoric that
inundate primary schools, beat columns in newspapers, whirl
around parliamentary speeches and roll in cascades over the
martial drum that drags children along city streets.*
(Ortega y Gasset cited by Marrero Cabrera 2006)

In 1931 the Second Republic was proclaimed after King Alfonso XIII
was forced to leave the country. Several changes of government
followed between 1931 and 1936 as conservative and progressive
governments alternated in quick succession until the elections of
February 1936. During this period the national rift over divergent
visions of Spain became radicalized into two camps, leaving little room
for alternative views as stand-points became increasingly intransigent,
stimulating a heightened aggressiveness of the opposed discourses.[19]
The mutual demonization and fabrication of myths escalated after the
violent suppression of an attempted revolution by Asturian miners in
1934 and the assassination of the conservative politician José Calvo
Sotelo on 13 July 1936. In February 1936 the Popular Front won a
narrow victory and five months later, on the 18th of July 1936, a military rebellion ignited what is known as the Spanish Civil War. The
Generals at the head of the revolt expected to perform a swift coup such
as the one that Miguel Primo de Rivera had managed in 1923.
However, by 1936 civil society had been mobilized to defend now radically opposing views of Spain. The following sections will show how
the vision of the 'two Spains' further crystallized during and after the
war.

Preston (2003) has argued that there were numerous contesting
visions at play, but they were simplified into a dual vision that gradually
became rooted in the Spanish national consciousness, influencing
discourse during the war, in its aftermath and creating a divided 'imagined community' which continues to permeate Spanish politics today.
Moreover, international interests and ideologies further drew the two
sides apart. The national clash within Spain – where the very definition
of the nation and its future shape were at stake – combined with the
more radical ideologies of Fascism and National Socialism on the one
side and Communism, Socialism, and Anarchism on the other, proved
explosive.

The *real politik* aspect of the conflict was the uprising of a part of
society that saw itself losing political and economic power under the
Republic. However, once the war began the conflict raged on ideological and cultural planes. In 1937 a Ministerial Decree literally opened a
'cultural front' when it created the *Milicias Culturales* – Cultural
Militias. These comprised an aggressive literacy program that was

presented as part of the fight of the people for their culture. They were soon followed by similar initiatives such as the *Guerrillas del Teatro* created by María Teresa León taking theatre to the frontlines.[20] The various sides also waged propaganda offensives promulgating a cultural model corresponding to their vision of Spain while delegitimizing the others'. Hence the keys to unlocking the reconstruction

---

Box 2.2   A Battle to define the 'Spanish woman'

As the war progressed values that had been commonly extolled by both sides, such as unity, began to take on different dimensions as they became imbued with ideological connotations. This dynamic is observable in the symbolic use and prescribed social roles of women. The Second Republic had made considerable advances in terms of women's rights, divorce was made possible, abortion was legalized in Cataluña, and images of strong women working and fighting alongside men were popularized. On the Nationalist side, women were seen as being the defenders of the Spanish hearth, family and the traditions of the Patria.[22] As the war evolved, despite the fact that women were doing similar work on both sides, propagandistic images became increasingly different emphasizing ideological differences.

The victory of one party in the conflict likewise meant a victory for the vision of Spain that they endorsed. However, the radicalisation of this vision during the conflict meant that the idea of women's roles in Spanish society promulgated by the Nationalists[23] at the end of the war was even more dogmatic than it had been before it. The vision of women upheld by the Franco regime went back not only on the advances made by the Republic but on those made since the beginning of the century – see writings by Carmen Martín Gaite, *Entre visillos* (1957) and Carmen Lafforet, *Nada* (1944). Examples of this backward trend, resulting from the association of traditional values with outmoded ways of life are apparent in all sectors of Spanish life as will be seen in the next chapter.

2.4   Photomontage in the Paris World's Fair, 1937, contrasting the two visions of Spanish women.

2.5   The version that 'won' on the cover of *Spain*, 1 November 1940.

after 1939 – the choices made, the reprisals and the underlying messages imbedded in it – originate in the war itself. The following section therefore outlines the use and abuse of cultural heritage during the war.

The cultural front and the 'Two Spains'

At the beginning of the war, both the government of the Republic and the rebel Generals drew on a common repertoire of historic symbols and myths. Both sides presented themselves as the heirs of 'heroic Spaniards' and called on their followers to emulate them and defend their *Patria*. In 1936, for example, the poet Rafael Alberti adapted Cervantes' play *La destrucción de Numancia*, which was presented in Madrid's *Teatro de la Zarzuela* in 1937 as Franco's troops surrounded the capital – equating the Iberian city of Numancia's legendary resistance to a Roman imperialist General to Madrid's resistance to international fascism. Thus, in one fell swoop, Alberti recruited the symbolism of both Numancia and Cervantes to rally popular support for the Republic. Nor was this original: Hermenegildo (1994:16) suggests that the play might have been put to similar use during the 1808 War of Independence, performed in the besieged city of Zaragoza.[21] These different uses of Numancia reveal that myths are made up of a densely woven combination of elements and layers of meaning that are reconfigured each time they are told. As different strands are emphasized or neglected at each re-telling, so the narrative and symbolic content itself shifts (Ball 1991). The myth acts in various ways: it is both inscribed by its telling and inscribes discourse; in turn it is transformed by the material used to communicate it and transforms the material, adding a symbolic dimension.

The attacks besieging Zaragoza at the hands of Napoleonic troops in 1808 and 1809 also became material for myth-making in 1936. During the sieges women had taken part in the defence of the city, firing canons from the ramparts and rallying others to do the same. Out of these actions the legend of Agustina of Aragón was born, a legend the Republic used to encourage women to take part in the conflict and which was taken up after the war, as will be discussed, by Franco to convey a very different message. Both sides also referenced Goya's emblematic paintings dating from 1814 – the *Second of May 1808 in Madrid* also known as *La carga de los mamelucos en la Puerta de Sol* and the *Third of May 1808 in Madrid* with its *fusilamientos*, also known as *Los fusilamientos en la montaña de Principe Pío* – to depict the 'heroism' shown by *Madrileños* in defence of their city. A common element in all of these myths was civilian participation, so crucial during civil wars, which both sides needed to rally. This illustrates a major characteristic of civil strife: no longer limited to the strategic movement of troops across predetermined battlefields, civilians become active participants to be won over, recruited, militarized and targeted. This element of the 'enemy within' further contributed to the dramatic vengefulness and paranoia of the post-war period that would be played out in the reconstruction.

Despite initially drawing on a common repertoire of symbols, as the war evolved the two sides increased their efforts to emphasize their differences. Both came to depict the other as a foreign invader; thereby denying the other's claim to Spanishness. For the Nationalists the war was presented as a Crusade against the red hordes of international communism. For the Republic, the aggressor was portrayed as a disloyal and rebellious military supported by the forces of international fascism (Figures 2.6 to 2.13). An important difference in the historical references that gained momentum throughout the conflict was the Nationalists' reference to the war as a Crusade with all the historical connotations of medieval Reconquest and Renaissance Empire that this word implied. This reference entailed a specific set of values by which the adversary was depicted as the antithesis of the Spanish *raza* – race – despite being Spanish (González Calleja and Limón Nevado 1988: 47). The interpretation of the war as Crusade was reinforced by the Spanish church and the Vatican, under Pope Pius XI and then Pius XII (Cooper 1976: 48–81). On 1 July 1937 the Spanish Episcopate published a collective pastoral (*pastoral colectiva del Episcopado español*) sanctifying Franco's position and the war, which only the archbishops of Tarragona and Vitoria – both in exile for having supported Catalan and Basque Catholics respectively – refused to sign (Sueiro 2006: 24–25, Cooper 1976: 48).

The battle lines of the war thus came to be drawn not only on ideological but also in cultural terms. Each side claimed to be the true defender of authentic Spanishness, its history, tradition and culture. The Second Republic had insisted so much on culture – through literacy programmes, touring schools, exhibitions and theatre, and through propaganda campaigns – that some Spanish observers came to describe the conflict as one of culture versus anti-culture (Giménez Caballero 1980: 112). The two key players of the confronted sides, and active in the propaganda battles concerning heritage, were Josep Renau, Republican Minister of *Bellas Artes*, and Pedro Muguruza, working for the Nationalist *Servicio Artístico de Vanguardia* and technical advisor of the *Comisión de Cultura y Ensenza de la Junta Técnica*.[24] Both sought to convince international public opinion of their efforts to protect heritage and so demonstrate their respect for Spanish history and culture.

The visual front and propaganda war

That the war inflamed passions worldwide can be seen in the estimated 45,000 international volunteers that went to Spain as the International Brigades to fight on the side of the Republic and against the international threat of fascism. In addition, some 80,000 Italians, both conscripts and

Republican posters against the 'invader' calling to defend culture by referencing bull fighting and the arts

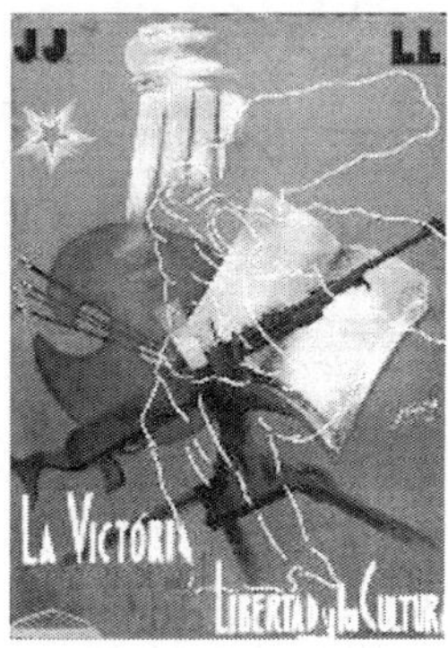

2.6   Bardasano. *Fuera el Invasor.* 1937. (España. Ministerio de Cultura. Centro Documental de la Memoria Histórica. Sig. PS-Carteles, 232.)

2.7   Fuentes, X. *La Victoria sera el puntal de la libertad y la cultura.* 1937. (España. Ministerio de Cultura. Centro Documental de la Memoria Histórica. Sig. PS-Carteles, 483.)

2.8   Martí Bas, *La Juventud en armas defiende la cultura*, 1938. (UGT: www.ugt.es/ugtpordentro/guerracivil/carteles.htm.)

volunteers and 15,000 Germans, fighting in rotations of 5,000, also fought in Spain on the side of the military rebels. Among the internationals engaged in this conflict were a significant number of artists. These photographers, poets, novelists, and artists together with their Spanish counterparts, generated an important body of literature[25] and visual art reflecting on and representing their experiences. This vast creative output was to constitute a form of heritage generated by the war and, like Lucilius and Polybius in Numancia, had an impact on its historiography and myth-making dimension. The context that made this possible was the result of a combination of factors both artistic and ideological. There were a significant number of Spanish artists at the visual vanguard, such as Pablo Picasso, Joan Miró, Juan Gris, and Salvador Dalí. Photography had increased in importance in terms of reporting, and experimenting with photomontage. The use of the arts for the purposes of propaganda spurred heated debates in the art world about the social uses, abuses and responsibilities of art, as well as stylistic concerns which pitted social realism against the experimental vanguard of expressionism and abstraction. As the Republic's *Director General de Bellas Artes*, Josep Renau organized the Republic's pavilion at the Paris World's Fair – a visual propaganda effort largely in the form of posters; and he was also responsible for the evacuation of the Prado Museum.

Nationalist posters emphasizing unity – reiterated by the yoke and arrows of the Falange and by the image of the Iberian peninsula, showing the war as a crusade, and the enemy as a devil incised with the acronyms of the parties of the Republic's Popular Front

2.9 Spanish Anonymous. 20th Cent. *España una, grande, libre.* c.1937–1940. (España. Ministerio de Cultura. Centro Documental de la Memoria Histórica, PS-Carteles, 2033.)

2.10 Teodoro Delgado. *Con el triunfo de los ejércitos, la unidad de las tierras de España.* c.1938–1939. (España. Ministerio de Cultura. Centro Documental de la Memoria Histórica, PS-Carteles, 2043.)

2.11 Morell. *Ha llegado España.* 1939. (España. Ministerio de Cultura. Centro Documental de la Memoria Histórica, PS-Carteles, 2116.)

Visual culture took Spain by storm from the very onset of the civil war, taking on the dimensions of a 'visual front'. City streets were plastered with mural newspapers[26] and posters but the visual frontlines also extended to postcards, pamphlets, flyers, stamps, money and eventually even lottery and ration cards. Colombo (1977: 17) has argued that with the Spanish war visual mass communication took off; images and photography added a new dimension to war reporting as did their ability to provoke feelings of indignation and exaltation. There was an explosion in the number of newspapers and especially illustrated magazines (Mendelson 2007: 342–345), all carrying illustrations, photographs, cartoons, and maps of the war fronts. This visual front, the battle to create an omnipresent landscape of images that could enlist the 'hearts and minds' of Spaniards, quickly became tangible throughout the streets of cities and towns all over Spain. They were an essential part of transmitting the political discourse in a country with high illiteracy rates.

The Spanish Civil War also coincided with the birth of photojournalism; the reproducibility of these images made it possible for the war and its dramatic events to have important echoes internationally. Robert Capa's "moment of death" photograph of a dying militiaman falling in a position that echoes the crucifixion pose of the central figure in Goya's *Third of May* became an iconic image of the war and of photojournalism.[27]

Stereotypical representations of *'Los Nacionales'*

2.12 "The Nationals", by Juan Antonio Morales for the Ministry of Propaganda, 1936. (España. Ministerio de Cultura. Centro Documental de la Memoria Histórica, PS-Carteles, 190.)

2.13 Depicted in a parade in Valencia, 1937.

The visual nature of this conflict helped capture the imaginations of artists and sympathizers, drawing them to Spain. As well as being instruments in the fierce propaganda war, images thus became part of the front line. They served as combative elements on the same level as political speeches and rallies, radio messages, slogans, demonstrations and parades. They were also central to constructing a visual stereotype of the enemy (Figures 2.12 and 2.13). There was little room for nuances in a Spain of 'reds' and 'fascists' in which neutrality was not an option.

Destruction and protection of cultural heritage during the war

Anti-clerical sentiment among Spanish liberals dated from the nineteenth century and attacks on church properties had occurred throughout, manifesting themselves in the period from 1931 to 1934. Hence, its manifestations during the civil war, which included the deliberate targeting of religious sites, came after a long history in which Spanish liberals and the Spanish Church had been violently confronted. Gaya Nuño (1964: 90–91) argued that the Spanish Civil War, in comparison with previous conflicts in Spain, gave rise to a remarkably low number of heritage sites being destroyed.[29] However, there were many instances of destruction, some of which were caused by military necessity and others which were acts of symbolic violence. The case of the Cathedral of Oviedo illustrates the former; while the *fusilamiento* of the monument of the *Cerro de los Ángeles* can be seen to illustrate the latter.

Box 2.3   The Cultural front: The Paris World's Fair and the Venice Biennale

Perhaps the two greatest cultural feats of the Republic during the war were the evacuation of the Prado museum's collections and the Spanish Pavilion at the Paris World's Fair of 1937. In the first instance Josep Renau was able to safeguard one of the greatest treasures of European painting. In the

second instance, he placed the war firmly on the landscape of the European imaginary as a significant event, and with the pavilion won a propaganda victory that was not to be matched militarily. The pavilion was remarkable in terms of architectural and artistic quality and became one of the main attractions of the Fair. Designed by architects Josep Lluís Sert and Luis Lacasa, it contained works especially commissioned for the exhibition by artists of the stature of Pablo Picasso, Joan Miró and Alexander Calder. It also proved to be an opportunity to showcase the plight of Spain and the cause of the Republic. Above the main entrance a quote by the President of the Republic, Azaña, read: "There are over half a million Spaniards standing ready with bayonets in their trenches, they will not let themselves be trampled" (Figure 2.14). Photomontage was extensively used to illustrate the war and its ravages, including the bombing of Gernika and the *fusilamiento* of the poet and playwright Federico García Lorca. The exhibitions also included

2.14   The Republic's pavilion, Paris, 1937.

displays of crafts and industry from various Spanish regions, and the Basque and Catalan governments were given their own exhibition spaces within the building. However, it was in its modernity that the pavilion was at the vanguard of architecture and the visual arts.

In contrast to the modernity of the Republic's pavilion was the display offered by the Nationalist side which was given exhibition space by the Vatican in its pavilion and thus was able to display its counter vision of Spain. The centre piece of this vision was a painting by Josep María Sert titled: *La intercesión de Santa Teresa en la Guerra Civil española* (*The intercession of Saint Teresa in the Spanish Civil War*).[28] The Nationalists tried to recover from the Republic's propaganda victory in Paris the following year when they, not the Republic, were invited by Mussolini to exhibit at the Venice Biennale. The Spanish Nationalist pavilion at the Venice Biennale, curated by Eugenio D'Ors, comprised an exhibition of realist paintings and sculpture – by artists like Ignacio Zuloaga and Gustavo de Maeztu – as well as samples of religious art (Alted Vigil 1984: 296). The pavilion's entrance was crowned by the coat of arms chosen for the new regime – an adaptation of the insignia of the Catholic Kings (Figure 2.15).

2.15   The Nationalists' pavilion, Venice, 1938.

More than acts against religion, however, they were acts against what was perceived as an oppressive institution that amassed wealth while colluding with the military and monarchy against the interests of the majority of the population (Brenan 2004: 37, 48–55; Jackson 1967: 245–246). The Republic tried to put an end to these attacks through public campaigns, emphasizing that these buildings and their contents represented a common heritage that belonged to all Spaniards and thus needed to be protected (Figure 2.16).

There are also several instances of religious sites on the front lines that remained intact for many months such as the churches of Santa María de Naranco near Oviedo and San Antonio de la Florida in Madrid (Gaya Nuño 1964: 90–91). Nationalist aerial bombings did significant damage to heritage sites and religious buildings; in the first two months of intense aerial bombings of Madrid (November to December 1936) incendiary bombs fell on the Prado museum, the Academy of Fine Arts, the National Library, the Liria Palace, the Museums of Modern Art and Archaeology, the church of Saint Sebastian and the Descalzas convent (Álvarez Lopera 2003: 38).

Three scholars have documented the efforts to protect cultural heritage during the war: Renau (1980) and Álvarez Lopera (1982) on the efforts of the Republic and Alted Vigil (1984) on the Nationalist efforts. On the Republican side several bodies were set up to protect cultural heritage, the main organising body was the *Junta de Incautación y Protección del Tesoro Artístico*[30] (Board for the Seizure and Protection of the Artistic Treasure). A campaign which attempted to put an end to the destruction of church property was launched as well as a more general one asking soldiers and civilians alike to respect and protect heritage sites. In Madrid monuments were sand-bagged for protection (Figure 2.17). The most impressive effort to protect Spain's heritage, however, was the already mentioned project to evacuate works of art, first by centralizing collections in key locations and then by moving them to safe areas. Among these evacuations, the most spectacular was that of the Prado museum which was moved to Valencia (November 1936 to February 1938), Barcelona (March 1938) and eventually to Geneva (February 1939). A selection of important works was exhibited in the Musée d'Art et d'Histoire (June to August 1939) until the Nationalist authorities recovered them in September 1939. This evacuation is documented by Álvarez Lopera (1982) and Colorado Castellary (1991 and 2008) and has been the subject of recent exhibitions, two documentary films and a movie.[31]

On the Nationalist side, protection efforts began in the summer of 1938 through the *comisarías de zona*[32] that were given a budget to inventory the monuments in their zone and attend to those most badly damaged. Alted Vigil (1984) has traced the evolution of various organisms involved with cultural heritage during the war such as the *Servicio*

Attempts to protect cultural heritage

2.16 Poster by Gaya produced for the Republic in 1937: "The art of Spain is a target of the Fascist aviation". (España. Ministerio de Cultura. Centro Documental de la Memoria Histórica. Sig.: PS-Carteles, 873.)

2.17 *Cibeles* fountain with her protective shield, Madrid 1937. (España. Ministerio de Cultura. Archivo General de la Administración. AGA-Cultura-124-Sig.: 17–8484.) (Archivo Alfonso. © DACS 2010.)

Nacional de Bellas Artes, the *Junta Técnica del Estado* (Culture and Teaching Commission and State Technical Board), and the reconstruction efforts that the latter began to undertake. She also documents the works of those organizations that gained greater protagonism towards the war's end, such as the *Servicio de Defensa del Patrimonio Artístico Nacional* (Service for the Defence of the National Artistic Heritage). This Service consisted of a *Comisaría General* (General Office) headed by Pedro Muguruza and offices for regional zones; many of its officers[33] were to play key roles as of 1939 working in the recovery, identification and return of works of art – including those that had been evacuated by the Republic.

Despite the Republic's efforts, on 5 February 1938 the magazine *L'Illustration* published a graphic report showing the destruction caused by 'the reds' (Alted Vigil 1984: 90). This accusation received prompt replies, namely an article in *Nuestra España* dedicated to the protection of cultural heritage during the war (April 1938). The 'foreign' element was here again important. On the Republican side, the justification for evacuating as much of the moveable heritage as possible out of the country during the war were the aerial raids (Figure 2.16) – bombs hit both the Prado Museum and the National Library in Madrid – attributed to the Italian and German air forces. On the Nationalist side, Republican leaders were accused of looting and selling Spanish cultural heritage to

2.18 Tourists visiting a site of the *Cinturón de Hierro* on one of the tours of the Northern Front organized by Luis Bolín. (BNE photo archive – *Sección Guerra Civil*, box 113-trip, envelope 29.)

foreign art merchants to the benefit of the Louvre's collections, and by so doing of emulating the actions of the Napoleonic troops in the War of Independence (Mora 1938: 32–33 cited by Alted Vigil 1984: 91). The city of Toledo became a focal point for the propaganda war, partly because of its rich cultural heritage and numerous religious buildings with important collections, and partly because its international renown made it an apt pawn on the diplomatic arena. One of the most influential actions by Renau was his speech to the League of Nations in 1937, published in the magazine *Mouseion* (vol. XI, n° 39–40, 1937: 7–64) on the protection measures adopted by the Republic. For his part, Muguruza, together with Juan Teixidor as head of the *Sección de Relaciones Culturales del Ministerio del Exterior* and the Duque of Alba, Nationalist Ambassador to London, sought to influence public opinion, particularly in Britain, on the side of the Nationalist efforts (Alted Vigil 1984: 92–93).

The propaganda war and mutual accusations of wholesale destruction were such that an interesting precedent was set for the role of foreign observers. As a result of a letter by Sir Frederic Kenyon, former Director of the British Museum, which appeared in *The Times* of 20 July 1937, expressing his concern over the fate of Spanish heritage, the Republic invited him to visit and observe their protection efforts. In August 1937, together with James Mann, Director of the Wallace Collection,[34] he visited Republican-held areas of Spain, including Madrid. Impressed by the protection measures they wrote a very favourable report on the work of the *Junta Central del Tesoro Artístico* as well as several articles (Kenyon 3 and 4 September 1937 in *The Times* and Mann 27 October in *The Listener*). A year later, in November of 1938, Michael W. Stewart of the Victoria and Albert Museum visited the Nationalist sites with a similar mission and reported his findings in *The Burlington Magazine for Connoisseurs* (vol. 74, n° 431, 1939: 72–76). International cooperation for the protection of cultural heritage during the war made possible the evacuation of the Prado's collections to Geneva through the actions of the International Committee for the Safeguard of the Spanish Artistic Treasures and the League of Nations.[35] This set yet another precedent, in this case for the role of international organizations in the protection of heritage threatened by war.

During the civil war cultural heritage was destroyed, severed, reinterpreted and recreated, thus transforming the landscape and heritagescape of the country and its 'imagined community'. Rather than physical damage to material heritage, however, it was through the mutual accusations of destruction as well as the propaganda campaigns seeking to disinherit the 'other' from any claims to Spanish culture or history that Spanish heritage received its most violent blows.

The war and the production of heritage

Many events of the war became myths, assisted by propaganda, mutual demonization and the need on both sides for heroes and martyrs. The battles that became the object of mythmaking included those of Brunete, Teruel and the Ebro; the massacres, those of Badajoz and the Malaga to Almería road, Paracuellos del Jarama and the Cuartel de la Montaña; the sieges, those of Madrid, Belchite and the Alcázar of Toledo; the strategic war elements, the *Cinturón de Hierro* (Iron Belt) and the *Alto de los Leones*; the martyrs, Federico García Lorca and Jose Antonio Primo de Rivera.

An activity that contributed to the creation of war-related myths was that of war-time tourism. Franco's first government (Burgos, October 1936) created the *Servicio Nacional de Turismo* (National Tourist Service) and by 1938 its director, Luís Bolín, was running war tourism trails called *Rutas Nacionales de Guerra* – National War Routes (Gutiérrez Valero 2005: 291).[36] The fall of the Northern front (Bilbao fell on 19 June and Oviedo on 20 October 1937) turned this area into a particularly attractive tourist attraction. As early as 18 October 1938, a tourist route was created called *Ruta de Guerra del Norte* within which Bolín organized visits to defeated Bilbao, the ruins of Gernika and the captured *Cinturón de Hierro* (Figure 2.18).[37] This officially organized war tourism was carefully controlled; neither maps nor cameras were allowed. Nevertheless, leaflets with the tourist routes were handed out and photographs were available for purchase (Ministry of Information and Tourism 1939 *Ruta de Guerra del Norte*).[38]

These tours had clear propagandistic aims, they were replete with references to and 'proof' of the barbarism of the enemy. For example, in the document *Itinerario turístico para el recorrido de la porción batida del Cinturón de Hierro de Bilbao* ("Tourist Itinerary for a tour of the defeated portion of the Iron Belt of Bilbao") a description of the visit to the church of Goicolegea reads:

> *This altar has been miraculously saved from the red-separatist*
> *horde that was preparing to take it apart and take it along with*
> *so many works of artistic value that were looted from their sites*
> *many of them lost for the national artistic treasure.*[39]

This is an early indication of the interest of the nationalist side in the rhetorical potential of ruins which was to be greatly developed in the postwar period. Diego Quiroga y Losada, Marqués of Santa María del Villar, who had been involved in organizing tourist activities under Miguel Primo de Rivera, also ran some of the war-tourism trips and photographed them. He later became one of the main photographers of the reconstruction, supplying many of the images used by the magazine *Reconstrucción* and national newspapers that today provide a valuable documentation of the process.[40]

Undeniably cultural heritage suffered physical damage during the Civil War, especially as a result of shelling and aerial bombings. Gaya Nuño (1964) has argued that despite attacks against church properties at the beginning of the conflict, there was not a deliberate programme of looting of collections and destruction on the massive scale seen in the wars of the nineteenth-century.[41] Both sides in the conflict claimed that they were the legitimate representatives and defenders of Spain, and made efforts to protect cultural heritage with the Republic spending considerable time and resources on the venture. The radicalization of Spain into two opposites and the false representation of these polarized sides as homogeneous wholes made this possible. Each side proceeded to construct a vision of Spain in which there was no room for the other and in which the other, represented as a foreign invader, had no claim to a Spanish heritage: past, present or future. The fact that one side won and transformed itself into a dictatorial regime without an arbitrated peace agreement or process of reconciliation meant that it was able to prolong its attack on the other side for the following 40 years.

The following chapter will lay out the reconstruction process that Spain went through to see how a fragmented heritage-scape emerged. It will first examine the administrative organization of the reconstruction then look at attempts to construct a New Spain – through selectively chosen historical narratives, visual styles, memorial and performative practices and moral parameters – and discuss how the process evolved through time.

3 Reconstructing Spain, 1938–1957

Final war dispatch corresponding to the 1st of April 1939, III Triumphal Year. On this day, captive and disarmed the red Army, the Nationalist troops have advanced on their final military objectives. THE WAR HAS ENDED.

Burgos, 1st of April of 1939. Year of the Victory.

EL GENERALÍSIMO: Franco

The war officially ended on 1 April 1939 with the fall of Madrid and the defeat of the Republic. If the war had divided Spain into two camps, the post-war maintained the division, now configured by the victorious and the defeated. The attitude toward the destruction caused by the war and how its aftermath would be dealt with was expressed by Diego Reina:

During it [the war] military necessity and waves of hatred destroyed works of art, demolished homes and laid waste to architecture. The passage of the red militias was signalled by systematic looting and a trail of fires. Finally, over these ruins the national spirit triumphed, and when on the 1st of April the headquarters of the Generalísimo emitted its final dispatch, the vibrations of combat ceased, it silenced the thunder in the air, and over the tortured fields there fell a monastic silence of Castilian monasteries. With the gaze fixed on the will of those who fell, Spain reformed its ranks to win the battle of the peace.

(Reina 1944: 126)

Before launching into the mechanisms and main actors of the rebuilding process, it is useful to provide a brief sketch of the atmosphere that reigned in Spain at the end of the war. Every aspect of life became imbued with new codes that were vital to understand within this radically altered state of affairs. Food, dress, professions, all became charged with new symbolic meaning. Since casual dress (overalls, short-sleeved shirts, women in trousers) was associated with the liberal and working classes now a new formality permeated dress codes so that hats and suits for men and skirts for women became the norm. A revealing anecdote is that of the astute hat maker who came up with the publicity slogan "the reds didn't wear hats" (Figure 3.43). Even the traditional dish called Russian Salad served in Spanish bars was renamed National Salad or Imperial Salad, while the uniform of the Spanish national football team was changed from the previously used red shirts to blue ones – echoing the Falangist uniform. These changes have significance beyond the merely anecdotal; they are indicative of an attempt to impose profound cultural change. As Pollock has commented: "cultural practices do a job which has major social significance in the articulation of meanings about the world, in the negotiation of social conflicts, in the production of social subjects" (Pollock 1988: 7).

As aspects of reconstruction can be seen as 'symbolic actions' (Geertz 1973: 10), the question becomes one of deciphering what is being said, what set of social codes and narratives are being relayed together with the bricks and mortar. This chapter sets out therefore to read the reconstruction in light of its various projects in order to then be able to examine the particular case of Gernika in light of the whole. The chapter will outline the reconstruction process in three main sections. The first will present the administration of the rebuilding and its dynamics: the institutions involved, the influential ideas about architecture and urban planning guiding it, and the communication of the process to the Spanish public. Second, the reconstruction project will be discussed in terms of the selective use of Spanish history, the memorialization and moralization of the conflict and the new heritage-scape that emerged as a result of these two veins. Finally, the evolution of the project through time will be addressed.

Administering the Rebuilding

In April 1939, the Nationalist government[1] faced the task of rebuilding the country. This was made more difficult by the advent of the Second World War only five months later, making materials scarce. This first Nationalist government established the main public organizations that would rebuild Spain (Table 3.1). Among these was the *Servicio de Regiones Devastadas y Reparaciones* (Service of Devastated Regions and Reparations) which became a *Dirección General* (General Directorate) with the reorganization of government institutions in August of 1939.[2] Both the General Directorate of *Regiones Devastadas* and that of *Arquitectura*, also created in 1939, were placed under the *Ministerio de la Gobernación* (Ministry of Interior) headed by Franco's brother-in-law Serrano Suñer – indicating a desire to closely control their activities.[3] While there was some overlap between these two organizations[4] it was *Regiones Devastadas* that had a specific *reconstruction* mandate, supplemented by the activities of the *Junta Nacional para la Reconstrucción de Templos* (National Board for the Reconstruction of Churches) which was created to restore and rebuild religious buildings. *Regiones Devastadas* also collaborated with the *Dirección General de Bellas Artes*,[5] which fell under the umbrella of the Ministry for National Education, and included the *Sección del Tesoro Artístico* and the *Servicio de Recuperación y Defensa del Patrimonio Artístico Nacional* (PAN).[6]

Table 3.1 Main State bodies involved in the reconstruction and in heritage

---

Dirección General de Regiones Devastadas y Reparaciones
    (DG of Devastated Regions and Reparations)
Junta Nacional para la Reconstruccion de Templos
    (National Board for the Reconstruction of Churches)
Dirección General de Arquitectura
    (DG of Architecture)
Dirección General de Bellas Artes
    (DG of the Arts)
Servicio de Recuperación y Defensa del Patrimonio Artístico Nacional
    (Service for the Recovery and Defence of the National Artistic Heritage,
    known as PAN)
Junta de Incautación y Protección del Tesoro Artístico
    (National Board for the Incautation and Protection of the Artistic Treasure)
Instituto Nacional de la Vivienda
    (National Housing Institute)
Instituto Nacional de Colonización
    (National Colonization Institute)
Instituto de Crédito para la Reconstrucción Nacional
    (Credit Institute for the National Reconstruction)

According to the decree of 25 March 1939 outlining its competencies, the function of *Regiones Devastadas* was to achieve the rapid restoration of the Spanish heritage, taking into account artistic value as well as the political and religious character of sites. Thus another role of the Directorate was its significant propagandistic agenda which resulted in the production of ample quantities of visual material for its magazine, exhibitions, and other forms of public communication. The mandate of *Regiones Devastadas* to define and manifest the "real representation" of the "Spanish spirit" played a central role in its activities:

> *Amongst the newly created state organizations is the Directorate*
> *of Devastated Regions and Reparations, its essential mission is to*
> *orient, facilitate and, in certain cases, directly put into practice*
> *the reconstruction of damages suffered in the towns and cities*
> *that were bloody stages of the saintly and victorious Crusade of*
> *liberation or irrefutable witnesses to the barbarous and cruel*
> *actions of the hordes that, guided by Russia, demonstrated their*
> *hatred towards all that signified the real representation of the*
> *basic and secular principles of the Christian and Spanish spirit.*
> (Reconstrucción, no. 1, 1940)

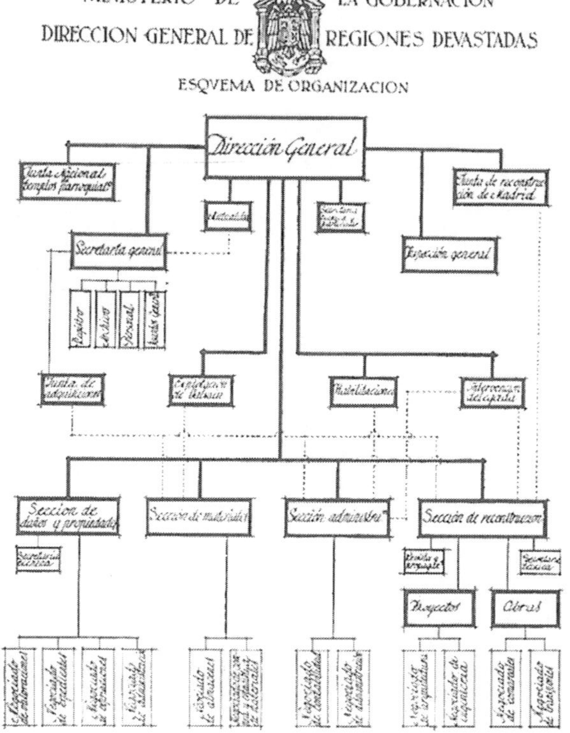

3.1 Organigram (*Reconstrucción*, no. 1, 1940: 3).

Regiones Devastadas was structured according to a hierarchy of various sections and 'juntas' (Figure 3.1). The *Sección de reconstrucción* was in turn divided into two main units, *Proyectos* which drew up projects for the reconstruction of adopted towns and official buildings and *Obras*, which actually carried out the projects that were approved. Orchestrated from Madrid, the rebuilding work of the Directorate was largely effected by its regional offices. Spain was divided into different zones and the Directorate established *Oficinas Comarcales de Proyectos y Obras* in each of them (Figure 3.2). The resolve of *Regiones Devastadas* to create an image of a unified Spain, explicitly laid out in its founding documents, meant that it tried to exert considerable control over all types of rebuilding, including private initiatives. Already in June 1938 it was decreed that no one could rebuild without authorization from its regional offices (Moreno Torres 1944). Furthermore, even structures not built by the state adapted an architectural language that corresponded to the official lines. For instance, the façade of the *Banco Hispano de Edificación* in Madrid, badly damaged during the war, was rebuilt by Fernández-Shaw in 1943–44 to resemble a triumphal arch (Figure 3.3). The explicit intention of this architectural form, as expressed by its architect, was for it to act as a monument to the reconstruction of Spain (Cirici 1977: 147, COAM 2003: 363).

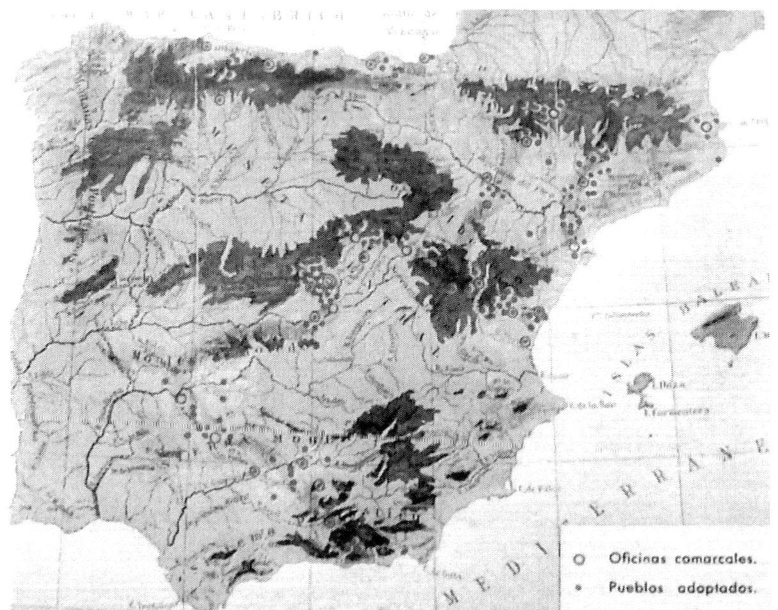

3.2   Distribution of regional offices, *Reconstrucción*, no. 12, 1941.

3.3 *Banco Hispano de Edificación*, Madrid (note the figure by Victor Macho on the pinnacle of a man holding up a building).

Along with these institutions there were a few influential individuals including the Directors of *Regiones Devastadas*: Joaquin Benjumea (1938–1939), José Moreno Torres (1939–1951) and José Macián Pérez (1951–1957).[7] Head Architect of *Regiones Devastadas*, Gonzalo Cárdenas, who was also the editor and a regular contributor to the Directorate's magazine *Reconstrucción*, Antonio Gallego Burin, President of the Monuments Commission for Granada, and Serrano Suñer, were also influential. Several other key figures — architects, art historians, politicians and ideologues— influenced the overall process (see Appendix A).

Scope of action

By law of 23 September 1939 a programme of *pueblos adoptados* was developed by which the Nation, and its Head of State, 'adopted' those towns and cities that had suffered the greatest destruction – those having had 75 percent or more of their habitable constructions destroyed.[8] In these localities, the State took on the reconstruction of buildings considered to be its responsibility: structures belonging to the church or provincial and municipal authorities (Moreno Torres 1944). By 1940 the *Caudillo* had adopted 102 towns, and by 1944 another 90, including several that had suffered destruction for reasons not directly related to the war such as floods and fires. In a speech given at the inauguration of the *Exposición de la reconstrucción de España*, later published as the paper *Datos sobre la reconstrucción de España* (Madrid, 22 June 1940), Moreno

Torres stressed that the importance of the reconstruction work in adopted towns lay in the need to prevent rural depopulation.

A large percentage of *Regiones Devastadas'* activities involved relatively small scale projects centred on the reconstruction of churches, town halls and *plazas mayores*, as well as official facilities such as *Guardia Civil* headquarters, Falange offices and public services such as medical dispensaries and markets. These projects focused around two urban nuclei, the *plaza mayor* and the church, demonstrating the Directorate's drive to redefine the political and religious centres of townships across the country (Blanco 1987: 17). Of these interventions, those relating to religious buildings clearly dominated. In June 1942, the Directorate published a report of its two years of work including lists of projects being planned, in process or already completed. Comparing the figures for town halls with those for churches is revealing of where priorities lay (see Table 3.2).[9]

Together with the acquisition of construction materials, one of the Directorate's challenges was the ability to procure labour. A solution was proposed by the priest José Pérez del Pulgar whose programme, *Redención de penas por el trabajo* (Redeeming of prison term through labour), came to supply much of the workforce for rebuilding projects *(Reconstrucción,* no. 1, 1940:28–31). The principles of the programme were that those held responsible for the destruction should repair the damage they had caused.[11] Thus the defeated were charged with the responsibility for the destruction and the regime portrayed as the rebuilder, adding a moral victory to the military one.[12] The system was put in place during the war (1938) with the use of prison labour reaching a peak at the height of the reconstruction efforts (1940–1945)[13] and lasting until 1970.[14] Prisoners provided labour for the public sector (mainly Regiones *Devastadas* and the *Instituto Nacional de Colonización*), for the church through the *Reconstrucción de Templos* programme and for private sector construction companies.[15] One consequence, resulting from the policy of moving prisoners to work camps away from their places of origin, meant that they were made to work in unfamiliar environments where they were unversed in local construction styles, traditions and materials, thus eliminating any possibility of drawing on the local expertise that they might have contributed. The use of political prisoners in the reconstruction not only reinforced the divide between the victorious and defeated of the war, it also added a further dimension to the emerging landscapes, as will be seen in greater detail in the case of Gernika.[16]

Ideology behind the rebuilding

At the end of the war, the victorious side consisted of a conglomerate of various groups: Falangists, Traditionalists, Monarchists,[17] the Catholic Church and the Military, as well as a large part of the aristocracy,

Table 3.2 Rebuilding and Restoring: town halls versus cathedrals and churches, 1942[10]

No.	Town Halls	No.	Cathedrals and churches
5	Town Halls completed (including Gernika) for 1,996,243.09 pesetas	48	Cathedrals and churches completed (including Belchite) for 5,810,084.54 pesetas
15	Town Halls under construction (including Brunete) budgeted for 5,710,597.87 pesetas.	97	Cathedrals and churches under reconstruction or restoration (including Brunete and Gernika) budgeted for 21,695,937.91 pesetas
23	Projects planned for the construction or reconstruction of Town Halls prepared (including Belchite)	77	Projects planned for the construction or reconstruction of cathedrals and churches prepared (of which 6 are cathedrals)

landowning and industrialist sectors of Spanish society. All of these were to vie for a part in shaping the construction of a new state. The Falange was the most powerful group at the end of the war,[18] and dominated the first stages of the rebuilding, informing ideas about architecture and urban planning.

During these early stages, architecture was considered to be the most important art of the new state. Giménez Caballero had written: "Architecture: art of the State, function of the State, essence of the State. Before her the other arts – like functional phalanx formations – must discipline themselves to occupy their rank in combat and order" (cited by Cirici 1977: 64). This policy was set out in an Official State Bulletin:

> (. . .) *the need to order the material life of the country in accordance with new principles, the representative importance of works of Architecture as an expression of the forces and the mission of the State in a determined epoch, induces us to bring together all of the various professional manifestations of Architecture under a Directorate at the service of public needs.*
>
> (BOE, 30 September 1939)

Even building materials were imbued with meaning. Giménez Caballero wrote deriding cement because it "crushed all hierarchy", and considered brick to be communist for being "cubist, naked, egalitarian, red, cellular" (cited by Bonet Correa 1996: 152). The preferred building material was stone, specifically granite, enhanced by wrought iron details. These choices had both political and historic readings. For while cement construction was associated with modernism and brick construction with traditional Mudéjar architecture (a style developed in the twelfth-century by Spanish Muslims), stone connoted castles and gothic churches, the Roman aqueduct of Segovia, the medieval walls of Avila, the Plateresque style of Renaissance Salamanca and above all the monastery of El Escorial.

Before the war, Giménez Caballero had set out that the Monastery of the Escorial should be adopted as the paradigmatic architectural model of the Spanish State:[19]

> *The Escorial is the State at its proudest, the most sublime and genial image of what Spain wanted to be, became, and wishes once again to be. The Escorial is, above all, Architecture: nothing to do with 'pure effort', with music and vagueness. It is construction. It is measure. It is conquest. All of it: hierarchy, harmony.*
>
> (Giménez Caballero 1935: 235)

The classicist renaissance building style of Philip II's empire, epitomized by the Escorial, came to be known after its second architect, Juan de Herrera (1530–1597), as *estilo herreriano* and was characterized by the use of granite, slate roofs, and geometric decorative elements such as spheres and pyramids. More than a traditional architectural style to be emulated, the significance of the Escorial lay in its association with the glory of the Spanish Empire and Philip II's reign. The choice of the Escorial as a model for the reconstruction was enunciated by two influential ideologues of the regime, Giménez Caballero and Rafael Sánchez Mazas; the latter calling it the "stone Carta Magna of Spain" (*Arriba*, 2 July 1939). The other historic architectural style that was selected as an expression of the 'authentically Spanish' by the regime, advocated by the architect Antonio Palacios and the art historian Fernando Chueca Goitia, was that of Juan de Villanueva (1739–1811), the foremost exponent of Spanish neoclassicism.[20]

The Imperial style of Herrera and the neoclassical style of Villanueva became the paradigms to emulate. Departing slightly from the purely historicist styles, Diego Reina (1944: 134) suggested an alternative that combined a sense of Spain's 'imperial mission' with a combined version of neoclassicism rooted in Herreran style but adapted to contemporary realities. These ideas occasionally translated into confused results with styles from different historical periods appearing on the same building.[21] An example of this conflation of styles is the police headquarters planned for Oviedo (*cuartel para policía armada*) which draws on styles from three different centuries: long Herreran side buildings topped with pinnacles, Medieval Mudéjar towers, and a pseudo-Plateresque entrance.

An example that clearly illustrates how Herreran style was emulated by the regime is the Air Force Ministry – *Ministerio del Aire* – in Madrid. The resemblance with the Escorial is such that the Ministry is often referred to as the *Monasterio del Aire* (Figures 3.4 and 3.5). Designed by the architect Gutiérrez Soto and built between 1943 and 1958, it was one of Franco's most monumental building projects in Madrid. It was not possible, however, mainly for economic reasons, to maintain this monumental and eclectic building style as a widespread practice. Historical styles were frequently referenced through architectural details. In *plazas mayores*, town halls, churches, official buildings and stately homes the Herreran style was replicated through the use of decorative elements such as round or pyramidal pinnacles.

Throughout the magazines *Reconstrucción* and *Revista Nacional de Arquitectura* (*RNA*) can be gleaned the motivations and priorities guiding the rebuilding, as well as its significant propagandistic elements. Tracing the evolution of the topics that the magazines addressed also reveals the contradictions and tensions between the various ideologies vying for influence within the regime. Despite attempts to develop a unified architectural style that could be followed in the construction of official buildings throughout the country, the fact that the regime was comprised of groups with different ideological tendencies manifested in the use of a variety of styles: historicist, imperialist, regional, folkloric, and rationalist. Although the rhetoric of *Regiones Devastadas* claimed that the architectural styles it used were inspired by traditional buildings and towns, in practice the urban plans of the towns it projected frequently disregarded original layouts (Blanco 1987: 19). Commonly, as in Brunete, only the location of the church or *plaza mayor* remained the same. The

3.4 Monastery of *El Escorial*, 1500s (Patrimonio Nacional).

3.5 Ministry of the Air Force, 1940s (COAM).

Directorate's mandate had a strong regeneration vein that, rather than seeking to preserve the past, involved taking advantage of the destruction to 'improve' the urban planning and infrastructure of towns – widening and straightening streets – rather than restore them to their pre-war state (Moreno Torres 1944). Pedro Bidagor's plan for Madrid and the work of architects in the *Instituto Nacional de Colonización* show that despite traditionalist rhetoric there was not a massive break with modern building and urban design practice. Bidagor's plans are largely a continuation of the Plan of 1929, and the work of architects in the Institute show a continuation of modernist approaches to housing and town planning. Furthermore, some Falange architects also rejected the eclectic approach and favoured the rationalist architecture of the pre-war 1930s (López Díaz 2003), exemplified in such constructions as Madrid's *Nuevos Ministerios* and the *Ciudad Universitaria*. Overall, 'return to tradition' remained on the surface, supplying decorative elements as a backdrop for the New Spain.

In the long run, a consequence of the regime's use of specific architectural styles, of historic moments and expression of folklore, is that these became associated with the regime's ideology. In "The Rest is Noise: Listening to the Twentieth Century" Alex Ross (2008) makes a related point. He observes that classical music in the wake of Hitler suffered both from the physical destruction of venues and musicians and by certain associations with the regime. This, Ross argues, lead to the pairing of classical music with violent aggression in Hollywood films for instance: "Now, when any self-respecting Hollywood archcriminal sets out to enslave mankind, he listens to a little classical music to get in the mood" (Ross 2008: 306).

Tradition and folklore

While the 'traditional' vein was mainly applied to official buildings, it was also a source of inspiration for decorative elements applied widely in modest constructions in rural areas. The 'traditional' was often conflated with folkloric and artisanal. Handicrafts were used both discursively and in rebuilding 'traditional' expressions. The attitude toward handicrafts was conveyed in an article by Manuel Pombo Angulo (*El Alcázar*, 14 February 1939) in which he played with the word for crafts, *artesanía*, calling it *arte-sano* (healthy art) and concluding that it is the appropriate form of expression for the populace. While architecture was meant to deliver monumentality in reconstruction, *artesanía* and folklore were to be the cornerstones of 'tradition'. The two came together in architectural details that referenced regionalist architectural styles through the use of folkloric and traditional decorative elements.[22] The outbreak of the Second World War meant that make-shift solutions had to be found as more state-of-the-art materials could not be found or afforded; the rupture of ties with Paris and London, the eventual cooling of ties with

Germany and Italy as the war progressed, and the consequent inward turn of the regime, all spurred its promotion of local Spanish traditions, encouraging a focus on regional crafts and architecture.

Folklore was the acceptable form of expressing regional identities within Spain. In reducing them to aestheticised and romanticised forms the intention was to denude them of their potential political rallying power (Ortíz 1999), though this intention was not entirely successful. Through *Sección Femenina* of Falange folkloric groups toured choruses and dances, the 'authentic expressions of Spanish culture', around Latin America at first and then North America and Europe. Not only did this provide members opportunities to travel abroad at a time when few Spaniards had possibilities to do so, but folkloric groups managed to recover and preserve crafts, techniques, dances and songs that might otherwise have been lost. Paradoxically, folkloric groups also became a vehicle for subverting the regime and its strict control of social gatherings. As a consequence of regional languages being outlawed, folkloric groups in Catalonia and the Basque Country became not only ways of preserving culture but also important social venues for contesting the regime. In Catalonia clubs formed around *sardana* dancing and in the Basque Country mountaineering and gastronomic groups became popular. The Basque gastronomic clubs, for instance, provided a means for men to gather together for several hours, something otherwise outlawed.

Of the folkloric architectural styles the *mediterráneo-andalucista* gradually became the most in vogue throughout Spain. This reflected an attitude towards culture that chose certain folkloric arts and styles – flamenco music, Sevillana dances, and whitewashed houses with wrought iron window-guards and red geraniums – as representing the 'authentically' Spanish. As early as 1938 this folkloric trend was manifest in the production of the first influential, Spanish, version of Mérimée's *Carmen* – Florian Rey's *Carmen, la de Triana*[23] – filmed in Berlin with Hitler's blessing and using German actors in supporting roles to Imperio Argentina's Carmen (Powrie, Babington, Davies and Perriam 2007: 163–168). The association to Andalusia was further encouraged in the following decades as relations with the US strengthened, given that this was the vision of Spain that American tourists were thought to have.

The idea of everything Castilian being the paradigm of Spanishness was largely used in the architecture of official buildings for which there was significant uniformity. A comparison of the Directorate's projects region by region shows the same basic elements repeated. This is especially the case with the centres and buildings of power: the *Plaza Mayor* and Town Hall whose structures are almost identical from one town to the next. A prototype model Town Hall was developed and then built in *plazas mayores* throughout the country, the similarities being occasionally masked with decorative elements with 'local flavour', again emphasizing

Town Halls (Images from various issues of *Reconstrucción*.)

3.6 Valdelugueros, León.

3.7 Arjona, Jaen.

3.8 Deifontes, Granada.

3.9 Siétamo, Huesca.

3.10 Model for town halls of Spain (*Reconstrucción,* no. 21, 1942).

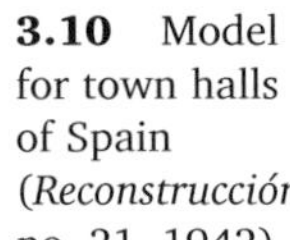

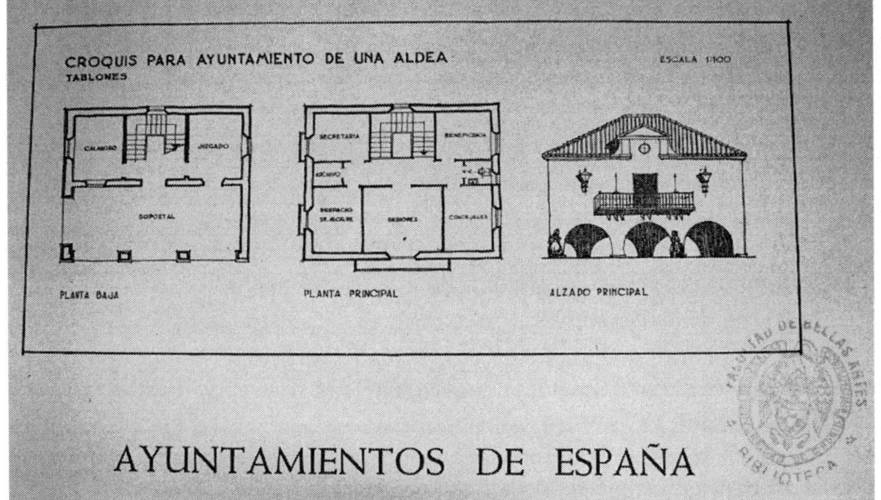

that to a large extent the more radical aspects of reconstruction rhetoric often remained at the level of façade (Figures 3.6 to 3.10).

Urban planning

One of the earliest documents laying out an ideological basis for the reconstruction of Spain was *Ideas generales sobre el plan nacional de ordenación y reconstrucción*, produced in 1939 by the Architecture Section of the *Servicios Técnicos de FET y de las JONS*.[24] In it, the plan for improving housing was expressed on three levels: the individual, family unit and social group. Further sub-sections indicating what the housing programme was intended to provide included: culture, "protection of the race", physical and pre-military education, and a "plan of popular, national and representative festivities" (*Servicios Técnicos de FET y de las JONS* 1939).

Partly as a result of the ideological influence of the Falange on early reconstruction plans, there was a strong emphasis on rebuilding rural areas. Ideologically this reflected the Falange's conviction that there lay the 'authentic' Spain, but practically it suited the regime's policy to stem massive population movements to urban areas. To these ends, the *Instituto Nacional de Colonización* was created in October 1939 under the auspices of the Ministry of Agriculture. While the term '*colonización*' in Spanish can refer to agricultural activity and rural development, there were nonetheless imperialist overtones to the actions of the Institute, albeit an internal kind. An article by Francisco Echenique published in *Reconstrucción* in 1942, entitled *Plazas Mayores en la colonización del Nuevo Mundo*, shows that these Spanish colonial towns were definitely present in the minds of architects working on the reconstruction. Also, an article by architect Alejandro Allánegui in *Reconstrucción*, no. 19 (January 1942: 23–30) reads: "The work that the Architects of Devastated Regions are carrying out in the Spanish countryside has much of the missionary, or crusade . . .", echoing both the Spanish colonial mission in the Americas and the *Reconquista*.

In addition to these recurring imperial connotations, urban planning was structured around one of the core values of the regime: order. Franco was depicted as the architect of the new state whose reconstruction project was a direct antithesis to the destructive 'red hordes' (López Gómez 2006:186), bringing order where there had been chaos. The *Plaza Mayor*, or main square, was the central element around which towns were structured and citizens' lives organized (Figures 3.11–3.14). It was made up of the Town Hall, Civil Guard precinct and Falange offices, and the nearby main church. The importance of the Plaza Mayor was explained by Victor D'Ors:

> *We mention with intent 'plazas mayores'. Because this traditional urban element in Spain, which resulted in creations of such*

Plazas Mayores

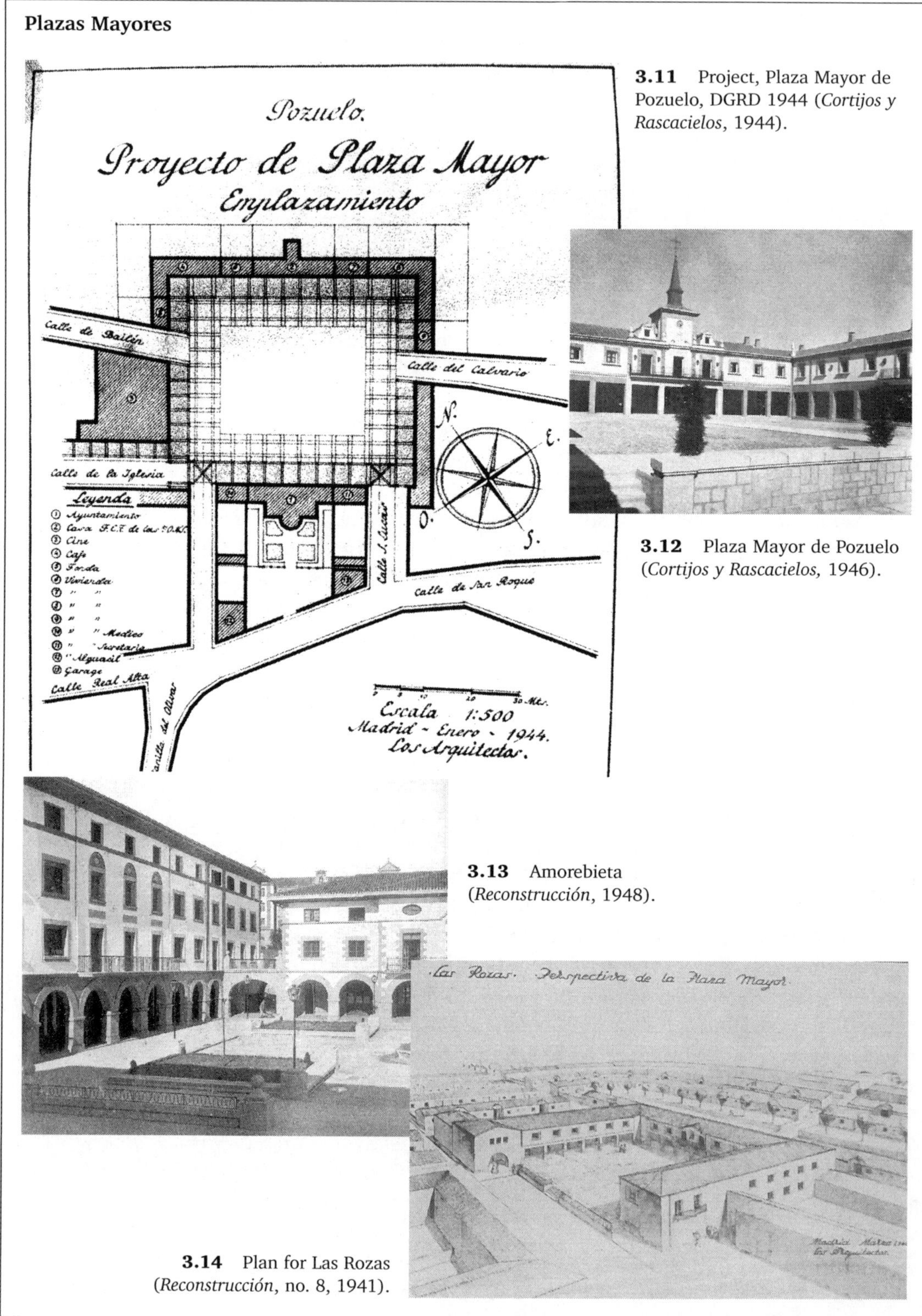

3.11 Project, Plaza Mayor de Pozuelo, DGRD 1944 (*Cortijos y Rascacielos*, 1944).

3.12 Plaza Mayor de Pozuelo (*Cortijos y Rascacielos*, 1946).

3.13 Amorebieta (*Reconstrucción*, 1948).

3.14 Plan for Las Rozas (*Reconstrucción*, no. 8, 1941).

beauty, adapted to the needs of contemporary life and re-established in the new spirit, must constitute the type of central nucleus in civic centres. It adapts better than any other type of square to public life and the conditions of our people.

(D'Ors, *Vértice*, no. 3, 1937)

The building plans of the Directorate clearly reveal a concern with the material ordering of a social hierarchy. The plans for towns like Nuevo Belchite, Lopera, Las Rozas and Villanueva de la Cañada show that housing types were classified according to the social rank of their destined inhabitants. The construction project for Nuevo Belchite reads: "Different types of housing of one and two floors are projected for seasonal farmers [*braceros*], for modest, medium, well-off and wealthy labourers and for industrialists"[25] (AGA-RD-Box 20702). Streets were designed to converge towards the axes of political, military, economic and religious power and memorialization. The buildings closest to the centre were built higher and with more 'noble' materials, including stone, wooden interior furnishings and iron window guards. This urban planning format was applied to cities throughout Spain. If Fascist Italy had chosen the ancient Roman Empire as the period on which to model itself Francoist Spain chose the Medieval and Renaissance periods, the austere Catholicism and the Imperial ambition of Philip II. This vision of Spanish heritage was reflected in the two veins that permeated the reconstruction rhetoric: the monumental and the traditional.

The rebuilding was accompanied by a further layer of redefinition as streets, squares, hospitals, schools and other public buildings were renamed referencing the regime's heroes (*Avenida del Generalísimo Franco, Calle del General Mola*); martyrs (*Avenida José Antonio Primo de Rivera, Calle de los Mártires*), religious and moral values (*Plaza de la Santa Trinidad, Glorieta de la Piedad, Calle de la Fe, Glorieta de Cristo Rey*), preferred historical periods (*Avenida de los Reyes Católicos*), and dates, battles and personages of the civil war (*Hospital 18 de Julio, Escuela José Antonio, Plaza de Belchite*). The project for the adopted town of Los Blázquez (Hernández Rubio 1941: 8–16) shows that the most strategic streets of this new urban plan – those running between the Town Hall and the Church – are all named after iconic battles: Brunete, Oviedo, Belchite, Teruel, and Virgen de la Cabeza. This standard street nomenclature was repeated in towns throughout Spain, thus contributing to the transformation of elements of the war into heritage, by inscribing them in the material fabric of the country. A lesser square in the town would contain a memorial, cross or obelisk, which would often double as an altar for outdoor masses.

The rebuilding was also marked by the memory of the war, as neighbourhoods were often financed and/or named after Nationalist military figures, such as the *Barrio Yagüe* in Burgos, named after one of Franco's

Box 3.1   Brunete: representation of a value-scape in urban planning

Brunete, a small town lying on the path of the Nationalist advance toward Madrid, was the stage of fierce fighting. Having represented an important advance for the Republic, the re-taking of Brunete was an important strategic and symbolic victory for the Nationalists. However, in the counterattack organized by the Nationalists, the German Condor Legion bombed the town. As a result, little was left when the Nationalists won Brunete back at the end of July 1937.

No longer militarily strategic at the end of the war, the symbolic element took over.[27] With 80–85 percent of inhabitable buildings destroyed, the reconstruction of Brunete offered a *tabula rasa*. The entire urban lattice of the town was wiped clean in clearing away the rubble, only the placement of the church remained as a point of reference between the old urban structure and new plan.

This opportunity to rebuild a town in a way that reflected the regime's ideology was not overlooked. The reconstruction of Brunete illustrates how urban terrains were charted according to coordinates of power: the Plaza Mayor and Town Hall, the Church, and the Monument to the Fallen. Furthermore, Brunete was used as a model for the ideal homes, both inside and out, as 'traditional new houses' were built from scratch. An article in *Reconstrucción*, no. 13 (June 1941) entitled *"Brunete: Reconstrucción del Hogar"* (Reconstruction of the home) shows the inauguration of housing in Brunete with Franco handing over keys of the new houses to their chosen residents. Rather than a *re*-building in the sense of restoring the old, the Directorate's projects consisted in rationalizing and ordering towns anew. As Sambricio has argued (1977), there is continuation here with the work set out by the Republic to rationalize and sanitize towns, providing them with basic modern infrastructures such as paved roads, electricity, schools, and medical facilities. The difference lies in the rhetoric and in the motivations. The first phase of Brunete's reconstruction was inaugurated in 1946 and it appeared frequently in the pages of *Reconstrucción* throughout the 1940s (Figure 3.15).

3.15   Franco with Moreno Torres inaugurating works in Brunete and presenting keys, June 1941 (*Reconstrucción*, no. 13, pp. 16–17).

While Brunete was an important symbolic marker in the regime's mythologizing of the war, it was, like Belchite, a small town and not heavily transited. While providing a successful reconstruction story that could be paraded through exhibitions, magazine pages and *NO-DOs*,[28] it was not a site that would be seen by many Spaniards. What Brunete did offer was a site whose name had become familiar to people during the

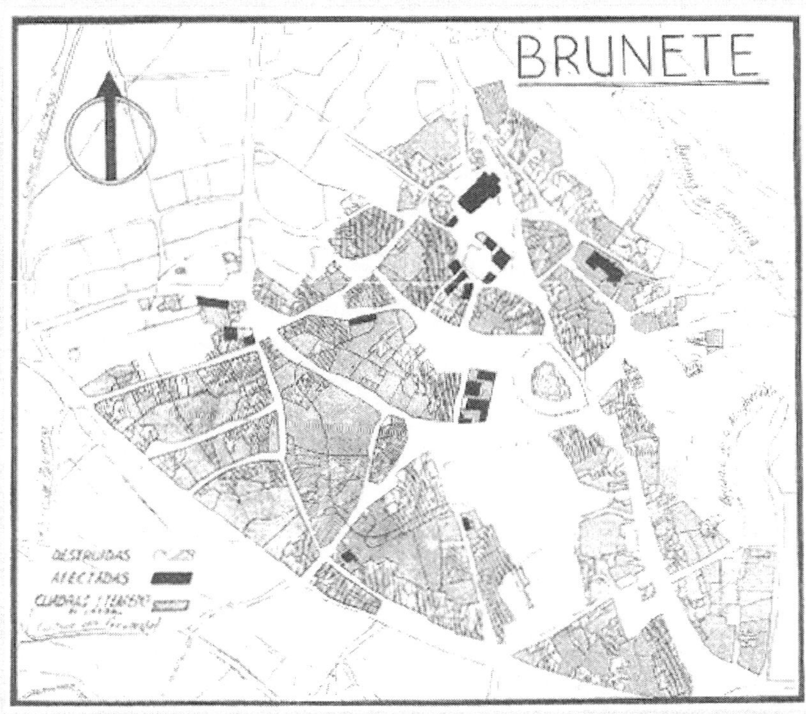

3.16 Brunete's original urban plan (shading indicates degrees of destruction).

war and whose site was small enough that a total reconstruction, following the regime's urban planning ideas was possible (Figures 3.16 and 3.17, both from *Reconstruccion*, no. 2, 1940). In reality, those that benefited the most from the reconstruction of Brunete were the Falangist landowners in the area for whom the town became a stronghold.

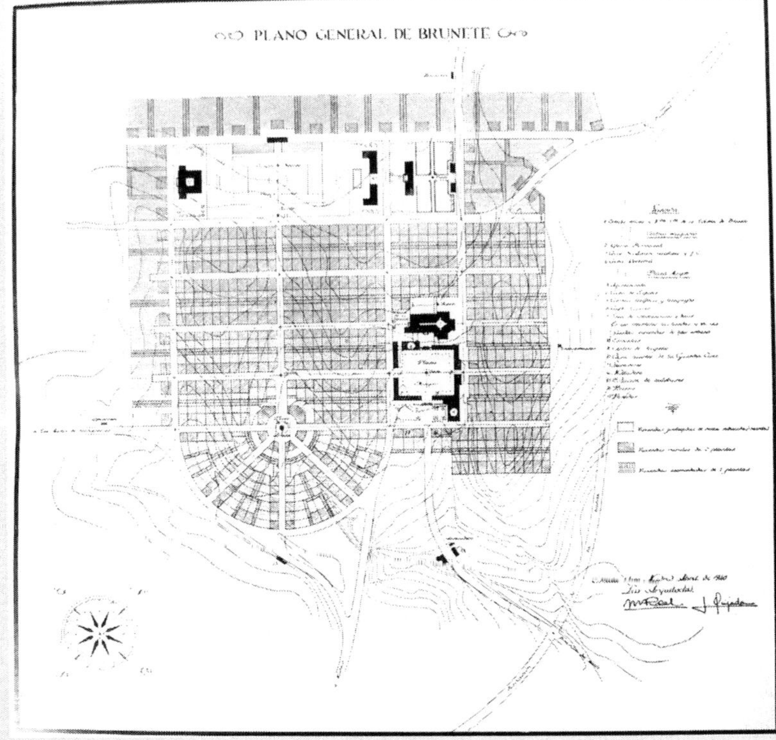

3.17 Brunete's reconstruction plan.

military collaborators. The construction of neighbourhoods specifically designated for particular social groups was another constant of the Franco period. In Madrid the *Barrio de Rosales*, entirely destroyed during the war, was rebuilt for high-ranking military officials. Housing barracks for the Guardia Civil and their families were also common, creating protected enclaves within larger cities.[26]

Propaganda and public communication

Aside from its announced role in coordinating the rebuilding efforts, *Regiones Devastadas* was also a significant propaganda tool. Its function was to communicate not only rebuilding activities but also the values of the new state, a link repeatedly made throughout official documents, magazines, newspapers, speeches and newsreels. The primary tool for the diffusion of the work of *Regiones Devastadas* was the magazine *Reconstrucción*,[29] administered by a section called *Negociado de Prensa y Propaganda*, also responsible for maintaining the photographic archive and relations with the press.

On 22 June 1940, an exhibition on the "Reconstruction of Spain" was inaugurated in Madrid's *Palacio de Bibliotecas y Museos* (today's National Library building). A special issue of *Reconstrucción* was dedicated to the exhibition, reproducing a report by Moreno Torres in which he explains the intention of the exhibition:

> *In its first number [of the magazine] we said that in the same way that all Spaniards lived the war day by day of those unforgettable days, today it is also necessary that we all become accustomed to living, if not day by day, at least every once in a while, the reconstruction of Spain. I know that all good Spaniards feel a patriotic interest in seeing Spain resurge, Spain's history begin to grow anew, and to this end we felt that this work should no longer remain hidden and that it was necessary to exteriorize it so that the Spanish people can know the work that is done in a Directorate, in a Ministry, in sum in a new State.*
>
> (Moreno Torres, *Reconstrucción*, no. 3, 1940: 21)

Over the next 15 years the Directorate held regular exhibitions throughout Spain on the reconstruction, producing a vast amount of visual material (Figures 3.18 to 3.21). An exhibition held in Seville, 11–20 October 1948, was reported to have had 10,000 visitors and contained a display of:

> *(. . .) over 70 models – some of entire towns – hundreds of photographs, statistics and numbers, leaflets, magazines, and*

*cinematographic documentaries, that give Spaniards an idea of
the work carried out during the past eight years by our General
Directorate.*

(Reconstrucción, no. 87, 1948: 323)

The *Junta Nacional para la Reconstrucción de Templos* also carried out its propaganda activities, mainly of exhibitions and inaugurations of restored buildings. Regardless of whether they had been destroyed by the Republican side or by Nationalist aerial bombardments, they were all included in the campaign of "reconstruction of churches destroyed by the Marxist horde" (Sánchez Erauskin 1994: 43).

It is difficult to establish whether the magazine and exhibitions were seen by enough Spaniards to have an impact on national consciousness; in 1941 an issue of the magazine cost 3 pesetas, the equivalent of the weekly salary given to prison labourers and their families. However, the Directorate and its activities were also omnipresent in newspapers, radio, and in the news programme *Noticiarios y Documentales* known as *NO-DO* (created by law in 1942, BOE 22-12-1942). The NO-DOs had a particularly wide reach as cinemas were obliged to show them from 1942 until 1976, and they began to appear on television in the early 1950s. From their inception and throughout the 1940s, the NO-DOs often presented a section dedicated to reconstruction activities. They displayed a quick succession of images of houses and public buildings being built, blessed, and inaugurated, including ceremonies in which keys were given to the new inhabitants.

Aside from their own internal press and propaganda sections, the activities of the organizations involved in the reconstruction were also publicized by the *Delegación Nacional de Prensa y Propaganda*. This body, created in 1941[30] and headed by General Arias Salgado, had a *Servicio de Arquitectura*, a *Jefatura de Ceremonial* and a *Sección de Organización de Actos Públicos y Plástica*. Each provincial office of the Delegation had to report to the central office in Madrid on a weekly basis detailing its activities and submitting participation figures for public events.

Reconstructing the Nation – history, memory and meaning

*Since a return to history most often occurs in moments of crisis,
it is not surprising to find that city tableaux repeat visual ideals
and normative views conservatively sanctioned by public
authorities, who attempt in this manner to regain a centred
world or a concrete system on which moral, political, or social
foundations can stand.*

(Boyer 1994: 377)

Reconstruction Exhibitions

3.18 *Reconstrucción* no. 3 of 1940 served as a catalogue for the first exhibition held in Madrid.

3.19 Postcard of a display on the reconstruction of Aragón from an exhibition held in 1944. (España. Miniesterio de Cultura. Archivo General de la Administración. AGA: F.04257-36-02.)

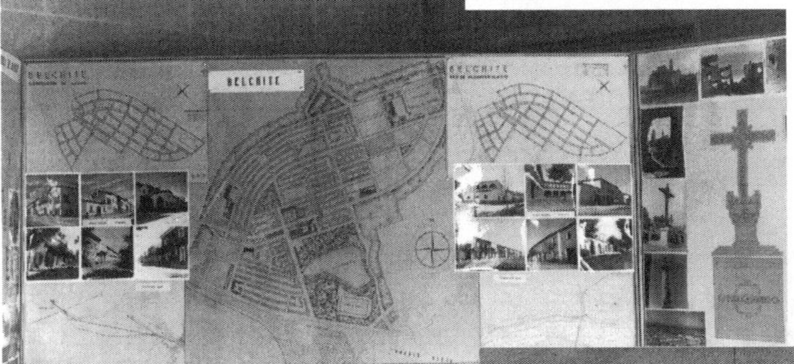

3.20 Stand dedicated to Belchite at the same 1944 exhibition. (España. Ministerio de Cultura. Archivo General de la Administración. AGA: F.04257-36-01.)

3.21 Model of new Belchite in a reconstruction exhibition, Seville, 1948 (*Reconstrucción*, no. 87: 329.)

As has been argued, the physical rebuilding was accompanied by a conceptual and ideological process of re-visioning and redefining the nation. This re-visioning was encapsulated in and communicated through the iconic projects of *Regiones Devastadas*. Unlike with building types, it is difficult to develop a typology for these projects because each one is so unique. This uniqueness springs from the role that each place was meant to play as a symbolic marker in the national narrative being constructed. In this way, each iconic site of the reconstruction illustrates a different part of a narrative that is at times complementary and contradictory. The regime paid particular attention to a few projects that stand out because of how they came to crystallize significant aspects of the ideology guiding the reconstruction. They include the *Alcázar* of Toledo, the towns of Belchite and Brunete, the *Ciudad Universitaria Complutense* in Madrid, the *Valle de los Caídos* in the Guadarrama mountains near El Escorial, and Gernika. References to these sites recur throughout the pages of *Reconstrucción* and in this research as well. Aside from these places, and following Pierre Nora's typology for 'sites of memory', other kinds of 'sites' will also enter the discussion, such as the Iberian sculpture known as the *Dama de Elche*, and also dress styles, food, popular songs, and comic books.

In certain cases, choices over what sites were to receive particular attention and resources were based on their significance during the war rather than on any heritage value that they might have had previously. The towns of Belchite and Brunete, for instance, had not been of any particular significance prior to the war and were remotely located, hence unlikely to be seen firsthand by many Spaniards. Yet they both saw fierce fighting and changed hands several times, resulting in their acquiring strategic and symbolic protagonism. In the postwar they became flagship projects in the work of *Regiones Devastadas* as evidenced by the numerous times they were featured in *Reconstrucción*, and especially by their generous budgets. Sambricio (1977: 23) notes, that the budget for the reconstruction of Brunete, a town of 1,600 inhabitants before the war, was nearly equal to that of the entire urban and industrial region of Bilbao (the city alone had an estimated population of 156,920 in 1930). The budget for new Belchite, whose entire municipality totalled 3,469 in 1930, was nearly four times greater than that of Oviedo, the destroyed capital city of Asturias (population of some 186,463 in 1930). Part of the motivation for this selection of sites is suggested by Franco himself; in a speech inaugurating the *Valle de los Caídos* in 1959, he referred to the heroic sacrifices made by "the defenders of a thousand small *Alcázares*" (Franco 1952). As we will see, the reconstructions of both Belchite and Brunete were surrounded by a discourse of heroism seeded with references to episodes of mythical significance in Spanish history, such as Numancia. Their significance lay in their contribution to the construction of a mythology of the new state, as markers on the emerging heritage-scape.

One of the values that these markers represented, especially until 1959, was that of martyrdom. This was materialized through public monuments and masses to the fallen, religious ceremonies and through an exaltation of ruins as symbolizing martyrs and fallen heroes – occasionally a combination of these (Figures 3.22 and 3.23). A specific set of values was imposed on society, by celebrating self-sacrifice and sending a reiterative message about a moral debt owed to the martyrs. Not only people, but towns and even buildings were portrayed as martyrs. The ruins of old Belchite became a proto-martyr town and the *Alcázar* of Toledo a proto-martyr building, spawning legends that were repeated in the media and intended for public consumption.

The most explicit method of inscribing memory in the landscape was through the construction of actual memorials.[31] Memorials to the fallen were such a central part of constructing a memory-scape, that it is impossible to ignore their contribution to the production of post-conflict heritage. Two layers deserve to be pointed out. The first is that both prisoners of war and eventually political prisoners were used as the manual labour to build some of these monuments. The task given to the first prison labour battalion, set up on 3 July 1937, was to build a memorial in the town of Alcocero, Burgos, to commemorate Nationalist General Mola[32] (Sueiro 2006: 88). The practice of making the defeated build monuments to the heroes of the victorious is most notable in the *Valle de los Caídos*; it can be understood as an indication of the vindictiveness of the post-war, as a means of recalling and maintaining a divided Spain – of guilty perpetrators having to atone for their sins and heroic martyrs to be honoured and remembered – and, consequently, as a source for deep-seated resentment.

The second layer is that, embedded in the memorials, plaques, prayers, anniversaries and ceremonies dedicated to those 'Fallen for God and for Spain', was a lesson about who ultimately had the right to mourn, and which dead had the right to be mourned and remembered. Every public act of remembrance on the side of the victors was simultaneously a sign to those who were not allowed to be remembered or mourned. The language used in the memorial plaques made this quite clear: "In memory of the Martyrs, sacrificed for the saintly cause of Religion and Patria", "To the glorious Martyrs that on these sites were sacrificed for God and Country (1936–1939)" (cited in Caprarella 1999:180). The memorial panorama also sent a gendered message in which women were ascribed the role of mourning mothers, sisters, daughters and wives of the 'heroic martyrs'.[33] Women did not appear on the commemorative plaques to the 'glorious fallen for Spain', theirs were to be the differently self-sacrificing roles of nursing the wounded, tending to orphaned children, 'righting' wayward women, and mourning the fallen.

Aside from the explicit moralizing theme of martyrdom, there were other more implicit ways in which a value-scape was inscribed. The

3.22, 3.23   Saying mass on the ruins of the 'liberated' *Cerro de los Ángeles* monument. (España. Ministerio de Cultura. Archivo General de la Administración. Sig. AGA F-1418. Sobre17.)

second half of this chapter focuses on three other dynamics of the reconstruction: the re-writing of history, the memorialization of the war, and the construction of a new value-scape. That discussion will conclude by examining how this reconstructed New Spain evolved and changed throughout the 1950s.

Constructing a selective past

When on the lands of our Patria each day dawns with some new ruin, we must forge the will to reconstruct from the deepest foundations, just as we have achieved the will for justice from the root.

(Victor D'Ors 1937)

The historiography of modern Spain has been concerned with three major issues – the origins of the Spanish Civil War, the course of the Spanish Civil War and the aftermath of the Spanish Civil War. In the interior, history under the Francoist dictatorship was a direct instrument of the state, written by policemen, soldiers and priests, invigilated by the powerful censorship machinery. It was the continuation of the war by other means, an effort to justify the military uprising, the war and the subsequent repression.

(Preston 1990: 30)

We must sweep aside that which has marred our History . . .
(Franco, 24 August 1942, La Coruña)

Having come to power after revolting against a democratically elected government and winning a civil war that had split the country, the regime needed to legitimize its right to power beyond the military victory. Thus despite the public discourse reiterating that Franco was building a New Spain, a convincing lineage and inheritance – *patrimonio* – had to be found in the Old Spain. This was done by selecting the historic periods, events, personages and legends that suited the new vision of Spain, constructing a historical narrative for which the regime would appear as both legitimate heir and protector. A dichotomy was therefore created by which the regime was both building a New Spain and restoring Old Spain to its former glory, a tension that recurs throughout the reconstruction projects. Amalia Avia's[34] recollection of her history classes as a schoolgirl in 1940s Madrid, were that they consisted of: "a little bit of history, the history of the Empire and the greatness of Spain, ending up with the Falange" (Avia 2004: 180). Until 1978 the school curriculum from primary education through to university included a subject called *Formación del Espíritu Nacional* – Forging of the National Spirit.

The historical periods – other than that of Philip II – that were favoured by the regime were related to the *Reconquista* (722–1492), especially the Middle Ages, and the *Guerra de la Independencia* (1808–1814), with their respective heroes and legends, El Cid Campeador and Agustina de Aragón. Other historical figures celebrated include monarchs like the Catholic Kings[35] and the Asturian King Pelayo; mythic warriors such as Viriato and El Cid; religious figures like Santiago, patron saint of Spain, and Cardinal Cisneros; and the explorers Hernán Cortés and Cristóbal Colón. Personages of the enlightenment or other liberal moments in history like the *Cortes de Cádiz* were largely ignored. As Tusell has written:

> *An idealized past provided the ground plan for shaping the future, and a particular vision of the past was promoted from which the former liberal tradition and cultural pluralism of Spanish society had disappeared: hence the large posters put up in Barcelona bearing the words: 'Speak the Language of the Empire'.*
>
> (Tusell 2007: 29)

Dent Coad further argues:

> *The return to historical models and the rejection of foreign avant-garde influences, was seen as a way of restoring religion, the family, patriotism, order and authenticity through a construction of 'Spanishness'. Many literary figures, artists and architects began investigating medieval culture, seen as compatible with nationalist values because of its association with*

> *unquestionable religious and hierarchical order. Roman classical*
> *themes were also investigated, and neoclassicism was revived in*
> *sculpture, painting and prose as well as in architecture.*
>
> (Dent Coad 1995: 223–224)

The Catholic Kings were celebrated as the creators of a Spanish Catholic Empire, for uniting Spain, for completing the *Reconquista*, and for the discovery of America. Of the two, Isabel was favoured over Ferdinand, not least because she was Isabelle of Castile, at a moment when Castile was being equated with 'authentic' Spain. As early as 1940 work was done at Guisando, Avila where she had been made heir to the throne of Castile in 1468, restoring and opening it to the public. A few years later the nineteenth-century monument to Isabel located in Madrid's old hippodrome was moved to the city's central artery, the Paseo de la Castellana, in front of the ministerial complex – *Nuevos Ministerios* (Ministerio de Cultura 1989).

'Restoring' the past: Preserving (some) heritage and traditions

While conserving traditional Spanish customs was a leitmotif of the reconstruction rhetoric, this too was done selectively. Those traditions that were not convenient or approved were 'forgotten' regardless of their Spanishness.[36] One example of this is carnival, which traditionally involved a parade on Ash Wednesday called the *entierro de la sardina* (burial of the sardine) and whose Spanish pedigree is evidenced by references to it in literature and the visual arts –including a painting and a drawing by Goya.[37] The wearing of masks, the use of firecrackers, pagan connotations, and the general public disorder caused by this traditional festivity earned the regime's dislike, and so it was banned. Furthermore, the regime's rituals – such as the fascist salute – began to interfere with its favoured customs, such as bull-fighting. Vizcaíno Casas (1996: 161) notes that bullfighters began using the fascist salute to address the tribune instead of the traditional gesture – placing right hand on sword and bowing the head (Figure 3.24). The vision of Spain constructed by the regime celebrated Isabel of Castile and rejected the Spanish Enlightenment. Yet Isabel had been against bullfighting, a favourite pastime of the regime that was celebrated as a Spanish tradition. Goya meanwhile was fêted, despite having moved in precisely those circles regarded by the regime as having been traitors to the 'true' Spain. A particular kind of site that benefited from the regime's appreciation of Spanish heritage were castles. On 22 April 1949, a Decree was passed for the protection of castles (*Decreto de Protección de Castillos*, BOE, 5 May 1949) and articles on castles appeared regularly in the *Revista Nacional de Arquitectura*. These examples illustrate a deliberate revisioning of history and tradition in constructing a selective past.

3.24 Poster from 1939 showing a bull-fighter doing the Fascist salute.

A further form of 'editing' history took place in actual conservation work. Occasionally, when the extant material culture did not fully conform to a preconceived image, restorations were used to make 'corrections' (Hernández Martínez 2008). An example is the Town Hall of the Asturian town of Potes. Here conservation work carried out on the building altered it to conform more closely to the image of the past that had been selected: opening up a grander entrance, enlarging and decorating the balcony, and making the building look more castle-like (Figures 3.25 and 3.26). One of the casualties of improving on the past were the Baroque choirs that were removed from medieval churches and cathedrals because it was thought that they disrupted this authenticity (Hernández Martínez 2008:

Restoring authenticity

3.25 Town Hall of Potes before . . .

3.26 and after 'restoration'. (Images from Blanco 1987: 26.)

164–169). There were instances in which pains were taken to make accurate restorations and scrupulously restore damaged areas, such as in the restoration work carried out on Oviedo Cathedral. The correspondence of Luis Menéndez Pidal, regional director of PAN for the north of Spain, shows that he requested detailed information on the baptismal font and other elements of the cathedral from the museum of reproductions in Madrid in order to restore them and where necessary make faithful copies (Correspondence from 1940 in AGA-BA-51/11208; *RNA*, no.3, 1941: 9; *Reconstrucción*, no.58, 1945: 316–344). Restoration practices varied from region to region depending on who was in charge (Rivera Blanco 2008: 96–108; Hernández Martínez 2008: 162–165).

Another strategy adopted by Franco was to usurp symbols from the past and make them his own; as a result 'his' symbol seemed to appear overnight on centuries-old buildings and monuments. The best examples of this are the royal standard of the Catholic Kings dating from the fifteenth-century and the 'victor' emblem of the doyens of the University of Salamanca, dating from the twelfth-century (Figures 3.27 to 3.30). Both were taken up as official symbols of the regime and were used on banners, parades, stamps, coins, buildings, medals, and during processions, parades and ceremonies.[38] However, they also existed already on architectural structures – porticos, façades – of heritage sites such as the sixteenth-century Visagra Gate in Toledo or the early sixteenth-century façade of the University of Salamanca. To a largely illiterate population that would not have known the origins of these symbols, the impression would have been that this regime had roots in Spanish history, culture and tradition. This use of symbols from the past illustrates a common practice also signalled by Hodder (2000: 398): "Material items are often central in the backward-looking invention of tradition, as when the Italian fascist movement elevated the Roman symbol of authority – a bundle of rods – to provide authority for a new form of centralized power." The Spanish Falange also adopted the symbol used by the Catholic Kings of the *yugo y flechas* (a yoke and bundle of arrows symbolizing unity in effort).

A selection of historic moments, personages, and values also made their appearance on postage stamps, banknotes, ration cards and lottery tickets. The images reproduced on these objects communicated the national narrative being woven by the regime, in a way that was accessible to the entire population, while simultaneously creating direct links between the person or object of significance being represented and the regime. The first banknotes printed by the Nationalist government in Burgos depicted monuments situated in Nationalist-held Spain. In subsequent years images representing historical figures or events that supported the regime's narrative of the past were used (see Table 3.3). As with tradition, folklore, rural and urban planning, and propaganda seen in the previous section, references to the past, the use of historic symbols, personages and architectural styles contributed to materializing and legitimizing the regime. Giving a physical form to the ideology of the new state and providing it with a repertoire of recognizable visual and historical references was central to the reconstruction programme.[40]

Archaeology under Franco

The principal archaeologists in Spain during the 1940s and 50s concentrated on demonstrating a vision of a unified Iberian history; Julio Martínez Santa-Olalla and Martín Almagro Basch are two examples of archaeologists who worked to this end. Even sites that were emblematic in terms of regional historical identification were integrated into this

Appropriating symbols of the past

3.27, 3.28 'Victor' anagram used to designate the rectors of the University of Salamanca (below) and used by Franco (right) in the first Victory parade held in Madrid on 19 May 1939.[39]

3.29, 3.30 Emblem of the Catholic Kings (left) on the façade of the School of *Artes y Oficios* of Toledo, and the official emblem of Spain developed for the regime.

Table 3.3 Historical personages appearing on bank notes, 1940s and 1950s

Historical figure	Monetary amount	Date
Hernán Cortés	1 peseta	1940
El Greco's painting *Burial of the Count of Orgaz* (detail)	500 pesetas	1940
Charles I of Spain	1,000 pesetas	1940
Ferdinand of Aragón	1 pesetas	1943
Isabel of Castile	1 peseta	1943
Isabel of Castile	5 pesetas	1943
Isabel of Castile and Christopher Columbus	5 pesetas	1945
Dama de Elche	1 peseta	1948

unified vision of the peninsula's history (Díaz-Andreu 2002: 131). A certain predilection was shown for what could be identified as 'Iberian' archaeology and – in the beginning – Roman remains (Tarrats and Sada 2002: 38–39). While Franco continued to show interest in the Roman amphitheatre of Tarragona in the early 50s, the interest in Roman heritage generally faded as Sagunto and Numancia gained increased attention and came to represent, as with El Cid and Agustina of Aragón, examples of heroic acts on the part of Iberians in defence of their lands.[41] Both Sagunto and Numancia involved legends of heroic self-sacrifice and thus were incorporated into the nation-building repertoire, what Stig Sørensen (1996: 26) has referred to as "a glossary of objects and images appropriate for the intended messages". Perhaps Franco's greatest early victory in terms of archaeological heritage, at least if we judge by the media hype surrounding it, was his success in negotiating the return of the *Dama de Elche* with France's Vichy government in 1941. Though other artefacts were returned to Spain in this deal, it was the restitution of this 'Iberian Queen' that took hold of the regime's imagination.

Constructing a narrative for public consumption

The reconstruction was creating a language for the new state, but Spaniards had to be taught how to read it. The regime's mythologizing of the conflict meant that it was fertile material for popular culture.[44] This transformed sites into beacons communicating both historical narratives and moral lessons. The prolonged period of reconstruction of these sites – often lasting twenty years – meant that they remained in a state of part ruin/part construction site and provided rich metaphorical sources. The

Box 3.2 – Recovering the Dama de Elche

3.31 The Dama de Elche exhibited in the Prado, 1941.

Discovered on the 4th of August 1897 near Elche, this female bust, estimated to be some 2,500 years old, was such a high quality, unique and well preserved find that it immediately drew attention. Despite efforts by a local expert, Pedro Ibarra, to have her purchased by the National Archaeological Museum in Madrid, fourteen days after being discovered the bust was bought by French hispanist Pierre Paris and taken to the Louvre. Here it became a popular exhibit and labelled as a treasure of Iberian art. The *Dama* had not been forgotten in Spain, reproductions appeared on stamps and currency, and efforts to recover the piece had begun the moment it left.[42] In 1941, as a result of negotiations between Franco and Marshal Pétain the Dama de Elche, along with other Spanish pieces, was returned to Spain in an exchange of art works.[43] In a letter dated 20 November 1940 from the Ministry of Education, signed by Jesús Rubio, to the Director General of Fine Arts, the reasons given by the Council of Ministers for recovering these works are given as :

The reconstitution and glorifying of our Nation with such good fortune begun requires that the spiritual aspect is not forgotten (…) they are essentially Spanish objects, as well as valuable documents some for the understanding of our artistic heritage and others for that of our history must return to Spain for the reintegration of that which is racially Spanish.

(AGA box 12/1104)

The return of the Dama de Elche – described in 1940 as a symbol of pre-Roman Spanish roots in antiquity and the greatness of the Iberian civilization – was portrayed as an important symbolic recovery and personal victory of Franco's in recovering the 'authentically Spanish'. First housed in Madrid's Prado museum, representations of the *Dama* were used on currency and stamps. She also appeared on posters, school books and even publicity where the image was used as a mark of authenticity on traditional Spanish products. She was also portrayed as the prototype of Iberian female beauty, coinciding in her layered garments and heavy ornaments with the image espoused by the regime (discussed in Text Box 2.2).

3.32 & 3.33 Used on currency (1938) and a stamp.

3.34 Used to illustrate a national census during the dictatorship.

most widely mined of these sites, and a foundational myth of the regime, was the Alcázar of Toledo (see Appendix B).

Until 1944 rebuilding efforts in Toledo focused on the Plaza del Zocodover,[45] religious buildings and infrastructure. A decision had not yet been made about the Alcázar and its 'glorious ruins'. In February 1941, two articles appeared in *Reconstrucción* dedicated to the Alcázar, one by Joaquín Arrarás entitled "*La nueva Acrópolis*" (*Reconstrucción*, no. 9: 2–8) and another by Aristides Fernández Vallespín on "*Orientaciones sobre la reconstrucción de Toledo*" (*Reconstrucción*, no. 9: 9–15). In 1943 the *Dirección General de Fortificaciones y Obras del Ministerio del Ejército* (General Directorate of Fortifications and Works of the Ministry of the Military) commissioned Manuel Carrasco Cadenas, Lieutenant Colonel of Engineers, with the task of putting together a proposal for the reconstruction of the Alcázar (AGA-RD. Alcázar de Toledo. Box 20779). In November 1944 an article appeared referring to the myth of the Alcázar and its martyrs – "*Cripta de los mártires del Alcázar de Toledo*" (Agrade in *Reconstrucción*, no. 47) – but there were still no signs of rebuilding. The greater part of the reconstruction eventually took place in the 1950s extending through to 1965 when work on the Alcázar was entering its twelfth stage. This final stage involved adapting part of the building to house a military museum (AGA-RD, Alcázar de Toledo, Box 20783).

While the physical rebuilding of the Alcázar was a lengthy process, the construction of the Alcázar as a symbol developed swiftly. This was done through infusing all forms of objects for public consumption, the media, education, and mass public events with the regime's mythologized version of the events leading to the destruction of the Alcázar.[46] This version inspired countless products of popular culture including songs, fiction and non-fiction books, movies and comic books during the Franco period. It was also mined by a wide range of entrepreneurs, who named newspapers, theatres and streets after it and used it to advertise a wide range of products (Figures 3.35 to 3.39). Through them, the Alcázar became a landmark in the physical and imagined landscape of the regime, marking both moral and aesthetic standards.

Popular culture was used to construct a mythology for the new regime with its repertoire of heroes, villains, epic battles and legends. Already in 1939 numerous movies were dedicated to the war, such as *Derrumbamiento del ejército rojo* (Antonio Calvache 1939) or *La Peste Roja* (1939). In 1943, the Madrid Delegation of the *Sección de Organización de Actos Públicos y Plástica* (Section for the Organization of Public Acts and Arts) organized an exhibition entitled *Así eran los rojos* – 'Thus were the reds' – in the capital's Círculo de Bellas Artes. This exhibition, much along the lines of those on 'degenerate art' being organized in Germany (Castillo 2010: 19), was intended to illustrate the barbarity of the 'reds', thus continuing the campaign of propaganda against the defeated. Popular culture also drew heavily on the historical periods favoured by the regime and supported the regime's mythologizing of its heroes and martyrs by dedicating to them movies, radio programmes, comic books, and other cultural products (Figures 3.40 to 3.45). Even advertising used the regime's symbols in its campaigns. Popular culture

The Alcázar of Toledo in popular culture[47]

3.35 Comic-book: *The Feat of the Alcázar of Toledo.*

3.36 Movie: *All Quiet in the Alcázar,* 1940.

3.37 Beer: *El Alcázar,* 1939.

3.38 Wine: *Imperial Toledo. Wine of Heroes,* 1939.

3.39 Cigarettes: *Alcázar.*

Popular culture and the regime's vision of Spain

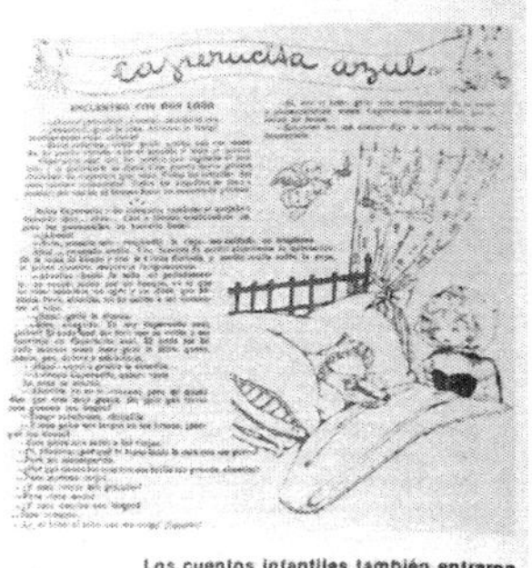

3.40 Board game "The Entry into Madrid", in which players battle to take over the capital, 1939.

3.41 "Little Red Riding-hood" became "Little Blue Riding-hood" (in Abellá 1978: 28).

3.42 Paper doll: "The Authentic Shirley" (Editorial Hergan, Vigo, c.1940), note the Falangist uniform and fascist salute option for Shirley Temple.

3.43 Advertisement for a hat store reads: "The reds did not wear hats", 1939.

3.45 Movie: "The Red Plague", 1939.

3.44 Movie: "The Collapse of the Red Army", 1939.

became an important vehicle through which the regime's myths could permeate into everyday life, supporting and communicating the regime's vision of the New Spain, its past, symbols and values. The 1940s and 1950s were a hey-day for radio and movies which were often set in historical periods populated with bullfighters and *majas*: *Goyescas* (1941), *Agustina de Aragón* (1950), *La Leona de Castilla* (1951), *Alba de América* (1951), *El Cid* (1961). Sports such as bullfighting and football also were heavily imbued with nationalist overtones.[48]

A nation revisioned

While the New Spain being built was a constant refrain in the regime's rhetoric, it was at odds with its other claim to be restoring and safeguarding 'authentic' and 'traditional' Spain. This duality required drawing a convincing lineage that linked Old and New Spain. To do so required an 'à la carte' selection of historic events, personages and legends that reinforced the vision of 1939. The resulting assortment of what was seen to constitute 'authentic and traditional' Spain formed an integral part of the overall reconstruction of its tangible and intangible heritage. In their now classic text, Hobsbawm and Ranger (1983) identified what they coined the 'invention of tradition'. The process in Spain was not so much an invention as a reinvention of the past, a reworking and an editing of tradition.

One example of this is the way in which past battles and wars in Spanish history were equated with battles of the civil war. The battles favoured in history textbooks and commemorations were the struggles against the Romans (at Sagunto and Numancia), battles during the 800 years of *Reconquista* such as the battle of Covadonga (722), battle of Lepanto against the Ottomans (1571), and the 1808 Napoleonic war (Boyd 1997: 243, 261). Episodes from all of these wars appear in a school map (Hernández y Fernández c.1940–42) in which the battles, heroes and martyrs of the civil war are also depicted (Figures 3.46 to 3.48). The ruins of Belchite have been placed next to the legendary Agustina de Aragón firing her canon against Napoleonic troops, and the ruins of the Alcázar exist on the same plane as those of Numancia. This map illustrates the vision of Spanish history which conflates several centuries in an assemblage sprinkled with references to the civil war. As a result it crystallizes the regime's imagined heritage-scape. Placing the historical events chosen by the regime as significant on the same plane as events and personages of the civil war gave a semblance of historical legitimacy and further mythologized the regime and its 'accomplishments'.

Constructing memory: memorials, martyrs and ruins

Avia (2004: 58) recalls how in the immediate aftermath of the war a park along the north-west border of Madrid (Rosales) which had been a front-line was full of placards from the war that read 'us' and 'them' (Figure

The topography of a selected past

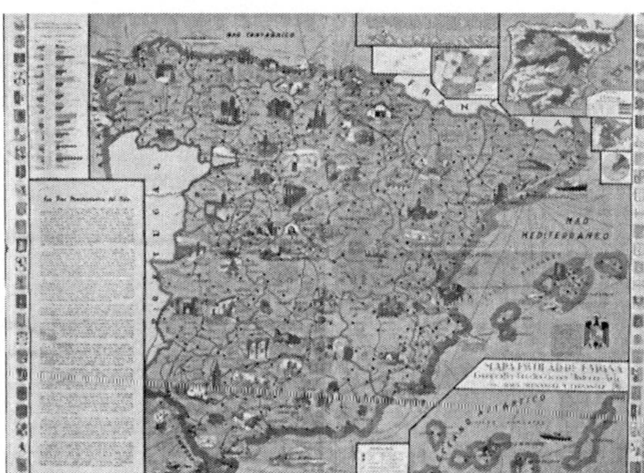

3.46   Hernández y Fernández, Jesús (and others). *"Mapa escolar de España. Geografía-Producciones-Historia-Arte. Los diez mandamientos del niño"* produced by Litografía "Arte", *c.*1940. (Biblioteca Nacional de España. BNE.Sig.Mr.16.1.)

3.47   Detail: The ruins of the Alcázar (bottom left) and the sacrifice at the siege of Numancia (top right).

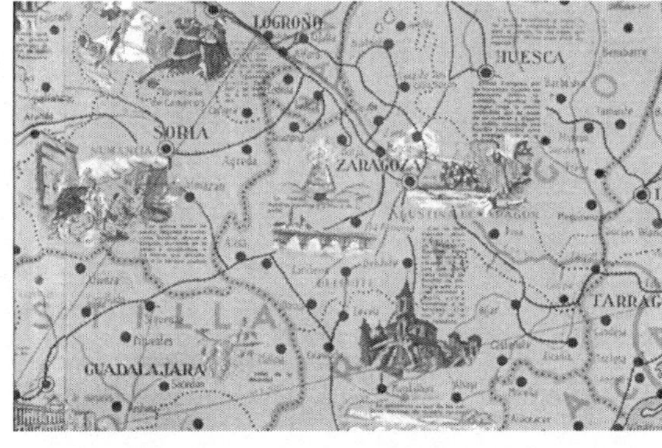

3.48   Detail: *Agustina de Aragón* firing a cannon (centre right) and the ruins of Belchite (bottom).

3.49). While these signs gradually disappeared, other, more permanent ones, memorials, were constructed, maintaining the divisions of the war through omnipresent reminders of a conflict that was not to be forgotten. In his analysis of Spanish Civil War myths, Reig Tapia (2006: 201–244) highlights the importance of heroes for both sides, yet it is the slightly different category of martyrs that predominated in moulding and keeping

3.49 Placard on a front-line that reads: "Us" (*Reconstrucción*, no. 8, 1941).

alive the memory of the war. In material culture this took the form of memorials and occasionally ruins.

The neoclassical pyramids and obelisks, two forms of mortuary architecture widely used in nineteenth-century Spain as symbolic forms to "honour a collective hero" (García-Gutiérrez Mosteiro 2005: 435), now

3.50 and 3.51 *Sueño Arquitectónico* by Moya Blanco, 1938.

made an emphatic return. Luis Moya's drawing *Sueño Arquitectónico* (Figure 3.50 and 3.51) for a pyramidal monument at the *Valle de los Caídos* was one fantastic expression of this return, but obelisks and especially crosses appeared throughout the country. Projects for the reconstruction of towns invariably included the installation of memorials to the fallen either as a plaque on the façade of town hall or church, or as a free-standing monument located on a square in their close vicinity.

The regime intended to carefully control their style, location and object of commemoration. In February 1938 the *Comisión de Estilo en las Conmemoraciones de la Patria* (Commission for the Style of Patriotic Commemorations) was created (BOE 22-2-1938), and in August 1939 an *Orden de Gobernación* was emitted concerning styles of monuments (BOEs 7-8-1939 and 22-8-1939), especially those dedicated to the Victory and the Fallen. The motivations outlined are:

> . . . *to give a unity of style and sense to the perpetuation,*
> *through monuments, of the events and people of the history of*
> *Spain, and in particular the events of the war and in honour of*
> *the fallen and to avoid that enthusiasm, often justified, might*
> *capriciously take over this kind of initiative, planting*
> *disillusionment when the projects are unrealistic.*
>
> (BOE 22-8-1939 cited in Llorente Hernández 1993: 277)

In the following year two further circulars were emitted by the *Delegación Nacional de Propaganda* outlining style guides for such monuments. This Delegation had the last word on all monuments, memorials, commemorative publications, celebrations and public acts.[49] Also in 1942 the *Jefatura de Ceremonial* and the *Sección de Organización de Actos Públicos y Plástica* were created. The *Servicios Técnicos* of the latter was responsible for approving or rejecting proposals and defining the artistic and historical criteria of their styles, with the aim of creating a uniform model and preventing a diversity of initiatives (Llorente Hernández 1993: 453–462). An article published in the *Heraldo de Aragón* (5 August 1941: 3) outlines the prescribed styles for memorials:

> *These monuments, brilliant mourning of the Crusade, must in*
> *the future be history made into stone, bronze and marble, and*
> *no other orientation must be allowed than that which*
> *corresponds to what these works symbolize: glorification of the*
> *fallen and exaltation of heroic Spain.*
>
> (cited in Vázquez Astorga 2006: 290)

The construction, styles and emplacements of memorials were carefully controlled. Early on, local governments received numerous petitions from individuals wishing to erect crosses marking the sites where family

Box 3.3   'El Valle de los Caídos': The Caudillo's memorial

The *Valle de los Caídos*, Valley of the Fallen, is a monument that Franco envisioned, commissioned and closely watched over after having personally chosen the spot for it in the mountains some 50 kilometres north-west of Madrid.[52] The decree that disposes for its construction dates from 1 April 1940, first anniversary of the Nationalist victory. The choice of date is eloquent of the symbolism intended for the site. The decree is explicit in signalling that this monument is to stand out from the rest, and expresses the intention of creating heritage:

> *The dimension of our Crusade, the heroic sacrifices that the victory encloses and the transcendence that this epic deed has had for the future of Spain cannot be perpetuated by those simple monuments with which towns and cities usually commemorate the salient events of our History and the glorious episodes of our sons. It is necessary that the stones that are erected here have the greatness of ancient monuments, that they defy time and forgetting and constitute a place of meditation and repose in which future generations can offer a tribute of admiration to those that bequeathed to them a better Spain.*
> (BOE, 2 April 1940, cited by Ureña 1979: 142–143 and Sueiro 2006: 24.)

The architectural project for the Valle was chosen from the results of a competition that was widely mediatized. The proposals were published in magazines and newspapers and exhibited in the School of Architecture in Madrid's *Ciudad Universitaria* (Llorente 1995: 275–303). The winning proposal was presented by Luis Moya and Enrique Huidobro, though the two architects involved in the actual construction were Pedro Muguruza and Diego Méndez (taking over entirely upon Muguruza's death in 1950), who also worked on Franco's personal residencies. Méndez expressed what the monument was intended to mean:

> *The monument is to symbolize and physically represent the racial virtues such as heroism, asceticism, the adventurous spirit, the thirst for conquest, the quixotic, that form the totality that inspires and defines Spain as a unit of sublime essence and a permanent aspiration to the eternal (…) it must be nothing less than the Altar of Spain, of heroic Spain, of mystical Spain, of eternal Spain.*
> (cited by Sueiro 2006: 168)

In the Valle the eclectic Herreran architectural style, the exaltation of the war's martyrs, the dominance of catholic dogma, the symbolic use of building materials such as granite and forged iron, the power of the military, even the symbolic use of cypress trees all came together, crystallizing the aesthetic vision of Spain celebrated by the regime.[53] The imagery that dominates inside the basilica is a combination of religious and military iconography with a predominance of archangels, saints battling evil in various manifestations, scenes of the apocalypse and virgins representing and protecting the different branches of the military.

Franco's cousin and secretary, General Franco Salgado-Araujo, comments in his memoirs that "possibly he [Franco] wanted to imitate Philip II, who built the monastery of the Escorial to commem-

3.52 Aerial for the Valle. (Patrimonio Nacional.)

3.53 Esplanade outside the monument planted with cypress trees.

orate the battle of Saint Quentin" (Salgado-Araujo 1976: 215, Sueiro 2006: 24). Certainly, the site chosen by Franco for the placement of the monument indicates the intended link with the Escorial as it is located along the same mountain range and only 9 kilometres away. Furthermore, the Valle was conceived not as a simple monument but as a complex that included a crypt, basilica, monastery, guesthouse and a School of Social Studies.

Despite the sense of urgency instilled in the construction of the Valle by Franco from the very start and repeated announcements of its near-completion, the monument took twenty years to build and was only inaugurated in 1959. By then even his cousin was not so convinced by the monument's relevance, Salgado-Araujo wrote of it:

3.54 Map in a 1973 tourist booklet about the *Valle* edited by *Patrimonio Nacional*; all the other sites illustrated had been royal palaces or residences.

In Spain there is not the atmosphere for this monument, for although the fear of another civil war remains, a large part of the population tends to forgive and forget. I do not think that the families of the whites or the reds feel the desire that their dead go to the crypt, if it is only for the whites it will instil for always an eternal disunion among Spaniards.

(Salgado-Araujo 1976: 215; Tranche and Sánchez-Biosca 2005: 496)

The completed structure was inaugurated on 1 April 1959, the 20th anniversary of the 'Victory'. In his inaugural speech, Franco did not present the monument as a place where all Spaniards could mourn their civil war dead. On the contrary, he emphasized continued confrontation, saying: "Our war was not a civil war but a true Crusade. The epic of our Liberation has cost Spain too much blood to be forgot-ten ... The battle between Good and Evil has not ended. (...) The anti-Spain was defeated, but is not dead. Periodically we see it lift its head ..." (speech reproduced in Díaz-Plaja 1972: 305–309).

3.55 Imagery of armed angels used on the inside. (Patrimonio Nacional.)

members had been killed. While there was at first some uncertainty about how to address these petitions, a strict policy was soon developed. The preamble to the construction project for the monument at *Paracuellos del Jarama* sets out that those monuments to the "victims of the red barbarism" should be grouped in predetermined sites. This document was used as a guideline by provincial delegations in deciding over individual petitions which were commonly denied. It was argued that "otherwise the roads would be filled with these small commemorative monuments",[50] and that "the Cross to the Fallen which exists in each of the towns that were once the object of Marxist persecution, is the monument destined to perpetuate the memory [of its victims]."[51]

Of the numerous grandiose plans drawn for the exaltation of the New Spain, its heroes and martyrs, only three were finalized to their full monumental intent: the Monument to the Heroes and Martyrs in Zaragoza (1943–1950), the Monument to the Fallen in Pamplona (1939–1959), and the Valle de los Caídos (1939–1959) outside Madrid.

In the same year it was inaugurated, a documentary was made about the monument entitled *El Valle de los Caídos*; the narrator's voice says:

> *(. . .) a monument to all those that fell in the civil war that*
> *between 1936 and 1939, bloodied the fields of the nation; to*
> *absolutely all that fell on one side and the other of the trenches,*
> *to those that were with the victorious or with the defeated,*
> *because uniting them in a single ossuary is the expression of the*
> *pure desire that the misunderstandings that once confronted*
> *them disappear forever.*
> (José Ochoa 1959, cited by Fernández Cuenca 1967: 72)

While seeming to endorse unity, the language continues to distinguish between the victorious and the defeated. In addition, the official criteria for being buried at the *Valle* included being Catholic and patriotic thus making the reconciliation of 'all' Spaniards dependant on their adhesion to the church and the regime (Sueiro 1977: 228). Another aspect that belies the reconciliatory claims of the monument is the fact that the workforce used to carry out the task consisted primarily of political and war prisoners. An estimated 20,000 Republican prisoners passed through it – many of them dying as a result of explosions, falling rocks and silicosis.[54]

Originally, the walls of the colonnade on either side of the basilica were intended to be filled with the names of the fallen whose remains had been placed in the crypt. Yet those walls remain bare to this day. The only named person to be buried in the Valle – in a place on honour in front of the altar – was none other than José Antonio Primo de Rivera, Falangist leader and proto-martyr of the war. On 30 March 1959 his remains were transported there, ceremoniously carried by a column of Falangists along the nine kilometres separating the Escorial and the *Valle*.[55]

Ruins as monuments – Buildings as martyrs

The martyr paradigm also extended to buildings and towns; this made the very act of reconstruction simultaneously one of memorialization. Serrano Suñer made this link explicit in an article that appeared in the first issue of *Reconstrucción*:

> *The work of the architect will be to continue the patriotic and*
> *Christian task (. . .) in order to communicate a better idea of the*
> *home and a higher idea of Patria, and so that all those that reap*
> *the benefits of our reconstruction, regardless of the comforts that*
> *they find in their new homes, will never forget that the new*
> *houses and the new towns of Spain are cemented on the*
> *exemplar lesson of those stones that war disturbed.*
>
> (*Reconstrucción*, no. 1, 1941)

Both Moreno Torres and Franco often alluded to the 'value of the ruin' as conceived by Albert Speer (Sambricio 1977: 23). The eighth issue of *Reconstrucción* includes an article by Francisco Cossío entitled "Death and resurrection of some towns" (1941: 1–6), in which he elaborates on ruins and the devastated landscape, incorporating them into the discourse of reconstruction.[56] Ruins featured prominently as a theme in post-war art, appearing in the magazines *Spain*, *Vértice* and *Reconstrucción*, in National Art Exhibitions as well as serving as a background for two portraits of Franco,[57] one by Alvarez Sotomayor and another by José Eugenio Martínez Gil (Llorente 1992: 687). The most frequently featured ruins were those of religious buildings, Belchite, the Alcázar of Toledo, and Madrid's University City.

At other sites symbolic elements were left in ruins as monuments to the crimes of the 'other'. In the reconstructed Sanctuary of Santa María de la Cabeza, another of the Directorate's much publicized projects, the corner where the Falangist Civil Guard Captain Santiago Cortés fell while defending the Sanctuary was left in ruin, and a *Vía Crucis* was built leading to his crypt (Ureña 1979: 140). At the Cerro de los Ángeles, remains of the famously destroyed monument dedicated to the *Sagrado Corazón de Jesús* – inaugurated by Alfonso XIII in 1919 on this supposed geographic centre of the Iberian peninsula – were preserved in situ and a broken piece of the Christ figure placed on a pedestal near the rebuilt structure.[58] Attached to the pedestal a plaque read: "Head of the Image of the Sacred Heart of Jesus profaned by the reds" (Figure 3.59). This was accompanied by another plaque requesting donations for the new monument, a common practice as the construction of many memorials was funded through a combination of municipal budgets and public subscription thus making people active participants.

There were other instances of particularly symbolic ruins being left *in situ*. On the site of Madrid's Cuartel de la Montaña, ruins were left in place, and on anniversaries of the siege an altar was placed amidst them for an outdoor mass. The town of Belchite became iconic in the regime's use of ruins (Text Box 3.4). A cleric from Belchite expressed it thus:

> *If the destruction of Belchite were not so profoundly tragic, we would say that the ruins of this town represent a touristic objective. Spanish pilgrims, with time, would come to see the old Belchite as the true patriots visit the ruins of Numancia. [. . .] When the war ends national schools will be obliged to organise excursions for the older children and presentations by teachers on the symbolism of these holy and precious ruins.*
>
> (Centellas *et al.* 2006: 69)

In other towns such as Seseña or Villanueva de la Barca, the volume of the destruction and the cost of clearing the resulting rubble were deemed too high, and so a new town was constructed rather than the original one rebuilt. However, none of these towns received the attention that Belchite did. Despite being a small, poorly communicated town, Belchite was turned not only into a symbolic motor of the reconstruction – generating references as to how the new Spain was springing from the ruins of the old – but also a practical one as both a large prison camp and a cement factory were set up there, the latter supplying many reconstruction projects throughout eastern Spain.

Codifying space: Inscribing meaning

Three modalities of the reconstruction have been discussed thus far: the rebuilding, the re-writing of a selective historical narrative and the memorialization of the conflict. The choices made and messages sent in each of these veins were instrumental in communicating new codes intended to shape thinking and behaviour. The regime explicitly attempted to influence behaviours and attitudes through the reconstruction. This aim can be observed in the emphasis on a set of moral values that were repeated in the regime's discourses. In the choice of Medieval Spain as the period to glorify and emulate, it was not only imperial but moral values (of austerity, piety, order and intransigent Catholicism) that were celebrated. The twin pillars of history and memorialization contributed to the construction of a new interpretative framework, redefining notions of 'insider' and 'excluded'.

Key symbolic values of the regime permeated the everyday life of Spaniards, often by directly expounding them – with newspapers called *Fe* and *Unidad*. In other cases it was done by referencing those key symbolic sites that the regime had chosen as beacons of moral lessons – periodicals titled *El Escorial* and *El Alcázar*. Few aspects of daily life were not injected with ideological tones as the regime tried to mould

Use of ruins in the visual rhetoric

3.56 Stamp created for the 25th anniversary of the *Alzamiento Nacional*, 1964.

3.57 Ruins of the Alcázar by Carlos Saenz de Tejada (popular reproduction, appeared in *Vértice*, © DACS 2010).

3.58 New monument built across the esplanade from the ruins of the old Sagrado Corazón. (España. Ministerio de Cultura. Archivo General de la Administración. Sig.: AGA(03)082F1418-sobre19.)

3.59 Ruins of the old monument with a donation box under the sculpture's damaged head. (España. Ministerio de Cultura. Archivo General de la Administración. Sig.: AGA-(03)082F1418-sobre18.)

behaviours and attitudes even cinemas were called things like *Cine Imperial* or *Cine Alcázar*. In her memoirs, Avia recalls how in the 1940s:

> *it felt and was believed as a sacred truth that Spain was different, the national day was spoken of with pride, and the scarce chauvinism of Spaniards was fuelled with words like bulls, carnations, bravery, mantillas, blood, fiesta, arrogance or señorío.*
>
> (Avia 2004: 159)

Box 3.4   Belchite and the politics of ruins

The town of Belchite, 40 km from Zaragoza, became one of the jewels in the Directorate's crown. Belchite embodied a tension within the regime of wanting to make rhetorical use of the war destruction and yet wanting to be seen as fuelling the country's rebuilding. The entire twelfth-century town, in which Mudéjar architecture predominated, was deliberately left in ruins and a New Belchite built only 500 metres away. The first issue of *Reconstrucción* shows a photomontage of Franco standing in front of the ruins of Belchite (Figure 3.60). Here we can clearly observe the explicit intention of the reconstruction to plant signposts in the topography of the new Spain. The article reads:

> *Reliquary of martyrs and heroes of a better Spain, by resolute decision of the Caudillo Belchite will conserve intact the prestige of its destruction, one further landmark in the long chain of epics that mark throughout the fields of Spain the renovation of our History that the Alzamiento Nacional has meant.*
>
> (*Reconstrucción*, no. 1, April 1940)

The link between old and new Belchite consisted in a 'monument to the fallen', placed on a hill visible from both towns. Planning maps for new Belchite show an axial radius drawn to determine the placement of the monument at the location where it would have the greatest visibility from the new town. The 'poetics of ruins' aspect of the reconstruction are evident in Old Belchite, while in New Belchite street names directly referenced the war and the regime.

Looking at the drawings made by the Directorate's architects for the two Belchites, the new one reflects a moral lesson, with its neat edges and straight streets laid out in a grid when juxtaposed with the chaos of the ruinous old town (Figure 3.62). Further emphasizing this point, a monument built in the new town to commemorate its construction consists of a broken column (Figure 3.61).

The article in *Reconstrucción* "The Symbol of the Two Belchites", illustrates the Regime's rhetorical and visual uses of the reconstruction: the juxtaposition between old and new, chaotic ruin and

3.60 Article from *Reconstrucción*, no. 1, 1940: 10–11.

3.61 Memorial column during inaugural ceremony led by Franco. (España. Ministerio de Cultura. Archivo General de la Administración. Sig.: AGA.F.04253-15-01.)

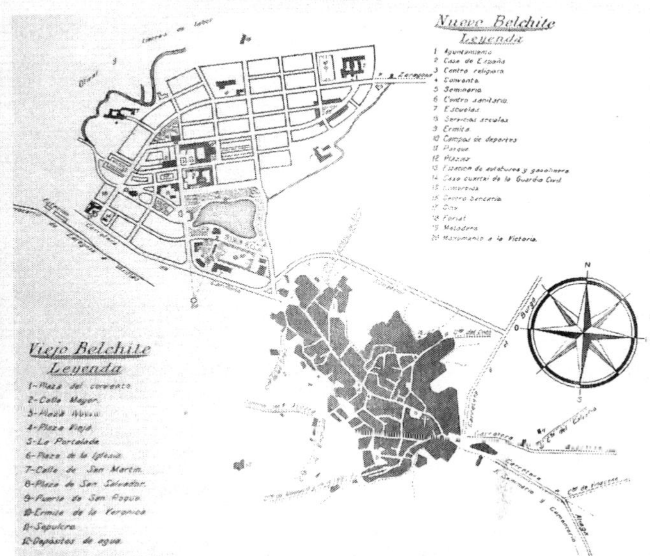

3.62 Diagram of new Belchite top left, old Belchite bottom right, the monument built on the hillside of the new town is shown on the South of the new town with vantage points calculated. (*Reconstruccion*, no. 1, 1940: 12.)

neat construction; as well as the personification of the Regime's moral paradigms of heroism, martyrdom, order, cleanliness and vertical hierarchy. The article begins:

> *Next to the heroic stones of old Belchite will be erected the cordial and welcoming line of the new Belchite; next to the rubble, the reconstruction; next to the mountains of ruins produced by Marxism as unequivocal trace of their brief passage, the happy monument to peace that Spain and Franco edify. Symbols of two epochs and two systems, the two Belchites speak, with the mute language of their rubble and white stones, of barbarism and culture, of misery and Empire, of materialism and of spirit, of the anti-Spain defeated and of the victorious and eternal Spain.*
>
> (Gómez Aparicio, *Reconstrucción*, no. 1, 1940: 6–9)

The reasons given for leaving it as a ruin include:

> *Because Belchite is a symbol, the Caudillo desired to conserve it with the pain of its burned walls. (…) There can be no higher monument to the memory of that remarkable handful of heroes than the grim panorama of the ruins.*
>
> (*Reconstrucción*, no. 1, 1940: 11)

As in other iconic cases of reconstruction, there is a considerable discrepancy between the rhetoric and the reality. After failed attempts to call it 'Belchite de Franco', new Belchite was inaugurated in

(continued overleaf)

1954 and it was only then that the approximately 3,000 inhabitants began to move in, having spent 15 years living in the remains of old Belchite (Cinca Yago, Allanegui Burriel, Archilla Navarro 2008). Even then, some inhabitants preferred to remain in their homes in the old town. Any significance that Belchite's ruined state could have had as a monument was limited to the realms of rhetoric, propaganda and mythmaking.

3.63 Ruins of the old *mudejar* church.

3.64 The new church of Belchite.

In the discourse surrounding the building of new Belchite, parallels with Numancia recur as references to another heroic town. For instance, in the newsreel *Noticiario* 616B (1954) dedicated to Belchite, the battles there are described as *numantine*. The newsreel continues that the new town was built 1 kilometer from the old with 700 homes and a church for the 'families of the heroic martyrs'.[59] The comparison between aerial images of the archaeological site of Numancia and the urban planning diagrams for New Belchite reveals resounding similarities (Figures 3.65 and 3.66).

3.65 *Regiones Devastadas* plan for new Belchite. (*Reconstruccion*, no. 1, 1940: 13.)

3.66 Map of the archaeological site of Numancia. (Ortego y Frias, 1975.)[60]

3.67 "Honour, Heroism, Faith, Authority, Justice, Efficiency, Intelligence, Will, Austerity". Poster, 1939. (España. Ministerio de Cultura. Centro Documental de la Memoria Histórica. Sig.: PS-Carteles, 1933.)

Thus far, this section has explored how the reconstruction project sought to imbue spaces with particular codes of significance. As shown earlier, the moral branches of the regime centred on the ideas of order, vertical hierarchy and unity. These paradigms reflected in the urban planning of places like Brunete and the Alcázar of Toledo both of which are well-documented examples in which the work of *Regiones Devastadas* is still clearly discernible today. Monuments were also used as explicit reminders of the moral values that the regime celebrated. An instance of this is a monument to José Antonio Primo de Rivera[61] – designed and erected in Badajoz on the occasion of the first millenary of Castile (943–1943) – on which was inscribed the following legend: "Unity between the lands of Spain. Unity between the classes of Spain. Unity in man and between the men of Spain" (Project document. AGA. 9.17.10-51/20601). The monument at the Cerro de los Ángeles already mentioned is equally revealing of the historical and moral panorama being constructed (see Appendix C).

Redrawing Madrid's symbol-scape

The reconstruction of Madrid was especially important to the new regime, aware that the war had only been won once Madrid had fallen. Some felt that Madrid should be punished for its resistance by taking away its status as capital (Sambricio, 1987: 79). Nevertheless, there were many elements in Madrid's favour. Symbolically, this was of primary importance to the regime's values of centre, unity and glorification of Castile as the most authentic region. It was, nevertheless, a delicate operation, as the city had to be cleansed of its 'red' elements and rebuilt materially and symbolically in order to fashion an "austere Imperial Capital that would set an example" (Álvarez Junco, 2002: 184). The tension was expressed by Serrano Suñer who said that work had to be done to end with the "tragic Spanishness of decadent Castilian Madrid, even if the *Puerta de Sol* has to disappear" (cited by Vizcaíno Casas 1996: 22). The regime's moral and stylistic doctrine was imposed on the urban fabric through the construction of monuments, changed street names, and a new topography intended to supplant the memory of the former capital of the Republic (see Appendix D). In April 1939 Madrid Mayor, Alberto Alcocer, created a Permanent Commission with the express mission of revising Madrid's toponomy. A letter sent from his office to the Commission on 24 April 1939 reads:

> *It is urgent that Madrid be cleansed of all symbols and names*
> *that a regime that was corrupt and harmful for the Patria left on*
> *its public avenues so that the traditional and clean sense of*
> *Spain prevails, in the continuation of the greatness impressed on*
> *it by the heroism of its children in defeating barbarism . . .*
>
> (cited by Caprarella 1999: 185)

The reconstruction of Madrid also involved many symbolic acts. For instance, the *Puerta de Alcalá*,[62] which had been used by the Republic as a support on which to hang images of symbolic figures, was used in the aftermath of the war both as a triumphal arch to Franco's victory and as an altar, supporting a crucifix and used for ceremonies and out-door masses (Figures 3.68 to 3.69). Historic monuments of Madrid were also re-interpreted, moved to different locations and re-inaugurated with new symbolism.

Such was the importance of the reconstruction of Madrid that a special body was created to direct it: the *Junta de Reconstrucción de Madrid*.[63] The 1939 document *Ideas generales sobre el plan nacional de ordenación y reconstrucción* (General ideas on a national plan for urban planning and reconstruction) describes the first four aspects of Madrid's reconstruction: dignity, tradition, façade and representation. The façade of the city was fundamental in planning what was intended be 'representative of national values' (Servicios Técnicos de FET y de las JONS 1939: 69), incorporating the Palace, the Cathedral, the Old Town and, towards the north, the buildings that would be erected to represent the new state.

Throughout the reconstruction there were considerable gaps between what was projected and what actually was built. Madrid was no exception. The *Plan de Ordenación* for Madrid was drafted in 1941 but it was not until 1946 that the *Ley de Ordenación Urbana* (Urban Planning

La *Puerta de Alcalá* as prop for different ideologies

3.68   The Puerta de Alcalá, 1936 with Lenin in the place of honour. (España. Ministerio de Cultura. Archivo General de la Administración. Sig.: AGA-Cultura-124-8962. Sobre17.) (Archivo Alfonso, © DACS 2010.)

3.69   The Puerta de Alcalá, 1939 with a Catholic mass being held replete with Falangist symbols and guard. (España. Ministerio de Cultura. Archivo General de la Administración. Sig.: AGA-Cultura-124-5725. Sobre17.) (Archivo Alfonso, © DACS 2010.)

Law) was passed, formalizing the plans that meanwhile had changed (Caprarella 1999: 160–162). Those five years were replete with polemic, debates, power struggles and changing realities – primary among them being the rapidly swelling shanty-town suburbs around Madrid.

Reconstruction as a stage-setting for performing the nation

By constructing spaces in which people lived and through which they moved, the reconstruction project provided a stage setting for the performance of the new state. Every building completed or begun, every street renamed and monument inaugurated, new and old holidays, saints' days and commemorations were marked with ceremonies and parades, thus further imbuing the spaces of these performances with new meaning. In addition to the Day of Victory on 1st of April, on every 18th of July the *Alzamiento* (uprising) was celebrated, and every 1st of October was designated as *Día del Caudillo*. Control of these events was in the hands of the propaganda departments of the Vicesecretaría de Educación Popular de FET y de las JONS (1936–1944), the Subsecretaría de Educación Popular under the Ministry of Education (1946–1951) and the Ministry of Information and Tourism (1951–1975) (Ramírez, 1981:

232). An indication of the importance given to these celebrations and the considerable amount of resources poured into them is the huge amount of preserved correspondence, invoices, budgets and memos. In 1948, for instance, the Negociado de Actos Público of the Servicio de Arquitectura requested vast amounts of ephemeral and decorative elements, including a large quantity of flags, for a variety of public events: book fairs, trade fairs, religious celebrations, sports events, honorary acts, and commemorations (celebrations of the fourth centenary of Cervantes' birth, the centenary celebrations of the first train in Spain) (AGA – 03.49.01-21/1856). Correspondence for this period between the head of the Almacén del Servicio de Arquitectura, the head of Protocolo de la Secretaría General de FET y de las JONS and the head of Patrimonio Nacional concerns the loan of rugs, tapestries and other ornamentation from the royal collections to use as decoration during these acts (AGA–03.49.01-21/1856).

One of the more important celebrations was the *Día de la Hispanidad* (the Day of Hispanicity) on 12 October – which also coincided with the *Fiesta de la Raza* (Celebration of the Race). In a period when post-imperial Spain was isolated from the rest of the world, it served to celebrate the regime's vision of a glorious Spain with international influence, a harbinger of civilization and Christianity. These festivities were orchestrated by the *Real Sociedad Colombina* (Royal Columbus Society) of each province, in collaboration with the provincial and national Delegations of Propaganda (under the auspices of the *Vicesecretaría de Educación Popular*). They involved a celebration of Columbus, religious acts, and speeches highlighting the cultural mission of Spain, with flags and marching bands playing the anthems of Spain and of the Falange.[64] Vizcaíno Casas (1996: 161) describes what he calls a "triumphant patriotic choreography" surrounding public acts.

On the *Día de la Hispanidad* 1944 an outdoor mass was held in Zaragoza in which Franco knelt and prayed at the memorial, consecrating Spain to the care of the *Virgen del Pilar* in the presence of the archbishops of Santiago, Tarragona and Barcelona. The choice of the city of Zaragoza for the celebrations of *Hispanidad* was no coincidence. As has already been mentioned, Zaragoza was the site of a legendary siege and defence during the 1808 War of Independence. Furthermore, the Palace in Zaragoza contains the throne room of the Catholic Kings, a room heavily laden with historical references to a glorious Catholic past that served to create the semblance of an unbroken historical continuation of the Hispanic family. This combination of religious, historical, military, political and folkloric imagery and activities was often repeated throughout the Dictatorship. Any occasion was a good excuse for such a performance of power[65] – moral, religious, economic, military and political – further emphasizing that the regime had the weight of tradition on their side.

Regardless of the day that was celebrated, provincial authorities were pressured by the central office to produce festivities with high visibility, participation and media coverage. Thus in the days prior to the celebrations articles appeared in the local press calling on the public to participate. Ceremonies were organized according to strict protocol, whether they consisted of a religious act (often a Te Deum or outdoor mass), military representation, speeches by local authorities, the consecration of a monument, placement of a wreath or positioning of a foundation stone for a new construction. These events were often accompanied by a parade, usually leading from the church to the *Plaza Mayor/Plaza de España/Plaza del Ayuntamiento* with a marching band playing the anthems of Spain and of the Falange.

The psychologist Erik Erikson (1972: 186) noted that "ceremonial permits a group to behave in a symbolically ornamental way so that it seems to present an ordered universe" and order is a sought-after value when seeking to rebuild a war-ruined country. More recent work has affirmed that our knowledge of the past and recollection of it is transmitted and sustained by performances (Connerton 1989); these take the form of rituals, ceremonies, festivals and commemorations (Winter and Sivan 1999; Müller 2002; Boissevain 1992). In Spain, the performances took place against a backdrop provided by the reconstruction. Although they rhetorically emphasized the unity of Spain, in reality they served to underscore divisions and exclude (Payá López 2002: 201). In the regime's performances can be seen the two sides of a discourse that altered between old and new. Events such as that by which Franco was made Lord High Admiral of Castile were orchestrated to resemble mediaeval ceremonies with all the relevant liturgy and iconography while other events were performed according to an aesthetic of National Socialism.

Dent Coad (1995: 223–224) describes the monumentalizing of existing public buildings by adding Herreran style decorative elements, porticos and grand entrances, and even boarding up key modernist buildings in Madrid for a brief period in the immediate postwar period. Ephemeral architecture was also widely used in public ceremonies and official events throughout the 1940s and 1950s as a stage set on which to perform the New Spain with scarce resources going towards creating temporary architectural structures (Bonet Correa 1981). When Eva Peron, 'Evita', the leading lady of Argentina, paid an official visit to Madrid in 1947, the city was still in such a ruinous state that officials erected false façades to line the streets along which her motorcade would pass.[66] This 'stage setting' concept ran through much of the Regime's reconstruction activities during the 1940s, and can be seen in ephemeral architecture, the focus on façades and prioritization of the *Plaza Mayor*.

The memory of the recent war was also performed through victory parades, masses to the fallen, inaugurations of monuments to the fallen, and countless activities commemorating events of the war and celebrat-

Table 3.4 Official days for remembering the war dead

30 September	Commemoration of the Liberation of the Heroes of the Straight of Quinto
28 October	Day of the Fallen
20 November	Day of Sorrow (Day in homage of José Antonio)
10 February	Day of the Fallen Student

These were in addition to larger celebrations during which the 'glorious martyrs' were also exalted such as:

1 April	Victory Day
18 July	Anniversary if the *Alzamiento*
10 October	Day of the *Caudillo*

ing both its heroes and its martyrs. For instance, the performative aspect of the reconstruction project of Belchite is explicitly detailed in the project documents:

> *The new Belchite is built in close proximity to the old, of accurate placement, taking advantage of its communications and services. Both towns are separated by a green zone, enhancing the ruins of the old [. . .] the layout [of new Belchite] is composed essentially of a transit route, a processional route drawn in relation to the square of the church, the square of the Town Hall, and linked to this a square for entertainment.*
>
> (AGA-RD, Belchite-20702)

Commemorative events invariably involved religious services with the presence of political and military authorities, as well as the placement of wreaths on the memorials to the fallen by a range of military, political and Falangist authorities, as well as representatives of public institutions and the private sector.[67] The majority of these memorials were designed so that they could double as altars for outdoor masses. On special occasions these would include the active presence of Franco, who would kneel at the altar at the base of the monument and read a formula of consecration of Spain to a Virgin or Saint.

Of all the celebrations, the most important in terms of the resources it mobilized, its media coverage and the participation of authorities and public alike were the Victory Parades. Held every year on the 1st of April, these acts were carefully planned. In October 1944, Madrid's Provincial Delegation of the *Vicesecretaría de Educación Popular (de FET y de las JONS)* developed a detailed project for the commemorative events marking the *Liberación de Madrid* (28 March) and the *Día de la Victoria* (1 April). Its aims are outlined in the first section of the document:

1. *To arouse the wholesome memory of the significance of our war: Spain laid waste and sunken by the hordes. Spain recovered and standing under Franco's flags.*
2 *Gratitude to the Almighty in the joy of being once again. Gratitude to the forger of the Victory. Gratitude to those that crushed the beast. Commemoration, remembrance of moved gratitude to the dead in the determination for triumph and of those that perished in the shadows, longing for light.*
> (Vicesecretaría de Educación Popular de FET y de las JONS, 1944)

These acts included parades, open-air masses and other religious services, concerts (by military bands) and the projection of four documentaries: *18 de Julio, Ciudad Universitaria, La liberación de Madrid, Desfile de la Victoria* (*Vicesecretaría de Educación Popular* 1944. AGA.03.49.01-21/1850). Despite the preponderance of parades and celebrations, starker aspects of daily life were reflected in memories, memoirs and biographies. Armando López Salinas' novel *Año tras Año* (1962), written on the basis of firsthand accounts and testimonies of Madrid's working class between 1939 and 1951, provides a valuable record of the living conditions of the period. In the novel, factory workers try to erase their personal histories, attempting to cleanse their political pasts in order to avoid prison and find employment. Once hired, the strong vertical hierarchies and a climate of fear pervade, dominated by informants, controllers, and regime spies. Even certain professions such as *porteros* (doormen), *serenos* (night watchmen) and eventually taxi drivers were associated with informant roles. Moral and cultural imposition, for which reconstruction in Spain was a vehicle, were intimately linked with the regime's aspirations to control attitudes and behaviour.

Contradictions, Responses, and Consequences

The success of the regime in imposing a uniform architectural style was limited. In 1944, Diego de Reina wrote:

> *A while ago already we Spanish technicians should have unified our efforts in order to achieve the creation and establishment of a new architectural style. However, save for the meetings held in 1939 by the Servicios Técnicos de FET y de las JONS and some possible isolated cases, we have paid little attention to such a complex topic. Undoubtedly the present circumstances,*

accumulating difficulties of all types, are in a large part to blame for the negligible appreciation to the aesthetic needs of the moment, but it is also necessary to confess that it is difficult to channel the liberal professions, taming that inherent aspect in them of eternal rebelliousness.

(Reina 1944: 10)

This criticism was echoed by others including Juan de Zavala, who spoke at the 1949 *V Asamblea Nacional de Arquitectura*. He criticized the architecture of post-war Spain for its mimicry of historical styles and its rejection of advances in modern techniques. Hence despite the image that *Reconstrucción* and the *Revista Nacional de Arquitectura* tried to give of a unified architectural style of the new state, in 1944 this was not yet a reality. Reina called for an "unmistakable, permanent and new stamp" to be put on national architecture, which he suggested would not be found in the picturesque or in the use of traditional handcrafted decorative details, but in a more grandiose style that, "inspired by past glories, adjusts to concrete realities" (Reina 1944: 120). He rejected the imitation of Herrera or Villanueva, saying that the style of the Escorial should be seen as a root "engendering new forms that, aside from enriching our architecture, represent the ideology of an Empire that resurges from its ashes" (Reina 1944: 120). The common denominator of this new style was not stylistic detail but a set of directive values translated into aesthetic, spiritual and material practice. He identified the essential characteristics as: "Religion, Historic Mission, Cultural Mission and Exaltation

2.2 Calle Genova, Madrid, July 2006. (Photograph by the author, 2006.)

2.6 Bardasano, *Fuera el Invasor*, 1937. (España. Ministerio de Cultura. Centro Documental de la Memoria Histórica. Sig. PS-Carteles, 232.)

2.8 Martí Bas. *La Juventud en armas defiende la cultura.* 1938. (UGT)

2.9 Spanish Anonymous. 20th Cent. *España una, grande, libre.* **c**.1937–1940. (España. Ministerio de Cultura. Centro Documental de la Memoria Histórica, PS-Carteles, 2033.)

2.11 Morell, *Ha llegado España*, 1939. (España. Ministerio de Cultura. Centro Documental de la Memoria Histórica, PS-Carteles, 2116.)

2.12 Juan Antonio Morales. *Los Nacionales*, Ministry of Propaganda, 1936. (España. Ministerio de Cultura. Centro Documental de la Memoria Histórica, PS-Carteles, 190.)

3.24 Poster announcing the 1939 Fair of Valencia showing a bullfighter doing a fascist salute. (Printed by the municipality of Valencia.)

3.29 Emblem of the Catholic Kings on the façade of the School of *Artes y Oficios* of Toledo. (Photograph by the author, 2008.)

3.30 The official emblem of Spain developed for the regime.

3.37 Beer: *El Alcázar*. (Vértice, September 1940.)

3.38 Wine: Imperial Toledo, Wine of Heroes, 1939. (*Revista de la Mujer*, January 1939.)

3.40 Board game "The entry into Madrid", in which players battle to take over the capital, 1939.

3.73 Poster: *Franco Mantiene la paz en España* ("Franco Maintains Peace in Spain") Published by the *Vicesecretaría de Educación Popular*. *c*.1944. (España. Ministerio de Cultura. Centro Documental de la Memoria Histórica. Sig.: PS-Careteles, 2110.)

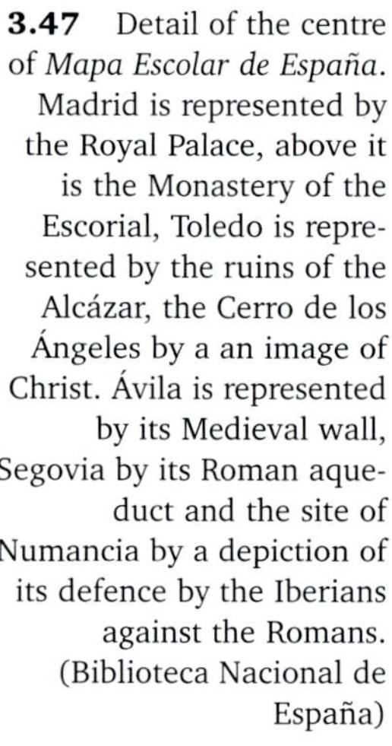

3.47 Detail of the centre of *Mapa Escolar de España*. Madrid is represented by the Royal Palace, above it is the Monastery of the Escorial, Toledo is represented by the ruins of the Alcázar, the Cerro de los Ángeles by a an image of Christ. Ávila is represented by its Medieval wall, Segovia by its Roman aqueduct and the site of Numancia by a depiction of its defence by the Iberians against the Romans. (Biblioteca Nacional de España)

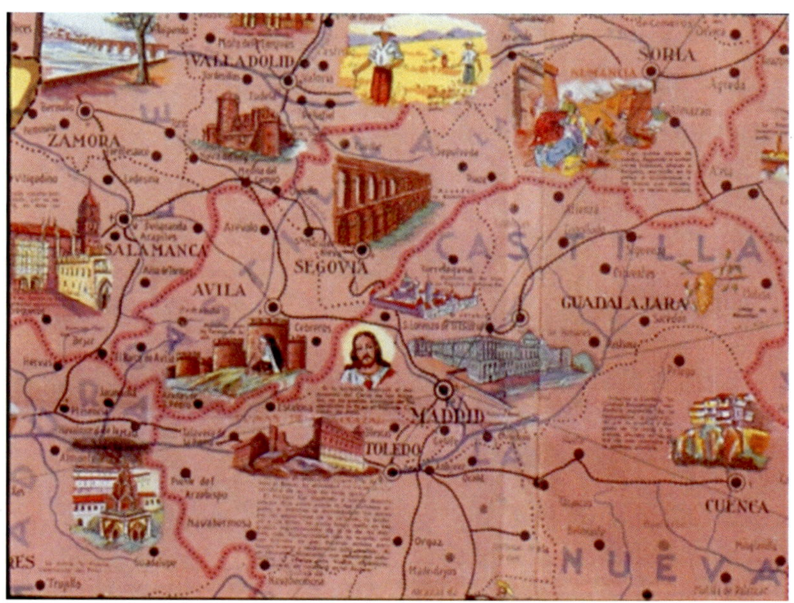

3.46 Hernández y Fernández, Jesús (and others). *"Mapa escolar de España. Geografía-Producciones-Historia-Arte. Los diez mandamientos del niño"* produced by Litografía "Arte", c.1940. (Biblioteca Nacional de España. BNE.Sig.Mr.16.1)

4.21 Front cover of *Reconstrucción* n°55 from 1945 with an image of Gernika's rebuilt Town Hall.

5.12 ETA flyer from *Aberri Eguna* in 1975 calling on people to gather in Gernika and using imagery of *Guernica* and the *ikurriña*.

4.44 Equipo Crónica. *El Intruso* (1969–1971). © DACS 2010.

5.21 Ceramic tile mural of *Guernica* on a street in Gernika.
© Succession Picasso/DACS, London 2010.
(Photograph by the author, 2006.)

5.20 Street name change in Gernika: From Fernando el Católico to Pablo Picasso.
(Photograph by the author, 2007.)

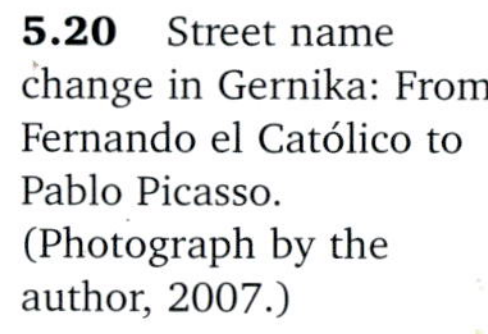

5.24 Mural of *Guernica* on a street in West Belfast, 2007.
(Photograph by Hannah Merron, 2009. © Succession Picasso/DACS, London 2010.)

5.23 A ceremony marking the 70th anniversary of the bombing at the base of the current Tree of Gernika.
(Photograph by the author, 2007.)

of Hispanicity", and the corresponding values and 'racial virtues' as "Austerity, Virility and Joy in labour or in sacrifice" (his use of capitals, Reina 1944: 123). A representative example of this style is the *Edificio España* (Figure 3.70), built in 1947 in Madrid, it fell within the urban policy of the Bidagor Plan with its intended "language of a nationalist character" (COAM 2003: 376).

Heritage and memory in exile and resistance movements

One of the most poignant ways in which the civil war caused a rupture in the course of Spanish history and culture was in the vast number of exiles that it engendered. Forced emigration encompassed the entire liberal political class as well as professionals, artists, intellectuals: university professors (12 percent of the national total), architects, doctors, poets, lawyers, engineers, and historians. This large-scale emigration began in 1936, and by the time the war ended there were 450,000 Spaniards in exile (Tusell 2007: 26). Among them were some of the more significant architects of the 1930s Rationalist movement: José Luis Sert, Juan de Madariaga, Tomás Bilbao, Francisco Fábregas, Félix Candela and many others. Their disappearance from the Spanish architectural scene caused a break in the modernist movement in Spain (Ministerio de Vivienda: 2007).

In exile other memories of the war were constructed and transmitted. Events and personages from the war, different from those memorialised inside Spain, also took on mythical dimensions in these communities and became part of their heritage (Figures 3.71 and 3.72). For instance, in 1944 several Spanish Battalions under General Le Clerc's orders were among the first to liberate Paris and arrive at the Place de

In exile a vision of Spain as a prison

3.71 Congress of the PSOE in Toulouse, 1946 (FPI).

3.72 Congress of the CNT in exile, 1940s (FAL).

l'Hôtel de Ville. All the armoured vehicles bore the names of battles from the civil war – Gernika, Brunete, Belchite, Teruel, Guadalajara. These exiles also had their own martyrs and heroes: the poet Federico García Lorca, the anarchist Durruti, *las trece rosas*, General José Miaja, Colonel Vicente Rojo and Dolores Ibárruri. Thus, among the exiled communities Spain too was reconstructed. The sensation that exiled Spain had carried with it and was safeguarding part of Spanish heritage was so strong that the exiled poet León Felipe would write: "Franco, thine is the land, the house, the horse and the gun, / mine is the ancient voice of the earth" (cited in Tusell 2007: 28).

Alternative visions of Spain and alternative memories of the civil war were constructed largely in exile, but inside Spain resistance to the regime's imposed narratives also took place. While the Maquis (resistance fighters) and a guerrilla movement (after 1945) tried to maintain an armed resistance, information and a spirit of resistance was communicated clandestinely through miniature newspapers or *octavillas*. In terms of the previous discussion it is important to note that one recurrent theme is that of remembering the dead on the side of the Republic.

Evolution of the reconstruction project

Throughout the nearly two decades in which *Regiones Devastadas* existed, both its discourse and its activities evolved. One of the determining factors in spurring change was the international situation. The outbreak of the Second World War seriously hampered Spain's ability to access construction materials, but provided two allies with strong ideological and aesthetic styles that the Franco regime could draw on. At first Franco sought to associate the regime with these two powerful allies, and the national press complied, linking Franco with Hitler and Mussolini. However, by 1944 as it began to become clear that the Axis powers were losing the war, inside Spain the tone changed and Franco was celebrated for keeping Spain out of the war (Figure 3.73). Correspondence between the Provincial Delegation of Seville and the national office in Madrid shows that 2,000 of these posters were intended for public places – "casinos, cafes, bars, movie theatres, official centres and entities, leisure centres, etc."[68] In the same year, when Moreno Torres presented the work of *Regiones Devastadas* at the *II Congreso de la Federación de Urbanismo y de la Vivienda* (Lisbon, Portugal), he started out by placing Spain at centre stage to Europe's foreseeable reconstruction work. Just as Spain had drawn on the post-1914 reconstruction experiences of France, Belgium and Italy, so, he said, Europe would now turn to Spain for its "small but solid" experience (Moreno Torres 1944).

Yet the end of the Second World War saw two contradictory movements in Spain. On the one hand, international isolation incited the regime to develop along more autocratic lines, becoming self-referential

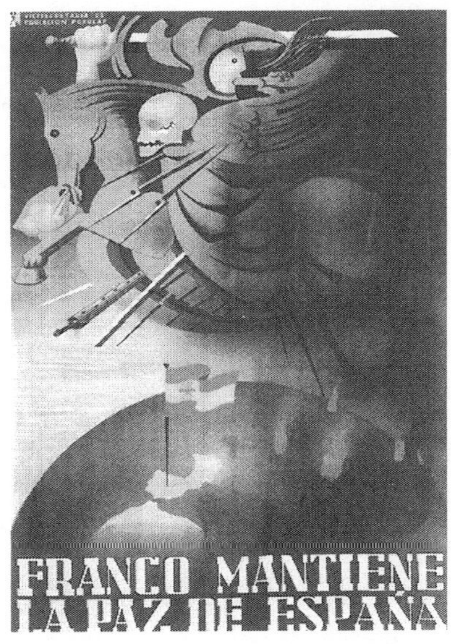

3.73 "Franco maintains peace in Spain", poster by the *Vicesecretaría de Educación Popular*, c1944. (España. Ministerio de Cultura. Centro Documental de la Memoria Histórica. Sig.: PS-Careteles, 2110.)

in its discourse and styles. A flyer produced by the Propaganda Department in 1948 quotes Franco as saying: "The Spaniard feels more united with the Americas of its same stock than with that miserable Europe that never knew how to understand our *Patria*" – a sentiment reiterated during his speech to the Cortes on 18 May 1949 during which he reflects on the rejection of the United Nations Assembly to accept Spain as a member state. Franco's speeches at memorializing events also illustrate this attitude. For instance, at the site of the *Alto de los Leones* in the mountains of the Guadarrama in 1952, he said:

> *Through the years transpired it can be clearly perceived that the Spanish Crusade did not constitute one more episode of our contemporary public life, one more revolutionary event of those that become lost amidst the episodes of History, but rather a true event that within the national frame links to and resembles what the Catholic Kings accomplished by changing the sign of the Nation in another epoch of revolts and turbulence, extending beyond the national borders to take on a part in international events, by constituting the first victorious battle that was fought in the world against Communism.*
>
> (Franco 1952)

On the other hand, the end of the world war initiated a period in which Spain began to open up in terms of architecture. Monumentalism and folklorism were put aside in favour of new building techniques making daring and innovative constructions possible; a prime example of this is the avant-guard Basilica of Aránzazu, Guipúzcoa, inaugurated in 1955.[69] As the decade came to an end, other dimensions of heritage began to be recovered. For instance, Madrid's cafés *El Gijón* and *El Comercial*, once associated with liberals, became meeting points for writers and artists again. Also, in 1948 the philosopher Ortega y Gasset and the artist Salvador Dalí returned to Spain.

In 1951 the social situation changed once again: the last of the Maquis resistance was arrested, there was an attempt at social mobilization through boycotts of public transportation, and evidence began to emerge of clandestine propaganda efforts. This year saw the publication of Camilo José Cela's novel *La colmena*, a forceful, realistic portrait of 1940s Madrid and the beginning of tentative negotiations with the United States. This rapprochement developed into an official cooperation agreement, initiating a quasi-Marshall Plan for Spain and affecting a marked change in architectural styles. The severe housing shortage (Figure 3.74) combined with the new US relationship prompted *Regiones Devastadas* to abandon its focus on the styles of 'traditional' and 'Imperial' Spain and turn to more practical solutions.[70] The shift is evidenced by articles on American architecture appearing in both *Reconstrucción* and the *Revista Nacional de Arquitectura*. While most of the reconstruction projects of *Regiones Devastadas* were planned and initiated in the 1940s, the majority were not completed until the 1950s. This decade also saw the reorganization of the architectural field and the beginning of an era in which construction would become one of the country's foremost economic motors. The Cold War greatly favoured Franco, for not only did it bring deals with the US, it also made it possible for Spain to participate in the international 'crusade' against Communism, thus further legitimizing Franco's civil war victory and subsequent repression, and providing little incentive for a radical change (Preston 1987: 7).

The development of relations with the US, aside from opening Spain to cultural products from abroad, provoked a series of side effects within the country. One of these was to reinforce the association of Spanish culture with a folkloric vision of Andalusia. This connection increased throughout the 1950s, as officials and hoteliers felt that American tourists expected to see cultural expressions of the south. This state of affairs was satirized with great sagacity and humour by Berlanga (1952) in the movie *Bienvenido Mr Marshal*,[71] which had an impact on how Spanish cultural heritage was valued. The image of Spain constructed for an international tourist market eventually transformed the image of Spain projected nationally as well. The advent of mass tourism was also a significant factor in initiating a new phase in the rebuilding of Spain as a wave of construction spilled out onto Spain's coasts to such an intense degree that it came to be known as the industry of *el ladrillo* (brick). Relations with the United States also stimulated a shift in the image of the country in other ways as well. The most visible level at which this occurred was that of popular culture as movies, music and television programmes from the US appeared in Spain showing an alternative way

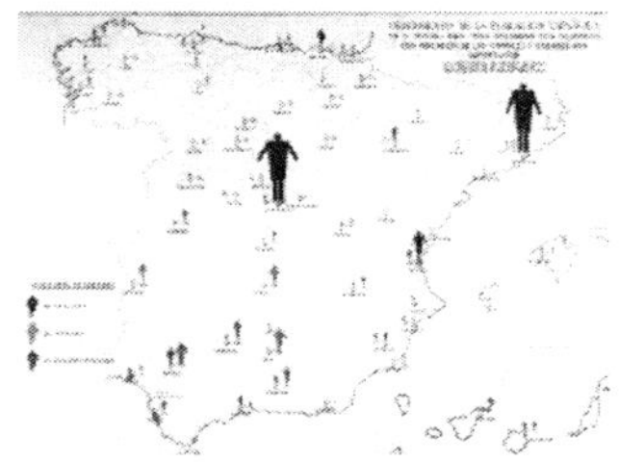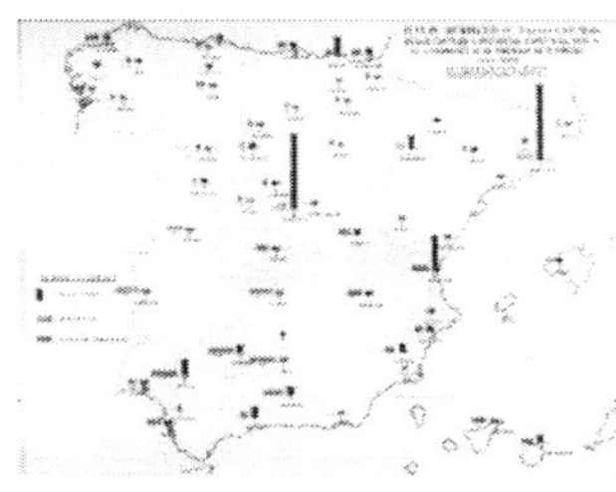

3.74 Maps showing the increase of urban populations, 1950. (España. Ministerio de Cultura. Archivo General de la Administración. Sig.: AGA-(3)082F04265. Sobre 10.)

of life. The less obvious ways included the CIA funding the Spanish branch of the International Association for Cultural Freedom (Díaz 1995: 296).

Regiones Devastadas was closed down in 1957, and by legal mandate (*liquidación*) in 1960 all of its materials, projects and archives were dispersed and distributed amongst other government institutes and ministries – most of its unfinished projects taken up by the *Ministerio de la Vivienda*. In 1964 the 25th anniversary of 'peace' was celebrated and from that point on Franco's image evolved from that of the re-builder restoring Spain's rightful glory, to that of peace-bringer and orchestrator of an 'economic miracle'. Franco was now portrayed inaugurating bridges, dams, reservoirs, and highways as well as new towns and neighbourhoods. In a speech given in May 1952 to inaugurate the *Pantano del Generalísimo*, he claimed that 32 reservoirs had been inaugurated and another 38 were in the process of being built. These inaugurations appear repeatedly in the NO-DOs of the 1950s and 1960s constituting a discourse of progress, economic development and modernity.[72] Paradoxically, in building these dams and reservoirs entire villages were submerged, thus losing the rural heritage that the reconstruction project had exalted as being the roots of 'authentic' Spain. This new discourse of peace-bringer clashed with Franco's own speeches, cited throughout this chapter, which continued to maintain a tone of confrontation.

In the previous chapter I concluded that the violence done to heritage during the war was inflicted as much through physical destruction as through the propaganda war that both sides waged and that the victorious side continued long after the war, disowning the other's vision of Spain and of its past. The architectural and artistic styles favoured, the historical periods celebrated, and the events and personages of Spain chosen for commemoration conveyed a clear message and imposed a vision of Spain with which the 'defeated' of the civil war could not identify. A Spain in ruins became the material on which Franco's regime could impress its image of the nation. In the process, a new historic, symbolic and mnemonic landscape – a heritage-scape – was forged, supported by official rhetoric, censorship of popular culture, and an array of public ceremonies and celebrations. The sites that were to be made iconic by the reconstruction were selected to a large extent on the criteria of their symbolic content including, most importantly of all, the story of their destruction during the war. This deliberate attempt on the part of a new regime to stamp its image on the country through a reconstruction process that draws on historical and folkloric elements, combined with a far-reaching policy of memorialization, is not unique to the Spanish case. However, as the aim of this research project is to understand it well enough to be able to extrapolate trends and dynamics that might be applicable to other case studies, it is necessary to delve even deeper into the process. To do so, we turn now to look at one particular story of reconstruction: Gernika, a town whose physical reconstruction has long been overshadowed by the symbolism of its destruction.

4 Reconstructing Gernika

The reasons why the Spanish Civil War offers a fruitful case study were outlined in chapter two; now we arrive at a further reason. Like Angkor Wat in Cambodia, the Mostar Bridge in Bosnia and Herzegovina and the Bamiyan Buddhas in Afghanistan, in Spain there was also a case of destruction of cultural heritage that became iconic: Gernika. There are various reasons for choosing Gernika as a primary case within the Spanish panorama; the two fundamental reasons are that it provides both a practical example of reconstruction with representative elements as well as a uniquely symbolic case.

As a representative case, Gernika allows a detailed look at some of the issues identified in the previous chapter and reveals some of the discrepancies between the national reconstruction project and local realities. Despite the vast amounts of literature about the bombing and the painting, comparatively little has been written about the rebuilding of this town. Since the 1990s a group of local historians (Gernikazarra) has been documenting, mainly through photographs, how the town was before the war, the devastation of the bombing, and the rebuilding. Nevertheless, the treatment of this heritage site during the reconstruction process has not been the subject of in-depth studies. The aim here is not to add to the significant historiography of the bombing[1] but rather to examine how it was woven into the reconstruction of the town and into its symbolic content. As we have seen, Spain was replete with symbols even before the war; many of them were transformed by the war and new ones engendered. Gernika provides concrete examples of all of these with the added advantage of its regional, national and international transcendence. The destruction of the town of Gernika and its crystallization in Picasso's painting would come to be seen as an omen of a new type of warfare – the aerial bombing of civilians and historic cities accompanied by propaganda battles waged to sway public opinion.[2] Both the bombing and painting gradually evolved into anti-fascist symbols in Spain and eventually anti-war symbols internationally.

The bombing of Gernika has been interpreted by observers of the event as a deliberate attack on a historically and symbolically important site in order to target a whole people: the Basques. The interest that the destructive act has for this study lies in the resonance it had, how it was "blown up, deflated, reconstituted, distorted, and reborn into two contradictory images, passionately argued" (Vilar 1977: *foreword, x*). While it is possible to pinpoint specific symbolic elements in the town – the Tree and the Meeting House – the town's symbolic significance lies beyond the sum

4.1 Visit of the *Gobernador Civil* to survey the reconstruction of Gernika, 1943. (España. Ministerio de Cultura. Archivo General de la Administración. Sig.: AGA: F.04246.09.01.)

of its parts. Gernika, long known as the "sacred heartland of the Basque Country", occupies both a physical and symbolic place in both the tangible and intangible heritage-scape. This is the way in which it is understood in the following discussion of its destruction and reconstruction. The fact that Gernika is such an important symbolic site for the Basque collective imagination makes it a rich case for tracing the evolution of its meaning, its interpretation and appropriation, throughout the reconstruction process. An in-depth look at the example of Gernika within the Spanish context provides useful insights into the treatment of iconic heritage sites in the aftermath of war.

This chapter will first provide brief historical outlines of the evolution of Gernika as a town and symbol prior to the war and its fate during the war, focusing on interpretations of and reactions to the bombing. The second part of the chapter will first look at the practical rebuilding of Gernika in the immediate postwar period – addressing some of the issues identified in Chapter 3 – and then finally explore the parallel reconstruction of its unique symbolism both within and outside of Spain.

Gernika: Symbolism and significance up to 1936

The Basque region in Spain consists of three provinces: Alava, Guipúzcoa and Vizcaya (Biscay). While Bilbao is the provincial capital of Vizcaya, Gernika has been its most symbolic town. The valley in which Gernika lies has been inhabited since prehistoric times. The caves of Santimamiñe – in the mountains five kilometres away and inhabited from around 15,000 BC – are adorned with Neolithic paintings and are a prominent symbolic landmark: references to them recur in writings on the history of Euzkadi, in its literature and visual arts. It is also the area of Vizcaya where the most Roman remains have been found to date.

The estuary of Gernika's river (*Mundaca* or *Río de Gernika*) was once a navigable waterway and important means of communication and trade for the region. The river estuary and its location at the intersection of the roads between Bilbao and the coastal town of Bermeo meant that Gernika was significant as a strategic trading point. This importance was officially recognized by Don Tello (Count of Vizcaya, *alférez mayor* to the King Don Enrique of Castile and main landowner in the area), who formally established Gernika as a town on 28 April 1366.

Throughout the Middle Ages (Figure 4.2), Gernika evolved as a meeting place where the *fueros* – a set of consuetudinary laws based on long-established customs – were proclaimed and councils met under an oak tree denominated *Arbol Foral* – Foral Tree.[4] Possibly due to its strategic location Gernika came to predominate over other places in the region. By 1370 when the King of Castile took on the title of Lord of Vizcaya (the highest authority governing the region) he was obliged to swear to respect the *fueros* of Vizcaya in a ceremony that took place around the oak tree of Gernika. The first King to do this was Juan I in 1371, but the most famous instance occurred on the 30th of July 1476 when King Ferdinand[5] swore to the *fueros* under the tree of Gernika (Figure 4.3). During subsequent centuries further developments consolidated Gernika's status as symbol of the Basque *fueros*: several wars, the building of the *Casa de Juntas* (Meeting House), a song and a political party (Sebastián García 1998: 91–146).

Víctor Ortega's account of the War of Independence coming to Gernika suggests that during this period the oak tree acquired a further mythical dimension:

> *On the occasion of the French war, at the start of the nineteenth-century the enemy soldiers that arrived in Gernika on encountering the Arbol Foral could not but present before it their weapons and salute it as the patriarchal symbol of so many trees under whose shade they had sworn the autochthonous liberties even in French territory.*
>
> (Ortega 1976: 34)

4.2 Gernika's layout in the Middle Ages (Gernika Peace Museum).

4.3 Painting from 1509 by Francisco de Mendieta of the *Jura de los fueros por Fernando el Católico* (30 July 1476).[3]

4.4 Print of the Meeting House and Tree of Gernika, *c.*1870.

In the Carlist wars of the nineteenth-century, the northern regions and in particular Navarra and the Basque Country backed the Carlist claimants to the Spanish throne. Both of the pretenders to the throne (Charles V and later Charles VII) swore loyalty to the *fueros* under the tree of Gernika. In reprisal the sitting King, Alfonso XII, suppressed the *fueros* in 1876. This did nothing to quell the growing significance of Gernika and its Tree. On the contrary, they now gained additional significance – that was to become primordial in subsequent centuries – based on the clash with a central power. While these wars waged, a *Casa de Juntas* was built next to the Tree. It served as a parliament building and became a site for royal visits, assemblies and public acts (Figure 4.4).

The significance of Gernika's Tree continued to gain renown within the Basque country and abroad. An often repeated reference is that Jean Jacques Rousseau alluded to Gernika as a site where, gathered under a tree, the peasants always made just decisions. In 1810 William Wordsworth wrote the poem *The Oak of Guernica*, dedicated to the tree. Two German linguists, Wilhelm von Humboldt in the nineteenth-century and Gerhard Bähr in the twentieth, visited Gernika and the Basque region and dedicated studies to the Basque language.[6] Then, in 1853 a musician exiled as a result of his participation in the First Carlist War, José María Iparraguirre, composed the song *Gernikako Arbola* – The Tree of Gernika – whose popularity spread to the point that it became a hymn of the *fueros* and was sung in assemblies and meetings related to autonomous movements in Euzkadi as of the early twentieth-century.

The *fin de siècle* saw the development of regionalist movements in Catalonia, the Basque Country, and Galicia[7] with the creation of nationalist parties and unions in all three regions. In the Basque Country they were: *Partido Nacionalista Vasco* (PNV, Basque Nationalist Party, 1895), *Solidaridad de Obreros Vascos* (ELA, Solidarity of Basque Workers, 1911), *Acción Nacionalista Vasca* (Basque Nationalist Action, 1930). Among these the most influential and enduring was the PNV founded by Sabino Arana, with which Basque nationalism gained an important political party, a leading source of ideology, and some of its key symbols – including the Basque flag (*ikurriña)* designed by Sabino Arana and his brother and still in use today. These political developments went hand in hand with an economic boom in these regions. In the Basque country in particular, its banks took the lead in the Spanish finance sector leading to an increase of wealth as the iron mines of Vizcaya began exporting massively to Great Britain. With its railway, river and pine forests, Gernika attracted industry and nine factories were established there during the first three decades of the twentieth century (Figure 4.5). Of these, two produced weapons – *Alkartasuna* (1912–1919), and *Astra, Unceta y Compañía* (1912–1997) – and at least one other also produced explosives – *S.A. Talleres de Guernica* (from 1916).[8] Both *Astra Unceta* and *Talleres de Guernica* produced regulation weapons for the military, and both were still functioning at the outbreak of the Civil War.

The political and economic growth within the framework of Basque nationalism paralleled the development of regional studies in the fields of archaeology, anthropology and ethnology led by José Miguel de Barandiarán (1889–1991). New regional newspapers and cultural magazines were founded, the study of regional languages was revived and idealized regional histories were produced. In the Basque country these new histories of the region include *El señorío de Bizcaya, histórico y foral* by Artiñano (1885), *La patria vasca* and *La nación vasca* by Aranzadi (1910, 1918). In 1918 the *Academia de la Lengua Vasca* was created and the first *Congreso de Estudios Vascos* was held. Throughout this period, the town of Gernika gained symbolic weight. The year 1908, first centenary of the 1808 War of Independence, saw an increased interest in defining Spanish nationalisms. In a lecture given in Gernika, Arturo Campión defined Basque nationalism as:

> *A demand for the immemorial rights of a country to live its own*
> *life: life that is an expression of its personality, constituted by*
> *race, language, public and private customs and history.*
> (Campión 1908)

That same year the *Comisión de Monumentos de Vizcaya* began publishing a Bulletin on the archaeology, art, history and monuments of the region. In its first run (1909–1914), the *Boletín de la Comisión de Monumentos de Vizcaya* published several articles dedicated to Gernika and its symbolic elements.[9] In the first issue of the *Boletín*, Carmelo de Echegaray published an article on the symbolic significance of Gernika's tree:

> *The Tree of Guernica, symbol of the liberties of a people whose*
> *origins become lost in the night of protohistoric times, has in its*
> *birth some of the obscurity that surrounds the beginnings of the*
> *race that it represents. No one knows when it began to serve as*
> *patriarchal canopy to the Council of Vizcaya: no one knows the*
> *reasons that moved the sons of this land to congregate under its*

> *shadow, and to convert it into the poetic personification of their*
> *most saintly loves. Only the august and mysterious voice of*
> *tradition is heard in its branches, and brings to us an echo of*
> *ancient things that nobody took care to write down, nor even to*
> *perpetuate by means of stone monuments in which might be*
> *found the date in which they were erected. We only know that*
> *when one of these symbolic and patriarchic Oaks fell from old*
> *age, a shoot from it would immediately replace it and inherit the*
> *emblematic significance that the other amassed in life.*
> *(. . .) the Tree that today symbolizes the memories, loves and*
> *hopes of the people of Vizcaya*
> *(. . .) the Tree that today represents in Guernica the*
> *Tradition, History, Aspiration and Honor of the Basque people.*
> (Echegaray 1909: 53–54)

All of these elements contributed to the cultivation of the town and its oak tree as symbols of the traditions and secular liberties of the Basque nation, with Gernika as its spiritual capital. This background sets the context for comprehending the impact of the bombing of Gernika during the civil war. In the period just before the war, Gernika's inhabitants rounded 7,000. In his memoirs José Antonio de Aguirre y Lecube described the town in the following terms:

> *As with all the towns of Euzkadi, [Gernika] was a conglomerate*
> *of clean little white houses, mutually facing each other across*
> *narrow and shaded streets. Distinguished from this group were*
> *the three buildings that stand out as symbols of Basque life: the*
> *church, indicator of the religiosity of our people, the town hall,*
> *representative of its civility, and the frontón, that speaks to us of*
> *the strength of the race.*
> (Aguirre 1944: 25)

Symbolism aside, the daily functioning of Gernika was like that of any other market town, making it an important social centre and locus of information exchange. Its famed weekly market traditionally held on Mondays attracted people from all over Vizcaya. On this day, the mercantile activities of the morning were followed by lengthy social meals in the eateries of Gernika where people would exchange news. In the afternoon matches of Basque handball – called *pelota* or *jai-alai* – were held at the *frontón* and traditional music and dances were performed in the main square (Figure 4.6) called the *Foru Plaza* or *Plaza de los Fueros* (Aguirre 1944: 25–26). Thus, in addition to being a key landmark in the imagined landscape of Basque culture, with political and symbolic importance, the town of Gernika also had a central role as a social space and commercial centre.

4.5 Gernika's railroad and factories.

4.6 Gernika's town hall, facing the *Plaza de los Fueros*, before the bombing. (Gernikazarra.)

Gernika during the Civil War

At the outset in 1936 the war split Spain into two main areas. The Basque region and Navarre, areas in which the symbolism of Gernika was especially meaningful, divided along opposing lines: Vizcaya and Guipúzcoa remained loyal to the Republic while Navarra and parts of Alava sided with the revolt.[10] Gernika thus found itself in the northern section which had sided with the Republic but was surrounded by the Nationalists (Figure 4.7).

In October 1936, three months into the war, Gernika's role as a symbolic place was reinforced. On the 1st a statute was passed by the Republican government in Madrid approving the election of a President of the Basque Government – a *Lehendakari*. Elections were held on the

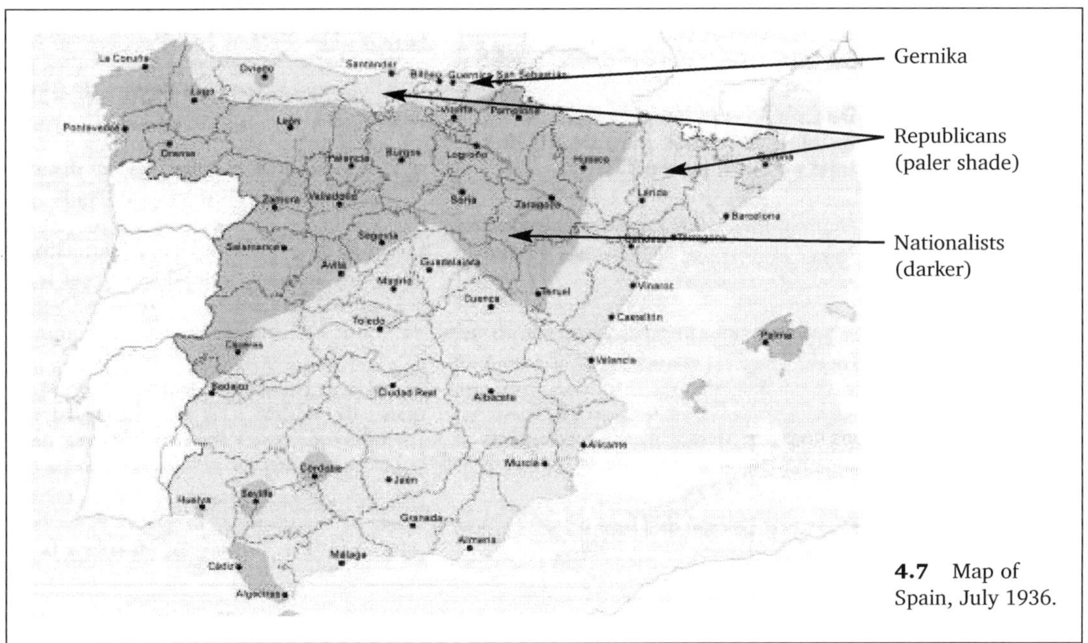

4.7 Map of Spain, July 1936.

7th of October and José Antonio de Aguirre y Lecube was elected, thereby forming the first Basque government since the *fueros* were abolished 60 years earlier. The ceremony took place around the Tree of Gernika and Aguirre swore using the traditional oath:

> *With humility before God,*
> *Standing on Basque land,*
> *With the memory of our ancestors*
> *Under the tree of Guernica*
> *I swear*
> *To faithfully fulfil my mandate.*

During the ceremony he read the programme of the newly established government, a document called *Pacto de declaración de Guernica*. These were significant events in reaffirming the symbolism of Gernika and its tree, in the *Lehendakari's* own words:

> *The tradition of our elders was once again reborn in us, and the sacred Tree that in Guernica grows, was no longer a relic, but became once again the living symbol of our history.*
>
> (Aguirre 1944: 17)

With the new government and president also came new symbols. A Presidential Decree of the regional government (*Diario Oficial del País Vasco*, no. 13) of 23 October 1936 established in its first article the emblem of the Government of Euzkadi, in the second article the flag (*ikurriña*) and in the third it declared that this flag should be flown together with the flag of the Republic. Thus the official distinctive symbols of the autonomous region and its government were set out (Grimau 1987: 244). The new Basque government likewise took it upon itself to create provisions for the protection of the cultural and historic heritage of the region. The legislation laid out to this end appears in the *Diario Oficial del País Vasco*; the first article, which was later developed in greater detail, reads:

> *In terms of protecting the Artistic Treasure, I have disposed: That the Department of Justice and Culture will adopt the necessary dispositions for cataloguing, protecting and depositing works of art, libraries, archival documents of interest as artistic, cultural and historic heritage in the Basque territory with the aim of preserving them from the threats of destruction inherent in a civil war. Bilbao, 12th October 1936. President. Jose A. de Aguirre. Minister of Justice and Culture. Jesús María de Leizaola.*
>
> (*Diario Oficial del País Vasco*, 12 October, 18 November, and 12 December 1936)

The battle-lines of the war in the Basque region, which was strongly Catholic, were not determined by religious issues.[11] Consequently, the symbols used on this regional 'visual front' differed to some extent from those used at the national level.[12] The *Lehendakari* Aguirre and the majority of his government belonged to the Basque Nationalist Party (PNV) and so the symbols that predominated on the side of the Republic were those associated with Basque nationalism. The recurrent images were the *ikurriña* (Basque flag), the tree (of Gernika), *txapela* (Basque beret), the *txistu* (Basque flute), the chimney, and the rifle (Grimau 1987: 241); images of the *Cinturón de Hierro* were also prevalent (Figure 4.8). The discourse accompanying these references advocated the safeguarding of Christianity, Basque liberties and ancestral lands, and the promotion of social justice. On Franco's side, symbols associated with Carlism and the *Requeté* factions of Navarre predominated.

The bombing

In March 1937 the Nationalist forces intensified their campaign on the northern front. The Basque town of Otxandio had already been bombed on the 22nd of July 1936, in what was perhaps the earliest instance of a civilian population being targeted during the war, and on 31 March 1937 the town of Durango was heavily bombed. Then, on Monday, market day, 26th of April 1937, beginning at approximately 16:00 and lasting for over three hours Gernika was bombed. Planes from the German Condor Legion and the Italian Aviazzione Legionaria took part in the various waves of bombing and it has recently come to light that planes from the Spanish Aviación Nacional might also have taken part.[13] The bombing flattened nearly the entire town: according to the report produced by Cárdenas for Regiones Devastadas – the *Informe Herrán* – 71 percent of buildings were entirely destroyed with only 1 percent remaining untouched (Cárdenas 1940a). Telesforo Monzón, Defense counselor of the Basque government,

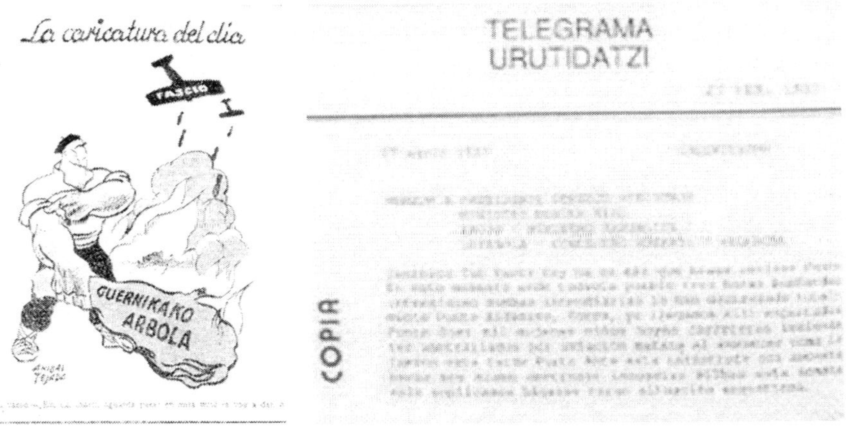

4.8 Wartime cartoon by Anibal Tejada with reference to the tree of Gernika (Gernika Peace Museum).

4.9 The telegram of 27 April 1937 (Gernikazarra Historia Taldea: 1991).

sent a telegram marked 'very urgent' on the day of the bombing to members of the Republican government (Figure 4.9) which began:

> *Guernica was. Today it is no more than ember-ashes. At this moment the town is still burning after three hours of very intense bombing, incendiary bombs have destroyed it completely.*
>
> (Telegram sent 27 April 1937)

Gernika was neither the first town to be bombed from the air, nor the first to be so attacked during the war.[14] Durango, a town of similar size and only a few kilometres away, had suffered comparable damage. Madrid, Bilbao, Barcelona, Valencia, Alicante and many other towns and cities were bombed throughout the war, with several involving the German and Italian air forces. Yet it was the bombing of Gernika that became symbolic.[15] From the very start the bombing caused a storm of reactions, denunciations, accusations of deliberate myth making, negations and contradictory accounts. Historians trying to discover the facts about the bombing have had to dig through several layers of propaganda, interpretations and memories when not through pure fabrications and deliberate lies (Southworth 1977). One of the most important eyewitness accounts of the bombing was that of the Basque priest Alberto de Onaindía (1973).[16] He described the atmosphere of the market, the panic as the first bombs fell and people ran to shelters, the use of incendiary bombs and machine guns fired from the planes, and the lack of any defenses. He communicated to the *Lehendakari* what he had seen and was subsequently sent abroad to disseminate his testimony.

Gernika's symbolism and interpretations of the bombing

The bombing of Gernika has been interpreted in many ways with different versions highlighting either its symbolic significance or its strategic military importance. Yet these explanations have their weaknesses in that neither the specific symbolic or strategic sites in the town were actually destroyed. In the same diary entry in which the commander of the Condor Legion, Wolfram Freiherr von Richthofen, recounted the success of the bombing campaign, he wrote:

> *Sacred oak tree in Guernica, beneath which for over a thousand years (old trunk under glass, new tree planted) the constitution and laws of Vizcaya were made. Beside that, a church and parliament. Nothing destroyed at all in the district at the edge of the town.*
>
> (cited by Patterson 2007: 47–48)

It is not clear whether he knew of the tree and its significance before coordinating the bombing, but he certainly became aware of it after-

4.10 Gernika burning, note the church of Santa María identifiable on the right (Gernikazarra).

4.11 Ruins of Gernika's *ferial* where the market was held (Gernikazarra).

wards. His reference to it has contributed to the interpretation that the town was deliberately targeted because of its symbolic significance. Of the one percent of the buildings that escaped harm many were known palaces or noble houses, religious buildings (save for the badly damaged church of San Juan), factories (including those manufacturing weapons) and the emblematic site of the Oak Tree and Meeting House (Figure 4.12). The fact that the clear symbolic targets represented by the tree and meeting house were not destroyed was used by both sides to back their divergent accounts of events.[17]

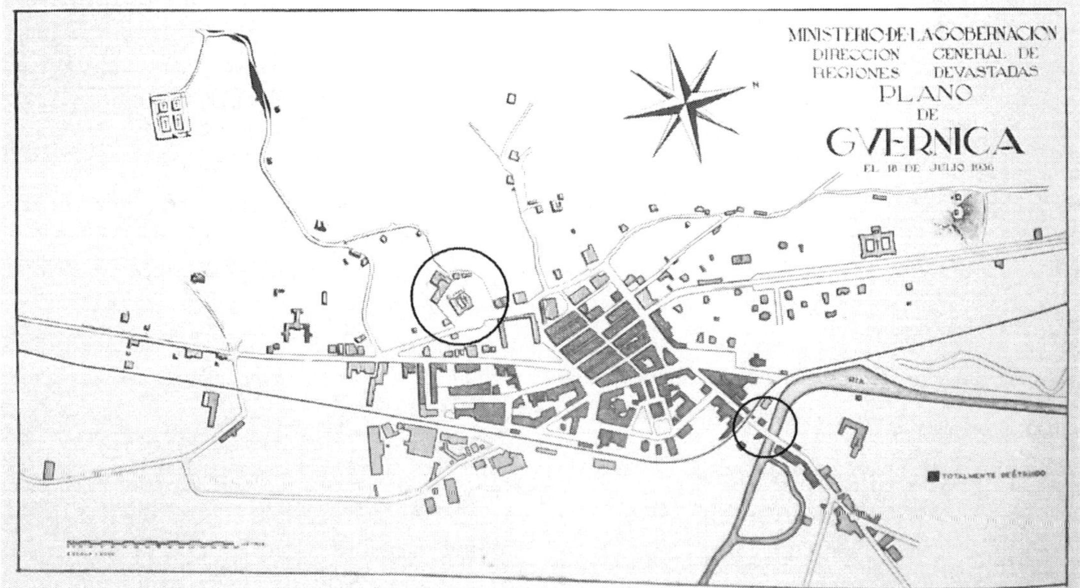

4.12 DGRD map plans for the reconstruction to be done in Gernika from *Reconstrucción*, no. 1 (April 1940: 26). The areas of the meeting house and tree (circled top left) and the Rentería bridge (circled bottom right) were not hit nor were the factories along the south side of the train tracks.

For those who witnessed the bombing, the symbolic element emerges strongly in explanations of why Gernika was targeted (Cava Mesa 1996: 257–259). Ortega has sustained this view, arguing that "The attackers chose Guernica in order to hurt the Basques in their most vivid patriotic sentiment" (Ortega 1976: 335). However, it is dismissed by analysts sympathetic to the Nationalists, such as de la Cierva: "the bombing of Guernica, of clear tactical intention, completely lacked any symbolic intention. In fact the *casa de los Fueros* and the famous tree remained pathetically immune" (Cierva cited by Reig Tapia 1987: 127).[18] De la Cierva explained further that Gernika was a strategic target because it had a weapons factory, two barracks and the bridge of Rentería strategically located on the road between Bilbao and the coastal town of Bermeo. The tactical importance of this bridge and of cutting off this passageway was often reiterated by Franco's side. Yet again, none of these structures were destroyed. Once more, this contrasts sharply with other appreciations; in his newsbreaking article in the London *Times*, George L. Steer reports that:

> *The raid on Guernica is unparalleled in military history.*
> *Guernica was not a military objective. A factory producing war*
> *material lay outside the town and was untouched [. . .] The*
> *object of the bombardment was seemingly the demoralization of*
> *the civil population and the destruction of the cradle of the*
> *Basque race.*
> (Steer, The London *Times*, 27 April 1937)

That claim was even contradicted by the Franco press, which sought to lay the blame for the destruction on the Republican side, as illustrated by an article from *Estampas de la Guerra*:

> *The Basque fugitives, that are in our units, tell us horrified of the*
> *tragedy of towns that, like Guernica, have been burned and*
> *destroyed by the intentional fire of the reds, almost in their*
> *totality, when our troops found themselves over 15 kilometers*
> *away. Guernica did not constitute in any case a military target*
> *for the national aviation, which only has military targets in*
> *combat and industrial ones in the enemy rearguard.*
> (*Estampas de la Guerra*, Album 1–undated–:23)

In his work on the bombing and its propaganda war, Southworth (1977) concludes that the Condor Legion bombed Gernika on the orders of Franco's military commanders, in order to break the defence of Bilbao by dealing a deft blow to Basque morale. Southworth comes to this conclusion after a meticulous study of correspondence, propaganda, journalism, and literature. Yet, even if the relevance of Gernika's symbolic dimension as motivation for its targeting could be contested, the symbolic impact of the bombing cannot. This can be seen in the responses aroused by the bombing (see Appendix E for a selection of reactions and interpretations) The interpretation of the town's destruction as a symbolic act added yet another dimension to Gernika's already multilayered significance. On 8 October 1937 the Government of Euzkadi declared Gernika 'spiritual capital' of Vizcaya.

For the Francoist side this was perhaps the largest diplomatic and propaganda fiasco of the war. The response was to deny the bombing and accuse Republican soldiers of torching the town while retreating.[19] There is some consensus (Southworth 1977: 388–389) on the authorship of this initial fabrication resting with Luis Bolín, Franco's press officer at the time of the bombing.[20] Within Spain, it angered Franco's allies in Navarre as well as those Basques who sympathized with him. Yet it was internationally that the most damage was done. The relevance of the attack on Gernika at the time was that the involvement of the German air force meant a violation of the Non-Intervention Pact that had been signed in August 1936 by 27 countries including Germany, Italy, France, the USSR, the US and the UK.

Once Franco's troops moved in they closed off the city for five days, during which, according to some, they planted evidence demonstrating their version of events. [21] Since the bombing had been a propaganda fiasco, the cover-up was fundamental for the Francoist side. In an attempt to repair some of the moral damage, a *Requeté* and a Falangist soldier were filmed and photographed mounting guard around the Old Tree (Gernikazarra 1991: 26). The images recur in several NO-DOs, newspapers and magazines (Figure 4.13) transmitting a message that Franco's troops respected Basque cultural traditions and implying that it was the 'other side' that posed a threat to them:

4.13 *Requeté* and Falangist guarding the Tree of Gernika. (España. Ministerio de Cultura. Archivo General de la Administración.)

> *. . . in Guernica, were found intact both the historic Casa de Juntas of Vasconia and the tree, symbol of Basque liberties and immediately they were placed under armed guard of the Basque Requetés, protecting such precious relics for the inhabitants of the region.*
>
> (*ABC, Andalucía*, 30 April 1937: 6)

In reality, the incursion of the Francoist troops caused further damage to remaining structures. North African troops under the command of Lieutenant Colonel Esparza set up camp in the church of Santa María – one of the few structures still standing – causing damage to its interior[22] and Italian troops painted slogans hailing Mussolini on buildings at the entrance to the town. Lieutenant Colonel Emilio Gómez del Villar, who entered Gernika with the IV Brigade of Navarra on 19 April wrote a letter to a colleague on the 11th of May 1937:

> *Before Guernica must have been lovely, but now it is a real disgrace for everything has been destroyed and ransacked and here there is a lack of everything and in these conditions there is no possibility of carrying out any fruitful work, because as they keep bombing the few people that remained are leaving and only the troops and a few families remain.*
>
> (*Aldaba*, no. 140, March 2006: 47)

The presence of these forces not only contributed to the further destruction of the town but also to the persecution of noted representatives of Basque culture. For instance, the poet and priest Esteban Urkiaga 'Lauaxeta', who entered Gernika on the same day as Franco's troops on 29 April, was later *fusilado* (executed) by those same troops. Bilbao fell on the 19th of June and the entire Basque front collapsed at the end of August, with over 150,000 Basques sent into exile, including the *Lehendakari* and his government. The official version of events continued to claim that the red-separatists had burned Gernika down while fleeing, and for the next 40 years contesting this account of events could be punishable with prison. At the end of the war, Vizcaya and Guipúzcoa were declared 'traitor provinces' while Navarra was rewarded for having sided with the rebelled Generals by being allowed to keep its *fueros*.

One of the instruments used in the revenge tactics that dominated the first decade of the postwar was a document called the *Causa General*. This report, administered by the Ministry of Justice, sought to create a record of all of the crimes committed in the Republican zones during the war.[23] Every Town Hall received three forms to be filled out, the first two related to number of deaths during the "period of red domination", and the third was:

*An account of torments, torture, buildings set on fire, destruction
of churches or cult objects, profanations and other offences that
because of their circumstances, the alarm or terror that they
produced must be considered as serious.*
　　　　　(*Causa General*, 1332–2, Archivo Histórico Nacional)

In the Case of the Town Hall of 'Guernica y Lumo' the completed forms
included a brief note dated 22 January 1941 and signed by the then
Mayor of Gernika, Juan Bilbao, detailing the following with regard to the
third point: "There were no offences of the kind requested in this form
since if buildings were set on fire it was during an act of war leaving the
entire centre of the municipality destroyed by the fire" (*Causa General*
1332–2). This neutral response is notable at a time when there would
have been considerable pressure to elaborate a version of events that
would back the official version of the destruction. His avoidance of the
word "bombing", however, is also revealing.

The Regime's Reconstruction of Gernika

The following section will pick up on the dynamics of reconstruction
identified in the previous chapter – the rhetorical uses of architecture and
urban planning, propaganda versus the reality on the ground, the role of
performance in the politics of space and aspiration to memorialize the
conflict. In further analysing these trends this next section will also indicate the cracks and alternatives of a seemingly homogenous reconstruction discourse.

Regiones Devastadas and the rebuilding

The rebuilding of Gernika was planned and publicized well before it actually began. Early in 1938 an exhibition organized by the Falange was held
in Nationalist Burgos which included plans for reconstruction projects.
According to an article by Angel Angoso (1938: 452–454) the plans on
display for Gernika were developed by the *Servicios Técnicos de FET y de
las JONS* and proposed the construction of the town as the National-
Syndicalist capital of the Basque region. The plans included an Imperial
Plaza situated below the *Casa de Juntas* and a monumental stadium for
parades in the area above it (Figures 4.14 to 4.17). Two other significant
elements were projected: a memorial and a *Jardín de lu Guerra* – War
Garden. The memorial was to be placed in a section of the *Plaza del
Imperio* as a monument to the 'Crusade' (Figure 4.15) and was to include
a wall with the names of the "fallen heroes of the war" and a range of
statues of "all the heroes of Spanish history". The *Jardín de la Guerra* was
to be created by preserving the central part of the city in ruins as a

Grandiose plans for Gernika (images from Angoso's 1938 article)[24]

4.14 Detailed plan of the stadium.

4.15 Detail for the memorial park.

4.16 Plan for the new Gernika showing the stadium and memorial park.

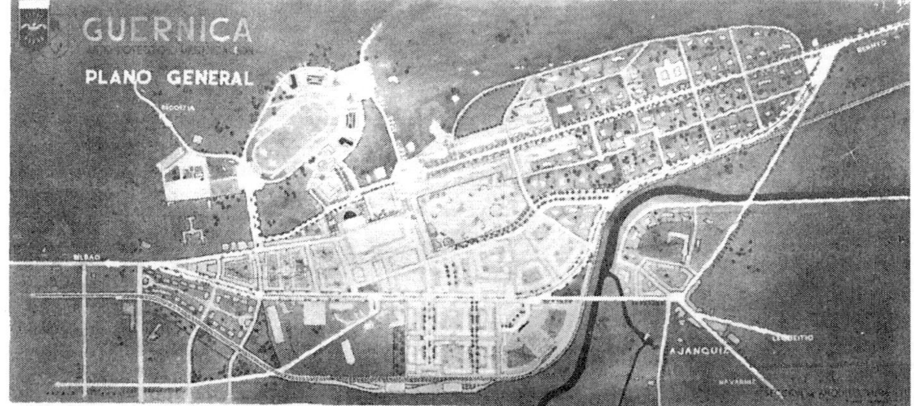

4.17 Gernika's urban layout.

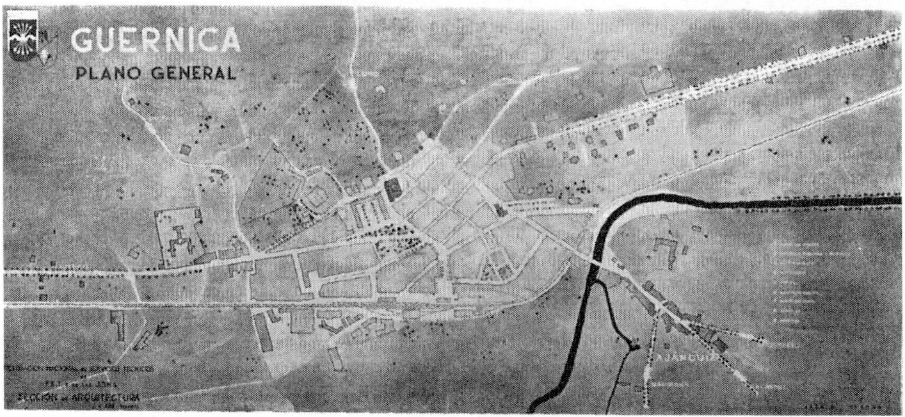

museum and garden. As with the other fantastic and ambitious reconstruction and memorialization plans of the war years, the end of the war proved otherwise. After *Regiones Devastadas* was established, a commission for the reconstruction of Gernika was set up on 3 July 1938.

By 1939 the plans for Gernika's reconstruction had changed drastically and the grandiose national-socialist influences disappeared. The first projects drawn up by *Regiones Devastadas* (Fernández-Shaw 1940) already show a tension that was to mark the entire reconstruction of Gernika: wanting to be seen to respect local urban planning and architectural traditions while at the same time wanting to mark the town with the imprint of the regime's ideology. At its heart was the dilemma presented by Gernika's complex symbolism: a significant site to the *Requetés* of Navarre and Basques that sided with Franco as well as being a powerful symbol to those that sided with the Republic against Franco. As we have seen, the dichotomy between claims to be building a New Spain while preserving tradition was also present at a national level. The most notable absence in the new project for Gernika was that of a significant memorial to the war,[25] indicating a shift in attitudes over how the town was to be treated. In 1941 a further project document for the reconstruction of the town states that the original urbanization project had been a bit ambitious, recommending that the rebuilding be undertaken in stages (AGA-RD-082.33. Guernica, Box 20684). The evolution in plans shows how visions for the reconstruction developed both ideologically and practically as a more realistic appreciation was made of the logistical and economic task it implied.

On 12 October 1939 Gernika subscribed to the 'Law of Adoption' passed the previous month. It was one of the first of the 102 towns and cities to be 'adopted' by 1940. After the propaganda fiasco that the bombing of the town represented for the Nationalists, an attempt was made to turn its rebuilding into a post-war miracle story, but before rebuilding could begin the town had to be cleared (Figures 4.18 and 4.19). In 1940, the architect Fernández-Shaw wrote a historical background of the town and its evolution indicating that the Gernika of 1936 had already gone through several phases of destruction and reconstruction (Fernández-Shaw 1940: 16). He cites floods, three fires (1521, 1537, 1835) and four wars (Napoleonic war, two Carlist conflicts and 'our Crusade') and observes that in clearing the rubble in 1939 to prepare the terrain for the rebuilding, layers of debris from past destructions were uncovered. This account of past cycles of destruction and reconstruction that the town had undergone was rarely referred to.

The first reconstruction plans drawn up by *Regiones Devastadas* were executed by Gonzalo Cárdenas, who was put in charge of the reconstruction of Gernika and became sub-director of the DGRD, and Luis Gana, Director of the *Comisión Provincial de Vizcaya*. Gernika appeared frequently in *Reconstrucción* in the first years (1940–1945) often having a prominent place (Figures 4.20–4.25).

4.18 Aerial view of Gernika in ruins (*Reconstrucción*, no. 1, 1940).

4.19 Gernika in the process of being cleared (*Aldaba*, no. 140, April 2006: 36).

Constructing place: Basque architectural styles and *Regiones Devastadas*

The directives of *Regiones Devastadas* were often contradictory, evolving through time and varying according to circumstances. The picture that emerges from examining it as an instance of reconstruction diverges from the apparently homogeneous and uniform vision presented by the regime and through the pages of *Reconstrucción* – those dichotomies already identified in the national reconstruction between imposing an imperial style and drawing on folklore, between renewal and the restoration of tradition. The project for the construction of Gernika's main square exemplifies a second tension inherent to the reconstruction project as a whole, between the desire to impose order and the scarce practical means to do so.

A doyen of Basque architecture, Manuel Smith Ibarra[26] was commissioned by *Regiones Devastadas* in 1939 to rebuild Gernika's *Plaza de los Fueros*. This was not a facile choice; the commission was delicate and there had been long deliberations to choose the architect capable of carrying it out (Paliza Monduate 1988: 367). The reconstruction project developed in 1939 by the *Comisión de Vizcaya* for *Regiones Devastadas* stated:

> *A city is never the arbitrary result of a capricious grouping of buildings, but rather it is always the logical consequence of a studied and imposed ordering; this is the fundamental problem of the city: order. (. . .) A city cannot be laid out without recalling and conforming to the norms of tradition and patriarchy of the genuinely Spanish cities; in them, the representative zone was always condensed in a square and a street. In one square were the most representative buildings of the State, the Municipality and the Church, and in one street were arcades for commerce.*
>
> (*Regiones Devastadas*, 1939)

Gernika in *Reconstrucción*

4.20   No. 29, 1943.

4.21   No. 55, 1945.

4.22   No. 8, 1941.

4.23   No. 29, 1943.

4.24   No. 1, 1940.

4.25   No. 55, 1945.

The square eventually planned by Smith Ibarra both maintained and broke with traditional Basque styles, producing a neo-Basque *Plaza de los Fueros*.[27] On the one hand, he maintained the portico arcade typical of Basque town halls since the fifteenth-century (Paliza Monduate 1988: 368); on the other, he broke with the closed, four-sided square creating an open three-sided one (Figures 4.26 to 4.29). At the start of the project document for the construction of the new town hall, Smith Ibarra outlines:

> *A primordial desire of the people of Guernica in the necessary*
> *mission of its rebuilding is that of re-establishing the ancestral*
> *home of the genuine representation of the people [. . .]*
> *It would be pointless to try and rebuild the old Town Hall,*
> *destroyed even to its foundations, but even if the destruction had*
> *not been so great, the needs of the municipality of Guernica,*
> *whose life continues ostensibly vigorous despite the misfortune*
> *suffered, would make it necessary to establish a perfect complex*
> *that links the administrative buildings, something impossible to*
> *develop in the old building.*
>
> (Proyecto Ayuntamiento de Guernica, 1939)

The urban layout of the city, especially its town hall and main square, were thus 'improved upon' in the reconstruction as streets were straightened and widened. This is clearly stated in a 1940 article on the progress of the reconstruction; regarding the Main Square it stated that: "its enlargement was projected giving it the traditional character of Spanish Main Squares" (*Reconstrucción*, no. 1, 1940: 46). The square was also supposed to emit a message of power: "all of the buildings of this square will form an obligatory and imposed architectonic whole" (Fernández-Shaw 1940: 31).

The project documents make the case for using a Basque style while simultaneously adopting an architectural language that coincided with the general lines of the national reconstruction:

> *The building is given the style that has seemed to us most*
> *characteristic of the tradition and adaptation to the land in*
> *which it is located. It is a Spanish Renaissance style, in which*
> *noble materials dominate, such as stone masonry and the iron*
> *common to these mountains.*
>
> (Proyecto Ayuntamiento de Guernica, 1939)

Also illustrating this approach is the placement of an ornamental freestanding column topped by a cross in the middle of the square, in substitution for the customary fountain. The architect explains that this solution is neater and provides a greater sense of cleanliness. It also coincides with the historicist styles of Regiones Devastadas and unites the symbolic materials of stone and wrought iron. The project document makes references to historical styles and "noble" materials as discussed in the previous chapter. The association of building materials with social and political values was manifest in other ways as well. For instance, in the minutes of a plenary meeting held at Gernika's Town Hall in 1937, the use of "red-separatist" bricks was grudgingly proposed for the installation of temporary stores in an arcade that had survived the bombing (*Aldaba*, March 2006: 43), and the intention to build a new town rather

Foru Plaza/Plaza de los Fueros

4.26 Being rebuilt, *c.*1941. (España. Ministerio de Cultura. Archivo General de la Administración. Sig.: AGA: F.04244.31.11.02.)

4.27 Finalized. (España. Ministerio de Cultura. Archivo General de la Administración. Sig.: AGA: F.04244.31.11.04.)

4.28 Being rebuilt, *c.*1947. (España. Ministerio de Cultura. Archivo General de la Administración. Sig.: AGA: F.04244.31.11.03.)

4.29 Finalized, *c.*1954. (España. Ministerio de Cultura. Archivo General de la Administración. Sig.: AGA. F.04244.31.11.01).

than restore the old one is reiterated. Furthermore, throughout the documents relating to Gernika's reconstruction there is a leitmotif as to how the reconstruction will provide both 'order' and an image of authentic Spanishness.

The project for the new town hall is detailed and includes a segment on the symbols that are to adorn the building's façade:

> *Presiding over the main facade, a niche with the Virgin, patron of the town, with the coat of arms of Guernica and Lumo, and in the prominent angle will be placed a large national coat of arms that will give brilliance to the classical roll of stone that resolves the said S.E. angle.*
>
> (Proyecto de Casa Ayuntamiento de Guernica, 1939)

But as soon became apparent, not all these prescribed symbols were locally meaningful. In 1952, when the three buildings forming the façades for the square were nearly completed, Smith Ibarra was commissioned to prepare a project for the construction of the square itself. In this project document, the architect notes that he has been asked by the municipal authorities to place an effigy of Saint Roque and not the Virgin in the niche of the Town Hall as *he* is the patron Saint of the town. In the document he also refers to a specific version of the Virgin of Begoña, patron saint of Vizcaya – suggesting that *her* effigy be placed in a niche of the facade of the *Artes y Oficios* building facing the Town Hall (*Proyecto de plaza de Guernica* 1952, AGA-RD 4.111.20682, box 1352). These changes were eventually made, demonstrating that Smith Ibarra was in dialogue with the local authorities and responsive to their suggestions. Respecting local wishes and replacing the more generally Spanish Saints originally planned for the building facades with more specifically Basque ones was a significant gesture considering that many Basque clergy were being persecuted. As Sánchez Erauskin points out:

> *In the task of acculturation Hispanic religious symbols are given priority, but the pillars on which Basque nationalist confessionalism is based were also dismantled in an attempt to empty them of any signs of identity. They were not destroyed instead they were reconverted by means of an astute cosmetic operation. Instead of making a tabula rasa of a bothersome past the Church of the new regime sought to straighten its course. Basque virgins and saints had to be turned into efficient means of communicating its message. With a convenient face-wash they were quickly prepared to preside over the patriotic ceremonies of national-catholicism.*
>
> (Sánchez Erauskin 1994: 62)

This sensitivity to local symbols and styles was clearly linked to the fact that Smith Ibarra was a prominent Basque architect. He was not the only architect that worked on Gernika's reconstruction, though; as has been indicated, Cárdenas and Gana were also involved, directing the reorganization of the urban layout of the town (straightening and widening streets and developing new residential areas), organizing the new market, and improving water distribution and sanitation systems.

As we have seen, a fundamental dimension of the reconstruction was its propaganda value. As one of the iconic projects of the reconstruction, Gernika was intended to serve as a model:

> *The square, which will soon be inaugurated, will serve as a model of the architecture of Vizcaya, marking a starting point for what the urban centres of the towns that have to be rebuilt should be like (. . .) achieve that the town of Gernika be a living example and best exponent of the new towns that are being built under the sign of Franco, the Caudillo.*
>
> (Fernández-Shaw 1940: 39)

The new market with its modern design was inaugurated in February 1943 (*Reconstrucción*, no. 31: 111). The importance of this structure lies not only in its practical and commercial function but in its symbolic meaning: the fact that Gernika was bombed on a market day had become an essential part of the mythology of the event.[28] Thus an attempt was made to create an open, modern facility for the market, and in order to take advantage of its propaganda power, its construction and inauguration received ample coverage in the media. Yet, perhaps this urgency to rebuild interfered with adequately deliberated planning. Testimony from an inhabitant of Gernika, collected many years later, underlines the point:

> . . . *they built a square that they could have made in Andalusia but not in Gernika. The market square, nobody liked it and I didn't either. Here nobody likes an open square because it rains constantly.*
>
> (Egido 1997: 75)

Of the public buildings destroyed in the bombing, two stand out for the fact that they were not rebuilt despite their social significance: the church of San Juan and the *frontón* (Figures 4.30 and 4.31). Plans for the reconstruction of both of these structures were made in 1940 and 1941, respectively, but were never carried out. The church of San Juan, built in 1910 on the site of a medieval temple (1463), was situated in the populous town centre, attracting many church-goers from this part of Gernika as well as from the port-town of Bermeo. This central location meant that it was badly damaged during the bombing, with only the outer walls left standing. Fernández-Shaw's 1940 report dismissed this popular place of worship saying that it "lacked artistic character" ("*sabor artístico nulo*"), arguing for its displacement to a more "convenient location" (Fernández-Shaw 1940:16) despite the fact that its location had made it so popular. In 1941 the remains of the church were torn down with the condition that *Regiones Devastadas* would build a new church and *casa parroquial* elsewhere in Gernika. Even though plans for these were presented to Franco in 1946 neither of the compensatory buildings ever materialized (Gernikazarra 1987: 140). While this church lacked artistic merit, the local community was attached to it and as will be seen in the next chapter, 70 years on its loss is still mourned.

The *frontón* is a court for playing the Basque sport called *pelota vasca* (*jai-alai* in Basque). The court can be covered or not, and can be more or less formal but it is a key fixture of Basque towns. The first recorded *frontón* in Gernika dates from 1854; and as the sport became increasingly popular an enclosed *frontón* was built in 1925. With its large windows, elaborate wooden carvings, ample public gallery and facilities for training in *cestapunta*,[29] this building became a focal point of the town. Again, while initially there were plans to rebuild it, *Regiones Devastadas* never implemented the reconstruction projects. It was not until 1962, with *Regiones Devastadas* closed down and the reconstruction officially over, that a new *frontón* was built in Gernika largely funded through public subscriptions.[30]

Also missing from the reconstruction of Gernika were the enclosed balconies that had been prevalent throughout the town. These glass-enclosed corridors ran along the outsides of buildings and are registered not only in photographs (Gernikazarra 1987) but in personal memories of the town prior to the bombing.[31] Instead of restoring this characteristic feature of Gernika, two parallel stone arcades were constructed along both sides of the main street (*Artekalea*) that passes in front of the *Plaza de los Fueros*. No uniform building style was developed for the town outside this symbolic central point and main thoroughfare.

Archives and libraries were also lost in the bombing of Gernika but these are not mentioned in reconstruction projects. The loss was poignantly described by Bonifacio de Echegaray, member of the Academy for Basque Studies in a radio broadcast on 4 May 1937:

> *The fire that suddenly glowed in this quiet place wiped out not only its beautiful habitations and churches, but the valuable papers and documents of its rich municipal archives. Carmelo de Echegaray, my brother and master died among them. Behind a gentle and modest exterior was a great mind consecrated to Basque culture. He owned the finest library in our country,*

Lost emblematic buildings of Gernika

4.31 Church of San Juan (Gernikazarra).

4.30 Old *frontón* (Gernikazarra).

renowned for the number and quality of books, rich in first
editions, unpublished letters and a vast collection of material
dealing with the history and folk-lore of our beloved country. My
brother's correspondence had been with outstanding personalities
in all parts of the world, librarians, scientists and men of letters.
Nothing of this was saved.

(Echegaray 1937)

The atmosphere and style of the old Gernika was lost without being
replaced by a coherent new place, resulting in an eclectic townscape
emerging that contrasted sharply with the orderly plan laid out by
Regiones Devastadas. In examining the gap between the propaganda side

4.32, 4.33 Moreno Torres
visits Gernika to inspect recon-
struction plans and works,
1943. (España. Ministerio de
Cultura. Archivo General de la
Administración. Sig.: AGA:
F-04246-08-02 and
F-04246-08-03.)

of the reconstruction and the reality of rebuilding we begin to see how the politics of space of Gernika were also transformed.

Another aspect of the reconstruction embedded in its discourse was an affirmation of the regime's account of the destruction. During the early 1940s, references to Gernika's reconstruction whether in official, professional or general publications refer to the destruction by accusing the *rojo-separatistas* – red-separatists – and avoid referring to a 'bombing':

> *Those who, with an absolute ignorance of the facts, falsified the history of Spain, the enemies of God and Fatherland, set fire like cowards to the town that they were not able to defend like men.*
> (*Reconstrucción*, no. 1, 1940: 25)

One of the motivations for the reconstruction of Gernika, then, became the cementing of the Nationalist narrative of its destruction. The following example text presents the project for the reconstruction of the town, illustrating how reconstruction could be used as a means to attribute blame for the destruction, de-legitimize separatist sentiments, and demonstrate the strength of the new State.

> *The reds, who were incapable of defending, let burn in a cowardly way what was once the legitimate pride of the lands of Vizcaya. With the destruction of Guernica a flag of rebelliousness was raised and flown and a campaign of falsities began, vilely encouraged by the enemies of God and Spain. A campaign that began first in our Patria and that then continued outside; a campaign that seemed to cease with the end of the Crusade; but of which there still remain some vestiges in those that, infected by the separatist virus, can not understand that the Spanish State, strong and decided, is going to be capable of rebuilding the town of Guernica.*
> (*Reconstrucción*, no. 15, 1941: 10)

Constructing space: social dimensions and realities

As we have seen, *Regiones Devastadas* was keen to rebuild Gernika's market structure, but while it was inaugurated in 1943, it took far longer for commercial activity and social, cultural and sporting events to recover anything resembling their pre-war levels. Gernika would have to wait until the 1960s for this and for a new covered *frontón*. Most of the rebuilding efforts focused on infrastructure, yet even this practical orientation affected the way the townscape was read and perceived, transforming its meanings and the politics of space.

Since Gernika's factories – producing weapons, heavy machinery, and milk products – had remained intact, providing housing for their employees was an early priority of the reconstruction. There were three types of housing built: high rent for 'middle classes', reduced rent, and cheap.[32] These housing projects were initially undertaken by the *Comisión de Vizcaya* of *Regiones Devastadas*, complemented by the work of other institutions.[33] In theory, housing was to be rented at affordable rates with apartments reserved for modest workers. However, by the time the buildings were completed the rents were set much higher (AGA Falange and Gobernación; Etxaniz Ortúñez 2007) or were of such poor quality that people were reluctant to move in.[34] The distribution of scarce housing was interpreted by locals as a manifestation of favoritism towards the most ardent supporters of the regime.[35] In order to be eligible for housing there was a long list of criteria that had to be met, with priority given to people working in key industries or services in the town[36] or who could provide 'political guarantees' in exchange for building permissions.[37]

In practice, much of Gernika was rebuilt by private initiative and companies, often local industry or banks. The factory "Talleres de Guernica" built housing, and individual families too requested permission to rebuild their businesses and houses, indicating that the reality of the reconstruction was far 'messier' than what the official discourse indicated. Control was exerted in the form of bureaucracy: in order to construct anything in Gernika plans had to be approved by *Regiones Devastadas*, the *Fiscalía de la Vivienda*, and the Municipal Architect[38] ("La reconstrucción de Gernika", *Aldaba* , no. 13, 1985: 19). Among the benefits awarded to organizations willing to undertake the construction of affordable housing was the forced expropriation of land (AGA-RD-082.33. Guernica. Box. 20679; Gernikazarra 1987). The property, terrains or lots of those who were not present to claim them – due to death, imprisonment, or exile – were expropriated, often without compensation. This practice imbued the new townscape with feelings of resentment that were to persist throughout the decades (Cava Mesa 1996: 245–246). Ultimately, both the politics of space and the population of the new Gernika changed almost as radically as its physical appearance. Foremost, the population had been sharply reduced as a result of the vast numbers of refugees and internally displaced persons from the bombing (Cava Mesa 1996: 249). Even those who began to return from France and Britain on the outbreak of the Second World War stayed in the homes of family members in Bilbao or other towns, with no homes to return to in Gernika. There were also few men, as one man from Córdoba, who in January 1943 was taken to the prison-labor camp in Gernika, recalled: "there were only women and children living in the town" (*Aldaba*, no. 13, 1985: 18).

This leads to another aspect that transformed the emerging townscape: the use of prison labour.[39] Already in 1938 *Regiones Devastadas*

4.34 Prison labour in Gernika, *Reconstrucción*, 1944.

transferred war prisoners to Gernika in order to clear away rubble. Eventually, a prison-labour camp was set up to provide the manpower for the reconstruction of the town (Figures 4.34 and 4.35). War prisoners were brought there from all over Spain. Various sites in Gernika were used to house the prisoners, including the school of the Augustine Brothers and the convent of the Josefinas.[40] The presence of prisoners in these buildings affected the meanings associated with them even after new uses were once again found for them.[41] Also, the fact that it was prisoners, and outsiders – to Gernika and to the Basque Country – who built the new town rather than the local population added a dimension of meaning that persists today.

The favoritism manifest in the allocation of scarce housing, the realignment of streets, the modification of existing neighbourhoods and creation of new ones, the altered population, the use of forced labour and the loss of popular meeting sites (San Juan and the *frontón*) all contributed to changing the politics of space within Gernika. This 'spiritual capital' lost its tangible old town, along with the intangible sense of age that had once permeated it. By May 1942 the new town hall had been built, along with a housing group of seven reduced-rent buildings. By 1945 the remainder of the buildings constituting the Plaza Mayor had largely been completed as well as other housing in the original plan, the market and slaughterhouse. The reconstruction then slowed until February 1947 when *Regiones Devastadas* passed responsibility for the remaining work to the municipal authorities.

Reconstructing Gernika's heritage-scape

Having examined the physical rebuilding and some of its impacts, we turn to how the town's heritage-scape was affected by the reconstruction

4.35 Working in front of the *Plaza de los Fueros*, c.1946. (España. Ministerio de Cultura. Archivo General de la Administración. Sig.: AGA: F-04244-32-02.)

and the performance of the new Spain. As occurred in the rest of the country during the postwar period, the cultural heritage of Vizcaya that was selectively valued was that which could be associated with the narrative of a national past favoured by the regime. Díaz-Andreu (1995: 51) describes an archaeological excavation carried out near Gernika but which sought to "document the presence of Celtic/Indo European invasions of the Basque", thus absorbing this region into the grand narrative for the rest of Spain and denuding it of any exceptionality.[42] Also, throughout the 1950s the *Servicio de Defensa del Patrimonio Artístico Nacional* (PAN) used the *Decree for the Protection of Spanish Castles* (1949) to preserve the fortified towers of Vizcaya,[43] integrating them into a national inventory of castles and favouring this manifestation of heritage over others. One instance in which Gernika revealingly stands out for its absence is in a report put together by Gallego Burín (1938) on the destruction of cultural heritage during the war. Leopoldo Ginard, then Vice-President of the *Comisión de Monumentos de Vizcaya*, and reporting on destruction in the region, makes no mention of Gernika, a notable absence given the prominence of the town and its symbols in previous publications of the *Comisión*.

This is not to say that Gernika's symbolic dimensions were overlooked. Aware of the symbolic importance of the Tree of Gernika, the representatives of the Franco regime made efforts to appropriate its meaning such that it was woven into the ideological fabric of the new state. Fernández-Shaw's report on the reconstruction of the town reads:

> *Guernica, cradle and symbol of the Spanish tradition, was the foral capital of Vizcaya, and the old oak existed there in whose shade the General Council of the Señorío met, to form its fueros, similarly to other Spanish towns and cities.*
>
> *At the foot of this tree was forged a tradition and a legend; tradition and legend genuinely Spanish, that only through a falsification of the facts and with absolute ignorance of History have been able to be exploited against Spain. The history of Guernica and its tree are tightly linked to the sacred name of the Fatherland [Patria].*
>
> *In the shade of the secular tree met the fathers of the Basque country to dictate the old laws of Spain, to offer their sons to a common Fatherland and march proudly over the seas of the world the invincible flags of our Empire.*
>
> (Fernández-Shaw 1940: 18–19)

Here *Patria*, Empire, History (all capitalized in the original text) are meshed into the symbolism of the tree, which now stands for the tradition and ancestry of Spain. This illustrates an attempt to absorb Basque identity into a sense of Spanishness and thus defuse its more contested dimensions. In the next quote, from the financial magazine of the *Banco de Vizcaya*, we see a further attempt to neutralize the symbolic power of the tree as a rallying point of contestation and resistance:

> *The tree of Gernika is one of love, peace and remembrance. One should not try to give it a meaning it has never had; in its branches a nest of hatred has never been built. It is a piece of the history of Spain, and symbolizes a people that have lived happily in its shade.*
>
> (cited by Egido 1997: 357)

As has been argued, an official narrative of Gernika's destruction was imposed through the rhetoric of the reconstruction, yet there were other forms of erasure implemented through the vehicle of the reconstruction. A decree (*oficio*) from 1949, for instance, emitted by the *Ayuntamiento* of Gernika, announces the order, issued by the Civil Government of Vizcaya, that all Basque language inscriptions on tombs in the local cemetery be removed and replaced with others written in Castilian.[44] In erasing traces of what had actually happened, in attempting to rewrite history and build

4.36 Falangist parade in Gernika, 1943. (España. Ministerio de Cultura. Archivo General de la Administración. Sig.: AGA: F.04246.09.03.)

a new Gernika, in trying to absorb the town's unique symbolism into a national ideology, the regime was consciously forging not a place of memory but a 'place of forgetting'.

Performance and ceremony further complemented both the discursive attempts to reinterpret the symbolism of Gernika and the physical efforts to transform it. They served to define the spaces created by the reconstruction imbuing them with prescribed meaning. In the 1940s Gernika was a place of both inaugurations and ruins. Official visits to inspect the progress of rebuilding were common, including a degree of ceremony involving the singing of anthems and a parade by the local Falangist group (Figures 4.36, 4.37, and 4.38). On 12 February 1943

4.37 The *Gobernador Civil* Vivar Téllez visits Gernika 1943. (España. Ministerio de Cultura. Archivo General de la Administración. Sig.: AGA: F.04246.09.02.)

Moreno Torres, Gonzalo Cárdenas and Vivar Téllez (the *Gobernador civil* and *Jefe provincial del Movimiento* for Vizcaya) travelled to Munguía, Gernika and Ajánguiz to inaugurate reconstruction works (*El Correo Español*, 13 February 1943). On this occasion the municipal market of Gernika was inaugurated with a ceremony that included the Archpriest of Gernika, monseñor Iturrarán, blessing the new market, a marching band playing the national anthem and the Falangist anthem (*El Correo Español*, 13 February 1943).

When the main square of Gernika was completed, a large festivity was organized comprising folkloric dances, speeches and the two anthems (Figure 4.39). Amidst the disorder of the reconstruction these performances projected a sense of control and order, reinforcing the regime's messages. Aside from inaugurations and official visits, the other festive and commemorative occasions encouraged by the regime centered on the foundation of Gernika by Don Tello (8 April 1366), and the date of the union of Gernika and Lumo (8 January 1882). The choice of these commemorations allowed for a celebration of Gernika's past that avoided associations with Basque nationalism and aspirations for autonomy. Furthermore, the bridge uniting Ajanguiz and Gernika along which the Nationalist troops entered Gernika on 29 April 1937 was used as a symbolic sites for official ceremonies ("La entrega de lo construído en Munguia, Guernica y Amorebieta", *La Gaceta del Norte*, 12 February 1943).

Aside from a plaque on the façade of the church of Santa María dedicated to those 'Fallen for the Fatherland', no major memorial was built in Gernika. This represents a break from the general town planning scheme developed by the regime's planners and architects, in which the three main loci of towns were to be the Plaza Mayor, Church and Monument (Blanco 1987: 21–30). Even in those towns where *Regiones Devastadas* only had small interventions, these often included provisions for construction of the Monument. The main square of Gernika built by the Directorate offered a perfect stage for such a memorial, but instead a column topped by an austere wrought iron cross was erected with no mention of the bombing or its victims. The only reference to the victims of the bombing was a stone cross situated in the cemetery on the fringes of the town.

In contrast to the symbols being implanted by the regime in Gernika, another layer of symbols emerged that demarcated the townscape over which officials had less control. Panels and posters appeared throughout the town as it was being rebuilt that fell into two categories: those announcing and pointing the way to businesses and those indicating allegiances to the new regime. In the ruinous landscape of Gernika the first type of panel indicated where the scarce functioning bars, businesses and stores were to be found. One of these signs *Paso al Café* (Passage to the Café) indicated a path through ruins to a café. The name stuck, and both

4.38
Inauguration of
housing, 1945.

the business and the reference exist today as *Bar el Paso* (*Aldaba*, no. 140,
March 2006: 42).[45] The second category of signs included two versions
remembered by those who were children during the period: "Here lives a
Falangist" and "Here lives a *Patriota*" (*Aldaba*, no. 140, March 2006: 42).
The creation of new pathways and the politicization of spaces with refer-
ence to the regime contributed to the demarcation of a new topography.

Aside from the physical and social reconstruction of Gernika, with its
architectural styles and urban planning, its rhetoric, intentions and
implementation, at the end of the war Gernika was more than just a

4.39
Inauguration with
folkloric dances,
c. 1954. (AGA:
F.04246.08.05.)

devastated town. Already a symbolic site before the war new layers were added with the bombing, irrevocably transforming the meaning and memories associated with the town.

The 'Other' Reconstruction of Gernika

In a few days the very name of Guernica had become a more burning subject than the flames of its conflagration. And this is indeed the first distinctive aspect of a symbolic event.

(Vilar in Southworth 1977: xi)

In the previous section we saw how the regime sought to reconstruct Gernika as both town and symbol. Now we turn to the other reconstruction that took place subversively in Spain, and throughout the world, at the hands of artists, journalists and politicians. This alternative reconstruction, while far from the stone and mortar going into the building of the new town hall, was no less powerful in shaping the meaning and symbolism of the place.

The bombing of Gernika proved to be one of the most furiously fought propaganda battles of the war, a battle that had long-term repercussions. Such was the degree of the polemic that Phillip Knightley deemed it the paragon of myth-making in war reporting (1975:192). In the three days that Gernika lay burning before Franco's troops marched in, a group of international journalists who had been covering the war from Bilbao rushed to Gernika and dispatched stories of what they saw. The article that made the greatest impact was written by George L. Steer for both the London *Times* and the *New York Times*, headlined: "The Tragedy of Guernica. Town Destroyed in Air Attack".[46] In the weeks after the bombing, many more articles appeared in the international press, thus spinning the web of memory, narrative and interpretation that would transform the bombing into a modern myth – along the lines suggested by Roland Barthes in *Mythologies* (1973). Both sides propounded the image of a martyred town regardless of their narrative of the destruction. On 2 May 1944, Eduardo Ortega y Gasset wrote in the Basque newspaper *Euzko Deya*: "The vultures, disguised as eagles, did not manage to wound it and soon, under the shade of the Gernikako Arbola, will flower anew the immortal dignity of the Basques." Buried in the discourse of martyrdom which portrayed the town as innocent victim was the fact that Gernika had been home to at least three factories involved in producing weapons.

Visual 'evidence' of the bombing – photographs, remnants of explosives, even eyewitness accounts – was used by both sides to prove their version of events. Thus, the same images appeared illustrating articles in *Le Journal* of 3 May 1937 and *Paris Soir* of 30 April 1937 that defended opposing accounts of the bombing[47] (Gautreau 2008). On one side the Franco-generated document *The Official Report of the Commission appointed by the Spanish National Government to investigate the causes of the Destruction of Guernica on April 26–28* used photographs and eyewitness accounts to attribute the destruction to the 'reds' (Patterson 2007: 38). On the other side, the propaganda services of the Basque Government used photography widely to illustrate news and information pamphlets. One such pamphlet simply entitled "Gernika" was produced shortly after the bombing and provided graphic reportage and testimonies of the event, with accompanying texts in English and Euskera (Tuñón de Lara et al. 1987: 271).[48] Testimony also became important. On 30th April the Mexican newspaper *El Nacional* published a story that included the testimony of a woman named María Hoitia, sparking a trend to collect and publish eyewitness accounts. The following day the magazine *Hoy* published a poignant testimony by the Mayor of Gernika, José de Labauria, which concluded by referring to Gernika as "the noble and loyal town martyred by the fascist fury" (José de Labauria, *Hoy*, 31 July 1937).

Throughout the war, the Republican government worked at the diplomatic level to gain international support. Being able to prove that the terms of the non-intervention pact were regularly violated by Germany and Italy was seen as crucial to this effort. Open letters of outrage were circulated and published internationally with noted figures from the arts and sciences adding their names. In the United States, Upton Sinclair joined his name to a list of 98 writers denouncing the bombing, and Albert Einstein, Theodore Roosevelt and James A. Angell united in a letter of protest (see Mexican newspapers: *La Prensa* of 9 May and *El Universal* of 10 May 1937, also Hensbergen 2004 and Patterson 2007). Part of the international impact of the bombing was that it was seen as an omen of the type of warfare that lay ahead: the idea of 'total war', the failure of non-intervention, and the use of propaganda to sway international public opinion (Knightley 1975; Onaindía 1973; Southworth 1977; Patterson 2007). Journalist Luigi Sturzo writing in 1937 reflected that "from now on, the history of future wars, in speaking of aerial bombings, will refer to Guernica as one now refers to the *Lusitania*, in speaking of torpedoing submarines" (cited in Patterson 2007: 34).

The myth-making propaganda war, the wide circulation of images of the destroyed town, the testimonies and eye-witness narratives, and its association to the price of non-intervention and to aerial bombing, all added further layers to the symbolism of Gernika. They also transformed its very name into an international sign for the horrors of war. However, it was an artist of Andalusian origin living in Paris who would crystallize the iconic nature of the event and create a visual representation that would become inseparable from it.

Guernica as a twentieth-century icon

Pablo Picasso was in Paris in the spring of 1937, worried about his family in Spain, scanning the French press for news of the war, and receiving regular visits from friends who were intensely involved with the Republican effort.[49] He had been appointed Director of the Prado museum in September 1936; a Prado in a besieged Madrid that was being bombed daily and that gradually became a hollow shell as its contents were evacuated. As Director General for Fine Arts, Josep Renau had asked Picasso to contribute to the Spanish Pavilion being planned by the Republic for the Paris World's Fair of 1937. José Gaos, Director of the Pavilion, together with a group that included the writer Max Aub (Cultural Attaché at the Spanish Embassy in Paris) and the poet José Bergamín, asked Picasso to provide a mural and prints on a theme related to the civil war. On 30 April 1937 the newspaper *Ce Soir*, produced by Picasso's friend, Luis Aragon, published photos of the destroyed town of Gernika. The following day, motivated by the news of the bombing, Picasso did six rough sketches that were to become the start of *Guernica*. Picasso's painting was by no means the only artistic or commemorative production related to the bombing (Appendix F). The man organizing the Basque section of the Pavilion at the Paris World Fair was a painter from the town of Bermeo near Gernika, José María Ucelay, and he gave the bombing of Gernika a prominent place in the exhibition. A photomontage was created using a photograph of the Tree of Gernika and the Casa de Juntas and then displayed with an aerial photograph of the town in ruins and a quotation by Aguirre: "Is it a crime for a people to defend their liberty?" The image of the ruined town was accompanied by the caption: "They destroyed our people and our language" (Figure 4.40). Yet another panel reproduced Paul Eluard's poem *La Victoire de Guernica* (Figure 4.41).

Picasso's painting was the piece that captured people's attention and imagination, becoming an iconic image of the Spanish war in particular and of twentieth-century war in general.[50] The reasons for this are varied: Picasso's notoriety, the stir caused by the painting at the World's Fair, and the painting's journey through a Europe on the brink of war – through Scandinavia (January–April 1938) and the UK (September 1938– March 1939). While the painting received mixed reviews at first, with some wishing that it had been less abstract, there was already a sense of its importance.[51] Shortly before the opening of the pavilion Max Aub said: "At the entrance, on the right Picasso's great painting leaps into view. It will be spoken of for a long time" (cited by Hensbergen 2004: 71). That the painting was to serve as an astute propaganda coup was clear even before it had been completed. As Treasurer of the Republic, Juan Negrín struck a deal with the Basque government to ensure that Picasso would be the artist to paint *Guernica* because he considered that

4.40 Panel on the bombing.

4.41 Panel with Eluard's poem exhibited.

it would amount to the "equivalent value in propaganda terms of a victory at the front" (Southworth 1977: 14, Hensbergen 2004: 35).

It was more than propaganda, though, for the painting also acted as a form of memorial. In the pavilion it was hung in proximity to an exhibit dedicated to a number of artists killed by the Nationalists, including the celebrated poet and playwright Federico García Lorca, executed on 19 August 1937. In a 1961 essay Jean Paul Sartre wrote that Picasso's *Guernica* was the commemoration of a massacre, as well as a revolt and a denunciation of it (Sartre 1963: 74–75). Picasso himself also added to the mythical dimensions of the painting over the years with his comments and attitude towards it. One frequently-cited anecdote tells of German officers visiting Picasso's studio in occupied Paris and on seeing *Guernica* asking "Did you do this?" and receiving the famous reply: "No, you did."[52]

Moreover, the painting served a very practical purpose. The touring exhibition in the UK was used to raise funds for Republican Spain, with the assistance of the National Joint Committee for Spanish Relief and the Artists' International Association. Picasso also agreed for *Guernica* to be

4.42 Representatives of the Basque government in front of *Guernica* in Paris. Aguirre is fourth from the right. (© Succession Picasso/ DACS, London 2010.)

4.43 The emplacement of *Guernica* and Calder's *Mercury Fountain*.

used by the Spanish Refugee Relief Campaign in the US, and so the painting travelled to New York on the *Normandie* with Juan Negrín, by then President of the Republic, arriving on 1 May 1939 to embark on a travelling exhibition around the country. Back in Spain, however, the Franco regime's attitude toward Picasso was mixed. During Picasso's last trip to Spain in the summer of 1934 an attempt had been made by the architect José Manuel Aizpúrua and Giménez Caballero to win the artist over to the ideals of the Spanish Falange. The failure of these attempts resulted in a backlash. In an article entitled "De arte y de España" Manuel Pombo Angulo recalls an exhibition of Picasso's paintings that took place during "the period of populist Spain which preceded red Spain" in Madrid's Salón de la Carrera. He writes:

> *I bring up this past because Picasso was for some time – I do not know if he still is – the top artistic hierarch of Red Spain. If art is the expression of the spirituality of a people, 'Guernica', the latest work of his that I know, between a geometric chaos and a slim horse leg in the first plane, shows us the exact dimension of the spiritual confusion of the other Spain.*
> (Pombo Angulo in *El Alcázar*, 14 February 1939: 7)

Hensbergen (2004: 5) suggests that had it not been for the rapid succession of aerial bombings and devastation wrought by the Second World War – Warsaw, Coventry, Dresden, Hamburg, Stalingrad, Pearl Harbour, Hiroshima, Nagasaki – the painting might have been rolled up, deposited in a corner of Picasso's studio and lost to the world's recollection. While this is unlikely given Picasso's fame, Gernika's symbolic nature and its significance were augmented by events of the world war.

Exile, resistance and the construction of another memory

The Franco regime did not have exclusive rights on the image of a phoenix rising from the ashes of a devastated town. The image was also used by the Basque government in exile to show that out of the ruins of a destroyed autonomous government, a new one would rise. On 8 October 1937 the Government of Euzkadi designated Gernika with the title of 'spiritual capital' of Vizcaya (Ortega 1976, album iii, introduction). The German invasion of Belgium caught the *Lehendakari* Aguirre in Belgium, and as he embarked on a rocambolesque journey throughout occupied Europe, the Basque National Council was set up in London in July 1940.[53] References to Gernika were a constant in the exiled *Lehendakari*'s speeches and communiqués, not only during the yearly commemorations of the bombing but also on the anniversary of the proclamation of the Basque Government, in his Christmas messages, and on the occasion of the *Aberri Eguna*. In Britain, a centre of operations for the exiled government, the "Information Bulletin of the Basques in England"[54] was called *Gernika*. It informed about the activities of the *Lehendakari* in exile and published his speeches and communiqués.[55]

From the end of the civil war until 1945 resistance activities in the Basque country and of Basques abroad concentrated on assisting the allies in the hope that, if victorious, they would invade Spain and restore a Republic. The world war and the widespread destruction of cities that it wrought also added further layers of meaning to Gernika. A booklet published in 1945 by the Delegation of Euzkadi in Colombia is entitled: "Rotterdam, Coventry, Pearl Harbour, Stalingrad, GUERNICA: Reminder of a Francoist Crime".[56] The text offers a symbolism of Gernika and its tree as miraculous survivor.

> *Guernica had been left converted into an immense pile of ruins,*
> *within which hundreds of innocent victims burned, in the*
> *holocaust of the barbarism sacrilegiously baptized as a 'Crusade*
> *for order, authority and religion'. The destruction of the town*
> *held sacred by the Basques had been accomplished but . . . the*
> *Tree of the Liberties remained miraculously unharmed,*
> *immutable, with its branches extended towards the reddened sky*
> *as if wanting to tell the world that, despite the hundreds of*
> *Basques lying at its feet sacrificed for defending liberty, the*
> *principles for which it stands will never pass.*
> (Delegation of Euzkadi in Colombia, 1945)

The name of Gernika was also perpetuated in other ways. The Basque government in exile insistently used the name and its symbolism almost as a synonym for Euzkadi (Rodríguez Fouz 2004: 261) and many initiatives received the name: a travelling Elai-Alai[57] group, a hospital in Cataluña, and even a spy network. Several Battalions of Spanish soldiers were formed in exile and fought on the side of France during the Second World War; one of these was the "Gernika", formed of Basque soldiers who took part in the battle to liberate Pointe-de-Grave. As mentioned earlier, Spanish troops also joined Leclerq's garrison in Algeria, forming an armoured battalion in which each tank was named after a battle from the Spanish war, including a "Gernika". The intentions behind these gestures were at least twofold: to maintain a sense of outrage and resistance against Franco among Spaniards and to remind the allies of the situation in Spain in the hope of rallying their assistance for an eventual removal of Franco. The perpetuation of the name Gernika contributed to its significance not only as a martyred town but as a symbol of resilience, resistance, and a refusal to forget.

The Basque government in exile worked intensely to rally support for their cause, but by the time the world war ended, a new balance of power was at play and neither France, Britain nor the US were willing to risk a communist Spain.[58] Once it became clear that the allies were not going to invade Spain and overthrow Franco, representatives of important political, economic and labour groups in the Basque Country met to create a committee that would offer resistance to Franco and continue to work for Basque autonomy. This group formed on 31 March 1945 in the French Basque city of Bayonne under the name of *Consejo Consultivo Vasco* – Basque Consultative Council (Clark 1979: 102–104). One of the key roles of this council throughout the Franco period was to ensure close communication between the Basque government in exile in Paris and the political forces that had remained in the Basque country. One of the outcomes of this collaboration was the jointly coordinated Resistance Committee – Junta de Resistencia. During its first years, activities included sporadic interventions of a symbolic nature, intended to demonstrate – in a climate of fear and oppression – that a resistance actually existed. These acts often revolved around public buildings, or sites – one frequent intervention was to paint the *ikuriña* on church towers or mountainsides. In one of these actions an explosive device was detonated at the base of the monument to General Mola (leader of the Francoist forces on the Northern front) in Bilbao. Clandestine celebrations of *Aberri Eguna*,[59] in itself an act of resistance, were often occasions for parallel actions.[60]

At the end of the Second World War, *Lehendakari* Aguirre presented a report to the Nuremberg tribunal documenting the involvement of the Condor Legion in the bombardment of both Durango and Gernika (*Oficina de Prensa Euzkadi*, OPE, 6 January 1947).[61] According to Southworth (1977: 242) however, the tribunal did not consider events before the Second World War. In 1949 on the 12th anniversary of the bombing of Gernika, *Lehendakari* Aguirre published the following statement:

> *Today it is 12 years since Gernika was destroyed by Hitler's planes at the service of General Franco. The material destruction of the sanctuary of Basque tradition would have been of relative importance were it not for the moral and physical kidnapping of the people by the totalitarian dictatorship of General Franco that continues today.*
>
> (Aguirre y Lecube 1981: 289)

It is estimated that from the siege of Bilbao to the end of the war some 100,000–150,000 Basques went into exile, a large percentage of them children (Clark 1979: 84), who remembered Gernika and took acorns from the oak tree to plant in their host countries.[62] These 'descendants' of the tree were planted in various places – Argentina, Brazil, and the US – and so 'offspring' of Gernika's oak grew in front of the Presidential Palace in Buenos Aires and the State Capitol of Idaho in Boise (Raento and Watson 2000: 719). According to Legarreta's study on Basque refugee children, those who were repatriated to Spain after having been in England later returned to the sites of their refugee colonies to plant "the traditional oak tree to symbolize the Tree of Guernica on British soil" (Legarreta 1984: 293).

The above illustrates how despite efforts made by the regime to silence accounts of the bombing and reshape the symbolism of Gernika, its influence was limited and strongly resisted in the Basque Country, by Basque refugees and by the Basque government in exile. Gernika was not forgotten.

Gernika and *Guernica*, 1945–1975

The social fabric of Gernika continued to be transformed: a result of the fatalities of the war, repression, exile, economic emigrations and internal migrations.[63] The once tightly knit society of the town, in which everyone knew each other by name, and shared customs and codes of conduct became less homogeneous. The use of prison labour for the reconstruction inadvertently contributed to this altered population, for even after they were freed they often still had a *pena de destierro* (banishment) that prevented them from returning to their places of origin (Etxaniz Ortúñez and Palacio Sánchez 2003: 112–115; conversations with Gernikans April 2007). Despite dramatic physical and social changes, the symbolism of Gernika proved resilient. A clandestine celebration of *Aberri Eguna* in 1964 drew two thousand people to the town. The regime, however, had not relented in its attempts to absorb the town into its ideological vision of Spain. Official celebrations in Gernika emphasized Hispanicity and focused on the more neutral historic period such as the town's foundation. On 12 October 1964 the Minister for Foreign Affairs, Fernando Castiella, chose the *Casa de Juntas* in Gernika to give a speech celebrating the *Día de la Hispanidad*. In 1966, amidst great festivities to mark the 600th anniversary of the town, a statue to Don Tello was erected in the Plaza Mayor. Considering that Don Tello had been *alférez mayor* to the King of Castile, the choice of this particular image to commemorate the event reflects a similar trend of infusing locally celebrated events with the regime's ideology and historic and symbolic preferences.[64]

During this period there was some evolution in the regime's narrative of the bombing. In 1967 the Francoist authority in Gernika, Francisco Javier Bilbao Amezaga, acknowledged that the Condor Legion had been responsible for the bombing, but insisted that it had been carried out without the knowledge of the National Command (Reig Tapia 1987: 125; Southworth 1977: 256). In 1970 the *Comisión de Investigación del bombardeo de Guernica* was created by twelve citizens of Gernika with a twofold purpose: first, to bring to light the facts of the bombing and second to have Picasso's painting (then on deposit in the MOMA in New

York) housed in Gernika (*Suplementos Deia*, Sunday, 29 January 1978: 7). The publication in 1973 of the memoirs of Alberto de Onaindía, the Basque priest present in Gernika during the bombing, made his eyewitness account of the attack more readily accessible.

During this time, the symbolic value of the painting also gained momentum, becoming an icon of contestation and protest. Reproductions circulated clandestinely inside Spain. From the early 1960s these reproductions began to be hung in the homes of those opposed to the regime – albeit in the least public rooms of the house. The painting took on the form of secret code in progressive circles, and revealing its presence in the home was equivalent to revealing opposition to the regime. Manuel Vicent remarks that: "There was a time when the reproduction of *Guernica* substituted that of the *Last Supper* in all progressive Spanish homes" (*El País Semanal*, no. 1.547, 21 May 2006: 44). The connection between the painting and anti-Franco resistance was further enhanced through two events. In the mid-1970s Xabier Gereño was jailed for having received by mail a letter with a stamp of *Guernica*. Also in November 1970 Picasso personally resisted attempts by Franco's government to obtain the painting, releasing a statement reiterating that it would only go to Spain when "public liberties are re-established" (cited by Hensbergen 2004: 265). Through the intermediaries of Pérez Embid, Carrero Blanco, Joaquín de la Puente and even the bullfighter Dominguín, Franco had made tentative attempts to negotiate the possibility of having Picasso's *Guernica* sent to Spain (Hensbergen 2004: 263–264). As a form of protest, the artistic partnership of *Equipo Crónica* produced a series of paintings during this period based on personages from Picasso's *Guernica*, several of which incorporated the *Guerrero del Antifaz* – a popular comic character and crusader figure associated with Franco[65] (Figure 4.44). These and other artistic challenges made during the period by artists such as Rafael Canogar, Josep Guinovart, Eduardo Arroyo, and Antonio Saura did not go unanswered. On 25 October 1971 the *Guerrilleros de Cristo Rey* (Warriors of Christ the King)[66] attacked 24 canvases by Picasso that were exhibited in the Theo art gallery in Madrid (Cooper in Preston 1976: 73).

What Gernika's destruction and reconstruction reveals

The transformation of Gernika by its destruction and reconstruction, and the evolution of its symbolic meaning through time, show that it is a polyreferential site (Kritzman in Nora 1996: *foreword*). It is a site densely packed with layers of meaning and with a variety of symbols that correspond to its different facets. The meanings, symbols, associations and version of history with which the reconstruction attempted to imbue Gernika added to but did not replace or erase its symbolic dimensions. The Francoist authorities, aware of the symbolic importance of the Tree

4.44 *El Intruso* (Intruder) painting by *Equipo Crónica*. (© DACS 2010.)

of Gernika, made an effort to appropriate its symbolism and interpret it so as to weave it into the symbolic fabric of the new state and its ideology. This was not about destroying the symbol, but rather manipulating its meaning through a cosmetic operation, a policy that coincided with the plan to build a new town rather than restore the old one. The reconstruction of Gernika undertaken by the Franco regime in the 1940s was tantamount to creating a *lieu d'oublie* – a place of forgetting. This contrasts with the regime's general policy of perpetually reminding the population of the war and who had won it – at once a source of legitimacy and mechanism for keeping fear alive: fear of stepping out of line, fear of another war. Instead, we see a deliberate attempt in the reconstruction to explicitly try and alter the meanings of symbols or symbolic sites. What we see in Gernika are the limits of this effectiveness, for while the reconstruction transformed the physical townscape, attempts at absorbing the town's symbolism into fitting with the regime's ideology did not result in replacing either its pre-war or post-war symbolism. On the contrary, efforts made to suppress the symbolism and identitarian narratives of the place – such as replacing Basque writing on tombstones or outlawing the Basque language – contributed to fueling resistance as well as efforts to preserve them either in secret in the interior or through the exiled communities abroad.

Gernika's roots in the historical narrative of Basque collective identity elevated its destruction to the status of a landmark moment in the struggle for collective affirmation. Hence despite the regime's attempts to overlay Gernika's old symbolism and neutralize its potential as a rallying symbol of Basque identity, Gernika's prior symbolism survived even where the town was radically transformed. Furthermore, not only did the old meanings, historical narratives and symbolism survive – of the *fueros*, autonomy, and ancestry – but new ones were acquired along the way – of resistance and denunciation – that were to prove powerful in the years to come. As we will see in the next chapter, this indicates that attempts to usurp powerful symbols on which communities draw their myths of origin are as likely to fail as attempts to impose new meanings on them. It also shows how the very act of destruction becomes absorbed into the narrative of a site, becoming an additional layer of meaning.

The destruction and reconstruction of Gernika functioned on at least three levels: physical, symbolic and human. At each of these levels further cross-cutting dynamics are identifiable, namely what was lost, saved, transformed, recovered, re-interpreted, new, and imposed. These categories are clearly porous: the Tree of Gernika exists physically, symbolically and socially, and its original meaning was preserved, recovered and expanded. The *frontón* was simultaneously a physical building, a symbol of Basque culture, and an important social venue for the community; while it eventually recovered its social and symbolic functions through the new one, the cherished old building was lost forever. We have also seen that meanings and memories associated to a place can be reconstructed away from its physical location. One of the most salient features of the Gernika case is the resilience of its symbols to persevere through time despite new layers of meaning being added. An address by Bonifacio de Echegaray, member of the Academy for Basque Studies, made on *Radio Euzkadi* on 4 May 1937, reinforces this point:

> *Yet something has been saved of Guernica. It is that which has given universal fame to our city – The Tree – it is the symbol of Basque freedom and there it stands upright before the house where lawyers of the Señorío held their meetings. Though our town has yielded its dwellings to the flames, though its streets are filled with the dust of its ruins, though from its squares and avenues the sad exodus of its people has taken place, still this, its most representative spot, remains unharmed. (. . .) The Beast of the Apocalypse has crossed through Guernica. It has killed her people, levelled her dwellings, churches and workshops, harassed her fields. Yet the most characteristic part of Guernica is still standing. But even if it had disappeared Guernica would live on for her soul is invulnerable.*
>
> (Echegaray 1937)

Gernika's symbolic meaning was resilient in spite of, not because of the physical reconstruction of the town. As has been shown, this meaning also gained new facets, one of which was an association with resistance. One of the most dramatic acts of protest made during the Franco period was in September 1970. As Franco presided over the world *jai-alai* championships in San Sebastián, Joseba Elósegui stood in centre court and set himself on fire shouting "long live the Basque Country" and "Guernica, Guernica" (Southworth 1977: 309; *Time* article, 2 May 1977). What linked the gesture to Gernika is that Elósegui had been in command of a military unit present in the town on the day of the bombing (Elósegui 1977: 32; Preston 2001: 76). By setting himself on fire in front of Franco he was making the General see the consuming flames of Gernika that he had denied for 30 years and which had obsessed Elósegui (Raento and

Watson 2000: 715). According to Southworth: "it is not too much to say that the flames from Elosegi's clothing also lighted the failure of the propaganda campaign to desymbolize the destruction of Guernica" (Southworth 1977: 309).

The work by *Equipo Crónica*, "Después de la batalla" (After the Battle), showing figures from *Guernica* scattered in an arid landscape, can be seen to represent the way in which both Picasso's painting and the memory of the bombing permeated the heritage-scape of Spain despite attempts to force it into a realm of silence. The re-emergence of once silenced memories will be the subject of the next chapter.

5 Reconstruction Continued: Transition and Recovery

Threats of violence are also violence.
(Johan Galtung 1990: 292)

One major motivation for this study has been to determine the medium-term repercussions of the post-war reconstruction of cultural heritage. The aim of this chapter is to trace how as concepts changed, cultural heritage was reinterpreted: new meanings were added and old ones were revived or lost their relevance. For this purpose, after a brief overview of the situation in the 1960s, the focus will be on two time periods: the political transition to democracy inaugurated by Franco's death in 1975, and the government of José Luis Rodríguez Zapatero's launch of a process termed 'recovery of historic memory' in 2004. First this evolution will be considered in terms of how symbols and identity were revisited, how notions of cultural heritage evolved and the idea of Spain was reconceptualized. The second half returns to Gernika to see how its meanings and memoryscapes evolved over time.

The fact that in studying the post-civil war reconstruction of Spain it is necessary to explore the 70-year period since the war bespeaks the difficulty of determining when a society stops being *post*-conflict. In Spain's case, this scrutiny is imperative due to the nature of the Franco dictatorship which comprised a form of sustained conflict permeated by violence, threats of violence, and reminders of the war. Moreover, the way in which historical symbols, events, styles and anecdotes are used to intimidate or assert the division lines of conflict is a form of violence that Johan Galtung has called 'cultural violence':

> *By 'cultural violence' we mean those aspects of culture, the symbolic sphere of our existence – exemplified by religion and ideology, language and art, empirical science and formal science (logic, mathematics) – that can be used to justify or legitimize direct or structural violence. Stars, crosses and crescents; flags, anthems and military parades; the ubiquitous portrait of the Leader; inflammatory speeches and posters – all these come to mind.*

(Galtung 1990: 291)

For this reason, since the beginning of this research, the Transition was seen as a second post-conflict period during which Spanish heritage was again revisited and reconstructed. Here the period of 'recovery of memory' initiated by the Zapatero government will be seen as a further stage in the process.

Reconstruction Continued

The 1960s: a new reformulation of Spain on the horizon

The major changes to affect attitudes towards cultural heritage in Spain during the 1960s were fuelled by the dynamics of emigration and tourism. Whereas since the end of the war there had been large migratory movements within Spain, now Spaniards began leaving the country to look for work.[1] This movement created new Spanish diasporas, in addition to those of the Republican exile. These diasporas tended to group around regional rather than political identities, creating social venues in the host countries such as the *Casa de Galicia* or the *Casa de Asturias*. In the face of a continued emphasis of the regime on a unified Spain, this emigration served to underwrite an economic and cultural fragmentation that would have consequences during the subsequent political transition. Tourism also took off during this period – despite opposition from the ecclesiastical and Falange hierarchies.[2] The influx of foreigners also propelled a new revalorization of Spanish heritage as an economic asset. This led to Spain's collaboration in an inventory project for the Protection of European Cultural Heritage which resulted in a report published in 1968 by the *Dirección General de Bellas Artes*. Another effect was the substantial development of the *Paradores*[3] which combined a pragmatic need for tourist infrastructure and a desire to cater to high-class tourism, with the symbolic need to portray the image of a medieval and imperial Spain.[4] Despite the unavoidable impact of this incursion of the outside world into Spain, introducing different attitudes and behaviours, the regime made efforts to impose its vision of Spain on visitors. Tourists to Madrid were guided along the 'Imperial route' that took them to the former royal palaces at La Granja, Aranjuez and El Escorial, with an obligatory stop at the Valle de los Caídos and past Franco's residence at El Pardo (also once a royal palace). Internationally, the New York World's Fair of 1964–1965 offered the Franco regime an opportunity to put its vision of Spanish culture and heritage on the international map. Masterpieces from the Prado museum were sent which, together with the flamenco shows, made the Spanish Pavilion popular among the public, press and critics. This proved an important symbolic achievement for the regime given the enormous success of the Republic's pavilion at the Paris World's Fair in 1936 (Alcoba López 2004).

An important landmark of the 1960s in terms of the reconstruction of the war narrative came in 1964, the year in which the "25 Years of Peace" were celebrated. By then, the rhetoric used to refer to the conflict had gradually changed from 'crusade' to 'fratricidal war'. Far from being conducive to reconciliation, however, this change meant that where previously the enemy had been portrayed as foreign – international Communism – now it was portrayed as being Spanish.[5] The distinction between the victorious and the defeated was reinforced by this renewed interpretation of the war. There was no political desire on the part of the regime to forget the war and move on; on the contrary, the narrative of the war dictated by the victors continued to be imposed on the collective conscience and consciousness through recurrent commemorative acts to its heroes and martyrs. Notably, it was not until 1969 that Franco passed a law (Decreto-Ley 10/1969) by which all crimes committed during the war could no longer be prosecuted.

La Transición

> *Don Cal-lo, it seems to me that this has ended. Now we can begin to talk, no? Although maybe not too loudly yet . . .*
>
> (conversation from 1976 remembered by Castilla del Pino 2004: 21)[6]

Franco died on 20 November 1975; the same day on which José Antonio Primo de Rivera had been shot 40 years earlier.[7] The two 'heroes' of the Crusade were thus joined in death, a union further emphasized by their shared burial place at the *Valle de los Caídos*. His death inaugurated a period of political, social and cultural transformation known as *La Transición*.

As had been the case with the regime during the 1940s, one of the first concerns of the political cadres following Franco's death was legitimacy. The challenge they faced was how to strike a balance between change and continuity, since the impetus towards modernizing and creating distance from the authoritarianism of the regime coexisted with an interest in retaining many of its structures, institutions, financial backers and chief representatives. Part of the problem lay in that on proclaiming Juan Carlos de Borbón y Borbón as his successor (22 July 1969), Franco clearly intended to root the future of Spain firmly in the military coup of 1936[8] and the victors of the war, declaring:

> *The Kingdom which we have established, with the consent of the nation, owes nothing to the past; it arises from that decisive act of July 18th, which constitutes a historical act of the highest importance which allows neither pacts nor conditions.*
>
> (*Spain Today*, no. 1, March 1970: 15–18, Proclamation is reproduced)

In 1977, however, the results of the first democratic elections since the war seemed to indicate that such roots were to be found in the elections of May 1936 rather than in the Nationalist victory of 1939. On the day after the elections, the newspaper *Diario 16* published an article headlined "Forty Wasted Years", for the percentage of votes received by the political left in 1977 were almost identical as those received by the Popular Front in 1936.

While the first stage of the Transition (1975 to 1982)[9] brought about significant changes, many institutions (and individuals) in power remained unchanged. In the interest of peace, prosperity, democracy and modernization, political parties approved an Amnesty Law (1979) that released the Franco regime's political prisoners but also exonerated its crimes, its henchmen and their beneficiaries. This law resulted in a largely unchanged status quo, reinforced by the fact that many of the new political leaders were the sons and daughters of Franco's oligarchy, a phenomenon that Preston refers to as "building a new world with the bricks of the old" (Preston 2001: 209–261). As a result, it was both difficult and undesirable for the new political elite to undertake a profound examination of the recent past. The tacit agreement among political parties to turn a blind eye to the crimes of the civil war and dictatorship was such a determining element in the politics of the Transition that it came to be known as the *Pacto de Silencio* (Pact of Silence) or *Pacto del Olvido* (Pact of Forgetting).[10]

The Spanish Transition was by no means free of violence, either threatened or real. It was partly the fear of a military coup that, politicians argued, forced them to compromise and to avoid the complexity of the past, and to risk antagonizing the military (Aguilar Fernández 2002: 140–145). Political violence claimed 20 lives between Franco's death and the 1977 elections. It continued throughout the decade carried out largely by groups on both extremes of the political spectrum. Evidence of this shaky ground was the uncovering in 1978 of a planned military coup, which on the 23rd of February 1981 was attempted when a group of officers held the parliament at gunpoint —an event known as the *Tejerazo* after the Colonel that lead it. It was only in 1982, with the electoral victory of the Spanish Socialist Worker's Party (PSOE) under the leadership of the forty-year-old Felipe González, that the transition to democracy was more securely cemented. Yet, the political consensus, amnesty and silence that made this victory possible also meant that the socialist programme for 'national regeneration' was undermined by a policy of keeping quiet about the recent past.

While this silence about the past reigned in the political spheres, especially about the dictatorship, in the academic and cultural arenas the heritage of this period began to be recovered. In 1977 an exhibition entitled *Arquitectura para después de una guerra, 1939–1949* was organized along with a catalogue published by the *Colegio Oficial de Arquitectos de*

Cataluña y Baleares. Then, in 1987 another exhibition was organized[11] at the Ministry of Public Works (MOPU) entitled *Arquitectura en Regiones Devastadas*, about the reconstruction work carried out in the 1940s and 1950s by the Directorate.

Two developments that affected notions of Spanish heritage during the Transition were the public recovery and reintegration of exiled Spain, and the administrative and political division of the country into autonomic regions through the 1978 Constitution. The first move reunited the 'two Spains' on the peninsula, and brought liberal and leftist Spain back to the country's social, cultural and political scenes. The second development saw a renaissance and rediscovery of Spain's regional cultures and the celebration of their differences.

Recovering the 'other' Spain

From his exile in Latin America, the poet Juan Larrea (1895–1980) published a magazine called *España Peregrina*. Over 30 years later this wandering Spain could return. The return of the 'other', exiled and silenced Spain was an essential part in the reconstruction carried out during the Transition. The involvement of illustrious exiles was central in adding legitimacy to the successive Socialist governments that would follow Felipe Gonzalez's electoral victory in 1982, as they banked on narratives of its leaders as having been protagonists in anti-Franco efforts. The regime had sought to create a direct lineage between itself and a particular vision of Philip II's Spain while projecting the idea of a 'New' Spain. Like Franco had done earlier in the century, the new Socialist government offered an *à la carte* version of the past presenting itself as an ideological and political heir of Republican Spain while projecting an image of a modern European Spain.[12] However, the association with the Republic was cautious and remained largely cosmetic. The modern European associations trumped the past of the civil war and dictatorship stayed off the political radar. This exercise of selection favoured the iconic figures of the Republic whose returns to Spain were highly mediatized events, woven into the political discourse as symbolizing the recovery of Spain's liberal past. After nearly 40 years of exile, figures such as Dolores Ibárruri, the legendary *Pasionaria*, and the poet Rafael Alberti returned to Spain to much acclaim and were given seats in Parliament. Artists and intellectuals who had lived internal exile within Spain were also re-discovered and celebrated publicly, as in the case of the poet Vicente Aleixandre, awarded the Nobel prize for literature in 1977. Yet others, executed by the Nationalists during the war or who perished in Francoist prisons afterwards, and whose work and memory had been absent from the public sphere, were now recovered. Such was the case of the poets Federico García Lorca and Miguel Hernández, whose writings enjoyed a renaissance.[13]

While the policy of the Socialist government regarding the Francoist past drew on the allure of mythical leftist figures, it did not dare to initiate more meaningful public actions recognizing the crimes of the regime. While it is possible to understand the motives for not undertaking such initiatives in the first Socialist mandate, given the ever-present threat of a military coup and frequent terrorist violence, the omission is more difficult to understand once the party had a clear majority and the country had joined the EC (1986) and NATO (1988).[14] By failing at that crucial moment to acknowledge the previously ignored and disregarded victims of the regime, the PSOE failed to give them an equal footing on which to claim rights and recognition, thereby making their suffering easier to dismiss in future debates. This political climate also inhibited a process of national reconciliation by which the past could have been studied and discussed, and those previously remaining silent become heard. On the contrary, distrust, recrimination and a silence fuelled by fear and insecurity continued to fester for another 20 years despite outward appearances of Spain as an economic and political miracle fast-tracked to modernity.

Spanish identity(ies) in transition

During this period, the change that came to mark the Spanish territory – physically but also politically, socially and culturally – was the rise in relevance of the regions. During the Franco period only Navarre was allowed to maintain its *fueros* and a small degree of autonomy – thanks to the support of the Carlists during the war. This changed with the Constitution of 1978. The political organisation of Spain was transformed through its administrative division into 17 autonomous regions.[15] After years of a forced unification that glorified anything Castilian and only recognized folkloric differences, the various regions of Spain celebrated their distinctiveness from the regime's portrayal of Spain. Differences emerged, real and imagined, profound and symbolic, old and new that imbued the Spanish topography with a renewed layer of regional and local meanings as old symbols such as flags and anthems were rediscovered and reinstated. This new decentralized framework had a major impact on the administration of cultural heritage, including not only museums but also architecture and archaeological sites as certain responsibilities and budgets were delegated to local governments. In part as a result of this decentralization, some archaeological sites came to be perceived as symbols of regional identity (Díaz-Andreu, 2002: 48): Empuries in Catalonia, Santimamiñe in the Basque Country and Medina Azahara in Andalusia.

This new administrative organization of the national territory, however, did little to reconcile regional populations with the repression suffered under Franco. Rather than extinguishing regional sentiments, Franco's intransigent centralism had spurred them. Regionalist groups emerged with significant anti-regime qualities, wide bases of social support, and in certain instances, armed units. García de Cortázar has argued that the failure during the Transition to truly break the silence imposed throughout the Franco regime fuelled regional and separatist violence:

> *Perhaps if the Spaniards of the end of the seventies and beginning of the eighties, instead of walling up the years of silence, had confronted the old and terrible stories of their sentimental education, the excluding nationalisms would not have been perpetuated throughout the democracy.*
>
> (García de Cortázar 2003: 325)

Cultural transition

While there was a clear absence of impetus for bringing the recent past to the foreground in the political spheres of the Spain being newly rebuilt, as Aguilar (2006: 250–265) argues, this was not the case in social and cultural fields. Spain's urban populations raced to catch up with the rest of Europe, cramming into a decade 30 years of social, political, economic and cultural developments. A Ministry of Culture was created in 1977. Called *Ministerio de Cultura y de Bienestar* under the Suárez government, it gradually shed those elements inherited from the regime (Semprún 1993: 115–116). The mood for change also inspired a renaissance in Spanish arts and entertainment that came to be known as *La Movida* (The Move). As one critic has said of this period:

> *In art this change had enormous consequences, principally by liberating the then emerging, or simply young, artists of the burden of 'the Spanish', that forced need to show in their own language the dictates, more or less folkloric or dramatic, of an imposed past.*
>
> (Calvo Serraller 2006: 33)

The end of strict state censorship in 1977 also instigated a period of intense productivity in Spanish cinema with some filmmakers presenting visions of the civil war and the dictatorship that departed from those that the regime had imposed[16] (Table 5.1). Others, like Pedro Almodovar, sought to break with the strict moral codes, values and taboos of the regime to define a new vision of Spain. This period also saw the planting of seeds that would germinate in the 1980s and 1990s into some of the most important cultural institutions of Spain.[17] The push towards a modern Spain did not exclude its cultural heritage. Spain first appeared on UNESCO's World Heritage List in 1984 with five

Table 5.1 Films on the subject of the Civil War and the dictatorship

Film	Director	Date
"El espiritu de la colmena"	Víctor Erice	1973
"Cría Cuervos"	Carlos Saura	1976
"La escopeta nacional"	Luis García Berlanga	1978
"El crimen de Cuenca"	Pilar Miró	1979
"Patrimonio nacional"	Luis García Berlanga	1981
"La colmena"	Mario Camus	1983
"Las bicicletas son para el verano"	Jaime Chávarri	1983
"Requiem por un campesino Español"	Francisco Betriú	1985
"La vaquilla"	Luis García Berlanga	1985
"Dragón Rapide"	Jaime Camino	1986
"Espérame en el cielo"	Antonio Mercero	1988
"Ay Carmela!"	Carlos Saura	1990

sites: two associated with its Al-Andalus heritage (Alhambra, Generalife and Albaicín of Granada and the Historic Centre of Córdoba), two with its Catholic – and royal – heritage (Burgos Cathedral and the Monastery and Site of the Escorial near Madrid), and one recognizing the architectural works of the twentieth-century Catalan architect Antoni Gaudí. This development, together with the rise of tourism, increased awareness about the preservation of built heritage and in particular that of historic old towns. By 1987 Spain was one of the countries with the greatest number of sites on the list with a total of 15 sites, six of them old towns.

The people chosen to fill the post of Minister of Culture in the first years of the Socialist government reveal just how strategic this office was. The first Minister was Javier Solana (1982–1988), one of the PSOE's central figures and close collaborator of Felipe González, who then acted as Government Spokesperson (1985–1988) and went on to be Minister of Foreign Affairs (1992–1995).[18] That Solana, a central party figure, was made Minister of Culture shows that the cultural portfolio was seen as important and strategic rather than purely decorative. Equally indicative of the Socialist government's attitude towards culture is the next selection for the post: Jorge Semprún (1988–1991). Semprún was an emblematic figure of resistance. He had been a member of the French Resistance, was deported to Buchenwald (where he ran cultural activities for the Spanish deportees), had been active as a leader of the Spanish Communist Party in exile and had a role in the underground resistance to Franco inside Spain. It is likely that with his appointment a gesture was being made to recover exiled Spanish culture and present a new image of Spain with international stature.

Change in continuity

One indicator of change and continuity during this period was the symbol-scape of the newly re-imaged Spain: its flag, images on stamps and banknotes, street names, people and events celebrated in its public spaces. The national anthem did not change,[19] but each of the autonomous communities began using their particular anthems for official events at the regional level. The flag retained the same red and yellow design, rather than reverting to the tricolour Republican flag, but the coat of arms used by Franco was replaced with the royal one. Franco's effigy on stamps and coinage was gradually replaced with that of the King, but statues of the dictator remained in many cities, as did the names of his generals and collaborators – including the Condor Legion – on streets, schools, and squares throughout Spain. The *Transición*, as a period of political redefinition, saw successive governments trying to strike a fine balance between change and continuity that would appease formerly opposed sides. In defining the laws that determine collective memory Halbwachs wrote that:

> *(. . .) it does not conserve the past, but rather reconstructs it,*
> *with the help of material traces, rituals, texts, and traditions*
> *that it has left, but also with the help of more recent*
> *psychological and social traits, in other words the present.*
>
> (Halbwachs 1925: 182)

Attempts to develop an alternative vision of Spain to the one built during the Franco period were nonetheless deeply rooted in the latter precisely because of its determination to distinguish itself from it.

The Spanish Transition was seen by outside observers as a model for the peaceful political transition from a totalitarian regime to a democratic system. Yet, this process has been seriously questioned within Spain and has become the subject of increasingly critical analyses (Aguilar Fernández 2002: 138–139). As we have seen (Chapter 3) there is no consensus on when the *posguerra* ended; it is equally difficult to find the temporal parameters of the *Transición*. It is as difficult to pinpoint the exact moment when the Spanish *posguerra* or the *Transición* ended. Some see that moment in 1982 when the PSOE won the national elections, and others in 1992, a year during which numerous events seemed to indicate that in just over 15 years Spain had become a modern country and international player in political, economic, cultural and social spheres.[20] The year 1992 also offered the opportunity for the emergent, democratic Spain to show a different way of celebrating and commemorating what had been one of the historic moments glorified by the dictatorship. A wide variety of events took place throughout the year commemorating the 500 year anniversary of Columbus's 1492 voyage. Many of these events – such as the symbolic marriage between the statue of Columbus in Barcelona and the statue of Liberty in New York staged by sculptor Antoni Miralda – had a markedly different tone from the sombre celebrations of Hispanicity that had characterized the regime. In addition the *Reconquista* was commemorated not as the glorious unification of Catholic Spain and the expulsion of Jews and Muslims, but through a series of exhibitions on the history and culture of Al-Andalus and Sefarad.[21]

That the Transition did not entirely end the looming silence that still weighed on Spanish society can be illustrated in 1999 in the small town of Castuera, Extremadura, on the final day of a conference on the nineteenth-century. The Mayor, after elaborating on the treasures of Castuera, offered to drive a group around the area – including history Professor Carlos Seco Serrano – to show them the landscape. On the car ride the Mayor expounded to us on the local sheep, cheese, almond trees and marzipan then stopped the car to allow his guests to step out and admire the scenery. Standing on a vast plain, surrounded by fields, with no buildings in sight and a harsh wind blowing Professor Seco Serrano pointed to a field nearby and revealed that it had been the site of a concentration camp and under the ground was a mass grave. This anecdote illustrates the persistence of a memory, the need to share it; but in 1999 there was still no public forum for so doing. While nothing in these vast fields indicated what had happened there, the knowledge of it persisted.

The restless past, 2004–2007

> *The profound and unresolved problem, the one that should set off*
> *some alarms and give rise to a profound and general debate, is*
> *that the democracy of 1978 has not yet found a perspective from*
> *which to narrate the past of Spaniards, of all Spaniards.*
>
> (Ridao 1999: 22)

In 1996 a centre-right party won the national elections, the Popular Party (PP) that had been created by a former Francoist Minister[22] and in the elections of 2000 the PP gained a parliamentary majority. That year, a study carried out by the *Centro de Investigaciones Sociológicas* (Centre for Sociological Research, CIS) on the evaluation of Spaniards of the years since Franco's death showed that, despite consensus on the significant changes that Spanish society had undergone in behaviour, attitudes, and "moral values", the remains of a divided past still lingered (Table 5.2).

During the years the PP was in power there was little incentive on the part of the government to revisit the Civil War and Franco regime. However, within civil society there began to emerge initiatives that aimed at breaking the 'pact of silence'. For instance, in 2000 the Association for the Recovery and Defence of Historic Memory (*Asociación para la*

Table 5.2 Change and continuity 25 years after Franco

Question 4 – Thinking about the recent history of Spain, do you think that Spanish society today . . . ?

	Yes	No	Does not know	Does not answer
Have forgotten the divisions and resentment that the Civil War created	42.7	50.9	6.1	0.3
Although the divisions and resentment of the past are forgotten, the deep mark left by the Franco period is still palpable	66.9	25.1	7.4	0.6
In general, the way people behave and think has very little to do with the past	72.4	18.9	7.2	1.5

Responses in percentage points out of a total of 2485 (CIS 2000: 2).

Question 13 – Speaking generally, do you think that in the last 25 years the moral values of Spanish society have changed . . . ?

A lot (*Mucho*)	34.0
Considerably (*Bastante*)	46.7
A little (*Poco*)	8.8
Not at all (*Nada*)	3.1
Does not know	7.0
Does not answer	0.4

Responses in percentage points out of a total of 2485 (CIS 2000: 4).

Recuperación y la Defensa de la Memoria Histórica) and in 2002 the Forum for Memory (*Foro por la Memoria*) were created. Efforts to create public platforms through which to unearth and share stories from these periods bore fruit in 2004, when a new socialist government began a process termed 'the recovery of historic memory'.

Rodríguez Zapatero's election, in the wake of Spanish involvement in the invasion of Iraq and the subsequent terrorist attack of 11 March 2004, is significant in terms of the story of the Spanish Civil War because he is the first President to have come from the side of the 'defeated'. This political change, together with the subsequent 70th and 30th year anniversaries of events linked to the war and transition respectively inaugurated a new phase in Spain's relationship to this part of its history. By 2006 there were 118 associations for the recovery of memory of these periods, including a State Commission for the Recovery of Historic

Memory. Thus a new phase began in the post-conflict reconstruction of Spain, as memories and narratives previously silenced began re-emerging. Examining this phase confirms the long arm of memory, but also reveals how unresolved issues can come back to haunt society and rekindle antagonisms.

The 'recovery of historic memory' 70 years on

Since 2004 a movement has arisen to uncover what was buried during the construction of the Franco regime's New Spain. In 2006 Zapatero's government began a process termed 'recovery of historic memory'. Though still popularly referred to as the "Law of Historic Memory", the text eventually passed by Parliament on 31 October 2007 was given the less evocative but more precise name: *Ley por la que se reconocen y amplían derechos y se establecen medidas en favor de quienes padecieron persecución o violencia durante la Guerra Civil y la Dictadura* (Law recognizing and amplifying rights and establishing measures in favour of those who suffered persecution and violence during the Civil War and the Dictatorship). There are two main lines to this law. The first addresses the victims, recognizing all the victims of the Civil War and of the Franco regime, including 'victims of the Transition'.[23] The second addresses symbols and documentation and provides for the creation of a documentation centre that will expand the Archive of the Civil War already extant in Salamanca. In a conflict where propaganda played such an important role, discovering what happened has been complicated by the destruction of documents that occurred during the war.[24] The new *Centro de la Memoria* in Salamanca will inventory all collections of documents relevant to these periods and gather them together to create a digital archive. One of the major polemics prompted by this line of the law relates to symbols of the regime: the numerous monuments, statues, plaques and street names that remain throughout Spain dedicated to the Nationalists and aspects of the war that they commemorated: *18 de Julio, División Azúl, Legión Condor* and *Héroes del Alcázar*. In the end, the Law established that symbols honouring only one side of the war must be removed from all state buildings and recommends that local governments do the same for all public buildings. This was a modified version of the original proposal, demanding that these symbols be removed from all public spaces including church and private property. In March 2005 the last equestrian statue of Franco remaining in Madrid was taken down, and on the 24th of August 2006 the equestrian statue that remained in the courtyard of the military academy in Zaragoza was removed. Monuments dedicated to figures on both the political left and right have been vandalized in recent years (Figures 5.1 and 5.2).

Amid this polemic, it can be difficult to gauge public reaction to this process. On the occasion of the 70th anniversary of the military uprising, *El País* published a special section dedicated to the event which included

5.1 Monument in Madrid to Pablo Iglesias, founding figure of Spanish Socialism; the nose of the bust has been broken off.

5.2 Relief bust of Franco in Salamanca's monumental *Plaza Mayor* with Republican graffiti, 2005.

the results of a series of opinion polls dealing with how Spaniards felt about this past (Table 5.3). Aside from the clear support to go ahead with the government's initiative to research the past and uncover graves (64.5%), there is nonetheless a clear split in attitudes towards the war and over 50 percent of respondents answered affirmatively to the question: "Do you consider that 70 years later, there are still two confronted Spains?"

The change in approach to the past between the governments during and after the Transition is further reflected in how the Republican exile has been treated. This has moved beyond the recovery of emblematic figures to attempts at estimating the social, intellectual, and cultural impacts that it had and which treat the exile as a violent amputation of Spain. For instance, an exhibition was held in May 2007 in the *Ministerio de Fomento* dedicated to exiled architects. Images of the buildings that they designed in exile poignantly evoked what Spain's reconstruction could have been, had they not been forced to flee. Moreover, the 9,000 Spaniards deported to German concentration camps – 5,000 of whom died – began to be the subject of research and exhibitions. In 2006 a report was published, *Libro Memoria* (Bermejo and Checa, 2006), which for the first time made public the names of those deportees who in Franco's Spain had been invisible.

Recently the memoirs of those who suffered under the regime have begun to be published, such as of the poet Marcos Ana (2007), imprisoned for 23 years between the ages of 19 and 41, and Andrés Iniesta López (2006) imprisoned at 17. They seek that the experiences of the 'other' Spain be taught and remembered. There is a particular sense of urgency about trying to collect oral testimonies and memories before the last witnesses of that period disappear. Furthermore, a different type of language has begun to be used when referring to the Franco regime's repression. Phrases like 'genocide' and 'crime against humanity', never before applied in this context, are now used, thus rewriting the country's recent past and suggesting a new moral spectrum with which to analyze it. [25]

In 2005 Amnesty International published a report requesting that Spain deal with the case of its 'disappeared'. Then on the 17th of March 2006 the Council of Europe agreed by unanimous vote to officially condemn the Franco regime.[26] It also drew up a set of recommendations

Table 5.3 Attitudes in 2006 about the memory of the Civil War

	Yes	No	Don't know/ No opinion
Do you think monuments, statues or street names dedicated to or commemorating the 18th of July and its protagonists should be preserved?	43.1%	40.9%	16.1%
Do you consider that 70 years later, there are still two confronted Spains?	54.6%	36.6%	9.2%
In your family do you speak about the 18th of July and the Civil War?	48.8%	50.1%	1.2%
The Government is preparing a Law of the Historic Memory. Do you think this appropriate?	54.9%	17.9%	17.9%
Do you support that everything regarding the Civil War be researched, that mass graves be identified and the affected persons rehabilitated?	64.5%	25.6%	9.9%

Information from *El País* (18 July 2006: 23) based on 800 telephone interviews.

to the Spanish government: creating monuments to the memory of the regime's victims; setting up a permanent exhibition in the *Valle de los Caídos* explaining how it was built with Republican prison labour; establishing an inter-ministerial commission to investigate the crimes of the dictatorship and reporting to the Council of Europe on its findings; and opening civil and military archives to historians (Cué, *El País*, 18 March 2006:26). This initiative was followed in June of 2006 by a petition from 199 deputies of the European Parliament to the European Commission requesting that the Franco regime be condemned and calling for the adoption of support measures for its victims. This is the first time that international institutions have condemned the regime. Furthermore, in February 2007 the first 'Truth Commission' was established in Valencia to explore the Francoist repression there between 1939 and 1953. The process of unearthing the past is rarely clear-cut though, as the case of Federico García Lorca illustrates (Box 5.1).

A new, but not unexpected repercussion following the efforts of the 'defeated' of the war and the dictatorship to recover that past, has been a counterreaction on the part of the 'victorious', who sense they are now losing the propaganda battle of a war they won. The revival of the

Box 5.1 To dig or not to dig: Symbol and praxis of Federico García Lorca's grave

5.3 Lorca in Madrid.

When local Falangists apprehended and killed Federico García Lorca in Granada on the night of 18 August 1936 they not only killed a gifted poet and playwright, they also created a martyr and powerful symbol. Lorca's creative work was known internationally and so was his death. A photograph of him was hung in the Republic's pavilion in Paris where his poems and plays were recited and performed. After forty years Lorca 'returned' to Spain after Franco's death through his poetry and plays where they began to be published, taught and performed. A statue of Lorca bearing the inscription "Madrid to Federico García Lorca" was inaugurated in 1986 on the square facing the National Theatre (Figure 5.3). Yet while Lorca's works were recovered, the question of his mortal remains went unresolved. A monument was erected and a park named after Lorca on the site where his remains, left in a ditch with his companions in death, are thought to lie. It became a place of pilgrimage for his admirers but also instigated a debate about whether or not to excavate the area. There are different positions in the debate, represented by Lorca's family, the families of the three others buried with him, and Lorca scholars and admirers.

In 2007 the position of Lorca's family was that the site be left undisturbed in order that his murder could continue to be a symbol of all of those who lost their lives for being artists, nonconformists, or liberals. They argued that in digging up the grave the symbolism would become vulnerable, easily usurped by different interest groups. Moreover, the gravesite where Lorca is thought to lie, along with a schoolteacher and two *banderilleros,* is close to the grave of other *fusilados*. Therefore, in order to identify the poet's remains those of many others would have to be examined, involving extensive DNA testing, and implicating people who would rather not be involved. The family also expressed their concern that those favouring the excavation of the area were motivated by the interests of real-estate speculators who wanted to build there. If the remains are dispersed, they further argued, the symbolism of the place would be altered. On the other side are the family members of the others thought to be buried with the poet who would like to recover their remains, and scholars like Gabriel Jackson who argue that admirers of Lorca want to know where he lies.[27] As in the case of Gernika, there are still many theories as to why and how Lorca was killed fuelling further myth-making of an act of destruction that became an enduring symbol of the war.

In 2009 family members of the three men believed to have been buried with Lorca used the provisions of a new law to force the excavation of the site and in December 2009 a team of forensic archaeologists excavated. No human remains were found on the site where for over 30 years people have gone on pilgrimages, deposited flowers, carried out commemorations, and where a monument to the poet was built. The initial silencing and confusions concerning his execution have resulted in perpetual reverberations.

What the bombing of Gernika and Lorca's murder have in common is that both actions quickly acquired mythical proportions and they were shrouded in silence during the extended dictatorship. One result has been to confound attempts to discover what actually happened. The silencing of facts contributes to making the interpretation of events malleable while simultaneously converting them into universal symbols.

dichotomy between the 'two Spains' accentuated the tone of the already tense political debate in 2006 so that it became not only the 'year for the recovery of historic memory' but also the year of *crispación* – extreme tension. Observers have commented that they do not recall a parallel climate of tension since the Second Republic, immediately preceding the Civil War (Carrillo 2006: 35). Part of the explanation for this lies in a generational change. For the most part the descendants – the grandchildren, nieces and nephews of those killed and disappeared – are now demanding answers. Rodríguez Zapatero himself exemplifies this generational change. Not only is he the first President to come from the defeated side of the war, he is also of the 'grandchild' generation for his grandfather, Juan Rodríguez Lozano, a captain in the Spanish military, who after a summary trial was executed by the nationalists for remaining loyal to the Republic.[28] One of the more virulent chants that were heard repeatedly in demonstrations organized by the PP and their supporters goes: "*Zapatero vete con tu abuelo*" (Zapatero go with your grandfather). Further tangible repercussions were seen in the revival of the 1930s confrontation, the multiplication throughout Madrid of posters of the Spanish Falange, and the fact that the annual celebration of the *Día de la República* (14th April) attracted more participants than ever to Madrid's *Puerta de Sol* in 2007, and in several demonstrations in Catalonia (Girona, Vic, Barcelona) photographs and effigies of the King and Queen were hung upside down and burned.

Another indicator of Spain's continued troubles with its recent past are the difficulties it has had with its flag and anthem, fundamental symbols of the modern nation-state. The flag has become a contested symbol not so much for its design as for its connotations. The PP uses the flag profusely in a proprietary manner in all of its public acts, demonstrations and public protests against the current Socialist Government, and this use has led to criticism (Figures 5.4 and 5.5). The appearance of the Francoist version of the flag at these demonstrations is not uncommon. In 2007 in an attempt to find lyrics for the Spanish anthem, a contest was organized to collect proposals, but it failed after the winning entry was criticized for being overly patriotic and reminiscent of Francoist Spain because of its refrain of "viva España" – a common salute under the regime.

Breaking the silence and battles over memory
> *The impulse to preserve the thread of continuity is a crucial instinct of survival.*
>
> (Marris 1974: 17)

> *I now know that there are two "memories" of any Spanish event.*
>
> (Vilar 1977: xvii)

A poignant example of how memory battles of the war have recently been fought in Spain took place in the summer and fall of 2006. The 70-

5.4 The ironic legend reads: "One demonstrator with a flag counts for 100" (El Roto, *El País*, 17 March 2007: 17).

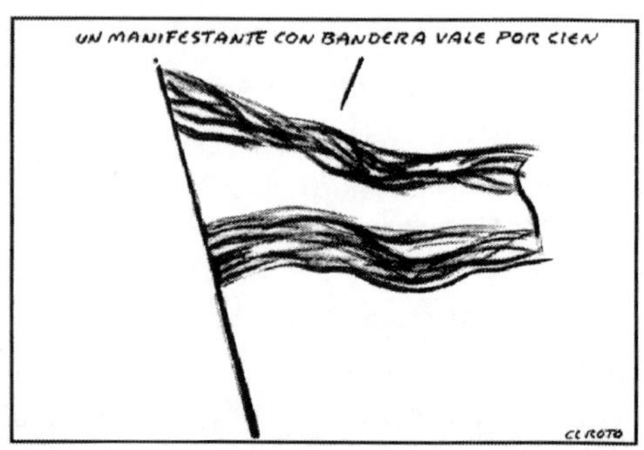

5.5 Photograph on the front cover of *El País* 2007; (23 March 2007; photo by Uly Martin), the caption reads: "The symbols of Franco and the Falange return to Madrid's avenues".

year anniversary of the military revolt inaugurated numerous commemorative events, television programmes, book presentations, articles, and special reports. Simultaneously, obituaries and commemorative death notices began to appear in newspapers on different sides of the political spectrum – *El País*, *El Mundo* and *ABC* – marking the anniversaries of people killed then. The tone of these obituaries often adopted the vocabulary of 1936: "vilely murdered by red hordes", "murderous bullets of the fascist repression", "genocidal coup leaders" (Figures 5.6 and 5.7). Grandchildren, nieces and nephews placed many of these notices. One woman who placed an obituary for her grandfather explained:

> *In my family we always knew that he had been executed, but we never spoke about the topic, my father never wished to tell us anything. I thought that now was the moment to do it. [...] It is up to us, the grandchildren, to do this, because it hurts the children too much. For them it is difficult. We have a bit more emotional distance, that is why it is our duty to do it.*
>
> (Tesón, *El País*, 10 September 2006: 29)

Her father seemed to agree:

> *I think it is good that my daughter published the obituary,*
> *although at first I objected. Perhaps because a lot of time has*
> *passed and facing all that is difficult for me. I was never able to*
> *pay homage to my father. In Spain Republican orphans were not*
> *allowed to mourn.*

(Tesón 2006: 29)

Occasionally, an obituary was placed by a son or daughter, such as José
Toribio Bravo who placed an obituary for his father. He explains:

> *For 40 years we could not do anything. I felt paralysed by that*
> *horrible dictatorship. Although with democracy we have begun to*
> *advance a little, it had to start being debated before we could*
> *dare to share what we carry inside.*

(Tesón 2006: 28)

Three themes have been leitmotifs of discussions around the recovery of
memory: duty (to remember), freedom to mourn, and daring to break a
silence and share experiences. There is also a recurrent idea throughout
the articles, interviews and 'letters to the editor' of the need for somehow
balancing out the scales, of a historic injustice that needs to be righted.
As many of these family members point out, the victorious had their

JULIÁN HERNÁNDEZ RUIZ

VÍCTIMA DE LA REPRESIÓN FRANQUISTA

Fue brutal y cobardemente asesinado, por conocidos elementos terroristas de Falange, en el salón de sesiones del Ayuntamiento de Santa Cruz de la Zarza (Toledo), en la madrugada del 30 de julio de 1947

Su sobrino, Félix Hernández Raboso, recuerda el valor de su sacrificio en la lucha por la LIBERTAD.

5.6 "Victim of the Francoist repression. Was brutally and
cowardly murdered, by known terrorist elements of the
Falange (. . .)", *El País*, July 2006.

†

70 ANIVERSARIO
RECUPERACIÓN DE LA MEMORIA HISTÓRICA DE

MANUEL BETETA CONTRERAS

VETERINARIO

Vilmente asesinado por las Hordas Rojas a los 36
años de edad el día 5 de septiembre de 1936 en
Socuéllamos (Ciudad Real).

Sus familiares RUEGAN una oración por su alma,
por el perdón de los culpables y por todos los
caidos de los dos bandos de la Guerra Civil.

5.7 "Vilely murdered by the Red
Hordes at 36 years of age (. . .)", *El
Mundo*, September 2006.

Causa General, their names on church walls, on streets and town squares. They had monuments, orations, and commemorations, while the other side had nothing, and was not allowed to memorialize, mourn, or retrieve the bodies of the loved ones lost during the war. Similar sentiments arise in the case of mass graves. In a letter to the editor of *El País* (Soto López, 9 March 2007: 18) a man writes to say that the name of his wife's grandfather, killed by the Republican side during the war, is on a plaque in the cemetery of the town where he was killed, near Toledo. Yet the body of his family member, executed by the Nationalist troops on entering Toledo, lies in an unmarked mass grave together with hundreds of other Republicans.

The Civil War and Dictatorship as heritage today

One of the activities that has attracted the most attention in the 'recovery of historic memory' has been the unearthing of unmarked and mass graves. This physical uncovering of a tragic buried past has become a metaphor for the process as a whole. It is thus revealing to note the reactions that these activities have provoked. The atmosphere described by archaeologists[29] coincides in that when working at these sites, usually situated on the outskirts of towns, locals were friendly when visiting the dig individually but then avoided any contact with the archaeologists encountered in town. Townspeople that visited the site were moved, curious, and anxious to share their personal memories or stories heard from others, yet preferred not to be seen by the rest of the community to be getting involved. The tension that still exists today in towns where people have cohabited for 70 years knowing who was on which side of the war and how they behaved during the Franco period, shows how restless the past can be and how long a spectre of fear can last.

The identification of mass graves is transforming the Spanish landscape both physically and symbolically: the new law promotes the creation of a map of Spain indicating the location of all unmarked graves. Furthermore, new memorials have now been built commemorating the International Brigades and victims of the Francoist repression, streets and squares are being named after Republican figures, and plaques are appearing on the façades of buildings explaining their past use as prisons.[30] Some neglected sites of the war are now being 'rediscovered', such as bunkers, or the subterranean passageways and shelters in Almería which was bombed for not having backed the military rebellion.

There are also new sites of memory emerging as a consequence of moves to recover the stories of those who lost the civil war. One example is the Carabanchel prison in Madrid which was built by the

Box 5.2   *The* Valle *in 2008*

The *Valle de los Caídos* and its future use has been a subject of heated debate. As part of Zapatero's government policy on dealing with the legacy of Franco, there have been discussions at the parliamentary level, among academics and in the media about how to deal with the *Valle de los Caídos*. The Law of the Historic Memory prohibits acts on the site that celebrate the Civil War or the Dictatorship. Nevertheless, in spite of pressure from several parliamentary groups, this law does not legislate for the transformation of the site into a museum about the dictatorship.

For those who spent time as prisoners constructing the *Valle*, an alternative would be to remove and transfer the remains of Primo de Rivera and Franco to their family graves, while creating an interpretation centre about the war, the dictatorship and the way the site was built (Sánchez Albornoz cited by Cue *El País*, 23 July 2006: 2–3). However, it is not only the political left that opposes the *Valle* remaining as it is. On the 20th of November 2007 tensions in and around the *Valle* were between Franco's supporters and the revived Spanish Falange. The latter demanded that José Antonio Primo de Rivera's body be removed from the site, where it lies as the 'proto-martyr' in a place of honour near Franco. The Falange claims that their leader has been made use of and should be returned to his 'rightful' burial place in El Escorial – traditional burial ground of the Spanish Kings and site where Franco originally permitted his interment.[33]

regime with prison labour (1940–44) and then used to interrogate and execute prisoners. The site was abandoned in 1999 and gradually became a ruin. In 2007, neighbourhood associations clashed with Madrid's local government over what to do with the site. One side wanted to turn it into a multi-purpose space with health, social and cultural facilities, including a permanent exhibition about the jail and the political prisoners once held there. The other side wanted to sell the space to a developer to build apartment buildings.[31] Other examples abound, including the *Valle de los Caidos* and the historic *Casa de Correos* (1766–68) on the *Puerta de Sol*, used by the regime as a detention and interrogation centre – and symbol of the repression and violence of the political police.[32]

Blatant in its intent and subtle in its impact, the reconstruction of Spain in the 1940s was inadequately funded, unevenly distributed and politically motivated. By creating monuments and memorials that were only valid for one side, the regime reinforced differences and prolonged a sense of division. Unexpressed memory and mourning continued to smoulder until a change in generation and circumstances made it possible for them to be revived and propelled by a 'need to know'. The troubled relationship that Spain still has with its recent past reveals a further stage in the reconstruction process which continues today, as the country struggles to come to terms with its historic and mnemonic 'inheritance' of the war and its aftermath.

Reconstructing *Guernica* and Gernika in the Transition

Guernica and Gernika in transition

In an attempt to seduce Picasso into the Falange in 1934, José Antonio Primo de Rivera told him: "One day we will receive you with an escort of the *Guardia Civil*, but as a guard of honour, and only then after we've insured your work" (Hensbergen 2004: 10). While Picasso would never again set foot in Spain, 47 years later Rivera's words came partly true, as *Guernica* arrived in Madrid escorted by an armed Civil Guard, and insured for far more than either man could have imagined in 1934. If Rivera had been the *Gran Ausente* of the Franco regime, *Guernica* was the *Gran Ausente* of the newly democratic Spain. Notably, both the Franco regime and the first government of the Transition led by Adolfo Suárez and the UCD performed symbolic acts of 'recovering' Spanish heritage. As seen earlier, in 1941 Franco's officials had orchestrated the return of the *Dama de Elche* spinning it into signifying Franco's recovery of 'authentic' Spanish heritage. Sixty years later, for the government of the Transition, a comparable act was the homecoming of Picasso s *Guernica*. The painting made its way from New York to Madrid on 25 October 1981, on the centenary of Picasso's birth, and 44 years after it was painted in Paris. Just as Gernika s destruction had come to crystallize the brutality of the Civil War, and *Guernica*'s exile was a reminder of the dictatorial nature and violent origins of the regime, so its homecoming symbolized the establishment of democracy and the return of exiled Spain. The significance of the event was captured in the words of Dolores Ibárruri who, standing before the painting, proclaimed: "The Civil War has ended" (Hensbergen 2004: 307). As a reminder that this democracy still stood on shaky ground, visitors to the *Casón del Buen Retiro* had to view the painting through bomb and bullet-proof glass and monitored by armed guards. In its first two days in Madrid over 5,000 Spaniards filed past the painting, and ten days later King Juan Carlos and Queen Sofía also paid homage.

A photograph showing Ibárruri standing in front of *Guernica* – two separate symbols, the woman and the painting, united – in turn became an icon of the Transition, revealing that new myths were created during this period.[34] The new myth constructed through this image was that the freshly born Spanish democracy was firmly established and contained enough freedom for the exiled symbols of the left to return and be welcomed publicly. One year later, in October 1982, the Spanish Socialist Party (PSOE) won the national elections. According to Hensbergen (2004: 309) "through its own transformation *Guernica* had helped psychologically to facilitate Spain's transition into a democracy." Yet, as we have seen, there were several other facets to the symbolism of both *Guernica* and Gernika, before this new one was added. This new meaning

5.8 Poster for the play *Cocidito Madrileño*, 2004.

5.9 Poster claiming *Guernica* for Gernika.

was at odds with some of the others and unsurprisingly the gesture lead to a conflict between those with claims to different interpretations.

In the first place, a polemic was raised regarding the 'rightful' destination of the painting. Among cities vying for the painting were Barcelona, Malaga, Bilbao and Gernika – the first two making claims based on Picasso's personal biography, Bilbao on the Basque element and Gernika on its undeniable link to its namesake. As already discussed, among the many cultural, political, economic and social transformations activated by the Spanish transition to democracy was the re-negotiation of national identity as regional groups asserted their identities and claimed varying degrees of self-government. The debates and conflicts over regional identity and autonomy critically marked this period within the Basque Country. As Gernika's symbolism as the capital of Basque liberty and self-rule was recovered publicly, both the painting and the image of the Tree were used to make political statements (Figures 5.8 and 5.9).

Guernica and Basque Nationalism

> *During the Transition, the history of the Basque exile was not written by historians but by journalists or by the protagonists themselves, the large majority of whom were nationalists. This contributed to creating an epic history of Basque opposition to Francoism, although with great differences between the visions of the moderate and the radical nationalists.*
>
> (de Pablo, *El País*, 7 October 2006, Babelia: 9)

The move of *Guernica* to Spain sparked an intense debate about where the painting should be exhibited, with many Basques arguing that it

5.10 Article from *El País*, 12 September 1981 reporting on protests in Gernika against installing the painting in Madrid (reproduced by Chipp 1989:187). The headline reads: "Protests in Euskadi against the installation of *Guernica* in the Casón del Buen Retiro. All the Basque political forces ask that the painting go to the town that inspired it".

should be in the Basque Country and not in Madrid. The language used was often confrontational, far removed from the peace symbolism that the painting had acquired. One way in which this was expressed was through a phrase coined by Xabier Arzalluz, President of the EAJ/PNV, repeated in various forms: "We put the blood and they keep the painting" (Rodríguez Fouz 2004:333). It was a fiery debate in a young democracy that had just survived an attempted military coup. The phrasing of some of the claims made no distinction between Franco's regime and the authorities of the Transition government when stating, for example, that the painting was going to be shown in the "capital of those who ordered the destruction" (*Deia*, 16 September 1981).[35]

Such claims over the painting also suffer from a selective vision of history. At the time of its exhibition at the World's Fair in 1937, Picasso offered the painting to the Basque Country saying: "if President Aguirre asks for it, the painting is for the Basque people". Aguirre declined the offer and Ucelay, the curator of the Basque section of the pavilion, criticized the work, calling it 'pornography' (Unzueta, *El País*, 22 November 1981). Claims for possession of the painting that accuse Madrid and the democratically elected Spanish government of the bombing obfuscate the past. On the one hand, at the time of Gernika's bombing in 1937 Madrid was itself being bombarded on a daily basis by Nationalist aviation.[36] On the other, it equates a democratically elected government precisely with the military rebels of 1937 that were trying to overthrow a democratically elected Spanish government. *Guernica* became the site of struggle and contestation, literal and metaphorical, through which political parties and interest groups in the Basque Country claimed it from Madrid. With the vast doses of symbolism and emotions that the painting engenders, this verbal battle over its fate took place within the larger context of redefining national symbolism and regional identity in post-Franco Spain. But the painting was not alone in being usurped for political purposes. The symbolism of Gernika was also used.

Symbolic violence: Politics, terrorism, and cultural heritage

The large number of Basque political prisoners in the 1960s and 1970s and the continuation of violence in the Basque Country after Franco's death meant that in this region the political pact of silence and forgetting was not easily accepted. Hence, the Transition was viewed differently in the Basque Country from elsewhere in Spain:

> *While in 1994 over 80% of Spaniards said they felt proud of the way that the transition had been carried out, less than 50% of Basques felt the same way (…) in 1985 over 45% of Spaniards affirmed that Francoism had been part good and part bad for Spain, only 20% of Basques responded in this way and over 55% said that Francoism had only been bad for Spain.*
>
> (Aguilar Fernández 2002: 148)

Here the Transition, while initiating a period of increased autonomy and prosperity, also inaugurated a new phase of conflict. The development of the cultural and social identity of the Basque Country has been so intertwined with the conflict that continued after Franco's death that it is often difficult to extricate one from the other. The main protagonists in this conflict have been Euzkadi Ta Askatasuna (ETA) and the central government, with its attempts to dissolve the group. This is not the subject of this volume and giving a brief overview would risk a counter-productive simplification of a complex issue. Nevertheless, there are cultural and symbolic elements associated with Basque separatist violence that are worthy of mention here as they reveal the multiple dimensions of material culture and its symbols.

Having been created in 1959, ETA's emergence on the scene as a revolutionary organization occurred in 1962 when its founding members issued a statement from exile defining ETA as "a clandestine revolutionary organization with three fronts: cultural, political and military" (Clark 1979: 157).[37] ETA's *Frente Cultural* had as its mission to counter "the destruction of Basque culture by the Spanish state" (Hollyman 1976: 223–224). Aside from military and police, ETA also targeted symbols. In 1972 in a town of Guipúzcoa called Villafranca de Ordica, the monument to the fallen was attacked with an explosive device and destroyed (AGA-CIFRA gráfica. 03.082-F/01343). The *ikurriña* had already been a contentious marker during the Franco period; as one man remembers:

> *On the feast of San Juan in Bermeo, I hung the ikurriña from the church spire. That was in 1959, twenty years after my return from France. Too early! They found out, and I spent months in jail. They beat me so that I still limp.*
>
> (Legarreta 1984: 290)

After Franco's death the *ikurriña* was used as an aggressive symbolic marker of territory and independence. Not only were claims made to legalize it, but *ikurriñas* were booby-trapped, successfully wounding and killing a number of Civil Guards as they tried to take them down (Preston 2001: 154, 246). Gernika was not free from symbolic violence, either. The statue of Don Tello erected in 1966 was repeatedly attacked with paint balls and dynamite (Urtea, *Aldaba*, 1987) and in 1994 a Molotov cocktail was thrown at the historic *Casa de Juntas* (part of a *kaleborroka* action)[38] provoking a flurry of accusations. Xabier Arzalluz lashed out in the newspaper *Deia* (28 November 1994) inciting a quick response in *Egin*,[39] which published a police report saying that the attack had targeted a policeman standing guard and not the building (Raento and Watson 2000: 731).

Gernika also began to renew its symbolic landscape, replacing Francoist symbols, such as the double headed imperial eagle taken down from the Town Hall, and changing street names.[40] In some cases former names were restored, in others new names were given – the *Calle de la Victoria* changed to *Esteban de Zabala*, among others – and in all cases street names were written in Basque[41] (Figures 5.11 and 5.20).

5.11 Market Street/ Azokakalea.

Gernika: breaking the silence and recovering memory

Silence is a method of internalizing of the human being faced with barbarism and desolation.

(Oar-Arteta March 2006: 24)

During and after the Transition a priority within Basque political and cultural circles became the recovery of the history and efforts of the Basque government during the war and in exile. In 1975 the Bidasoa Institute was set up as the historical wing of the PNV;[42] one of its main missions was to ensure that documentation of the activities of the Basque government from 1936–37 was not lost (Rankin, *TLS*, 6 July 2007:5). From 1975 a number of publications appeared dedicated to the bombing of the town. After 1975, a change occurred in the significance given to various commemorations. Gernika became an important site for the celebration of the *Aberri Eguna*. Both ETA and the PNV made use of a different symbol associated with the town to call for participation in the *Aberri Eguna* held in Gernika on 30 March 1975 (figs 5.12 and 5.13 both use the red, white and green *ikurriña* flag); a flyer distributed by the PNV entitled *Aberri Eguna 1975 en Gernika* read:

> *On the 5th of November 1933 the Basque people manifested through a plebiscite their desire for autonomy. After 38 years the regime that suppressed our liberties is in the process of disappearing. During the Aberri Eguna of last year, President Leizaola came here clandestinely to be under the tree of Gernika and make blatant to our people and also to the regime the permanence of that government born of the will of our people. This year, 1975 the Basque Nationalist Party calls to all those affiliated to it and to all the Basque people to come to Gernika to peacefully manifest their will for liberty their will to decide their destiny and their solidarity with all of their men in prison or in exile for their defence of the Basque people*
>
> (signed "Gora Euzkadi, Azkatuta, PNV").[43]

The momentum to recover a silenced history was evidenced in other ways. On the 26th of April 1976, five months after Franco's death, and on the occasion of the first public commemoration of the bombing to be held in Gernika, the *Gernika Batzordea* (Gernika Commission) was created with three principle aims: to clear the Basques of all responsibility for the destruction of Gernika, to investigate the bombing and discover responsibilities for it, and to obtain *Guernica* for Gernika. In the history of the recovery of memory in Gernika, the decennial anniversaries of the bombing proved to be important catalysts spurring subsequent flurries of publications.[44]

5.12 ETA flyer using the painting.

5.13 EAJ/PNV flyer using the Tree. (Note they both use the *ikurriña*).

Anniversaries of the bombing

The 40th anniversary in 1977, the first not celebrated in secret, addressed the historiographic problem surrounding the destruction of the town. Key historians of the event were present, and they gathered symbolically under the tree: Fernando García de Cortázar, Ángel Viñas, Luis Ruiz de Aguirre, Herbert Southworth and Manuel Tuñón de Lara (Figure 5.15). This was the first time that the 'other' historiography of the bombing could be voiced publicly in Spain to contrast the official version still being supported by some historians.[45] The event echoed in the Basque press – in particular the recently established *Deia*. On this significant occasion *Guernica* made a public appearance in the town in the form of a massive banner reproducing the painting (Figure 5.14). Then, on 25 October 1979 the *Estatuto de Autonomía del País Vasco* (Statute of Autonomy of the Basque Country) was approved, establishing a system of regional government and reinstating the position of *Lehendakari*. The Statute is known as the *Estatuto de Gernika*.

5.14 Demonstration during the 40th anniversary in Gernika, April 1977.

5.15 Historians gathered in Gernika, June 1977.

The 50th anniversary was especially important for generating a series of initiatives. In February 1986 the *Comisión de Trabajo para Conmemorar el 50 Aniversario del Bombardeo de Guernica* (Working Group for the Commemoration of the 50th Anniversary of the Bombing of Gernika) was created. This Commission recognized the peace symbolism of Picasso's painting and reached an agreement with the Department of Culture of the Basque Government to commission a monument.[46]

> *We want to commemorate the anniversary of this massacre, not from a negative viewpoint, masochistically, but rather in order to gain a positive lesson, to propose Gernika as an international symbol of peace, more so when considering the global fame of this crime, not for the number of dead nor the circumstances that produced it but because Picasso's painting that symbolizes the event has taken root on a world scale.*
>
> (Basque Counsellor of Culture quoted by Abrisketa, *DEIA*, 20 February 1987)

In the end, two monuments were added to Gernika's heritage-scape. Sponsored by the Basque government, Eduardo Chillida's *Gure Aitaren Etxea* and Henry Moore's *Large Figure in a Shelter* (Figures 5.16 and 5.17) were followed by others on the 60th and 70th anniversaries (Appendix G). In Gernika's complex symbolism, the Chillida sculpture is the most significant. As the Basque visual artist of greatest international renown, Chillida was commissioned to create a 'monument to peace'. The title of his creation *Gure Aitaren Etxea* is revealing as it means 'Our Father's House'. The large sculpture creates a semi-circular space in which the viewer stands next to the *estela* (a traditional funerary marker) while

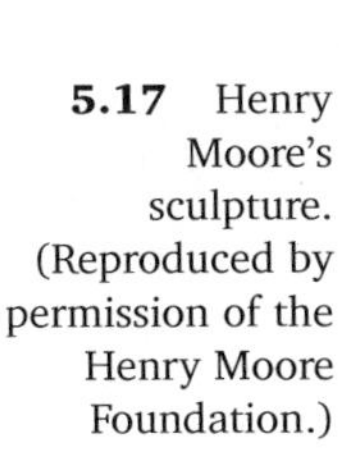

5.16 Eduardo Chillida's monument.

5.17 Henry Moore's sculpture. (Reproduced by permission of the Henry Moore Foundation.)

looking out through the cut stone toward the Tree of Gernika.[47] It thus links by means of its name and its physicality the concepts of peace, monument, memorial, and the confirmation of Gernika as the spiritual home of the Basques.[48]

The association of the commemoration with a symbolism of peace was carried through with a meeting held in the *Casa de Juntas* on the day of the anniversary with representatives of the *Unión Mundial de Ciudades por la Paz* (World Union of Cities for Peace).[49] Further initiatives from 1987 include the creation of a Gernika Peace Forum, a peace research centre *Gernika Gogoratuz* (Remembering Gernika) and a town twinning initiative launched with the German town of Pforzheim.[50] Thus, the anniversary brought about considerable developments in the association of Gernika with a symbolism of peace. Furthermore, it was on this occasion that survivors of the bombing were invited to participate in the commemorative events. The inclusion of this group was a valuable step for the recovery of the memory of the tragedy and for Gernika's community to come to terms with its history. This first experience had mixed results however, as some participants felt used and paraded like museum pieces, rather than being heard.[51] One of the missions of *Gernika Gogoratuz* over the next few years was to improve this situation. The anniversary also spurred publications and exhibitions about the bombing (Figure 5.18).

In the 1990s the memorial landscape of Gernika was transformed by two further additions. In 1994 a mausoleum was built in the town's cemetery to house the remains of the victims of the bombing. On the wall outside the mausoleum, the façade of which simply has the date of the bombing and the word *pax*,[52] hangs a bell from the disappeared church of San Juan (Figure 5.19). This bell is tolled each year on the anniversary, as a reminder of when it rang in 1937 to warn of the enemy planes approaching. In 1996 another addition was made in the form of a full-scale ceramic mural reproducing *Guernica*, commissioned by the City Council, and placed at one end of a centrally located street (Figure 5.21).

5.18 1991 Exhibition in Gernika.

5.19 Mausoleum and bell in Gernika's cemetery.

The 60th anniversary events were held in Gernika's market and were significant for three developments: the reconciliation with Germany, the voicing of testimonies by the survivors of the bombing, and the talk of peace contrasting with demands that the Spanish government take responsibility. The reconciliation with Germany was a result of ten years of negotiations by Petra Kelly of the German Green Party, who lobbied the Bundestag for a gesture of reconciliation and acknowledgement of the Condor Legion's participation in the bombing. On the occasion of the 60th anniversary, a letter from the German President Roman Herzog was sent to each individual survivor and then read publicly during the ceremony by the German Ambassador to Spain on 26 April 1997. In the statement he acknowledges the participation of the German Condor Legion, expresses a desire to join the surviving witnesses in mourning and makes a plea for reconciliation (full statement reproduced in Appendix H).

The survivors of the bombing responded with a statement of their own, read by Luis Iriondo, who lived through the bombing as a child and who has become their spokesperson:

> *And they rained down fire, shrapnel and death on us. And they destroyed our town. And that night we couldn't go back home for our supper, or sleep in our beds. We had no home anymore. We had no house. But that event, which was so incomprehensible to us, left no feelings of hate or vengeance in us – only a huge, immense desire for peace, and for such events never to happen again. A flag of peace should rise up from the ruins of what was our town for all the peoples of the world.*
>
> (Iriondo 1997)

The active participation of survivors in voicing their memories publicly was of great significance. This development was partly the result of an attitude shift in Spanish historiography that had previously prioritized scholarly research over personal memories and accounts regarded as unreliable. In Gernika, the appreciation of oral history and in particular of the power of witness and testimony was strengthened by the publication of the book *Memoria Colectiva del Bombardeo de Gernika* (Cava Mesa 1996), a collection of oral histories of the bombing assembled by Professor Cava Mesa and her colleagues at the Universidad de Deusto. This publication and the numerous interviews entailed in producing it helped to legitimize the memories silenced for so long and confirmed the testimonial value of their keepers.[53] Some of this material was used for the documentary *The Mark of Men* edited by *Gernika Gogoratuz* (1998). For the first time, those people who had witnessed the bombing were called on to share deeply buried and previously censored memories.

The gesture by the German government, while welcomed by Gernikans, also spurred controversy.[54] Namely, it rekindled demands for the same gesture to be made by the government in Madrid. During the ceremony and in response to Herzog's letter, the Mayor of Gernika, Eduardo Vallejo, ended his speech saying:

> *I want to demand that the great lie, coined by the dictator, that made the pain of the tragedy more acutely felt, venting his anger on the Basques, who were accused of having destroyed our own town, be officially undone and free the Basques from that infamy, that while cleared by history since the first instance, has never been officially recognized by Spanish governments.*
> (Vallejo, speech 26 April 1997)

The transfer of the grudge from Germany to the Spanish state exhibits an amalgamation of the perpetrators of the bombing with the Spanish government. This discourse, cemented throughout the 1980s and 1990s, is still recurrent today and has provoked frustration on the part of those working toward developing Gernika as a symbol and generator of peace.[55] By using the peace-bearing message of Germany as a stick with which to attack the Spanish state, the gesture was undermined. As argued earlier, demands that today's democratically elected government apologize for the actions of military insurgents who overthrew a democratically elected government demonstrate the selective nature of 'memories' being called on in this conflict.[56] Yet the conflation of contemporary demands and grievances with historical injustices is one that recurs repeatedly in situations of conflict, and requires examination.

Despite these tensions, the recovery of memory and association with peace movements continued to be a motivating dynamic. The project "Initiative 60 Years Gernika – Against Forgetting" was launched and an international conference was organized in 1999 entitled "The Basque Exile, 60 years on". The identification of Gernika with peace work also continued to develop. The Gernika Museum, which had been created in 1998, was refurbished and reopened on 8 January 2003 as a Peace Museum. It joined the International Network of Museums for Peace and became a member of the International Committee of Memorial Museums for Remembrance of Victims of Public Crimes.

Gernika and *Guernica*: evolution of a relationship

Once it became clear that the painting would be transferred to Spain, the town of Gernika made a move to create a more explicit link between itself and its namesake. Thus, in Gernika, the painting's 'return', was marked not only by controversy but also by the change of a street name. The street *Fernando el Católico* that runs along the site where the old market area had been was renamed *Pablo Picasso* (Figure 5.20). The initiative for the name change was taken by the *Comisión Informativa de Cultura* and

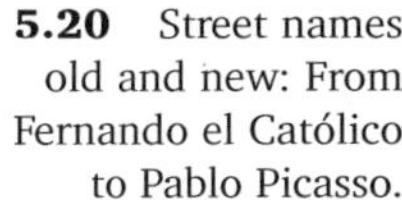

5.20 Street names old and new: From Fernando el Católico to Pablo Picasso.

a memo attached to the official document of the report, dated 9 July 1981, states that the street in question runs "next to the Ferial (reminder of the *Guernica*) and is an important and authentic street" (*Ayuntamiento de Gernika*. 1981. Doc. no. 1557. Sig. 2328/9). By doing so, Gernika paid tribute to the artist who had made the town's suffering known around the world. But the relationship between the town and the painting has been more complicated. As we saw, one of the goals of the *Comisión Investigadora del Bombardeo* (created in 1977) was to claim Picasso's *Guernica* for Gernika. In April 1987, a group from the *Comisión Gernika 37–87* went to the Casón del Buen Retiro where *Guernica* was being exhibited and demonstrated through a sit-in in front of the painting (*Punto y Hora de Euskal Herria*, 16–30 April 1987: 32–33). In an article from 1988 the spokesman of the *Comisión Investigadora del Bombardeo*, Karmelo Landa, was quoted as saying: "The symbolism of Gernika has to be united with nationalist claims" (Jauregi in *Egin* Sunday, 24 April 2008:8).[57]

The debate about where the painting should be exhibited has been repeatedly revived at the time of the anniversaries of the bombing and on other occasions such as the construction of the Guggenheim in Bilbao. In 1996 a mural was commissioned by the city Council of Gernika from a Catalan ceramics company (*Cerámicas Queralt*) based in Berga, a town twinned with Gernika. Based on a proposal from the *Ayuntamiento* (exp.2926/20. 1996) approved and carried out by *Kultur Extea*, this ceramic mural of Picasso's *Guernica* was planned "in order to be able to count with a ceramic reproduction of Picasso's *Guernica* painting in the town". There are two revealing points concerning this monument (Figure 5.21). The first is that beneath the reproduction was included the legend: "Guernica Gernikara" (Guernica to/for Gernika), thus inscribing in the

5.21 Mural of *Guernica* in Gernika. (© Succession Picasso/DACS, London 2010.)

town's landscape its demand for the painting. According to the City Council, "Its presence (the mural and its inscription) has the testimonial value of a popular social petition" (that of having Picasso's painting in the town of Gernika). The second is that despite the fiery statement, the City Council had to argue at length with the residents of the buildings on whose wall (the enclosure of a car park) the mural was to be installed. In the end the Council was obliged to build a fake wall in front of the existing one to position the tiles. Furthermore, these residents refused to have their property altered so that the mural could be centered; with the result that the image is misaligned in what could have been a dramatic perspective.[58] This conflict flags up a dichotomy between the symbolic and the quotidian life of Gernika that will reemerge.

For the *Comisión de Investigación del bombardeo de Guernica* the painting is "a living denunciation of the fight against fascism and symbolizes the fight for the attainment of democratic liberties" (*Suplementos Deia*, Sunday, 29 January 1978: 7). Basque prisoners have painted copies on their prison walls, and in the 1998 regional elections a reproduction of *Guernica* was used as the backdrop for the reading of the electoral results. Each appearance underscores the symbolic nature of the painting but also adds a new layer to that symbolism. As has been pointed out by Rodríguez Fouz (2004: 240–241), the choice of *Guernica* as a backdrop for the *Lehendakari* to read the election results was revealing. As an act of performing Basque democracy it was not the tree of Gernika, symbol of the *fueros*, that was called on but the painting of the town's destruction. Fouz suggests that this indicates the extent to which the painting has become a unifying Basque symbol – assimilated even by Basque institutions – but it also demonstrates how the conflict with Madrid is ubiquitous in Basque politics. The painting is used simultaneously as an accusation, reminder and demand of the central government in Madrid:

accusation of responsibility in the destruction and violence then and now, reminder of the historic crime, and demand for the painting to be given to the Basque Country. The painting thus becomes shorthand for the conflict with Madrid, as well as a symbol around which Basque society can gather, with the ensuing danger that these two strands become conflated.[59]

Gernika in 2007

The false narrative constructed, imposed, and repeated by the Franco regime in relation to Gernika's destruction was a constant affront to those who had witnessed the bombing. The imposition of the 'official story', accompanied by the threat of punishment for contesting it, made it almost impossible for alternative narratives to be heard. These narratives, when they were voiced, were relegated to the domestic sphere where only children or grandchildren ever heard them.[60] According to Juan Gutiérrez, it produced a "culture of silence that penetrated even to the survivors" (prologue to Cava Mesa 1996: 11). This part of the story explains why publicly giving voice to the testimonies of the event that refuted the false narrative that had been imposed for nearly 40 years continues to be so important.

Today in Gernika the story of the bombing has a public platform, though not all of the remaining survivors have been willing to speak about their memories and experiences. Those who have been willing and able to speak have been heard through various supports that comprise the 'public sphere': radio, television, books, newspapers, ceremonies, school classrooms and cafés. There is, however, a fragment of history over which there is still silence, and that is the Franco period: the memories of this period are not so readily shared.

Evolution of Gernika's meanings: Peace symbolism and the 70th anniversary
While the Zapatero Government declared 2006 the Year of the Recovery of Historic Memory, the city of Gernika has been recovering its memory of the bombing since the very moment of the event. The anniversaries have acted as catalytic events and offered a sort of catharsis, becoming platforms through which to negotiate the painful past and finally 'set the record straight'; they have also spurred a growing emphasis on the town as a motor for peace.

Significantly, after each of the anniversaries a shift of emphasis can be observed in the cultural institutions of Gernika. From focusing on trying to right the historical record and collecting the living memory of the events and the testimony of witnesses, an emphasis on the construction of peace progressively gained ground (Table 5.4). In the context of ETA's

Table 5.4 Evolution of Gernika's symbolism since the 50th anniversary

2001	Gernika and the museum participated in the EU project "Paths of Memory" (www.pathsofmemory.net)
2002–2003	Gernika receives UNESCO's Cities for Peace Prize
2003	Museum of Gernika (1998)was re-inaugurated as the Gernika Peace Museum
2003	Bombing Documentation Centre is inaugurated
2003	Basque delegation protests at the covering of the tapestry of *Guernica* that hangs outside the Security Council meeting room.
2005	Gernika hosts the 5th International Conference of Peace Museums
2005	Gernika joins Mayors for Peace
2006	Bust of the journalist G. L. Steer is inaugurated
2007	Manifesto *Gernika for Peace* is presented and read
2007	Nobel Peace Prize winner, Adolfo Pérez Esquibel's speech

activities the word 'peace' in the Basque Country is politically charged, and the fact that the city that represents the 'heart and soul' of the region chooses to identify itself with the concept of peace is significant. This constitutes a further stage in the reconstruction of the city.

This concept of peace being drawn is far from straightforward though. The last half of the Franco period emphasized the regime's success in maintaining peace, in order not only to strengthen support for the regime but to insinuate a persistent threat. Such was the success of this rhetoric that in the public opinion polls held in 1966, 1975 and 1976, Spaniards chose peace over justice, freedom or liberty as the most significant political value (Aguilar-Fernández 2006: 263–264). Furthermore, by the time of the 50th anniversary in 1987 the Basque Country had experienced twelve years of violence since Franco's death in which ETA continued their attacks despite the autonomy gained by the 1978 Constitution. The democratic government had also responded to ETA's violence with violent measures, prolonging a climate of conflict. In this context, loudly claiming for peace from the symbolic site of Gernika was a daring act.

The 70th anniversary in 2007 strongly emphasized the peace symbolism that had been developing, and it did so significantly at both the Basque and international levels. The *Lehendakari* Ibaretxe took advantage of his planned presence at the commemorative events to launch a Peace Manifesto. This Manifesto was presented in a special exhibition set up in the *Plaza de los Fueros* which included a reproduction of *Guernica* made up of passport photos of locals (Figure 5.25). In his speech Ibaretxe called on

70th Anniversary ceremonies, 26th April 2007

5.22 Ceremony at the *casa de Juntas* with Mayors of other 'martyr cities' in the front row.

5.23 Lighting an 'eternal flame' and signing a Peace Manifesto by the Tree.

5.24 Memorial service at the cemetery.

Gernika's symbolism to be a motor for peace building. On the international level, during the commemorative ceremony held in the *Casa de Juntas*, the Nobel Peace Prize laureate Adolfo Pérez Esquivel received the Gernika Peace and Reconciliation Award, thereby calling on Gernika's symbolism to make a call for peace. The ceremony also included speeches by the Mayors of other 'martyred' cities such as Hiroshima and Dresden. The public at these ceremonies included representatives of Gernikan and Basque institutions, participants in the colloquium organized by *Gernika Gogoratuz* and survivors of the bombing[61] (Figures 5.22 to 5.27). A new documentary, "The Gernika Story – *El bombardeo de Gernika*", including testimonials from several Gernikans, was shown, and a lunch was offered for the survivors of the bombing. Those invited to the latter included

At the Plaza de los Fueros

5.25 *Guernica* reproduced using photos of locals.

5.26 A survivor relating his war memories.

5.27 Three former *Lehendakaris* in Gernika.

Representatives of the three War Children Associations of the Basque Country, representatives of the survivors of the bombings of Otxandio and Durango, as well as Ernst-Albrecht von Moreau, nephew of Rudolf von Moreau, officer of the Condor Legion.

The presence of mayors from other bombed cities introduces a further issue in the creation of meanings in Gernika during the anniversaries, for depending on the comparison that is made a different set of meanings are implied. Linking Gernika and Dresden, for instance, sends a different message than linking Gernika and Hiroshima. By referring to Pearl Harbour in 1944, an event which three years earlier had launched the United States into the Second World War, the message that Aguirre y

Lecube (1944: 29–30) intended to transmit was that Gernika's bombard-ment should have sparked Allied involvement in Spain. Likewise, refer-ences to Gernika during the siege of Sarajevo in the mid-1990s, during the bombing of the Old City of Nablus in 2002 and during the aerial attacks on Gaza in December 2008 were intended to raise international attention and ultimately intervention.

The recovery of memory in Gernika today

On 17th April 2007, as part of the activities surrounding the 70th anniversary, a colloquium was organized in Gernika's *Elai Alai*, on the bombings of Durango and Gernika. The historian Vicente del Palacio addressed what he described as the decalogue of points about the bombing still in dispute.[63] In the auditorium there was a group of elderly women sitting together who had experienced the bombing as children. When the floor was opened for discussion some of these women picked up on the point, briefly mentioned by Palacio, about the looting that had taken place in the hours and days immediately following the bombing. One woman in particular recounted that her mother had told her of objects – family heirlooms, silverware, and wedding rings – that had disappeared from the ruins of their house. This reproach reflects one of many ways that the bombing changed Gernika's community, becoming an unspoken undercurrent of resentment.[64] Another aspect of tension that still exists in Gernika concerns the issues of participation and repre-sentation. While some people are more willing and ready to share their experiences than others, those that lived through the bombing but are not invited to participate can feel that their experiences are not equally valued.[65] For there are still Gernikans that do not want to speak about the bombing they witnessed as children.[66] These two anecdotes illustrate how memories of perceived injustice and injury persist, and how they can affect community relations, even 70 years after the event. They also reveal the complexities of giving voice and testimonial roles to individu-als to relate the traumatic experience of a group, and how to represent and not exclude those unwilling or unable to speak. The reasons for silence might also be the result of an amnesia that is not willed but a self-defence mechanism that consists of self-censorship. In her study of Basque refugee children, their experiences in exile and return to Spain, Legarreta quotes one of her interviewees:

> I don't know how we survived, or brought something to eat to
> my father in Larriñaga prison. I believe we lived in a state of
> amnesia because I can't remember anything except from time to
> time we ate, sometimes carob beans we got from animal
> nosebags and turnips foraged from the fields.
>
> (Legarreta 1984: 285)

Another of her interviewees gives an explanation for her silence:

> *A family member, whom I was unable to draw into a political conversation, told me, 'Dorothy, for forty years we could only talk about the weather or the crops; now we are unable to talk about anything else.'*
>
> (Legarreta 1984: 290)

The public acknowledgement of all that was lost in the bombing is a relatively recent phenomenon dating from the 60th anniversary. One of the projects of *Gernikazarra* has been to create a map of pre-war Gernika, collecting images of the buildings, streets and people that made up the town. Ricardo Arrien, who lived through the bombing as a 10-year-old, has run a programme called *In illo témpore* (In that time) on the local television station *Oizmendi* (Mount Oiz) in which he shared anecdotes, songs, photographs and documents from pre-war Gernika. He explained the importance of showing Gernika's past: "We do it because for a time everything was erased from us"[67] (cited by Lamarca 2007: 50). This thirst for images of Gernika before the bombing recurs in the accounts of those that, as children, survived the bombing. There is a yearning for photographs of friends and family members never seen again, of one's own youthful innocence pre-bombing, of the condition that family homes were left in by the bombs; the few images that do survive have become treasured objects, framed and taking place of honour on mantelpieces. The absence of images together with the trauma of the event provoked some amnesia; Consuelo Aguirre-Amalloa lost all memories of her first communion which took place 15 days before the bombing (Lamarca 2007: 54). The absence of images not only from the public sphere but also from the most intimate corners of survivor's memories also helps to explain the iconographic significance that Picasso's painting has for this town. Furthermore, memory can be fickle. Research by local historians has only recently revealed the existence of a military hospital for prisoners – *Hospital Militar Nacional de Prisioneros de Guerra de Gernika-Lumo* – situated in Gernika and used both as a hospital and as a prison for the *Batallón de Trabajadores* of Gernika (Etxaniz Ortúñez and Palacio Sánchez 2002: 41). Despite the evidence they found few traces of the hospital and its function in the memories of Gernikans.[68]

Gernika's heritage-scape 70 years later

For those who remember the pre-war town, today's town-scape includes a phantom layer of houses and streets remembered. When looking at today's market square, Luis Iriondo sees the place where his childhood home used to be. Near this market square, where the bust commemorating George L Steer stands today, some still see the

5.28   Bust of Steer inaugurated in 2006.

5.29   The Old Tree in its *templete*.

5.30   The New Tree planted in 2005.

phantom building of the church of San Juan. These phantom sites do not only exist in the memories of those who knew the original buildings, they also crop up in paintings by local artists, in newspapers, magazines, radio shows, publications and in the imaginations of those who have heard the stories of the 'witness generation'. This vision of how Gernika used to be will disappear as those who knew it firsthand pass on, but it will linger among their descendants, local artists and historians who have imagined that lost town-scape. Paintings of the lost church of San Juan, for example, were included in an exhibition by a local painter Julen Munitis in the *Kultur Etxea* – Culture House – in September 2006. Memories of lost childhood homes also linger[69] and remains are cherished like the bar *El Paso* that recalls a pathway through the rubble of a town in ruins. Also vividly remembered are those scarce objects rescued from ruined houses, such as the gold coin that Ricardo Arrien's father had hidden under a leg of the dining room table (Lamarca 2007: 50).

Gernika's symbolism as 'spiritual capital' remains intact and is the one most frequently cited when Gernikans are asked about the town's symbolic importance (Cava Mesa 1996: 259–262). Thus the town has also retained its close ties with the *Fueros* and the associated concepts of autonomy and democratic rule. This meaning is regularly reinforced by references to the *Estatuto de Gernika*, by the numerous ceremonial occasions organized there by the Basque government, and by the speeches made there by successive *Lehendakaris*.[70] This symbolism is intimately linked to the Tree.

On the ceiling of the *Casa de Juntas* is a 235 m^2 stained glass window representing the Tree and peoples of Vizcaya. In the park outside this meeting house are three generations of sacred trees: the *arbol viejo,* whose trunk stands in a small neo-classical *templete* built especially for it; the acting tree standing in front of the shrine, and the designated heir growing behind it (Figures 5.29 and 5.30). There is a plantation of saplings of descendants of The Oak, so even if the individual trees die, its replacement is held to be of the same hereditary lineage. Several trees have successively held the 'post' of Arbol Foral (see Appendix I for a chronology). In 1991 the Tree became infected with a fungus and died in 2004. As there were fears that its 25-year old successor had also been infected, a generation was skipped and a younger uninfected tree (15–20 year-old) was selected, essentially taking a 'grandchild' instead of a 'child'. The planting of a new tree in 2005 – an event that had not occurred since 1892 – was widely reported in the media thus providing a revealing source of material on the significance of the Tree today. [71]

The newspaper *Deia* (31 July 2004: 12) highlighted three statements made by Ana Madariaga, President of the *Juntas Generales* of Vizcaya, by putting them in separate textboxes under three categories: eternal, bombing and peace. The excerpts read as follows: "Our Tree is a symbol and a symbol never dies, it is eternal"; "Aguirre swore his charge under the Tree shortly before the bombing"; "The new one will be a witness of times of peace and liberty for all of Euskadi". In these comments is the core of the tree's symbolism: its resilience and continuity, its ability to create an unbroken link between the past and the present that resists and perseveres over the bombing. The tree continues to be a 'living symbol' even though the oak tree that survived the civil war did not survive the Transition. It is no coincidence that the Basque 'Archive of Genealogies' is housed a few meters away from the current tree. In 1999 the Tree and the Meeting House were included on the list of sites that Spain submitted to UNESCO for inclusion on the World Heritage List.

The ceremony that takes place annually in the cemetery of Gernika evokes the event of the bombing by starting at half past four in the afternoon, the approximate hour at which bombing began, with the ringing of the same bells that announced the arrival of enemy planes. In this moment the event as a reality and as a symbol are merged. As a reality, Gernika's bombing is still a site of contestation today as the facts of the bombing continue to be researched and clarified. Yet, these facts have long been obscured by the powerful symbolism of the event. As Elorza remarks:

> *The disaster of Guernica was to be a key piece in the affirmation of Basque nationalism during the twentieth-century, it was to become one of those great symbolic moments that work against those that cause them and become decisive pieces in favour of the historic destiny of the victims.*
>
> (Elorza in Tuñón de Lara 1987: 13)

So much myth-making has informed the bombing that it is difficult to separate the two. Gernika's destruction combined with the painting became such a powerful symbol that not only did it obscure the aerial bombing of many other cities and civilians during the war, but it also came to obscure the everyday reality of the destruction suffered by the city. The resilience of Gernika's pre-war symbolism is remarkable, especially given the degree of destruction it suffered with observers saying "Gernika has ceased to exist".[72] Yet that symbolism is today interwoven with the events of its destruction and all the new meanings that followed.[73]

As described earlier, reproductions of *Guernica* became a sign of resistance in the homes of progressive Spaniards during the 1960s and 70s. On 17 May 1999, shortly after being re-inaugurated as the Gernika *Peace* Museum, International Museum Day was celebrated by giving away reproductions of Picasso's *Guernica* to the first 100 people to visit the museum (*Deia*, 16 May 1999: 10). Reproductions of the painting, often appearing on tiles or as a small mural, can today be found hanging in the entrance halls of many homes in Gernika; in some cases it has even moved to the front façade of houses. As we saw earlier, reproductions of the painting became symbolic objects, so much so that Manuel Vicent remarked:

> . . . *to me it always seemed that the "Guernica" that arrived in*
> *Spain was false, because the authentic one was the small*
> *postcard format that we all had stuck to a wall of the studio*
> *with four thumbtacks.*
> (Vicent, *El País Semanal*, 21 May 2006)

The move of the reproductions to the façades of Gernika's houses can be interpreted as an act of affirmation and defiance, a public statement, and a marker of place and meaning on the visual plane of the city. Reproductions of the painting now co-exist on the same visual plane as images of Gernika's Tree (Figures 5.31 to 5.33).

Guernica and Gernika as international symbols

On an international level, the painting trumped the event, becoming *the* image that came to mind in response to the sign that is the word: Guernica or Gernika. In 2007, Gernika existed both as a physical *lieu de memoire*, a town that could be walked through and 'read', but also as a symbol in a common international repertoire. It is in this latter aspect that Picasso's painting has had the biggest impact, its name being associated with an image of the horrors of war. In the immediate aftermath of the Second World War, US Senator Borah said of it: "Here fascism presents to the world its masterpiece; it has hung on the walls of civilisation,

5.31 Façade in Lumo using both images.

5.32 Restaurant and bar 'Gernika' using Picasso's painting.

5.33 A local bakery and café using the image of the tree.

a painting that will never be taken down nor erased from the memory of man" (cited by Aguirre y Lecube 1944: 30). The power of this symbol still today is illustrated by a brief anecdote. In the same way that 70 years ago photographs of the bombing were used to back accounts of radically different versions of events, so today *Guernica* is referenced to support calls for armed intervention and, more frequently, in calls for peace. US Senator John McCain,[74] addressing the Senate on 23 September 1998, made a reference to Picasso's *Guernica* in his call to back military intervention in Kosovo (Hensbergen 2004: 6). Only two months later Kofi Annan also made a reference to the painting, calling it a 'political masterpiece', as a reminder of the need for peace.[75] The fact that these two politicians called on *Guernica* is explained in part by the fact that a tapestry reproduction of the painting hangs outside the Security Council meeting room of the United Nations in New York as a reminder of why the organization was created.[76] Revealingly, the tapestry was covered up in January 2003, as the Security Council became the site of a struggle for influence over the invasion of Iraq. News of this controversial gesture reached Gernika and the town responded by drafting an open letter to Kofi Annan protesting that the reproduction of the painting was there precisely to remind international delegates of the horrors of war to be avoided. With this action Gernika was claiming its voice as the reality on which the painting was based and the symbol forged. This claim has been central to Gernika's recovery of its past and the management of its heritage-scape. The use of the painting as a symbolic call for peace can also be seen through its appearances in Belfast and protests against the Vietnam war (Figures 5.34 and 5.35).

According to Juan Gutierrez, founding director of *Gernika Gogoratuz*, the aspects of Gernika's symbolism that have resonated differently at

5.34 Mural in West Belfast, 2007.
(© photograph Hannah Merron, 2009;
© Succession Picasso/DACS, London 2010.)

5.35 Poster protesting the war in
Vietnam, 1966. (Chipp 1988: 193.)

various levels – the Basque, the Spanish, and the international – started
coming together as of the 50th Anniversary of the bombing. However,
while they may have begun to coincide they have not melded into one.
The desire among Gernika's institutions to draw on its peace symbolism
to develop the town into a meeting ground between the Basque Country
and the world still has not completely coalesced, as continued violence in
the Basque Country has proven a major hindrance to this end. These
institutions recognized this and have begun to address the issue of
violence in the Basque Country. The Peace Museum has a section dedicated to this theme and *Gernika Gogoratuz* has been developing
programmes along these lines.

Contradictions: Gernika's heritage today?

While memorials and sculptures were being built in Gernika, some scarce
buildings that had survived the bombing were being demolished. In
February 2006 the *Villa Arriaga*, dating from the early twentieth-century
and according to *Aldaba* (no. 140, March 2006: 30) 'one of the most
emblematic buildings in Gernika', was pulled down. In the same issue of
Aldaba (no. 140: 31) there is criticism concerning the Chapel of Santa
Ana, which was allowed to fall into disrepair despite being over 500 years
old, while in other towns similar chapels were being conserved. For a
town whose inhabitants lament the lack of an 'old town centre' or
'historic feeling', and annually recall its tragic destruction, this new loss
of scarce pre-war vestiges seems incongruous. The very nature of having
a living Tree as a symbol suggests one explanation: the significance does
not lie in the materiality of the site but in how it is remembered, felt, and
experienced. On the 40th anniversary of the bombing Joseba Elósegui
was quoted as saying: "Guernica's significance does not lie in its stones,
you can change those. What you cannot change is its legend, its face as
a spiritual center for the Basques" (*Time* article, 2 May 1977). The *Villa
Arriaga* was subsequently rebuilt, imitating the architectural style of the
original and preserving its aesthetics. Now housing the *Ertzaintza*
(Basque police force) this reconstructed villa has combined the symbolism of its architecture with that of the Basque police. This emblematic

building thus associates the *Ertzaintza* with Gernika's heritage and past as well as indicating their power and importance in the town.[77] Another occurrence that stands out is the regular vandalism to which both the Moore and Chillida sculptures are subject. Most frequently it takes the form of graffiti and refuse left over from picnics and *botellones*.[78] Such has been the damage that in April 2007 the City Council decided to reinforce security measures, build a fence around the area and commission a cleaning of these two monuments to peace (Luzarraga, *El Correo*, 20 April 2007). These developments indicate a possible disparity in how the monuments are perceived, with the local officials giving them more importance than do other parts of Gernika's population.

To return to Gernika's new *frontón* discussed in the previous chapter, after its inauguration in 1963 Gernika became a centre of *jai-alai* for some two decades, attracting *pelotaris* from around the world and hosting historic matches. By the mid-1990s, however, the *frontón* was starting to show its age. In the early 2000s there was talk in the Town Hall of demolishing the building and selling off the land, but this sparked a public outcry with Gernika's inhabitants reminding the town authorities that the building had been partly financed through public subscription, and thus it belonged to them. After negotiations it was agreed to convert the building into a multi-purpose venue that could host theatre, conference, concerts, film viewings and the occasional *jai-alai* match. Shortly after its re-inauguration the centre was used in April 2007 for the public viewing of a new documentary about the bombing of the town. The space filled up with whole families of Gernika's inhabitants: grandparents, children and grandchildren arrived in large groups. They commented on the documentary during the viewing and occasionally called out when a fellow Gernikan appeared on the screen being interviewed. As people left each one was given a copy of the documentary on DVD. The story of Gernika's *frontón* – its rebuilding and reuse – illustrates how a community can become actively involved in the construction and preservation of a building deemed meaningful to it.

The Monday market still takes place in Gernika and its composition is revealing of developments in Basque society. The weekly trip to the market continues to be a relished opportunity to catch up on gossip and comment on the week's developments. Numerous stalls are run by people from the region selling the produce from their *caseríos*. However, the vast majority of these sellers are elderly (Figure 5.36) and many *caseríos* have been turned into guest houses, often as part of a development scheme of enhancing rural tourism.[79] The tension between preservation and modern development is not unique to reconstruction periods and Gernika is facing it today as apartment blocks are built around its outer periphery.

Attempts to use reconstruction to impose meaning and memory had limited success, and as recent developments in Spain show it was and is not possible to bury a conflict through a policy of imposed oblivion and

5.36 Gernika's market today.

silence. Historic narratives are central to establishing the identitarian codes of communities whether they are publicly aired or privately transmitted; passed on in families through generations, they are not easily suppressed. Gernika illustrates the importance of narrating experiences and giving testimony – particularly in response to imposed official narratives – for the process of reconciliation. It was only after the previously suppressed narratives of the bombing of Gernika began to be expressed publicly that the town's symbolism gradually began to shift from victimhood and resistance to engaged peace building. Today Basque political parties and interest groups all vie for a bit of Gernika's 'magic' either by holding official acts there or by planting their marks on the city – in the form of monuments and events. This trend, along with the urban development of the town are having their impact on its physical and symbolic nature which today is constituted of many layers of meaning that are often at odds: peace versus conflict with the Spanish government, historic town versus expanding urban centre, Basque heartland versus international symbol. While these different layers are not mutually exclusive, it remains to be seen how Gernikans, after years of silence, take ownership over their town's history and symbolism.

6 Deconstructing the Reconstruction Process

The previous chapters sought to demonstrate how Spain was reconstructed and its heritage-scape revisioned in the aftermath of the 1936–1939 war. To that purpose, we examined how the Civil War itself, combined with issues of the physical protection and destruction of cultural heritage it provoked, gave rise – through the accompanying propaganda war – to radical changes in how that heritage was reinterpreted and to whom it was understood to belong. We saw how opposing sides portrayed themselves as defenders of those symbols, values, and rights of the collective now divided and in confrontation. The war also generated the emergence of new heritage sites, myths, heroes, monuments, and memorials, along with the reinterpretation of existing ones (Chapter 2). Once the war ended, the Franco regime attempted to control the reconstruction process by keeping the responsible organizations under the tight control of the Ministry of Interior, as well as through the propagandistic use it made of reconstruction. It was shown that the directives for reconstruction purposely selected specific historical periods, monuments, and architectural styles to serve as paradigms, reinforcing the dominant ideology and creating a stage-setting for the performance of the new state (Chapter 3).

The case of Gernika (Chapter 4) illustrated the way in which the profound crisis wrought by civil war can divide a community that shares a set of symbols, material images and codes. This process of division was explored, including the efforts of different sides to impose their hegemony on the others and to disqualify them from the collective, in part by appropriating those symbols that had constituted a shared heritage, and in part by turning them into points of contention, and justifications for aggressive action. We also analyzed how the responses to this can vary, for those symbols can be reinterpreted with regard to the past or questioned *vis-à-vis* the future. Their manipulation can be denounced or counteracted. Or, as in the case of the Bamiyan Buddhas and the Mostar Bridge, the symbols can be denied as such and attacked. Regardless of the forms taken by actions and reactions, it is clear that rarely can previously collective symbols remain unscathed by the ravages of civil war, for even if they survive materially, as did the Tree of Gernika, new meaning is added, thus transforming them.

Another dimension likewise revealed was that, in the long term, unresolved issues are taken up by subsequent generations (Chapter 5). Refusing to address a troubled past does not make it disappear from individual and group memories or conscience. Building memorials only to one side does not erase the memories of the other side. Reconstruction, when one-sided, can thus contribute to prolonging division in a society for generations to come.

At the beginning of this study, reasons were given for the selection of Spain as a fruitful case to scrutinize in order to test some ideas and intuitions that originated from direct observation of UNESCO's work in the former Yugoslavia. As the investigation draws to a close, it has become apparent that Spain presented an excellent case due to the unique circumstances that led to a 40-year dictatorship and to the relative immutability of its main protagonists, with the dictator as well as the political, ideological and economic elite remaining in place. Yet, as we saw in the previous chapter, the Francoist ambition for a New Spain failed over time in its attempts to impose silence, engender oblivion, or eradicate alternative visions of the country and its heritage. One aim of the present chapter is to synthesize the main trends of the reconstruction: which ones succeeded, which ones failed, and also which ones could be relevant to other reconstruction scenarios.

Clearly, the social and spatial topography of cities throughout Spain changed as a result of the reconstruction project, and so did their symbolic landscape. The reconceptualized vision of the country and its people was supported by an *à la carte* selection of the past, some historical moments being glorified while others totally disappeared from the public sphere. As new historical sites, narratives, legends, and myths were emphasized, so a new heritage-scape emerged to support the desired re-visioning of the nation. The historical periods chosen as direct precursors did not only provide guidelines for the visual construction of the newly defined nation; they were also associated with particular values and visions of the nation's place in the world. Inevitably, these narratives also redefined notions of otherness, excluding groups that once formed part of the nation. A comparative look at other aftermaths of civil war reveals that these mechanisms of the reconstruction process are not unique to Spain; the reconstruction in Bosnia and Lebanon, for example, show similar dynamics and fissures.

The other aim of this chapter is to depart from the specificity of the Spanish case, by taking the lessons and observations gleaned from it and looking at the broader picture of post-war reconstruction of cultural heritage. The intent is to draw out those elements from the Spanish experience that are relevant in order to develop a framework of analysis that might be applicable to other post-conflict scenarios. The proposition is thus to deconstruct the reconstruction by, as Geertz suggested, "sorting out the structures of signification" (Geertz 1973: 9) that it inscribed.

Physical, Symbolic, Social

Reconstruction, we have seen, is an evolving process that goes through various phases that are inevitably affected by national politics and the international context. Reconstruction can have a dimension that involves redefining group identities by inscribing the physical landscape with new meanings that situate it within narratives of belonging. It is in the formation of this symbolic landscape that cultural heritage plays a major part, planting landmarks in city, town, or countryside to reinforce a particular vision of the group, its history and identity. This is the reason that particularly symbolic sites are revealing to study, even if they constitute a relatively small part of the rebuilding effort. The reconstruction of cultural heritage takes place on a number of different levels, which have been identified and examined in this research along with its possible impacts.

Four main channels of reconstruction have been identified (Table 6.1), which although interrelated and overlapping have distinct dynamics. The category of 'revisioning the nation' deliberately alludes to the notions of revising and seeing anew. This course indicates a deliberate attempt to create an idealized vision, both physical and intangible, of the nation. Part of this process involves the architectural styles chosen for the reconstruction, the ways in which the nation is represented to its own population in the aftermath of a civil war, and the resulting visual landscape. It also includes public acts that perform the nation through parades, celebrations, or other official events. The 're-writing of history' involves the selective editing of the national historical narrative in order to account for the conflict, its outcome, and to give legitimacy to the group that wins the political power. Celebrating certain historical figures and events, while 'forgetting' others, allows the new regime to construct its own genealogy, associating or disassociating itself from its predecessors. This selection process also applies to how the recent conflict is commemorated or memorialized. Another part of the reconstruction is related to value, for what is valued will guide decisions about what parts of the national history to preserve or not. This process of selection and valuation is deeply linked with the moral paradigm that the new regime is seeking to establish. While the case study chosen for this research is a civil war a comparable situation might be the post-war construction of national-historical narratives in East and West Germany.

Throughout the previous chapters, the three recurring facets of reconstruction have been the physical, symbolic and social. The subdivision of history, heritage and its uses, into different categories is not new (Table 6.2). In his *On the Advantages and Disadvantages of History for Life* (1874) Nietzsche lays out three kinds of history that correspond to the ways in which "history belongs to the living man": monumental, antiquarian, and critical (Nietzsche 1980: 14). In his *The Modern Cult of*

Table 6.1 Breaking down the reconstruction process

	REvisioning	the forging of a new vision of the nation, visual landscape, and performing within it
	REwriting history	retelling the national past in light of the conflict
Reconstruction	REmembering	constructing memory, monuments, commemoration, *lieux d'oubli*
	REcodifying space	politics of space and place, symbolscape, new moral paradigms and values

Monuments, Riegl (1903/1982) identified various kinds of values associated with monuments: history-value, age-value, use-value, and art-value. In an essay from 1984 Lipe breaks down the ways of giving value to cultural resources into four types: associative/symbolic value, information value, aesthetic value, and economic value. Lefebvre (1974) subdivided his conceptualization of space into three planes which correspond, in part, to those that Nora later identified with the *lieux de mémoire* (1989: 19; 1996: 14). Nora further indicated that these aspects always coexist.[1] A further insight is that the manner in which objects – and sites – are used adds meaning to them. Geertz argues that they "draw their meaning from the role they play in an ongoing pattern of life, not from any intrinsic relationships they bear to one another" (Geertz 1973: 17). This is especially relevant for the post-war scenario when objects and sights have been 'used' either propagandistically, militarily, or both during the conflict.

While the five concepts – history, monuments, cultural resources, space, and *lieux de mémoire* – are different, it is nonetheless useful to contrast these multiple attempts to grapple with similar problems, when analyzing uses of the past and its tangible remains. For the task ahead, and in order to maintain the themes that have gradually gained in strength throughout the present study, it would be useful to adopt a combination of Lefebvre and Nora's categories. The advantage of this combination is that it results in more robust concepts with which to analyse the many dimensions of the agency[2] of heritage in post-conflict scenarios. Thus, the materiality of the object and its situation within a delimited space with which it interacts becomes one category. The symbolic content, or significance, of a site can be explored as well as its topographical location within the individual and collective *imaginaire*, the transformed imagined community and haunted landscapes of a post-

Table 6.2 Identifying the realms and dynamics of heritage

Nietzsche, 1874 (history)	Riegl, 1903 (monuments)	Lipe, 1984 (cultural resources)	Lefebvre, 1974 (space)	Nora, 1989 (*lieux de mémoire*)
Monumental	History-value	Associative/symbolic-value	Physical	Material
Antiquarian	Age-value	Information-value	Mental	Symbolic
Critical	Use-value	Economic-value	Social	Functional
	Art-value	Aesthetic-value		

war. Finally, the function given to the site, the social impact it has and the responses it elicits of affirmation or rejection also become a useful lens. By now it will be evident that these subdivisions are porous and that a dogmatic segregation of the three categories would impoverish our understanding of them.

On materiality and physicality (or the place in space)

Reconstruction as a generator of places and spaces can be broken down into those trends observed in the Spanish case (Table 6.3). A fundamental aspect was ideology, for it determined attitudes and policies about architecture and urban planning that were then translated into reconstruction plans. Although the material difficulties encountered in the reconstruction process frequently impeded turning these plans into reality, propaganda instruments continued to project the ideological vision of the reconstruction. This projection was sustained well after it became evident that the reconstruction originally devised would not materialize, or that it would do so on a reduced scale and only on selected sites. Partly as a result of this realization, the selected sites were promoted for all the symbolic content they could generate, resulting in the repeated reference to limited iconic sites that served as showpieces of the reconstruction.

Another consequence of the contrast between grandiose plans and their delayed realization was that, by the time some projects were finalized, they no longer reflected the general atmosphere of the times (see Text Box on the *Valle de los Caídos,* Chapter 3). The degree to which the reconstruction project was infused with ideology can also be gleaned by the way in which each reconstruction plan – whether of a building, square or town – was developed in terms of the message that it would transmit. This was clear in the care given to the types of materials used for different purposes and what those materials were understood to signify. It can also be seen in the way in which town halls, churches and memorials were planned in relation to the rest of the town, and

Table 6.3 Reconstruction trends

Trends and aims	Manifestation
Use of propaganda to communicate the ideology of the reconstruction	Exhibitions, magazines, inaugurations, ceremonies.
Political and strategic relevance of architecture	Architecture becomes an element of 'high' politics with impact on stability, security, social planning.
Building place	Town Hall, Church.
Structuring space	Plaza Mayor, street names, urban organization.
Use of performance to imbue sites with prescribed meaning (ideology)	Parades, official visits, consecrations, inaugurations, key-giving ceremonies.
Profusion of symbols	A new panoply of flags, anthems, uniforms, rituals performed repetitively.
The focus on façades, surfaces, stage-setting	Reconstruction rhetoric often remained at the level of facade and decorative detail, indicating a move beyond the building of infrastructure to the realms of propaganda and nation building.
Use of historicist architectural styles	To visually construct a narrative, historical lineage, highlight perceived values and accomplishments from that period.
Control	Decrees were made that none could rebuild without the regime's authorization and approval.
Representing the new status quo	Focus on central elements representing the state: the *Plaza Mayor* and Town Hall.

surrounded by streets named after moral paragons of the regime – in the shape of military leaders, martyrs, battles or moral values. During the reconstruction new power structures are not only built politically but also through urban planning and architecture; through these interventions the physical and symbolic topography of the country is transformed. The urban fabric is remoulded; as buildings, streets and neighbourhoods become associated with the new regime through their use and by the choice of architectural styles, name changes, and monuments. New meanings etched into the urban and national landscape thus transform the semiotics of the heritage-scape. Departing from Garden's (2006) understanding, the heritage-scape here is the cartography of meaning and memory that individuals and collectives 'read' in a particular space

Reconstruction was thus not only about building places but also about structuring spaces and their meanings. This trend was reinforced by the performance of rituals including Falangist parades, official visits, consecrations, inaugurations, and key presentation ceremonies. Through these events, spaces were sowed with the regime's symbols: flags, emblems, anthems, and uniforms. The propagandistic aspirations of reconstruction can also be seen in the emphasis on façades and on the efforts vested in ephemeral structures used for public ceremonies whose utility lies in communicating a message which can be altered and replaced with new temporary structures. Yet another manifestation of how architectural styles chosen for the reconstruction were intended to be eloquent of an ideological vision of the country can be seen in the use of historical styles. Linked to these trends was an aspiration to exert an absolute control over the reconstruction, as demonstrated by the regime's decrees outlawing rebuilding activities not formally validated, as well as by the substantial number of administrative instruments – and regional offices – that the regime dedicated to reconstruction. The reason for this exertion of control was that reconstruction was intended to crystallize both the new vision of Spain, its past, and the new status quo. Reconstruction was intended not only to act as a reminder of who had won the war and what they stood for, but also to condition behaviour and attitudes to comply with that vision by structuring space and filling it with signifying markers.

Despite the differences in motivations, many of these trends can also be found in instances when reconstruction projects are led by international organizations. Such is the case with the politics of space. Franco's dictatorial regime sought to impose repressive ideological values and organize space through urban planning with clearly demarcated centres of power and moral paragons. In a parallel manner, and with significantly different aims, international organizations apply their humanitarian and human rights values, set up high-security citadels within the cities in which they act (Sarajevo, Kabul, Bagdad) and use highly visible symbols (such as white land-rovers and institutional emblems). Thus they act on and create spaces that transmit messages of power and difference, inclusion and exclusion, thereby potentially alienating those that are denied access to the coveted safe areas and associated privileges (Smirl 2008: 236–53). Though international organizations generally intervene in reconstruction motivated by the aim of enabling a reconciliation – the opposite of the Franco regime's aims – the process of reconstruction itself has an impact on heritage-scapes and societies in comparable ways.

Table 6.4 Dichotomies imbedded in the reconstruction

Rhetoric versus reality	Central planning gives a significant uniformity in the buildings and urban plans throughout the country.
Urban versus rural	Influx to cities in post-conflict scenarios, internal displacement and emergence of slums on city outskirts.
Old versus new	Emphasis on tradition and folklore while claiming to be building a 'new' nation.

Another characteristic that emerged from the research was the existence of several dichotomies within the reconstruction project that occasionally led to tension, often resolved creatively, but which at other times led to manifest contradiction (Table 6.4). The first of these, already alluded to, was the gap between the rhetoric of the reconstruction, its plans and propaganda, and the reality of what it was possible to do given the circumstances. This dynamic also worked in the opposite direction: the reality which determined decisions about reconstruction approaches was construed in such a way as to appear to be a manifestation of the regime's ideology. In some towns the devastation was so extensive that it was more practical, and less costly, to simply build a new town nearby rather than try to clear the rubble and rebuild on the same site. Such decisions were presented, as in the case of Belchite, as intentional acts to preserve the ruined towns as monuments to 'heroic martyrs'. A major difficulty impeding some of the more ambitions reconstruction and memorial plans was that of the limited resources available which had to be divided up among all aspects of reconstruction.

Another tension the reconstruction organizations had to deal with, heavily influenced by the former, was that between rural and urban centres. Whereas ideology and rhetoric exalted the first, the reality of mass population movements to city centres created situations not foreseen and which imposed different priorities. The difference with which cities and towns were treated offered a practical solution to stylistic conflict in the regime's ideology between the imperial and the folkloric. While the two coexisted rhetorically, architecturally the imperial style was more frequently used for official buildings in cities, while folkloric elements were more widely applied in towns.

Finally, and perhaps the most problematic of the three, was the constant tension implicit in aspiring to build a new country versus the assertion that tradition was being restored, and 'authentic' Spain with its historical roots recovered. A constant in reconstructions, regardless of how its rhetoric has been spun, is the tendency to take advantage of them in order to modernize urban planning and infrastructure. In Spain, the straightening and widening of streets were not simply a question of crystallizing an ideology that emphasized hierarchy and order but also of improving water, sanitation and transportation systems – projects that had been conceived before the war broke out. One way that this tension was resolved relates to the above-mentioned approach to façades: restoring façades to their original style while modernizing the buildings they fronted (as in Toledo's *Zocodover* Square). Another solution was the use of regional architectural details that added local and traditional flavour to formulaic models implanted throughout the country. The dichotomy between preservation and renewal is not unique to post-war scenarios but exists in urban regeneration plans generally. However, in the post-war scenario the trend can be revealing when looking at what sites and towns are selected for 'regeneration', or modernization, which ones are selected with the aim of restoring them to their pre-war state, and which are preserved as ruins.

These trends and dichotomies identified in the Spanish reconstruction can be found in other post-civil war scenarios. Furthermore, they often conflate in the case of iconic sites of heritage destruction and reconstruction. The focus on iconic projects is also a recurrent theme found in all of these parallel situations. As we saw in Chapter 2, the propaganda battle waged during the Spanish Civil War had an important international dimension; Toledo and the Prado became the focus of propaganda because of their international fame and hence the widespread attention they would generate. This dynamic has been witnessed again in more recent conflicts: the Mostar Bridge in Bosnia, the Bamiyan Buddhas in Afghanistan, and Babylon in Iraq. Iconic sites have elicited attention from international organizations interested in reconstruction or the safeguarding of heritage, often at the cost of a global vision and with the result that these sites become political pawns. These trends can also lead to the neglect of other lesser-known sites. In Bosnia, for instance, while the international community focused on heritage sites of world renown, monuments to the partisan struggle of the Second World War erected by Tito throughout the former Yugoslavia were being torn down. Likewise, other important sites were being neglected, such as the bridge at Visegrad.

The symbolic plane: meaning and memory of the imagined community

One lesson confirmed by the Spanish reconstruction is that symbolic meaning evolves: it is neither static nor can it be fixed in time. One of the ways in which meaning is affected is through the comparisons and associations that occur when a symbol has a wide-ranging echo, as is the case of Gernika/*Guernica*. After Spain, George L. Steer went on to cover the European war in Finland and compared what he saw there – the bombing of Viipuri – with that of Gernika. Frequently recurring comparisons with the Basque town are the cities of Hiroshima and Dresden, and each comparison sends a different message thereby altering the significance of Gernika as a symbol (see Chapters 1, 4 and 5). As Hensbergen (2004: 5) observed, today "each act of devastation begs the question — shall this be the Gernika of our age?".

Earlier (Chapter 2) we examined how Madrid's *Puerta de Alcalá* was used first by the Republic and then by the Franco regime as an emblematic site on which to hang their own symbols. In this way, they each linked the site and the city with their respective signifiers, on the one hand international communism and socialism and on the other, fascism and national Catholicism. In the context of Gernika's bombing and its depiction in the contemporary media (Chapter 3), we observed the ways in which images of the destruction were used by both sides to back contradictory accounts of events. These examples clearly indicate that a symbol can have different, even opposing, meanings, a frequent locus of debate:

> *For example, in his insightful essay on Joan of Arc, Michel Winock dramatizes this phenomenon by demonstrating how that historical figure emerged as a political emblem simultaneously functioning for the mythology of both the left and the right alike. For xenophobic groups such as the paramilitary fascist leagues of the 1930s or the acerbic neo-nationalism of Jean-Marie Le Pen, Joan of Arc represents a totemic figure capable of forestalling foreign incursions into the homeland whereas for the left she incarnates courage in doing battle against the corruption of the church.*
>
> (Kritzman in Nora 1996: foreword, x)

The construction of war heritage through memorials often gives preference to one group or version of events to the detriment of others. In the Spanish case, while the defeated could not build public memorials inside the country to contest the official ones, this did not stop practices of mourning, commemoration and memorialization from taking place within the private sphere or amongst the exiled communities. This process is clearly traceable in the case of Gernika; not only was the bombing commemorated in exile, but the painting became a form of memorial that powerfully contested the official ones. Since Franco's death, memorials have been built to commemorate the wartime experiences and loss of life on the Republican side (Chapter 5). Such actions illustrate a need for the public commemoration of the 'other' side of events even seventy years after the war. The contentious character of memorials is also evidenced by how often they are targeted: public images of Franco and memorial plaques to his regime continue to be subjected to vandalism and graffiti.

The memorial plaques that at the end of the war were hung across Spain on the walls of churches, town halls, and squares bore the exclamation: *¡Presentes!* ("Present!"), accompanied by the slogan *Caídos por Dios y por España* ("Fallen for God and Spain"), and a list of the names of Nationalists killed during the conflict. The names on the plaques were supposed to indicate those to be remembered and the names absent those to be forgotten, yet the plaques served as mementos to the family members of those missing from the memorials. These commemorative plaques were therefore transformed into mementos not only of their loss during the war but also of the injustice of the post-war; the memorials maintained the 'us' and 'them' alive during decades throughout the country.

The dynamics witnessed in Spain have counterparts in the former Yugoslavia. In the context of 'revisionist history' prevailing in the 1980s, the subject of Second World War dead in Yugoslavia (one million Yugoslavs killed, mainly by their own countrymen) gained even greater protagonism in 1991. They became a source of mutual recrimination and demonization, as clamours were made for bodies to be returned to their 'rightful homes' and for the 'unnamed' soldiers and civilians previously commemorated through communal monuments to the anonymous 'dead soldier' to be named (Petrovic-Štreger 2005). The capacity of memorials to perpetuate division within society can be seen in the case of the memorialization of Srebrenica. In July 2005, just prior to the 10th anniversary of the massacre in Bosnia, police discovered bombs at the site of the memorial. Another response has been the profusion of parallel memorials commemorating the deaths of Bosnian-Serbs that have cropped up throughout the villages of the now predominantly Serb area surrounding Srebrenica as a sign of contestation and demand for recognition of those 'other' victims. Partial memorials do not erase the 'other' memory, but they do infuse it with an element of confrontation.

National culture is fragmented and essentialized during civil wars through the formulation of an inner enemy. International interventions can further exacerbate this violent breach by choosing sides, thus reinforcing the propagandistic images of 'good' and 'evil', 'perpetrator' and 'victim'. When these attitudes are maintained during reconstruction, violence continues to be wrought on the society and its *imaginaire collectif*.

Function and social impact

The question of whether meaning and memory can be imposed on sites queries whether *lieux de mémoire* can be deliberately created. As discussed earlier, Riegl distinguished between 'intentional' and 'unintentional' monuments (Riegl 1903/1982: 21), while Nora (1989: 23, 1996: 19) distinguishes between 'dominant' and 'dominated' sites. As most heritage sites with long histories, Gernika offers a complex scenario of symbols at once 'intentional' and 'unintentional', 'dominant' and 'dominated': its tree, its bombing and Picasso's painting all took on dimensions of monumentality and additional layers of symbolism that were not originally present. The town became, in part, a memorial to the event. What is clear is that in none of these instances are meanings permanently fixed, for as Stuart Hall (1997:61) indicates: "It is us – in society, within human culture – who make things mean, who signify. Meanings, consequently, will always change, from one culture or period to another". The reconstruction effected by the Franco regime was not able to resist this dynamic of change despite its otherwise long-lasting effects.

Gernika has recovered the richness of its multifaceted meanings, memories and interpretations and has gained many others in the process despite attempts to stifle them. In another case, the international community tried to impose the symbolism of rebuilding Mostar's Old Bridge in such a way that it would come to stand, both physically and metaphorically, for linking the two divided communities and re-opening dialogue. Yet, as was already indicated in the preface there is little evidence that this imposed meaning has taken hold among the town's population. Whether it is an autocratic regime that rebuilds a monument or an international organization, both inevitably do so with a particular set of values in mind, adopting a methodology that complements them. In Spain, a regime with every possibility of controlling the reconstruction – the meanings it took on, the version of history that it fostered, and the memories that it validated publicly – did not in the long term succeed (despite having power over all the available resources) in imposing its historic, memorial or moral vision. This is not to say that it did not have long-term effects. It managed to maintain a divided society, creating a far-reaching structure and culture of power, and a status quo that largely withstood the Transition (González Duro 2005). It also succeeded in silencing alternative versions of the war and its events, promoting a distorted vision of Spanish history that subsequent generations are still working to dismantle. Finally, it succeeded in planting its symbols and rituals throughout the towns and cities of Spain, creating a sense that these were the norm.

One indication of how successful the Franco regime was at implanting symbols is the way monuments and rituals created during that period came to be regarded as tradition, heritage, or to use the Spanish expression, *de toda la vida*.[3] This is revealing of the temporal perception of monuments that take on an aura of permanence quickly, at least if they go uncontested. This observation helps to understand how constructed structures become naturalized or normalized so that they are no longer perceived as constructions. Implied in the use of the phrase *de toda la vida* is a reference to what is considered normal, understood as "it has always been this way," and yet it is applied to traditions, monuments, and forms of behaviour that were actually created or reinvented during the Franco period. Critical reactions against some of the changes that have occurred since Franco's death reinforce this perception. Remonstrations are based on the attitude that things should be left 'as they always were', as if the Franco regime represented the beginning of history, and thereby denying not only the Republic but also everything that came before it. These attitudes reveal how selective memory can become internalized in popular culture, commemorative events, and monuments when it has been imposed on a collective through repetition and rehearsal.

Of the various sites, the town of Brunete is perhaps the only one in which Franco's dictum of leaving everything *atado y bien atado* (firmly sealed with no loose ends) came true. In Brunete the reconstruction was successful in that it crystallized the regime's values and the architectural, memorial, and urban planning ideas of the Falange. As such, it served as a model for other reconstructions. Brunete played a significant role in the attempted coup (*Tejerazo*) of 1981 through the participation of the *División Acorazada Brunete,* and it has remained a Falangist stronghold to this day (Figure 6.1). However, it failed in becoming a national *lieu de mémoire* or in having any significant repercussions on a national level, either as a moral or urban paragon. In Brunete it is also possible to identify a hint of one of the more pronounced failures of the Spanish reconstruction: the second phase of the reconstruction plan was never put into effect because of a decrease in population. This example of failure to

6.1 Falangist cross, Brunete, 2007.

stem population movements to urban centres is again embedded in the dichotomy between rhetoric and reality.

In Spain then, attempts to impose a set of values on the reconstruction that determined the selection of sites met with variable success. The impact of population movements in undermining reconstruction can also be observed in Bosnia. There, population movements that occurred during the war did not reverse, a trend resulting in many cities and towns having a significantly different population than before the conflict. The internally displaced populations caused by the conflicts in Rwanda, Iraq and Democratic Republic of Congo – to name but a few examples – indicate that this trend is unlikely to come to an end. The misalignment between the values of reconstruction and social attitudes can also be seen in Bosnia, for, while international organizations were focused on the Mostar Bridge and Sarajevo, communities were looking towards other sources and sites of symbolic meaning. In 2004, in Mostar the local population chose to erect a bronze statue in honour of the Kung-fu legend Bruce Lee. In the words of one local citizen: "Lee is an international hero to all ethnicities in Bosnia and that's why we picked him" (Gatalo quoted in BBC, 2 September, 2004). The dichotomy of reconstruction practice resulted in many diverse visions of post-war Bosnia emerging that have had implications for reconciliation and peacekeeping in the medium term. Alternative symbols for unity, such as Bruce Lee, surprising to an outsider, show a refusal to comply with an imposed vision of reconstruction.

In choosing Spain the intention had been to apply this research to a historical case study. Yet as research progressed between 2005 and 2008, memory wars unfolded in the country, and history seemed to be catching up with the research. In September 2008, Judge Baltasar Garzón of the *Audiencia Nacional* (National Court),[4] who became internationally known for prosecuting such figures as the Chilean General Augusto Pinochet for crimes against humanity, turned his attention to Spain and ordered that all the names of those killed during the civil war and dictatorship be submitted to the court. It took 20 years to build and rebuild certain unique sites of memory (the *Valle* and the *Alcázar*), but other less tangible sites of memory and heritage are still being recovered over 70 years after the end of the Civil War (35 years after Franco's death). The temporal question has been a constant in this research and it will be treated in the following section.

From Common Trends towards an Analytic Framework

There have been two main themes driving this study and one general outcome that have guided the work. The first has been to explore what is understood as heritage. The intent here has been to take into consideration the evolution of heritage as a concept from the monumental to the *lieux de mémoire*. This was necessary in order to be able to gauge its importance in shaping group identity and therefore appreciate how prone it is to be manipulated, interpreted, and re-interpreted in cases of conflict, especially civil wars. The second theme has been reconstruction once conflict has wrought its destruction. Here too reconstruction was understood broadly, to encompass not only the physical re-building but also the selective rewriting of history, social codes, moral values, symbols, and ultimately the entire heritage-scape. The case of civil war is a particularly poignant one in this examination, as with the triumph of one side over the other reconstruction becomes decisive in imposing the old, revered symbols once shared by the whole of society in revised and exclusionary versions to which the defeated side no longer has a right – neither a right to 'own' them nor to interpret them differently:

> *These ritual operations were carried out as mechanisms of socialization, geared at the symbolic integration of some, and paradoxically, the exclusion of others, eliminating a series of attributes that potentiated one integration at the same time as it left the excluded without references.*
>
> (Payá López 2002: 201)

The general outcome towards which this research was geared was to see what lessons could be learned and what useful tools could be gleaned from the study of one case that could then be applied to others, and so to this we now turn. Examination of the Spanish case has enabled the identification of several trends that deserve examination in order to determine whether they might be analogous.

As we have seen, reconstruction can cement the narrative of these events through rhetoric, commemorative events and memorials, thereby further demarcating difference between the opposing sides of the conflict. A further incursion on the heritage-scape comes in the form of the new layers of sites added to it by the events of the war. This means that the reconstruction, regardless of how faithful it seeks to be in restoring what was destroyed, will always be a new construction in that it will reflect a new state of affairs, a transformed cartography of meaning and power with shifted boundaries and allegiances. This changed landscape is equally pertinent for the population, which through internal displacement, the purging of public institutions, exile, imprisonment, persecution or death is significantly different from the pre-conflict one. The relevance for the heritage domain is, on the one hand, that intellectuals, university professors, and artists are often targeted in these conflicts. On the other, these professionals can become politicized to the extent of reinterpreting the past and fuelling the political rhetoric of difference and prioritizing the protection of 'their' heritage over that of the 'other' (which occurred in Spain and in the former Yugoslavia). Furthermore, in the case of civil wars a victor can appropriate and reinterpret symbols, adding new elements in order to reinforce the pretence of being the rightful representative of the collective. The response from the defeated coalition(s) can be to refuse to recognize the new meanings until time or changed circumstances offer the opportunity to reclaim alternative interpretations of those symbols, heritage sites and values. Enforcing memory (and forgetting) has limited results, as the public remembering of the past is central to group identity, but there are multiple readings of past events and ignoring these alternatives can foster division or camouflage it.

Two further common areas that are closely related are the protagonism of myth-making and the impact of propaganda and censorship so rampant during civil wars. If truth is the first casualty of war (Knightley 1975),[5] it certainly takes a long time to be resuscitated, as myths born during the war take years to be dispelled and can be reinforced in the reconstruction. We have only to look at the case of Gernika and Herbert R. Southworth's (1977) considerable efforts to dispel the myths fabricated by the Francoist regime. Reconstructions bearing these myths at their foundations continue the violence that engendered them and can perpetuate divisions of 'us' and 'them', 'perpetrator' and 'victim'. The divisive myth-making dimension is also crystallized in the reconstruction by the idolization of heroes and martyrs. The memorial landscape that results both constructs memory and articulates a moral code, setting up paragons to be emulated by celebrating patriotic self-sacrifice. Memorials also serve the purpose of representing group loss; together with commemorations they can be vehicles for expressing a sense of collective mourning. As we have seen, however, memorials can also retrench divisions when they exclude parts of society or serve to lay blame.

As we have seen in the previous chapters, one of the dimensions of reconstruction is that it is heavily influenced by ideology, which in turn establishes a prescriptive moral framework intended to shape behaviour and attitudes in the new environment. One aim of reconstruction is thus to crystallize the changed moral framework and ethical lessons of the conflict; to rebuild according to a set of values that includes both a conceptualization of the conflict (who were the victims and who the perpetrators), and an agenda (influenced by budgets, political manoeuvring and perceived time-frame for action). All of these areas impose a vision and rhythm on the reconstruction that will determine how heritage is regarded and valued. In Spain it meant that the austerity and Catholicism of the Middle Ages was given priority. In Lebanon it meant that in Beirut the citadel model took precedence over the Riviera model determining the shape of the city as it was rebuilt (Shehadi 2006; Farchakh Bajjaly 2006). Especially when civil wars end in the victory of one party or in fragmentation there is a propensity for partisan reconstruction, supporting one vision and ideology.[6]

Two intimately related notions that also recur in these scenarios are those of legitimacy and authenticity. In the aftermath of civil war, when one part of society seeks to demonstrate its legitimacy – beyond military victory – to rule over the other, authenticity becomes an instrumental tool. Post-conflict rhetoric is often laden with claims of recovering, establishing, or restoring power to the authentic. As we saw in the case of Potes in Spain, restoring authenticity may mean remodelling sites to fit a regime's vision of how that authenticity should look (Chapter 3). The object of this reaffirmation of authenticity can be a group – ethnic, political, religious, social – but to back these claims it is invariably material culture that is applied, often in the form of archaeology and built heritage. Archaeology is used to create the semblance of a direct lineage of the ruling group with the past, thereby establishing their historic links to a territory and supporting a myth of legitimacy (Meskell 1998). This was done by Enver Hoxa in Albania, who used the archaeological sites of Apollonia and Butrint to develop a narrative of Albanians being the direct descendants and heirs of the Illyrian civilization, thus neglecting the Byzantine heritage of places like Voskopojë because they did not suit the narrative being constructed. Franco used archaeology at the height of the regime's isolation and autarchy to develop a narrative of Iberian culture as resilient, self-sufficient and distinct from the rest of Europe. Cultural heritage is selectively drawn on to support historicized narratives of the nation that legitimize the regime in power. We can perceive the selective construction of a nation's past like the galleries of an imaginary museum – precedents for this kind of exercise are Warburg's 'Mnemosyne-Atlas' (Gombrich 1970: 283–306) or Malraux's *musée imaginaire* (1947). Thus, in order to draw conclusions, one must differentiate between what part of the past is framed and displayed in the gallery of honour, composing the visual narrative of the nation; what is relegated to badly lit secondary rooms; what is deliberately left in storage hidden from view, perhaps to be taken out again when appropriate, or neglected and allowed to decay; and what is sold off or exchanged.

Underlying all of these aspects is the temporal element that comprises the notions of change and evolution. The consideration of time is fundamental to dissect reconstruction as a process consisting of various stages. This is more so since there seem to be different appreciations of time at work in the process and these do not necessarily coincide: reconstruction plans versus the time needed to realize them, the length of projects versus the needs of individuals, appreciation of events of those who live through them versus the appreciations of future generations. The temporal issue is fundamental to reconstruction projects today, as project time and human time run at different speeds. There is a dichotomy between the time needed to rebuild a bridge or building and the time needed to mourn its destruction and be willing to see it replaced. This dichotomy can be illustrated in the difference between the reconstructions of the Mostar Bridge and the Frauenkirche in Dresden. The bridge, whose reconstruction was lead by international organizations, was inaugurated 11 years after its destruction, while the Frauenkirche remained in ruins for over 50 years under the DDR whose policy was not to rebuild it. The reconstructed church was only inaugurated in 2005 after 13 years of rebuilding amidst much controversy and as the result of a lengthy process of negotiations with local authorities and stakeholders involved at different stages. Furthermore, there are different allocations of time, resources and emphases, relegated to the planning, execution and evaluation phases of projects. Reconstruction is not an end but rather a process made up of various levels of action, stages and cycles; it is not linear but moves in starts and stops as motivations and circumstances change. In other words, the national rituals explicitly commemorating and presenting a single version of history and the conflict: public agendas versus private memories that resist being erased.

The final elements, which are not about change but about durability through time, are those of resilience and recurrence. As has become evident in many conflicts (Spain, the former Yugoslavia, Lebanon), when a contested past is simply dropped from textbooks, monuments and official history it continues to be transmitted privately in communities and families. Even buildings that no longer exist can continue to be a presence for those who knew them, spectres, and signposts in a remembered and imagined heritage-scape. This was the case with the church of San Juan in Gernika which 70 years after its destruction was being painted back into the townscape by an artist on his canvas. In other cases, discussions about whether or not to rebuild emblematic sites can continue for generations, as was the case with Dresden's Frauenkirche[7] and Berlin's Hohenzollern Palace.[8] Exiled or silenced culture also endures as seen both in the Basque Country, and in the return of the Russian Orthodox Church after 70 years[9] following the collapse of the Soviet Union.

Resilience, recovery, reconciliation, and the "consequences of peace"

An indication of what prompts resilience was suggested in the discussions that were stimulated in Spain as a result of the 'recovery of historic memory' and the confrontation in the obituary columns of newspapers (Chapter 5). The sentiments frequently expressed by those wishing to discover the burial places and recover the remains of their lost family members were: duty (to remember), freedom to mourn, daring to break a silence and share experiences, and the sense of debt, of needing to right a historic injustice. Along with resilience, recovery and reconciliation are fundamental to reconstructions that seek to be instrumental in peace-building.

In 1919 John Maynard Keynes published *The Economic Consequences of Peace* as a commentary on the Treaty of Versailles that ended the First World War, which, he argued, planted the seeds for a future war. The problem of one-dimensional interpretations of heritage is that they are excluding and more apt to be used in constructing opposite, radical, and equally one-dimensional narratives of group identity. In the aftermath of war, heritage more than ever becomes a site of contestation and dissonance (Ashworth and Tunbridge 1996) as both a focus for opposing interpretations of the conflict and the ensuing uses made of it. Only by recognizing this and dispelling the nomenclature that characterizes heritage as a container of exclusively positive values and narratives is it possible to understand it in the post-war context. Only by recognizing its potential to impart messages of fear, domination and violence can its potential as a resource in reconciliation be engaged and any historical grievances linked to it addressed (for the role of culture in peace-building and reconciliation see Galtung 1990, 1996; Lederach 1997).

The element of choice is central to any moral framework. Reconstruction demands a series of choices in determining what sites of cultural heritage are to be rebuilt or not, and the narrative that binds these decisions together gives rise to a new value-scape. The legacy of history can be a heavy burden in the effort to move towards peace and stability. In instances when the destruction of cultural heritage has been heavily used for propaganda purposes in wartime rhetoric, the reconstruction process is especially delicate as memories of the destruction can prolong fear and resentment. The decisions made concerning what elements of cultural heritage are rebuilt and how they are presented will inevitably affect the future development of meaning and symbols in their surrounding communities, as well as influence how they are perceived and interact with the 'other'. Research presented here has made clear that reconstruction itself can destroy heritage and create the circumstances for a recurrence of war. Thus, though it might be possible to use it as such, the reconstruction of cultural heritage in the aftermath of war is not inherently a peace-building activity.

In Spain, attempts to deny the involvement of one part of society in the reconstruction with the intent of eradicating traces of their heritage were not successful in the longer term, even using the means available to a dictatorial regime. There is little chance, then, for organizations involved in the reconstruction of cultural heritage to have peace-building effects unless they work over a longer period of time and in close collaboration with the various groups that were involved in the conflict. There are neither easy answers nor easy questions, but one sincerely hopes to have contributed to formulating the latter in such a way that it is possible to advance this line of thinking. Based on the key points identified

Table 6.5 Lines of questioning

What has been . . .	At the level of . . .		
lost forever saved transformed newly added imposed illicitly preserved recovered re-interpreted Continues to be destroyed	Physical	Symbolic	Social

thus far, a question framework can be developed to help analyze reconstruction work or to serve as a guideline for developing projects that will bring to light various dimensions and implied choices.

The legacy of the Franco reconstruction is that there is still work to be done in dismantling the myths of the Civil War and dictatorship. Far more than an academic exercise, it is essential in order to understand the threat of violence that looms over Spain every time a political party resorts to reviving historical grievances in order to sow division. This process, to which heritage is often instrumental, applies to many places other than Spain. Aside from a continuation of this type of work, which is being taken up by Spanish researchers and civil society groups, comparative studies would be invaluable in two ways. One would consist of studies carried out across different countries, historical periods and types of conflicts. This would help develop a typology of reconstruction practices, identify differences and similarities in the aftermath of different types of conflicts, and trace a wider evolution in reconstruction theory and practice. The other would cut across fields by comparing, for instance, the reconstruction of heritage with that of educational systems in order to see how heritage compares with other areas. This work is necessarily cross-disciplinary and collaborations among political scientists, sociologists, psychologists, historians, architects and art historians could produce insights impossible to formulate within a single field. Collaborations would be particularly imperative in order to explore the psychological dimensions of post-conflict scenarios, the attachment of individuals and groups to symbols in these contexts, and the transmission of wartime experiences across generations. A final dimension of joint work to highlight is that among academics, practitioners and policymakers, bringing these different scopes of expertise and experience together is essential for developing a more comprehensive understanding of post-conflict reconstruction which, as we have seen, is never the process it claims to be.

Conclusion: "The minds of men"

> *Someone has said, if my memory serves it was André Malraux,*
> *that a ministry for cultural affairs is a useless luxury unless the*
> *ministers are given a decent budget and time to work. Because*
> *the time needed for reforms in this field is long; it is not only a*
> *case of intervening in the materiality of places and objects, but*
> *also in the spirit of society, its behaviours, beliefs, and the*
> *collective ghosts.*
>
> (Semprún 1993: 313)

As indicated in the Preface and Introduction, the spark that led to my interest in the relationship between cultural heritage, conflict, and its aftermath lay in the Yugoslav wars of the 1990s. It was the motivation to understand these conflicts, and the processes witnessed there, that provoked my search for a historic case study which might reveal long-term impacts. The Spanish example clearly shows that cultural heritage unquestionably plays a significant role in long-term post-war reconstruction and reconciliation. Heritage can create a sense of place within space and time, of history and belonging, at once anchoring the present and inserting it within a flowing narrative with deep roots and a forward momentum. Post-conflict situations are ones in which such places are transformed, often deliberately, through their destruction and reconstruction.

Every state develops its policy towards heritage on the basis of a framework of values that informs decisions about that which is worth preserving. The preserved sites are in turn woven into a meta-narrative that seeks to fuel a sense of national cohesion and belonging. Moments of acute crisis within a society, such as that brought about by the extreme case of a civil war, cause radical shifts in these meta-narratives. In the aftermath of such conflicts there is a rush to redefine the emerging state and its population in order to situate it within a new narrative of the nation. The sense of urgency and emergency surrounding this process makes it all the more overt.

Post-civil war societies offer a lens through which we may examine the fragmentation of a country, and the emergence of competing claims for national and historical pre-eminence. In this type of conflict, myths of national unity are replaced by divisive discourses, often reliant on and relaying of improvised narratives of alleged historical injustices. Despite the context-specific differences of civil conflicts, their aftermaths do retain some common elements – such as an emphasis on re-inventing tradition and re-envisioning history, a form of historical territorialism in which dialogue and reconciliation have little place. History and heritage are represented in new ways as the nation's identity is tested, split apart, and ultimately redefined. This reconceptualized vision of the country, its past and its people is supported by an *à la carte* selection of the past: some historical moments are glorified while others disappear from the public sphere. As new historical sites, narratives, legends and myths become emphasized, so a new heritage landscape emerges to support the emerging *re-visioning* of the nation. The historical periods chosen to mythologize as direct predecessors or heirs do not only provide guidelines for the visual construction of the newly defined nation, but they also create a substance for nationalist narratives and construct meaning through the association of values derived from that selection. Inevitably, these narratives also redefine notions of otherness, excluding groups that once formed part of the nation.

Reconstruction can foreseeably contribute to scenarios that will lead to the next emergency. The first line of UNESCO's constitution states: "That since wars begin in the minds of men, it is in the minds of men that the defences of peace must be constructed". But we should likewise remember that it is also in the minds of men that heritage can be destroyed and reconstructed.

Notes

Preface

1 The Dayton Peace agreements were internationally brokered by the United Nations to end the wars in the Former Yugoslavia between Serbia, Croatia and Bosnia in the period 1992–1996. The agreement included active 'peace implementation' which involved peace-keeping and reconstruction activities mainly focused on rebuilding political, legal, economic and police institutions. UNESCO's mandate in the implementation was in its relevant domains: cooperation in educational, scientific and cultural issues.

2 That the confrontation between these two teams goes beyond the realm of football is further suggested by the names of their fan clubs, Red Army Mostar (Velež) and Zrinjski Ultras with clear political allegiances to the left and right of the political spectrum.

3 This division is still the case today, 13 years after the war and six years after my initial observations.

4 The article was a review of George L. Steer's book *The Tree of Gernika* published while Orwell was completing his *Homage to Catalonia*.

5 The official name of the town today is Guernica-Luno (Castilian) or Gernika-Lumo (Basque).

Chapter 1   Cultural Heritage and Post-Conflict Reconstruction

1 Johst wrote the play *Schlageter* in 1933 on the occasion of Hitler's birthday and to celebrate the Nazi's coming to power in Germany.

2 Since 1989, 115 of the world's 122 wars were intra-national rather than international. See the Human Development Report 2005 (Chapter 5 "Violent Conflict": 151–181), the Correlates of War data on intra-state wars and on international governmental organizations (2003) and Armitage (2008).

3 A historical overview of the cycles of construction, destruction, reconstruction and the corresponding waves in the re-invention of place can be found in Mark Mazower's (2004) study of the city of Thessaloniki.

4 On destruction and looting see Treue (1960), Gamboni (1996), Lambourne (2001), Bevan (2006), Nicholas (1994); on protection measures and legislation regarding heritage during wartime see Boylan (1993, 2001), Toman (1996), Hladík (2001), O'Keefe (2006); on the material remains of war see Schofield, Johnson and Beck (2002), Schofield, Klausmeier, and Purbrick (2006). Important exceptions to this are Ashworth and Tunbridge (1996) and Meskell (1998) which explore various ways in which heritage, conflict and identity have converged.

5 One exception during this period is the Universal Copyright Convention (1952) in which the idea of knowledge, creativity, innovation and know-how are recognised as a cultural good or property.

6 The former Yugoslavia was divided by conflicts between 1991 and 2001, the most intense and wide-spread fighting took place during the conflicts between Serbia, Croatia and Bosnia 1991–1995.

7 For more on culture and peace-building see Galtung (1990; 1996) and Lederach (1997 and 2002).

8 Two theorists on peace-building and reconciliation that have built the cultural dimension into their work, John Paul Lederach and Johan Galtung, have nonetheless overlooked the role of material culture.

9 Barahona de Brito, González-Enríquez and Fernández-Aguilar 2001; Jelin and Langland 2003; Edkins 2003; Amadiume and An-Na'im 2000.

10 Mary-Catherine Garden (2004 and 2006) coined this term in her PhD dissertation and with the article "The Heritagescape: Looking at Landscapes of the Past" in the *International Journal of Heritage Studies*, vol. 12, no. 5, pp. 394–411. She used it to refer to how one may analyze the extent to which heritage sites more or less successfully convey a sense of a particular kind of place. This differs from how the term is being used here, which is to give a sense of layered symbols, narratives and interpretations. It is closer to the idea expressed in the quote used of Moore and Whelan (2007: introduction *x*) a "site of representation, a locus of both power and resistance", for a particular valley might contain memories of battles, unmarked graves, anecdotes, associations with emotions and values as well as memorials or heritage sites of various types. See also Ashworth, Graham, and Tunbridge (2000).

11 The 'reading' of built heritage and landscape is not without precedents in the heritage field and has been carried out by Tilley (1994), and many others.

12 For more social performance as symbolic behaviour see Alexander, Giesen and Mast (2006).

13 For more on the creation of place see Keith and Pile (1993).

14 The notion of 'thick description' was first developed by Gilbert Ryle in his *The Thinking of Thoughts: What is 'Le Penseur' Doing?* (1968), it was further developed by Clifford Geertz in his essay "Thick Description: Toward an Interpretative Theory of Culture" in *The Interpretation of Cultures* (1973).

15 This is a simplified use of the symbol of the bull in its association with Spain used here simply to illustrate the dynamics of this form of analysis.

16 A prior research visit was made in September 2006 as well as a follow-up one in April 2009.

Chapter 2   Spain: Background and Context

1 Resina (2000:74–75) remarks that Spanish society was under the "state of war" formally declared by the *Junta de Defensa Nacional* until 1948. Martín Gaite (1987: 12) situates the end of the Spanish post-war in the 1950's with the renewal of relations with the United States but she acknowledges that others see this end only with the death of Franco in 1975.

2 Casanova 1993:944–945; Di Palma 1990:64–65, 105–106; Przeworski 1986:61, 1991:8; Huntington 1991:101–103, 126–127, 173–174.

3 The Zapatero government declared 2006 the "Year for the Recovery of the Historic Memory".

4 Palmieri (2006) has addressed the problematic involvement of the Red Cross in the Spanish Civil War, with the governing committee sympathizing with the Nationalists and workers on the ground favoring the Republic.

5 Namely the 1935 Roerich Pact for the Protection of Artistic and Scientific Institutions and Historic Monuments.

6 After the First World War, Article 247 of the Versailles Treaty included compensation in kind for the destruction of Louvain and its library.

7 Karl von Clausewitz: "War is politics by other means" (1976: 87).

8 As Toman (1996) has indicated the cultural dimensions of conflict and its long term impact on cultural life have generally been inadequately analyzed and little understood.

9 Álvarez Junco notes that this war against the Napoleonic invasion only came to be known as the *Guerra de la Independencia* when it was baptized as such in history books a quarter of a century later. He points out that it came to be the central event of the nationalist mythology which was to dominate the nineteenth and part of the twentieth centuries (Álvarez Junco 2005: 31–32).

10 *Patrimonio Nacional* is a specific part of a larger whole referred to as *Patrimonio Histórico Nacional*. Its sites and collections consist of royal palaces or monasteries and their contents, there is a specific administrative and professional body that looks after this heritage.

11 Their most influential works in developing their thoughts on conservation are, respectively: Violet le Duc's *Dictionnaire raisoné de l'architecture française du XIe au XVIe siècle* (1854–69), and John Ruskin's *The Seven Lamps of Architecture* (1849).

12 In the inauguration he was accompanied by high dignitaries from both the military and the arts – a frequent partnering in the construction of national narratives and myths.

13 In 1914 a *Real Orden* set up the *Museo Numantino de Soria* and the 1929 *Exposición International* held in Barcelona included 67 pieces from this museum.

14 The patio was acquired by a French art dealer in 1913 from whom George Blumenthal purchased it. Taking the patio to New York he installed it in his house on Park Avenue. On his death in 1941 it passed to the Metropolitan where after a long study it was installed in 1964. (www.metmuseum.org/special/velez/velez_more2.htm)

15 Purchased by William Randolph Hearst in 1925 and shipped to the US, it was reconstructed in the early 1950s ("Jigsaw Puzzle", *Time*, 11 January 1954)

16 This first line of an often cited quote is from a text entitled "En defensa de Unamuno" it appears in *Obras Completas. Volume VII (1902–1925)* published by the Fundación José Ortega y Gasset in 2007: 391.

17 Such as in the book by Juan Rey Carrera (1938) entitled *El resurgir de España previsto por nuestros grandes pensadores: Donoso Cortés, Jaime Balmes, Aparisi y Guijarro, Menéndez y* Pelayo, *Vázquez de Mella* (San Sebastián: Editorial Española).

18 *España invertebrada* (Ortega y Gasset 1921), the *Institución Libre de Enseñanza* created in 1876 and directed by Ginér de los Ríos, *España en su historia* (Américo Castro 1948); *España, un enigma histórico* (Sánchez-Albornoz 1957); *España* (Madariaga 1931).

19 The two sides had different levels of success in setting aside internal differences in order to focus on presenting a united front. The failure on the part of the Republic to unite the various political and ideological factions on its side, famously depicted in George Orwell's *Homage to Catalonia*, is often cited as a reason for its defeat in the war.

20 Max Aub and Rafael Alberti both wrote plays for these *Guerrillas*.

21 According to Hermenegildo, Cervantes' play was represented three more times in Spain: 1949, in the Roman theatre of Sagunto; 1956 in Alcalá de Henares; 1966 in Madrid's *Teatro Español*.

22 This was according to a 1936 ordinance of the women's traditionalist organisation the *Margaritas* (Tuñón de Lara 1986: 336).

23 Franco's side during the war were referred to as *los nacionales* which translates as nationalists; this is not to be confused in Chapters 4 and 5 when Basque nationalists are discussed. To avoid confusion, when referring to the Francoist side the word is capitalized.

24 These two organizations were the main instruments for the protection of heritage until the creation of the Nationalist government in January 1938. The main actors then became the *Ministerio de Educacción Nacional*, the Church and

the Falange with its National Delegations for Culture and Education (Alted Vigil 1984: 25).

25 Over 40,000 works according to Esteban (1998:133).

26 Newspapers were plastered on street walls; some of them were home-made, written and illustrated by hand (Mendelson 2007: 355–357).

27 The photograph, known as *The Death of a Militiaman* or *The Falling Soldier* was published in *Vu* (23 September 1936), *Regards* (October 1936), and *Life* (12 July 1936). Two years later a photo reportage in the *Picture Post* deemed Capa "the best war photographer of the world" (3 December 1938: 13–24).

28 These two pavilions also illustrate how the war split families. One of the two architects of the Republic's pavilion was Josep Lluís Sert, nephew of Josep María Sert who participated in the Nationalist exhibition in the Vatican's pavilion with this painting.

29 "Here I must point out that the Spanish Civil War of 1936–1939 caused a ridiculously small amount of destruction to ancient buildings" (Gaya Nuño 1964: 90–91).

30 Presided by Roberto Férnandez Balbuena and later to become the *Junta Delegada de Incautación, Protección y Salvamento del Tesoro Artístico* adding the word 'rescue' and with it a sense of urgency.

31 Exhibitions: *Du Greco à Goya. Chefs-d'oeuvre du Prado et des collections espagnoles. 50 ième anniversaire de la sauvgarde du patrimoine artistique espagnole 1939–1989* (Musée d'art et d'histoire de Genève, 1989); *Protected Art* (Palais des Nations, Geneva, 2005), documenting efforts to protect Spanish heritage, and *Arte Protegido. Memoria de la Junta del Tesoro Artístico Durante la Guerra Civil* (Museo del Prado, 2003). Documentaries: *Salvemos el Prado* (Arteseros 2004). Movie: *Las Cajas Españolas* (Porlan 2004).

32 These were under the control of the *Comisaría General del Servicio de Defensa*.

33 Juan Contreras y López de Ayala (Marquise of Lozoya), Manuel Cárdenas, Luis de Villanueva, José María Muguruza, Pedro Gamero del Castillo and Antonio Gallego Burín.

34 They were not the only international observers, Dutch and Swedish conservators and English artists also visited Spain during the war to assess the situation.

35 It worked through the International Council of Museum, office of the International Institute for Intellectual Cooperation, a predecessor of UNESCO.

36 Bolín was regional delegate for Andalucía of the *Patronato Nacional de Turismo* before the Second Republic, during the war he was a spokesman for Franco and was later named Director of the *Dirección General de Turismo* under the *Ministerio de la Gobernación*. According to David Clay Large (in Cowley 1992: 387) and Southworth (1977: 33) Bolín was the person responsible for initiating the official denial that Gernika had been bombed and for fabricating the story that it was the retreating 'reds' who burned the town.

37 Reminiscent of the Maginot Line, the latter was a system of bunkers and trenches of some 200 kilometers in length built to defend Bilbao. It was portrayed by both sides as an invincible bastion until the fall of the Basque region in August 1937.

38 Archive reference: AGA:03.049.002.12025-22/44

39 Archive reference: AGA:03.049.002 – 12025-12028 – 22/44 The Spanish National Library (BNE) has photographs of these excursions (BNE box 113 trip) showing tourists visiting sites on this route, looking at ruins and getting off their tour bus (Fig. 2.18).

40 He photographed ruins, inaugurations, and officials visiting sites at various stages of the reconstruction.

41 The looting of private property did occur on a massive scale during the Spanish Civil War; both sides requisitioned material and looted, and the North African

mercenary troops brought over by Franco were given a green light to loot as part of their payment.

Chapter 3 Reconstructing Spain, 1938–1957

1 Formed during the war in Burgos on 30 January 1938 with General Francisco Franco at its head.

2 This Directorate will be referred to as '*Regiones Devastadas*', the name by which it was commonly known.

3 Serrano Suñer was at this post until 1941 when he became Minister of External Affairs.

4 Evident from their publications – *Reconstrucción* and *Revista Nacional de Arquitectura* (*RNA*) respectively – founded in 1941 with the same architects often writing in both.

5 Although the General Directorate of the Arts was not directly in charge of reconstruction it played an important role in the restoration of monuments, the design of memorials and in validating the use of items from national collections as decoration in public ceremonies. Eugenio d'Ors was at the head of the 1938 version, from 1939 to 1951 it was directed by Juan de Contreras y López de Ayala, Marqués de Lozoya.

6 An earlier version of the PAN had existed since 1938 directed by Pedro Muguruza Otaño until 1939 and then Luis Villanueva Echevarría, 1939–1941.

7 Although the engineer Benjumea was only at its head for the first year, he continued to be a powerful figure in Spain's reconstruction becoming Minister of Agriculture, Minister of Hacienda (Treasury) and Director of the Banco de España. For his part, Moreno Torres, Conde de Santa María de Babio, combined his Directorship with several other posts including Mayor of Madrid (1946–1952).

8 There is a discrepancy here in that the magazine *Reconstrucción* repeatedly refers to these towns as having been adopted by Franco, whereas in public speeches Moreno Torres refers to them as having been adopted by "the Nation" (Moreno Torres 1940, 1944).

9 The projects outlined in the report refer to adopted towns in which new urban plans were being designed (at the time there were 36 of these projects being prepared including Belchite, Brunete and Gernika) as well as projects involving smaller scale interventions on town halls and religious buildings.

10 These figures do not include 30 religious buildings of other types (convents, monasteries and charitable institutions) that had been completed by 1942. The data is taken from *La Reconstrucción de España. Resumen de dos años de labor* published by the *Ministerio de la Gobernación* (1942). The discrepancy in figures reflects both the nature of the destruction and priorities for reconstruction.

11 In return for every day worked, two days of prison sentence were discounted and prisoners and their families received a small salary. Through their work prisoners were meant to be politically re-educated.

12 This discourse was a leitmotif of the 1940s, the destruction and scarcity caused by the war was blamed on the 'reds' (see Payá López 2002: 200–201, Tranche and Sánchez-Biosca 2005: 230–231).

13 In a talk at the *Instituto Técnico de la Construcción* Moreno Torres (*Reconstrucción* May 1941) notes 400 prisoners in Brunete prison-camp and 1,000 in Belchite's. He later said that the Directorate had had up to 7,000 prisoners working for it at one time but that by 1944 there were 1,000 (Moreno Torres 1944).

14 In 1970 the last known battalion of prison labour was used by the constructor José Banús to build a neighborhood of elegant houses in Mirasierra, Madrid (Lorente-Fuentes 2006: 38).

15 *Regiones Devastadas* was the employer with one of the highest mortality rates (Lorente-Fuentes 2006: 38).

16 The use of prison labour in reconstruction is not unique to Spain but is noteworthy for this study because it added further meaning to sites, especially the *Valle de los Caídos*.

17 Monarchists were divided into two camps with the Carlists of Navarre, called *Requetés*, favoring the regime and those Monarchists supporting the return of a Bourbon King having their reservations.

18 This was the Spanish version of the fascist ideologies that existed throughout Europe at the time.

19 The monastery of El Escorial, located some 50 kilometers northwest of Madrid, was envisioned and commissioned by Philip II as a monument to commemorate the Spanish victory in the battle of Saint Quentin, 1557. It was from there that he administered and reigned over the Spanish Empire at its height. Built between 1563 and 1584, first under the architect Juan Bautista de Toledo (d. 1567) and taken up in 1567 by Juan de Herrera (c.1530–1597), the complex of the Escorial includes a monastery, royal palace, library, basilica, and pantheon to the kings and queens of Spain.

20 His most important work is the Prado museum with its rigorous symmetry and straight lines. Plans for the building were approved in 1786 and it was nearly completed when the War of Independence erupted in 1808 and caused much destruction to the building – the lead roofs were melted down to make bullets – and it was not inaugurated as the Royal Painting Museum until 19 November 1819.

21 Eclecticism was not a novelty in Spanish architecture; neo-renaissance and neo-baroque styles were popular at the end of the nineteenth-century. It was also at this time that regionalist architectural styles became popular, reaching a peak in the first three decades of the twentieth-century.

22 Throughout the early 1940s, special sections of *Reconstrucción* were regularly dedicated to traditional architectural details, decoration, and folklore.

23 In the version of the story that this film presents, the character of don José departs from the original; he follows Carmen only because he has been kidnapped by her band; his sense of soldierly duty and honour prevail over his attraction for her, he sacrifices himself to save his fellow soldiers and is buried with military honors (Powrie, Babington, Davies and Perriam 2007: 165–166).

24 FET y de las JONS is the acronym version of the Spanish Falange's full name: *Falange Española Tradicionalista y de las Juntas de Ofensiva Nacional-Sindicalista.*

25 The main differences in these constructions are the number of floors and rooms, the building materials and their placement within the town. The more modest constructions were one floor, had little decoration, were intended for 2–4 families, had out-houses by the animal quarters, and were in the outer periphery of towns (AGA – Box 20702, folders 2, 3, and 4 for detailed construction plans). 'Nobler' constructions were usually intended for one family, incorporated greater decorative detail, had toilets indoors and were located near the church and *plaza mayor*. This was a widespread approach that can be seen in many projects of the INV, INC and *Regiones Devastadas*. A good example is the town of Guadarrama where clear distinctions of housing types were developed (Martínez Cubells 1942: 195–210).

26 During the political transition of the late 1970s and early 1980s these places became targets of the armed groups ETA and GRAPO, adding another symbolic dimension to them.

27 While for the Nationalists Brunete became a symbol of heroic martyrdom and victory in the aftermath of great sacrifice, for the Republican side, or at least its international supporters and reporters, the Battle of Brunete was associated with the death there of the photo-journalist Gerda Taro in July 1937.

28 *NO-DOs* were state controlled filmed newsreels produced from 1943 to 1981.

29 The architect Gonzalo de Cárdenas shaped the conceptual and stylistic focus of the magazine.

30 Under the auspices of the *Vicesecretaría de Educación Popular de FET y de las JONS*.

31 For more on memorials to the fallen: Llorente Hernández (1995); Vázquez Astorga (2006: 285–314).

32 The monument was intended to mark the spot where Mola had died when his plane crashed earlier in the year. The crash was deemed to be an accident though leftist popular myth has suggested that Franco was involved as it conveniently removed one of his rivals for power.

33 This is significant in the context of a war in which women on the side of the Republic had fought alongside men.

34 Amalia Avia's autobiography about the Madrid of her childhood and adolescence, the 1940s, has been chosen because she describes the visual landscape vividly.

35 Composed of Ferdinand of Aragon and Isabel of Castile who united Spain with their marriage, the Catholic Kings became symbolic not only of this unity but also of the Reconquest – and expulsion or conversion of the Jewish and Muslim populations – and the expansion of its empire to the Americas.

36 This dynamic, in different versions, is not unique to this context or to Spain but is common to moments of radical change when a society goes through a process of reinventing itself.

37 Francisco de Goya y Lucientes. "The burial of the sardine" c.1812–1819, Madrid, *Real Academia de Bellas Artes de San Fernando* and the preparatory drawings for this painting in the *Museo del Prado*.

38 The other aspect of this strategy is that images of Franco and José Antonio were in high demand and their distribution was coordinated by the *Ministerio de Educación Nacional* and its *Secretaría de Educación Popular* (Secretariat of Popular Education). Images of both men – often situated on either side of a crucifix – appeared in official buildings, school-rooms and places of commerce throughout Spain. The heads of Franco and José Antonio, together or separately, were stenciled on the facades of buildings all over Spain.

39 Note the use of tapestries hanging from the official podium. Tapestries from the royal collections were often used in official ceremonies and were also hung on the wall of the *Valle de los Caídos* thus adding a layer of history and 'authenticity' to the newly created ceremonial and memorial structures.

40 For this reason, it is also possible to observe some of the contradictions and divergent branches of that ideology in the reconstruction as Falangists, Traditionalists, Carlists and increasingly as time went on the Opus Dei all vied to impose their vision.

41 Illustrations depicting the sieges of Sagunto and Numancia were frequently used as representations of the past in school text books in the 1940s and 50s (Ruíz Zapatero and Álvarez-Sanchís 1997: 624).

42 The first serious efforts were made in 1928 when Pierre Paris was made Director of the new French cultural institute in Madrid, Casa Velázquez, the idea being that the bust be located in the institute, itself situated within the University campus then being developed (Storch de García 2006: 18–25).

43 Together with the Dama were requested a Murillo painting, the Visigoth Treasure of Guarrazar, a collection of Iberian artefacts and documents that had been in the

Archive of Simancas. In exchange, the Spanish side offered one portrait by Velazquez that the Prado had in duplicate, one El Greco to be chosen from a selection, and a tapestry based on a cartoon by Goya (letter from Ministry of Exterior to the Director General of Fine Arts, 23 June 1941, AGA legajo 12/1104).

44 By popular culture here is meant a wide variety of supports such as comic books, radio programs, clothing fashions, songs, film and publicity.

45 Toledo was unique in that the entire city was declared to be a National Monument (Moreno Torres 1946: 15). Initial reconstruction efforts concentrated on the Plaza de Zocodover, Toledo's *plaza mayor*, where entirely new buildings were built with a false facade imitating what had been there (Fernández Vallespín 1941: 9–15).

46 This selective process regarding what objects and images of the past are chosen for public consumption is not unique to post-conflict scenarios (Stig Sørensen 1996: 24–25).

47 For more on the symbolic uses of the Alcázar in the media see Sánchez-Biosca 2000 and 2008.

48 For instance the bullfighter Manolete being backed by the regime, or in football, Marcelino Martínez Cao's goal against Russia in the 1964 European Cup, which was celebrated as a political and moral victory.

49 At first the Delegation was housed within the *Ministerio de la Gobernación* but soon passed on to the *Vicesecretaría de Educación Popular*, henceforth charged with managing monuments in general and those relating to the 'alzamiento' and the war in particular.

50 A letter dated 22 January 1941 from the Head Engineer – *Ingeniero Director* – of Vías y Obras of the Madrid Diputación to the President of the *Diputación Provincial* asking for advice reveals the uncertainty (Archivo Regional de Madrid). In the same letter he suggests that the document designating Paracuellos as a memorial should set a precedent and determine a policy of limiting memorial sites to those predetermined by the regime.

51 Document signed on 15 July 1941 by the President and Secretary of the *Comisión Gestora, Diputación de Madrid* in response to a request from a man living in Colmenar de Oreja seeking to have a cross placed at kilometer 14 of the road from Aranjuez to Brea, in the memory of a family member fallen 'for God and for Spain' (Archivo Regional de Madrid).

52 The final monument consists of the underground basilica and crypt measuring 260 metres. The cross, which measures 150 metres from its base (rising 300 metres above the esplanade, with a 40-metre span at the arms), is visible from Madrid on clear days despite the distance.

53 In Spain, cypress trees are traditionally planted in cemeteries, and are a distinct marker in the landscape. On approaching a town, the location of the cemetery can be identified by their distinctively tall, slender shapes. They were used explicitly at sites like the Valle and the Complutense.

54 The high mortality rates in the construction of the Valle are important in terms of recent debates about how the site should be interpreted today (see Chapter 5).

55 The Valle also became a place of contestation for Falangists angry with Franco for diverting from its ideology, gradually taking political power away from the Falange and moving José Antonio Primo de Rivera's sepulture from the Escorial where they felt it rightfully belonged, buried with Spain's royals.

56 See articles: "Arquitectura Hermosa de las Ruinas" (*Vertice*, No. 1, April 1937: 41); "Elegía a las ruinas de la Ciudad Universitaria" (*Vertice*, No. 4, July 1937: 106); Francisco Cossío, "Muerte y resurrección de unos pueblos" (*Reconstrucción*, no. 8, January 1941: 1–6)

57 A portrait by Parraga of Franco with the dictator in military uniform shows an intact Alcázar in the background.

58 Construction of the new monument began in 1944 creating a larger version than the original – the Christ figure now measures over 11 metres and the pedestal 26 meters. It was inaugurated in 1965 with the legend under the Christ figure reading: 'I reign in Spain'.

59 The 'NO-DO' newsreel Noticiario 616A is about the *Fiesta Oficial de la Hispanidad*. Noticiario 616B is about Belchite.

60 The map has been rotated slightly anti-clockwise for the sake of comparing the shapes.

61 He was made prisoner by the Republic during the first days of fighting and, after failed attempts on the part of the Republic to exchange him for prominent Republican prisoners, shot on 20 November 1936. Immediately he became the proto-martyr of the Nationalist side and the only effigy that would hang in public buildings next to Franco's for decades to come. His father had been dictator of Spain from 1923 to 30, his sister, Pilar Primo de Rivera, was influential in the post-war and lead the female branch of the Falange, *Sección Femenina*.

62 The monument, designed in 1769 (by Francisco Sabatini and built 1774–1778), is one of the most symbolic architectural elements of Madrid. In historical maps of Spain, Madrid is often represented by an image of this grand five-arch stone portal and several popular songs are dedicated to it.

63 The *Junta* was created in April 1939 and was officially a dependant of *Regiones Devastadas*, but was guided in its actions by a *Comisión Técnica Asesora*, a subordinate of the *Dirección General de Arquitectura* presided over by Pedro Bigador.

64 Information for this is taken from various reports sent from Provincial Delegations of Propaganda to the national office in Madrid describing the celebrations of the *Día de la Hispanidad* in their localities for the year 1944 (AGA.09.17.10-51/20590, 51/20601, 51/20649).

65 See 'NO-DO' Noticiario 616A for news coverage of these celebrations, including the outdoor mass, images of the throne room and of the image of the Virgin being paraded along the streets of the city as Franco and his wife look on and wave from the balcony of the regional government headquarters.

66 Conversation with archivist at the *Consejería de Medio Ambiente y Ordenación del Territorio* (Council for Environment and Urban Planning), Madrid, July 2007.

67 Reports (1944) from the Provincial Delegations of Huelva, Salamanca, Oviedo to the *Delegado Nacional de Propaganda* on how their commemorative acts were celebrated (AGA.03.49.01-21/1850).

68 Letter of 2 August 1944 from the Provincial Secretary to the National Delegation of Propaganda with 'approved' seal of the Provincial Chief. Actos Públicos y Plástica, Delegación Provincial de la Vicesecretaría de Educación Popular de FET y de las JONS (AGA – Gobernación-01.0344/3311).

69 The design for the new Basilica was projected by Javier Saenz de Oiza and Luis Laorga, and including pieces by sculptors Jorge Oteiza and Eduardo Chillida and the painter Lucio Muñoz, all amongst the Spanish artistic vanguard of the time. Its daring design caused controversy and its construction was frequently delayed as a result.

70 A 1950 census revealed the persistence of an acute housing deficit (Dieguez Patao 1981: 74) which contributed to the creation of a law on 15 July 1954 facilitating the construction of low income housing (*viviendas de renta limitada*).

71 In the movie, a village in the central region of La Mancha is asked by the authorities to put on a good face for visiting American officials who will decide whether to build a railroad through the town. After much deliberation the Mayor decides to camouflage the town as Andalusian. Cardboard façades of typical whitewashed houses are erected with geraniums at the windows, flamenco dresses are distributed and the entire village is taught to dance 'Sevillanas'.

72 *In the first decades the commemoration of 18 July, like Victory Day, was aimed at evoking the Civil War as the basic source of legitimacy for the Franco regime. But during the change in the legitimizing discourse of the late 1950s and early 1960s, the commemoration of 18 July increasingly emphasized the legitimacy derived from the achievements of the Franco regime [. . .] the anniversary was increasingly commemorated by the inauguration of many important public works.* (Aguilar and Humlebaek 2002: 125)

Chapter 4   Reconstructing Gernika

1 The most complete study remains Southworth's (1977). See Preston (2007) for a reflection on its impact; other valuable contributions include: Tuñón de Lara (1987a), Cava Mesa (1996), Rankin (2003, 2007) and Patterson (2007).

2 Pierre Vilar writes that the bombing of Gernika served as a warning of what was to come, signalling a realization of the shape that a future European war would take (Vilar 1977: *foreword*).

3 Legend has it that the painting was found in a London tavern by the Basque Captain of a merchant ship and that he sent it to the Diputación which in turn sent it to the *Casa de Juntas* (Ortega 1976: Introduction).

4 These types of proclamations – and the use of trees – were not unique to Gernika or to the Basque region, as they existed throughout Spain and Europe at the time. They involved meetings of regional lords and landowners in order to establish political allegiances and establish common regulations.

5 Husband of Isabel I of Castile with whom he comprised the already mentioned 'Catholic Kings'.

6 In 1821 von Humboldt wrote a text entitled: *"Research into the Early Inhabitants of Spain with the help of the Basque language"* and Bähr defended his PhD thesis in Gottingen in 1940 on "The Basque and the Iberian".

7 These regions partly blamed Spain's troubles on the centralisation around Madrid. The Basque region had a system of taxation and military conscription different from other parts of Spain – amongst the privileges originally conceded with the Spanish King's respect of the *fueros*.

8 Astra Unceta produced the *Astra 400* gun for the Spanish military and exported it widely abroad. Alkartasuna and Astra saw a sharp rise in their businesses during the First World War (in which Spain was neutral) and Talleres de Guernica during the Third Rif War in Spanish Morocco (1921–1927). An interesting historical note is that in this war, the Spanish military dropped bombs containing chemical weapons, including a precursor of mustard gas, on the Rif (Balfour 2002: 132).

9 January 1909: "El Árbol de Guernica" by Carmelo Echegaray, "Lápida sepulcral de Guernica"; April 1909: "¿Cuando se plantó en árbol de Guernica?"; January 1910: "Monumentos de Vizcaya: La Antigua de Guernica" by Eugenio Zameza; Cuarto trimestre de 1912: "La villa de Guernica y Luno", "La villa de Guernica: Apuntes para su historia" by Eugenio Zameza.

10 For an explanation of how this division came about in the Basque Country see Juan Pablo Fusi (1984: 182–200).

11 When the PNV decided to side with the Republic it first consulted with priests and religious authorities in Guipúzcoa (Granja 1987: 76–77). Even the Nationalist side acknowledged the lack of religious persecution in the Basque region during the war. The *Causa General* report on Vizcaya reads:

> *It is true that because the Basque nationalists are Catholic the phenomenon occurred in Vizcaya that the Catholic cult was not interrupted, nor were profanations, sacrileges or mass executions of clerics carried out in equal amount to other regions.* (Section viii, 'Religious persecution', p. 23).

12 In fact, in this region the clergy was often targeted by the Francoist forces for defending Basque nationalism.

13 For more on the participation of Spanish aviation in the squadrons that took part in the bombing see Echaniz Ortúñez and Palacio Sánchez (2003: 111), in which they cite a document from the *Jefatura del Aire, Estado Mayor, 3a Sección, "Resumen de Operaciones del día 26 de abril de 1937"*.

14 For a history of aerial bombing including precedents to Gernika see Lindqvist (2001).

15 Even the infamous bombing of refugees on the road joining Almería and Malaga came to be known as the *Guernica Andaluza* (Suerio and Díaz Nosty 1977: 298).

16 His eye-witness account was reproduced in several formats – radio, newspapers, pamphlets, speeches, communiqués– as well as his autobiography from 1973.

17 Luis Bolín (1967), in charge of Nationalist propaganda, was central in disseminating the version of events by which Asturian miners and Basques destroyed the town; in his memoirs he presents the fact that the Tree was spared as proof that retreating Basques forces set the town on fire.

18 As Reig Tapia observes (1987: 125), Cierva is the same historian who went from saying in 1970 that the bombing of Gernika was a myth and that barely a dozen were killed to saying in 1977 that it was "an enormous reality, an enormous myth, and enormous symbol, an enormous painting". The first opinion was expressed by him in an article entitled "La guerra del 36, su historia y su circunstancia" in the Falangist newspaper *Arriba*, 31 January 1970, and the second statement appeared in *Historia Nueva*, no. 4, 1977. See Southworth 1977: 311–314 and Preston (2008: 352–362, 2007: 52–55) for an account of how Cierva repeatedly revised his account of events.

19 The panoply of lies that the bombing stimulated became an important subject in itself. The French revue *Esprit* dedicated a substantial section of its June 1937 issue to it, entitled "Guernica or the technique of lying"; Southworth (1977) provides an exhaustive account of the lies constructed identifying their origins and how they were transmitted.

20 This public relations gaffe likely caused him his job (Southworth 1977: 389), but as we have seen in Chapter 2 it did not stop him from organizing tourist trips to visit the ruins of Gernika.

21 Several authors (Lindqvist 2001: 159) suggest that this period was used to cover-up the bombing and plant evidence against Republican troops.

22 This seems to have especially shocked the population (Cava Mesa 1996: 240–241).

23 A complementary study has never been carried out of the crimes committed in the zones controlled by Franco's troops.

24 Photographs of the exhibition in Bilbao that Angoso reports on and in which he saw these projects are in the BNE box 113 trips "Exposición de Burgos de proyectos de reconstrucción de Guernica".

25 In the 1952 project for the main square of Gernika (AGA-RD-4.082.33. Guernica, box 1352) there is a plan for a commemorative obelisk but the intention is said to be ornamental, replacing the traditional fountain; there is no mention of a commemorative function for it.

26 Sixty years-old at the time of the commission, a monograph dedicated to Smith in 1933 attributed over 300 construction projects to him (Jaime Engaña 1933 cited by Paliza Monduate 1988: 16).

27 The neo-Basque style emerged as a result of the conjoint evolution of Basque regionalist architecture and Basque nationalism in the first three decades of the twentieth-century. It was influenced by Basque palaces and house-towers but took as its basis the *caserío* – traditional farmhouse, bastion of the family and a veritable Basque social institution (Paliza Monduate 1988: 336).

28 It recurred in accounts of the bombing. For instance, on the 5th of May 1937 *L'Humanité* had published a report by the priest Onaindía describing the bombing and affirming that it had been a market day.

29 *Jai alai*, which resembles squash, can be played with bare hands or with a narrow *cesta* –basket– usually made from chestnut wood and reeds.

30 The company Guerestu was created and with a combination of public subscription and nominal actions raised the necessary funds so that on 29 June 1963 the new *frontón* was opened. After over 25 years Gernika recovered part of its lost heritage through a combination of local initiative and private investment on the margins of the national reconstruction project.

31 One of my informants in Gernika (Luis Iriondo) remembered that the buses used to have a hard time passing through the streets because of the corridors, and spoke of them with nostalgia lamenting that Gernika no longer had an 'old town' or even a feeling of an old town.

32 'casas para la clase media' , 'viviendas de renta reducida', 'casas baratas'

33 The *Instituto Nacional de la Vivienda* had a programme for building subsidized housing in Gernika.

34 This came up repeatedly in conversations with Gernikans with respect to the *casas de sindicatos*.

35 During my stay in Gernika in 2006 a woman (early 30s), after hearing that I was studying the reconstruction of Guernica, expressed to me her view that the first and best buildings were "of course" not given to the original inhabitants but to "friends" of the regime.

36 The document "*Informe sobre la adjudicación de las 84 viviendas del grupo construido por la Dirección General de Regiones Devastadas en Guernica*" includes a detailed list of applicants for this housing (AGA). The successful applicants were public functionaries (postmen, civil servants), industrial workers (from the factories Unceta, La Industrial, Los Pirineos, Talleres de Guernica or Amurrio) or had important trades (baker, tailor, butcher). A further six apartments were allocated to functionaries of *Regiones Devastadas*. The dossier includes a list of the people living in Gernika on 18 July 1936, and whether any family members had been "victim of the bombardment of the town by the reds".

37 An application (of 27th March 1945 by Juana Echebarría) for building a house in the centre of Gernika also includes a "certificate of adhesion to the Glorious National Movement" (AGA-RD).

38 This paperwork required such means that only those with connections to the local authorities or with enough financial resources to 'ease' the process had a real chance of acquiring the necessary building permits. There was a vigorous black-market – estraperlo – during this period in which not only goods and services but also 'influences' were traded.

39 In project document for various phases of the rebuilding in Gernika architects frequently asked for extensions of time giving the reasons as the difficulty in procuring materials and the "scarcity of labour in the town caused by its depopulation" (AGA-RD-082.33.Guernica. Box 20682).

40 A project to build a concentration camp for prisoners was never carried out ("Campo de concentración de prisioneros en Guernica", Archivo del Bombardeo, Museo de la Paz de Gernika).

41 Today a school, the building of the Agustinos was signaled out to me on numerous occasions during my stays in Gernika for its past use as a prison.

42 In 1982 an important Roman site and necropolis were discovered in Forua, a town a few kilometers away from Gernika.

43 Examples of such interventions include the Torre de Salazar in Portugalete, and the Torre Larreaco.

44 Sabino Arana archive, *Notificaciones* / 1949 / Pnv_nac_ebb, k.00226, c.3

45 This example was mentioned to me in conversations with Luis Iriondo and Juan Gutiérrez.

46 For an excellent account of Steer's experience of the bombing and the pressures faced by journalists reporting at the time see Rankin (2003).

47 Not only newspapers but also official reports on the bombing did this, for instance, the Report prepared by a special Nationalist Commission for the British government (1938) and that prepared by the Comité Franco-Espagnole (1938).

48 A note on these appeared in the newspaper *Tierra Vasca* of 3 June 1937, cited in "Fotografía y Guerra civil en Euskadi", by Josu Bilbao Fullaondo in M. Tuñón de Lara ed. *c.*1987: 271.

49 This is extensively documented by Juan Larrea 1947, Herschel Chipp 1989, Laurent Gervereau 1996, Gijs van Hensbergen 2004.

50 There have been several thorough studies of *Guernica* from the art historical perspective and others that have combined this with political and social analysis: Juan Larrea 1947, Herbert Southworth 1977, Herschel Chipp 1989, and Laurent Gervereau 1996. The most recent and complete study of the painting is Gijs van Hensbergen's (2004). There is no need to repeat this material here where the interest in the painting resides in its contribution to the symbolic construction and evolution of Gernika.

51 The response of the Basque officials in Paris and of the *Lehendakari* Aguirre in particular was unenthusiastic even though they accepted to have their picture taken in front of the painting (Figure 4.42).

52 This anecdote is cited by many authors, most recently by van Hensbergen (2004: 139).

53 This Council initiated talks with General de Gaulle, developing a quid-pro-quo agreement that attempted to ease the difficult conditions of Basque refugees who found themselves on French soil in exchange for the voluntary enlistment of Basques in the Free French army (Clark 1979: 89).

54 *Boletín de información de los vascos en Inglaterra*

55 This first issue of *Gernika* contained a Christmas greeting from the *Lehendakari* to all Basques – "Mensaje de Gabón a todos los Vascos".

56 The booklet includes texts from Aguirre's autobiographical writings (1943, 1944).

57 Traditional Basque dance.

58 Once the war ended, Basque government in exile shifted its policy to one of close collaboration with the exiled government of the Republic. Such was the close working relationship that Aguirre was nearly made President of the Republic in 1947.

59 *Aberri Eguna* is the Basque National Day celebrated during Easter to coincide with the day of resurrection. It was created by Sabino Arana, the first one being celebrated on 27th March 1932 in Bilbao.

60 While propaganda remained a foremost objective, the most successful tool used by the Consultative Committee was the organization of strikes. Though the civil war ended in 1939 armed resistance continued until 1952 in the form of guerrilla fighting, often in mountainous regions.

61 In the document, a moral reparation is requested as a means of leaving the door open for future requests for material reparations "once the Government of the Basques is re-established by the restoration of democracy in the Spanish State", *Oficina de Prensa Euzkadi*, OPE, 6 January 1947.

62 In doing this they were continuing a practice initiated by Basque immigrants in previous centuries who had thus extended the scope of the Tree of Gernika's symbolism beyond Vizcaya.

63 From the early 1960s the industrial development of the Basque Country attracted internal migration and the population increased rapidly in a short time.

64 The statue replaced the column and wrought iron cross of the reconstruction, which was moved to another location in the town.

65 The popular comic, created by Manolo Gago, ran from 1943 to 1966. Between 1969 and 1971 *Equipo Crónica* used this quintessential representation of the regime to denounce it.

66 An ultra rightist group active at the end of the Franco period and during the subsequent transition to democracy.

Chapter 5   Reconstruction Continued: Transition and Recovery

1 The regime actively encouraged this from 1961, providing Spaniards assistance to work abroad. By 1973 there were an estimated 620,000 Spaniards working in France; 720,000 in West Germany; 136,000 in Switzerland; 78,000 in Belgium; 40,000 in Britain and 33,000 in Holland.

2 Growth of tourism to Spain: 1950 – some 750,000 tourists visit Spain; 1960 – over 6 million tourists; 1970 – over 24 million (Criado 2006: 7).

3 The *Junta de Paradores y Hostelerías del Reino* – a committee that administered the *Paradores* – had been created in 1928, in 1962 their administration came under the Ministry of Information and Tourism headed by Fraga Iribarne who opened 43 new ones (Criado 2006:21).

4 The creation of *Paradores* involved restoring castles, palaces, monasteries, *alcázares* and cloisters and turning them into luxury hotels and restaurants where the 'authentic' Spain could be experienced. The restaurants in Paradores were expected to serve 'traditional' food from the region in which they were located and the interiors were decorated with period objects and traditional handicrafts.

5 In effect this justified the continued persecution of Spaniards opposed to the regime.

6 The psychiatrist Castilla del Pino recalls in his memoirs (2004: 21) these words of a shoe-shine man whom he had known since 1949. Only in 1976, after 27 years and after Franco's death, did he dare to tell him that he had been a guide for the International Brigades and had been interned in a concentration camp as a result. His observation skills and professional training as a psychiatrist make his memories of the period especially insightful.

7 There has been some speculation concerning the role played by his doctor, and son-in-law, in deliberately choosing this date to shut off the life support system that Franco had been on for months.

8 A perception further emphasized by the fact that Franco chose the young prince over his father, thus breaking the line of succession.

9 Though the political transition officially began with Franco's death it would not have been possible without various developments in the last years of the dictatorship and the transformation of Spanish society that had begun in 1960 and had gradually accelerated.

10 Aguilar Fernández has argued that the central dynamic was not so much one of amnesia or forgetting but one of silence (2006: 246–249) and recent developments seem to support her analysis.

11 Through the initiative of some of the same architects and historians that had been involved in the first exhibition such as Carlos Sambricio.

12 A thus edited vision focused on a carefully chosen gallery of legendary figures.

13 The works of these poets had never entirely disappeared from Spain but had continued clandestinely to be recited and performed; Lorca's plays were performed in prisons such as the one in Burgos (Escalera 1994: 16–18).

14 Felipe González has since said that this omission is his one regret from his years as head of the government (González and Cebrían 2001: 36–46).

15 Although, as we have seen, there were only three historic regions – Galicia, Catalonia and the Basque Country – the Constitution divided the country into 17 administrative regions thereby diluting some of the potential of the three original regions to claim more independence.

16 Some of these films sought to denounce crimes of the past and their continued impunity; others sought to tell the story of the 'other' side; others attempted to capture the tense mood and realities of the war and dictatorship; and yet others tried more optimistic and even comic notes.

17 Valencian Institute of Modern Art (IVAM, 1989), National Museum Art Centre Queen Sofía (MNCARS, 1990), Museum of Contemporary Art of Barcelona (MACBA, 1995), Kursaal Auditorium and Congress Centre in San Sebastián (1999).

18 Solana went on to be Secretary General of NATO (1995–1999) and High Representative of the Common Foreign and Security Policy of the EU (1999–2009).

19 The *Marcha Granadera* chosen by Charles III in 1770, as opposed to the nineteenth-century *Himno de Riego* which had been used by the Second Republic.

20 The summer Olympics were held in Barcelona; the Parliament ratified the Maastricht Treaty on European Union; Sevilla hosted the International Expo; Madrid was European Capital of Culture, and hosted the Middle East Peace conference.

21 *Al-Andalus las Artes Islámicas en España* (Ayuntamiento de Granada – Ministerio de Cultura and Metropolitam Museum of Art, 18 March–19 June 1992, exhib.cat, La Alhambra, Granada), *La Vida Judía en Sefarad* (Centro Nacional de Exposiciones-Ministerio de Cultura, Nov.1991–Jan.1992, exhib.cat., Sinagoga del Tránsito, Toledo).

22 Fraga Irribarne founded the PP in 1989; he had held various posts within the Franco regime since 1945.

23 This relates to family members of those killed between 1 January 1968 and 6 October 1977 'in the defence of democracy' (*El País*, 3 August 2006: 24). In all three categories, pensions have been increased for living persons and compensatory payments arranged; also local governments are obliged to facilitate the excavation of mass or unmarked graves.

24 Often, as in the case of Gernika's municipal archives, bombing caused the destruction. In other instances, the destruction was deliberately carried out in order to protect people from reprisals.

25 Juan Luis Cebrián and Paul Preston have used these terms to refer to the acts of the Franco regime.

26 The decision was made by a unanimous vote of the Permanent Commission of the Parliamentary Assembly.

27 Information about this dispute is taken from a series of newspaper articles and radio programmes on the topic that have come out over the years and in particular around the date of the 70th anniversary of Lorca's killing. See: Nuria Labari. "La familia de Lorca rechaza la exhumación de los restos del poeta", *El Mundo*, September 2003. Fernando Valverde, "Los fusilados junto a García Lorca. Un libro recuerda al maestro y a los dos banderilleros fusilados junto al poeta", *El País*, 7 May 2007. Luis García Montero, "Setenta años de un crimen", *El País*, 18 August 2006. Ian Gibson, "Lorca: setenta años después", *El País*, 18 August 2006:11. In 2008 as a result of Judge Garzón's initiative to pursue a more active investigation of the crimes of the civil war and the dictatorship Lorca's family said they would not try to impede the uncovering of the grave but they contin-

ued to be against it (see Jesús Ruiz Mantilla, in *El País*, 18 September 2008 and 18 October 2008:12).

28 This said it is also noteworthy that several members of Zapatero's government are descendants of Falangists.

29 Conversations with Layla Renshaw, forensic archaeologist at Kingston University working on the exhumation of civilian mass graves from the Spanish Civil War, and the return of these remains to relatives and communities (Bristol, July 2006), see also Jimenes (2007).

30 For instance in las Palmas and in Telde, both in Gran Canaria, there have been streets, a square, a hospital, two schools, and a scholarship all named in honor of Dr Juan Negrín, as well as a sculpture.

31 The Madrid local authorities won and in 2008 the remains of the prison were torn down.

32 The debate surrounding this site is captured in the play by Jerónimo López Mozo "*El arquitecto y el relojero*" (1999), which is set in this historic building and structured around a conversation between the architect commissioned to transform it and the watchmaker in charge of maintaining its clock (a highly symbolic clock, as it is the one that chimes in the New Year, like Big Ben in London).

33 This was not the first time that the Falange's attitudes, in contradiction with the regime's, have caused tensions at the *Valle*.

34 Barthes's method of dissecting modern myths, which he applies to a front cover of *Paris Match* (discussed in Chapter 1), can be applied to this photo to reveal the layers of meaning-making involved.

35 Cited by Marta Rodríguez Fouz (2004: 333); she gives more examples of the same type of claim, but also of Basque leaders who did not feel any particular attachment to the painting.

36 The Nationalist government was in Burgos and the Republican one in Valencia.

37 According to Clark, originally the organization had been a "patriotic, democratic and non-confessional movement" (Clark 1979:157); he suggests that the severe repression of the organization on numerous occasions in 1960 and 1961 spurred its radicalization and turn to violence. ETA's first assembly took place in May 1962.

38 This is a form of street violence commonly used by youth groups affiliated with or sympathetic to ETA. They usually attack public property, banks or state symbols.

39 *Deia* supports the PNV while *Egin* supported ETA.

40 These changes took place throughout the Basque Country. One particularly symbolic replacement was in Bilbao's Albia gardens where the Monument to the Fallen of Bilbao, inaugurated in 1950, was replaced by a statue dedicated to Sabino Arana.

41 Victor Cerabitia, Counselor for the Basque Language at Gernika's Town Hall, spoke to me about the importance of recovering the Basque spelling for streets and provided me with a list of Gernika's street names including recent changes (April 2007).

42 This archival material is housed in the Sabino Arana Foundation and Museum in Artea, Vizcaya.

43 Archive of Basque Nationalism, Artea.

44 Southworth 1977; Onaindia 1987; Salas Larazabal 1987; Talón 1987; Cava Mesa et al. 1996.

45 As mentioned in chapter 4, even during the Transition revisionist historians continued to support the regime's version of the bombing of Guernica albeit gradually changing the story (see references to Ricardo de la Cierva in Reig Tapia 1987: 125).

46 The first meeting of the Commission took place on 26 February 1986 in the Meeting Room of the Department of Culture and Tourism of the Basque Government in Bilbao. A copy of the *Convenio* signed with the *Departamento de Cultura del Gobierno Vasco* is in the archive of Gernika's Town Hall (exp. 2487/23.1986. no. 8789).

47 The work measures nearly 8 meters in height and 18 meters in circumference.

48 Following its installation, Chillida was told that from its vantage point the place in the proximate mountains where the caves of Santimamiñe are located could be observed. The sculptor was delighted to learn of this unexpected addition to the symbolic dimension of his creation.

49 The 1987 annual congress of this organization was held in Madrid following the wishes of Enrique Tierno Galván who had been the first president of this Union– as well as Mayor of Madrid (1979–1986).

50 Pforzheim is in Baden-Wuerttemberg, it is of comparable size to Gernika and was destroyed by an aerial bombing on 23 February 1945.

51 From conversation, 27 April 2007.

52 Using the Latin word diplomatically avoids the conflict that would arise from using the Castilian or Basque words: *paz* and *bakaez*.

53 In 2006 another publication came out which compiled 136 testimonials on the civil war in the Basque Country collected by the Basque anthropologist José María de Barandiaran in the immediate aftermath of the war (Barandiaran 2006).

54 There was talk of a form of monetary donation to be made by Germany but there was no consensus about to whom it should go, how much it should be, or what it should be used for.

55 Conversation with Juan Gutiérrez.

56 Over the years there have been recurrent demands on the part of various sectors of Basque society for post-Franco governments to acknowledge that Gernika was not bombed by 'Basque separatists' but by the Francoist military command, and to apologize (Arruti, *DEIA* 25 April 2007). These claims fail to acknowledge that many cities, including Madrid, were severely bombed throughout the war. The debate attests to the instrumentalization of the Civil War past in the current conflict in the Basque Country and also to the symbolic nature of Gernika.

57 In the article he refers to the symbolic meaning of Gernika as being the pre-war historical one to which was added those of the bombing and Picasso's painting.

58 The mural was placed at the end of a central street in Gernika which slopes up towards it.

59 In exchange, the number of voices in Madrid that accuse Basques of overplaying their 'victimization' card gradually increases.

60 In many cases survivors of the bombing never spoke about the event even to their children.

61 Participants were composed of very specific groups, not necessarily of the general population of Gernika, either because they were the ones invited, informed or interested. As I stood observing the events that took place in the *Plaza de los Fueros*, I was approached a number of times by older Gernikans who asked me what was happening. I explained that they were events related to the anniversary, and pointed out to them that the *Lehendakari,* and two previous *Lehendakaris*, were present. The latter observation drew much more interest than the former and a couple of these people paused to observe the events from a distance, not entering the square or the exhibition.

62 In this photograph we see several layers of Gernika's heritage: the church of Sta María which survived the bombing, the statue of Don Tello inaugurated in 1966 and which commemorates the town's foundation in 1366, three *Lehendakaris* who have served since the 1978 Constitution was signed, all of them coming together

in Gernika's *Plaza de los Fueros* built by the Francoist reconstruction and today housing both the *Ayuntamiento* and the Peace Museum.

63　The number of people in Gernika that day, the aim of the bombing, the number of casualties, the air-forces that took part, whether there was a market, whether Franco ordered it or knew about it, who ordered it if not Franco, and what the strategic value of the bombing was.

64　These feelings are also expressed in some of the interviews carried out by Cava Mesa (1996: 183–184).

65　One of the activities of the anniversary was a luncheon offered for the survivors of the bombing. Prior to the event, within a group of elderly Gernikans, one complained that she had not been invited even though she had lived through the bombing. According to her, the same people were always invited. She wondered aloud why some survivors were 'better' or their memories more 'valuable'.

66　A woman (38) that I spoke with said that while she knew that her grandmother had lived through the bombing she had only mentioned it to her once, spurred by a television programme, but that her parents never spoke about the bombing. Since she had not learnt about it at school and it remained a taboo subject in her family she felt that she did not know anything about it.

67　Treasuring pre-war photographs is common to the survivors interviewed by Eva Lamarca (2007: 50).

68　Local historians have continued to investigate the pre and post-war periods, for instance, Delgado Cendagortagalarza (2000), *De la capital foral al bombardeo. Gernika-Lumo entre dos guerras (1876–1937)*.

69　In interviews Luis Iriondo frequently indicates the place where his house had been, now the market square.

70　A Gernika–Bilbao bus driver was asked by a couple of tourists to recommend a day trip to which he responded that if they wanted a nice coastal town they should go to Bermeo but if they were interested in Basque culture should go to Gernika as "after all it is the spiritual capital of the Basque Country".

71　These were the terms used in the media at the time (*DEIA*, Section Euzkadi, 31 July 2004: 12). The fungal infection and the solution of looking to the younger generation was interpreted in some articles as a metaphor for the troubles in the Basque Country.

72　Variations of this statement appeared in various formats, two examples are: the brochure from 1937 *Algunos datos sobre la tragedia* (AHN Salamanca) and *Tierra Vasca* no. 27 April 1937.

73　While the perseverance of Gernika's old symbolism is the dominant sentiment, there are divergent points of view: "Before there was more importance given to the Tree now it is more overlooked"; "They should give it another name because it is no longer Guernica. Guernica no longer exists. Guernica no longer belongs to Guernicans. It is not Guernica, it is not anything"; "Before it had more meaning than today. Today between the politics of one and the other . . . before there were only two or three parties", "Guernica today is and is not. Before we were all one, now no, there is more envy than before" (Cava Mesa 1987: 263).

74　The Republican presidential candidate for the US elections of 2008.

75　Gernika's ruins were once used to back their divergent accounts of the destruction, now reproductions of *Guernica* are used to call for peace or for armed intervention, a dynamic that came to the fore in 2003 in the run up to the invasion of Iraq.

76　A gift from Nelson D. Rockefeller in 1985.

77　The *Ertzaintza* is a powerful symbol in the Basque Country, a sign of its independence from Madrid and the persistent conflict and threat of violence.

78　A *botellón* is a youth culture trend involving large gatherings in public spaces to drink cheap alcohol.

79 Today's version of the *Paradores* initiative of the 1920s.

Chapter 6   Deconstructing the Reconstruction Process

1 For instance, referencing a generation, like the 'generation of '68', can refer to a demographic, or to a community of memory by hypothesizing that a set of memories are crystallized in this group, or to a symbol in that "the experience of a small number of people can be used to characterize a much larger group that did not participate in the central event or events" (Nora 1996:14).

2 This is not to suggest that heritage has agency in itself but that such agency is projected on it so that it would appear to speak in support of a determined, selected, narrative.

3 In response to queries about how long a monument or religious festivity had existed, I often heard *'de toda la vida'* or *'desde siempre'* (from always), even for those that dated from the Franco period and/or had been put up within the informant's life time – for instance the statue of Don Tello in Gernika inaugurated in 1966.

4 This court deals only with a category of crimes that has national or international scope such as human rights, terrorism, drug trafficking, and large-scale financial scandals.

5 This is the title of Philip Knightley's 1975 book on war correspondents, which was inspired by a statement made by US Senator Hiram Johnson in 1917: "The first casualty when war comes is truth".

6 This is likewise the case with international organizations. UNESCO embarked on reconstruction projects in Sarajevo with a firm conviction for the need to uphold and if necessary enforce 'multiculturalism' – a value that shaped many of the organization's interventions.

7 Attempts by East German authorities to clear away the ruins were blocked over the years; in 1982 they became the site for a peace movement and protests against the government. Since then a citizen's initiative, an NGO, members of the diaspora, a Nobel Prize winner, the Duke of Kent and the Bishop of Coventry have been involved in the Frauenkirche's reconstruction. The project has not had unanimous backing, and some survivors of the bombing were angry at the reconstruction thus bringing to light the different understandings of the site held by East and West Germans.

8 This proposed reconstruction is significant because on the same site the GDR had built the *Palast der Republik* housing its parliament. This building was demolished after 1989 (it was found to contain asbestos), a move which was criticized for destroying part of Germany's past. In 2003 a controversial decision was made to rebuild the seventeenth- century palace; however the project is still on hold.

9 Lenin's Decree of 23 January 1918 on the Separation of the Church from State and School.

Bibliography

Abellá, Rafael. 1978. *Por el imperio hacia Dios. Crónica de una posguerra (1939–1955)*. Barcelona: Planeta.

Abellá, Rafael. 1996. *La vida cotidiana bajo el régimen de Franco*. Madrid: Temas de Hoy.

Agarde, Eduardo. 1944. "Cripta de los mártires del Alcázar de Toledo". *Reconstrucción*, no. 47.

Aguilar Fernández, Paloma. 1997. *La Guerra Civil en el discurso Nacionalista Vasco: Memorias Peculiares para un Aprendizaje Político Diferente*. Madrid: Instituto Universitario Ortega y Gasset.

Aguilar Fernández, Paloma. 2002. *Memory and Amnesia: The Role of the Spanish Civil War in the Transition to Democracy*. New York and Oxford: Berghahn Books.

Aguilar Fernández, Paloma. 1996. *Memoria y olvido de la guerra civil española*. Madrid: Alianza.

Aguilar, Paloma and Carsten Humlebaek. 2002. "Collective Memory and National Identity in the Spanish Democracy: The Legacies of Francoism and the Civil War". *History & Memory*, vol. 14, no. 1/2, Fall 2002: 121–164.

Aguilar-Fernández, Paola. 2006. "Presencia y ausencia de la guerra civil y del franquismo en la democracia española. Reflexiones en torno a la articulación y ruptura del 'pacto de silencio'". In J. Aróstegui and F. Godicheau (eds), *Guerra Civil. Mito y memoria*, Madrid: Marcial Pons, pp. 245–293.

Aguirre y Lecube, José Antonio de. 1944. *De Guernica a Nueva York pasando por Berlín*. Buenos Aires: Editorial Vasca Ekin.

Aguirre y Lecube, José Antonio de. 1981. *Obras completas de Jose Antonio de Aguirre y Lecube*. Donostia (San Sebastián): Sendoa argitaldaria.

Alcoba López, Antonio. 2004. *El Pabellón que hizo Patria: 40 años después (historia de la joya de la Feria Mundial de Nueva York, 1964–1965)*. Madrid: Antonio López Alcoba.

Alexander, Jeffrey C., Bernhard Giesen and Jason L. Mast. 2006. *Social Performance: Symbolic Action, Cultural Pragmatics and Ritual*. Cambridge: Cambridge University Press.

Alexander, Jeffrey C., Ron Eyerman, Bernhard Giesen, Neil J. Smelser, and Piotr Sztompka. 2004. *Cultural Trauma and Collective Identity*. Berkeley, CA: University of California Press.

Allánegui, Alejandro. 1942. "Proyectos de reconstrucción en le región de Aragón". *Reconstrucción*, no. 19, January.

Alted Vigil, Alicia. 1984. *Política del nuevo estado sobre el patrimonio cultural y la educación durante la guerra civil española*. Madrid: Ministerio de la Cultura.

Álvarez Junco, José. 2002. "La nacionalización del paisaje urbano madrileño". In *1702–2002: Madrid tres siglos de una capital*, Fundación Caja Madrid. exh.cat. Conmemoraciones del tercer centenario de Caja Madrid, Madrid: COAM.

Álvarez Junco, José. 2005 (9th edition). *Mater Dolorosa: La idea de España en el siglo XIX*. Madrid: Taurus-Santillana.

Álvarez Lopera José. 1982. *La política de bienes culturales del gobierno republicano durante la Guerra Civil española*. Madrid: Ministerio de la Cultura.

Álvarez Lopera, José. 2003. "La Junta del Tesoro Artístico de Madrid y la protección del patrimonio en la Guerra Civil". In Argerich and Ara (eds): *Arte Protegido*.

Memoria de la Junta del Tesoro Artístico Durante la Guerra Civil. exh.cat. June–14 September, Madrid: Museo Nacional del Prado.

Alvesson, Mats and Kaj Skoldberg. 2000. *Reflexive Methodology: New Vistas for Qualitative Research*. London: Sage.

Amadiume, Ifi and Abdullahi A. An-Na'im (eds). 2000. *The Politics of Memory: Truth, Healing and Social Justice*. London: Zed.

Ana, Marcos. 2007. *Decidme cómo es un árbol*. Barcelona: Umbriel.

Anderson, Benedict. 1991. *Imagined Communities: Reflections on the Origin and Spread of Nationalism*. Revised edition. London and New York: Verso.

Angoso, Angel. 1938. "Projet de reconstruction et urbanisation de la ville de Guernica (Vizcaya). Étude réalisée par les Services Techniques de FET y de las JONS". *La Construction Moderne*, year 53, no. 27, 5 June 1938, pp. 451–454.

Antze, Paul and Michael Lambeck. 1996. *Tense Past. Cultural Essays in Trauma and Memory*. New York and London: Routledge.

Argerich, Isabel and Ara, Judith (eds). 2003. *Arte Protegido. Memoria de la Junta del Tesoro Artístico Durante la Guerra Civil*. exh.cat. June–14 September, Madrid: Museo Nacional del Prado.

Armitage, David. 2008. "The Idea of Civil War From Rome to Iraq". Lecture given at the University of Cambridge, December 2008.

Arrarás, Joaquín. 1941. "La nueva Acrópolis". *Reconstrucción*, no. 9: 2–8.

Arruti, Joseba. 2007. "El Gobierno vasco exige que el Estado pida perdón por crímenes como el de Gernika". *DEIA*, 25 April 2007.

Arteseros, Alfonso. 2004. *Salvemos el Prado. El Frente del Arte en la Guerra Civil Español*. Madrid: Borderdreams. (Documentary film).

Ashplant, Tim, Graham Dawson, and Michael Roper. 2000. *The Politics of War Memory and Commemoration*. London: Routledge.

Ashworth, Gregory and John Tunbridge. 1996. *Dissonant Heritage: The Management of the Past as a Resource in Conflict*. Chichester: Wiley.

Ashworth, Gregory, Brian Graham, and John Tunbridge. 2000. *A Geography of Heritage: Power, Culture, and Economy*. London: Arnold.

Augé, Marc. 2004. *Oblivion*. Minneapolis: University of Minnesota Press. (Translated by Marjolijn de Jager).

Aull Davies, Charlotte. 2008. *Reflexive Ethnography: A Guide to Researching Selves and Others*. London: Routledge.

Avia, Amalia. 2004. *De puertas adentro. Memorias*. Madrid: Taurus.

Balfour, Sebastian. 2002. *Deadly Embrace: Morocco and the Road to the Spanish Civil War*. Oxford: Oxford University Press.

Ball, Mieke and Norman Bryson. 1991. "Semiotics and art history". *Art Bulletin*, no. 73: 174–208.

Ball, Mieke, Jonathan Crewe and Leo Spitzer. 1999. *Acts of Memory. Cultural recall in the Present*. Hanover & London: University Press of New England.

Ball, Mieke. 1991. *Reading Rembrandt: Beyond the Word-Image Opposition*. Cambridge: Cambridge University Press.

Barahona de Brito, Alexandra, Carmen González-Enríquez and Paloma Aguilar Fernández. 2001. *The Politics of Memory: Transitional Justice in Democratizing Societies*. Oxford: Oxford University Press.

Barakat, Sultan (ed.). 2004. *Reconstructing War-Torn Societies*. Basingstoke: Palgrave Macmillan.

Barakat, Sultan, Jon Calame, and Esther Charlesworth (eds). 1998. *Urban Triumph or Urban Disaster? - Dilemmas of Contemporary Post-War Reconstruction Symposium Report*. Cambridge, MA: University of York and The Aga Khan Programme for Islamic Architecture at MIT.

Barakat, Sultan. 2001. "The challenges and dilemmas of the restoration of cultural heritage". In Layton, Stone, and Thomas (eds), *Destruction and Conservation of Cultural Property*. London: Routledge.

Barandiarán, José Miguel. 2005. *La Guerra Civil en Euzkadi: 136 testimonios inéditos recogidos por José Miguel de Barandiarán*. Milafanga, Villefranque: Bidasoa SL.

Barthes, Roland. 1957 (1973). *Mythologies*. Translated by A. Lavers. London: Paladin.

Berlanga, Luis García. 1953. *Bienvenido Mr Marshall*. Unión Industrial Cinematográfica (UNINCI). (Film)

Bermejo, Benito and Sandra Checa. 2006. *Libro Memorial: Españoles deportados a los campos Nazis 1940–1945*. Madrid: Ministerio de Cultura.

Bevan, Robert. 2006. *The Destruction of Memory: Architecture at War*. London: Reaktion.

Bilbao Fullaondo, Josu. 1987. "Fotografía y Guerra civil en Euskadi". In M. Tuñón de Lara, J.P. Fusi, M. González Portilla, A. Reig Tapia et al. (eds), *La guerra civil en el País Vasco: 50 años después.*. Bilbao: Universidad del País Vasco.

Blanco, Miguel Angel. 1987. "España Una". In *Arquitectura en Regiones Devastadas*, exh.cat. Madrid: MOPU.

Bloch, Maurice E.F. 1998. *How We Think They Think: Anthropological Approaches to Cognition, Memory, and Literacy*. Boulder, CO; Oxford: Westview.

Boissevain, Jeremy (ed.). 1992. *Revitalising European Rituals*. London: Routledge.

Bolín, Luis. 1967. *España: Los años vitales*. Madrid: Espasa Calpe. (Published in English in the same year in both London: Cassell and Philadelphia: J. B. Lippincott Company.)

Bonet Correa, Antonio. 1981. "Espacios arquitectónicos para un nuevo orden". In *Arte del franquismo*. Madrid: Cátedra.

Bonet Correa, Antonio. 1996. "La arquitectura efímera en el primer franquismo". In an issue of the *Bulletin d'Histoire Contemporaine de l'Espagne* entitled "Imaginaires et symboliques dans l'Espagne du franquisme", no. 24, December. Paris: Centre National de la Recherche Scientifique, Maison des Pays Ibériques.

Bourdieu, Pierre. 1984. *Language and Symbolic Power*. Cambridge, MA: Harvard University Press.

Bourdieu, Pierre. 1986. "The Production of Belief: Contribution to an Economy of Symbolic Goods". In R. Collins (ed.), *Media Culture and Society*. London: Sage.

Bourdieu, Pierre. 2000. *Pascalian meditations*. Cambridge: Polity Press.

Boyd, Carolyn. 1997. *Historia Patria: Politics, History, and National Identity in Spain, 1875–1975*. Princeton; Chichester: Princeton University Press.

Boyer, M. Christine. 1994. *The City of Collective Memory. Its Historical Imagery and Architectural Entertainments*. Cambridge, MA: MIT Press.

Boylan, Patrick J. 1993. *Review of the Convention for the Protection of Cultural Property in the Event of Armed Conflict*. Paris: UNESCO. Report ref. CLT-93/WS/12

Boylan, Patrick. 2001. "The Concept of Cultural Protection in Times of Armed Conflict: from the Crusades to the New Millennium". In K. Walker Tubb and N. Brodie (eds), *Illicit Antiquities*. London: Routledge.

Brenan, Gerald. 2004. *The Spanish Labyrinth: The Social and Political Background of the Spanish Civil War*. Cambridge: Canto, Cambridge University Press. (First published in 1943.)

Buchli, Victor (ed.). 2002. *The Material Culture Reader*. Oxford: Berg.

Calvo Serraller, Francisco. 2006. "Arte Español del Siglo XX en la Colección BBVA: El Progreso de una Historia". In exhib. cat. *Arte español del Siglo XX en la Colección BBVA*. Bilbao: BBVA. pp. 15–35.

Campión, Arturo. 1908. *Conferencia Acerca del Nacionalismo*. Lecture given in Gernika on 19 April 1908. Published by Antonio de Egurrola.

Caprarella, Marcelo. 1999. *Madrid durante el Franquismo. Crecimiento Económico, Políticas de Imagen y Cambio Social*. Madrid: Consejo Económico y Social, Comunidad de Madrid.

Cárdenas Rodríguez, Gonzalo de. 1940. "Estudio de un pueblo adoptado, Guernica. [Vizcaya]". *Reconstrucción*, no. 1 abril; p. 22–27.

Cárdenas Rodríguez, Gonzalo de. 1940a. *Datos para la reconstrucción del pueblo adoptado de Guernica*. Madrid: Dirección General de Regiones Devastadas y Reparaciones.

Carrillo, Santiago. 2006. "Entrevista: 70 aniversario del estallido de la Guerra Civil". *El País*, interviewed by Joaquin Prieto, 18 July.

Caruth, Cathy. 1996. *Unclaimed Experience: Trauma, Narrative, and History*. Baltimore, London: Johns Hopkins University Press.

Casanova, José 1983. "Modernisation and democratisation: Reflection on Spain's transition to democracy". *Social Research*, Winter 1983, 50(4): 929–973.

Casar Pinazo, José Ignacio and Julián Esteban Chapapría (eds). 2008. *Bajo el signo de la victoria. La conservación del patrimonio durante el primer Franquismo (1936–1958)*. Valencia: Pentagraf Editorial.

Castilla del Pino, Carlos. 2004. *Casa del olivo. Autobiografía (1949–2003)*. Barcelona: Tusquets.

Castillo Cáceres, Fernando. 2010. "Dos Miradas, Una Visión. Los dibujos de guerra de Carlos Sáenz de Tejada y Joaquín Valverde". In J. de la Mano (ed.), *Dos Miradas, Una Visión. Los dibujos de guerra de Carlos Sáenz de Tejada y Joaquín Valverde*, exh.cat. Madrid: Galería de Arte José de la Mano.

Causa General. c.1940. *Informe sobre resultado de las actuaciones relativas a la provincia de Vizcaya*, section viii, 'Religious persecution', Archivo Histórico Nacional (AHN): leg. 1332–2.

Cava Mesa, María Jesús. 1996. *Memoria Colectiva del Bombardeo de Gernika*. Gernika: Gernika Gogoratuz.

Centellas Salamero, Ricardo, Carlos Forcadell Álvarez and Alberto Sabio Alcutén (eds). 2006. *Paisajes para Despues de una Guerra: el Aragón devastado y su reconstrucción bajo el franquismo (1936–1957)*. Zaragoza: Diputación Provincial de Zaragoza. Servicio de Cultura Zaragoza.

Certeau, Michel de. 1984. *The Practice of Everyday Life*. Berkeley: University of California Press.

Chipp, Herschel B. 1989. *Picasso's Guernica: History, Transformations, Meanings*. London: Thames and Hudson.

Cinca Yago, Jaime, Guillermo Allanegui Burriel, Angel P. Archilla Navarro. 2008. *El Viejo Belchite. La agonía de un pueblo*. Zaragoza: Programa Amarga Memoria del Gobierno de Aragón.

Cirici, Alexandre. 1977. *La estética del franquismo*. Barcelona: Editorial Gustavo Gili.

Clark, Robert P. 1979. *The Basques: The Franco Years and Beyond*. Reno, Nevada: University of Nevada Press.

Colegio Oficial de Arquitectos de Madrid. 2003. *Arquitectura de Madrid. Vol. 1, Casco Histórico*. Madrid: COAM.

Colombo, Furio. 1977. *Fotografía e Información de la Guerra de España 1936–1939*. Barcelona: Gustavo Gili.

Colorado Castellary, Arturo. 1991. *El museo del Prado y la Guerra Civil. Figueras-Ginebra 1939*. Madrid: Museo del Prado.

Colorado Castellary, Arturo. 2008. *Éxodo y exilio del arte. La odisea del museo del Prado durante la Guerra Civil*. Madrid: Cátedra.

Comité Franco-Espagnol. 1938. *La destruction de Guernica*, Paris: Comité Franco-Espagnol.

Comité Pour la Défense de la Culture Espagnole. "La protección del tesoro artístico de

España durante la guerra". Special number of *Nuestra España*. Paris: *Comité Ibero-Americano para la defensa de la República Española*, April 1938.

Commission to investigate the facts regarding the bombing and destruction of Guernica. 1938. *Guernica: Official Report of the Commission Appointed by the Spanish National Government to investigate the causes of the destruction of Guernica on April 26–28, 1937*. Introduction by Sir Arnold Wilson M.P. London: Eyre & Spottiswoode.

Connerton, Paul. 1989. *How Societies Remember*. Cambridge: Cambridge University Press.

Cooper, Norman. 1976. "The Church: From Crusade to Christianity". In P. Preston (ed.), *Spain in Crisis: The Evolution and Decline of the Franco Regime*. Sussex: Harvester Press.

Correlates of War. 2003. "COW Intra-State War Data, 1816–1997 (v3.0)", http://hdl.handle.net/1902.1/10167 UNF:3:CNvDCxPKBfL79NImc++3Cw== Murray Research Archive [Distributor] V1 [Version]

Correlates of War. 2003. "International Governmental Organization (IGO) Data (v2.1)", http://hdl.handle.net/1902.1/10177 Murray Research Archive [Distributor] V1 [Version].

Cowley, Robert. 1992. *The Experience of War*. New York & London: W.W. Norton & Company.

Criado, Míguel Angel. 2006. "Auge y caída del cuñadísimo". In *El franquismo año a año*, vol. 2, 1941–1942. Madrid: Biblioteca el Mundo.

Cue, Carlos E. 2006. "Represaliados después del 39", *El País*, *Domingo* section, 23 July 2006: 2–3.

D'Ors, Victor. 1937. "Hacia la Reconstrucción de las ciudades de España". *Vértice*, no. 3, June.

Das, Veena, Arthur Kleinman, Mamphela Ramphele, and Pamela Reynolds (eds). 2000. *Violence and Subjectivity*. Berkeley, CA: University of California Press.

de Pablo, Santiago. 2006. "Visiones del exilio vasco". *El País*, *Babelia* section, p. 9, 7 October 2006.

Deák, István, Jan Gross, and Tony Judt (eds). 2000. *The Politics of Retribution*. Princeton, NJ; Chichester, UK: Princeton University Press.

Delgado Cendagortagalarza, Ander. 2000. *De la capital foral al bombardeo. Gernika–Lumo entre dos guerras (1876–1937)*. San Sebastian: Txertoa.

Dent Coad, Emma. 1995. "Constructing the Nation: Francoist Architecture". In H. Graham and J. Labanyi (eds), *Spanish Cultural Studies: An Introduction*. Oxford: Oxford University Press.

Denzin, Norman K. and Yvonna S. Lincoln (eds). 2000. *Handbook of Qualitative Research* (second edition). London: Sage Publications.

Di Febo, Giuliana. 2002. *Ritos de guerra y de victoria en la España*. Bilbao: Deesclée de Brouwer.

Di Palma, Giuseppe. 1990. *To Craft Democracies: An Essay on Democratic Transitions*. Berkeley, CA: University of California Press.

Díaz, Elías. 1995. "The left and the legacy of Francoism: Political Culture in Opposition and Transition". In H. Graham and J. Labanyi (eds), *Spanish Cultural Studies: An Introduction*. Oxford: Oxford University Press.

Díaz-Andreu, M. and Champion T. 1996. *Nationalism and Archaeology in Europe*. London, Boulder and San Francisco: UCL Press and Westview Press.

Díaz-Andreu, Margarita and Gloria Mora (eds). 1997. *La cristalización del pasado: Génesis y desarrollo del marco institucional de la arqueología en España*. Málaga: Universidad de Málaga.

Díaz-Andreu, Margarita. 1995. "Archaeology and Nationalism in Spain" in Kohl and Fawcett (eds), *Nationalism, Politics, and the Practice of Archaeology*. Cambridge: Cambridge University Press.

Díaz-Andreu, Margarita. 2000. *Historia de la Arqueología en España. Estudios*. Madrid: Ediciones Clásicas.

Díaz-Andreu, Margarita. 2002. *Historia de la Arqueología*. Madrid: Ediciones Clásicas. Estudios

Díaz-Plaja, Fernando. 1972. *La España política del siglo XX en fotografías y documentos*. vol.4. "Del final de la Guerra Civil al Principe Juan Carlos" (1936–1969). Barcelona: Plaza & Janés.

Dieguez Patao, Sofía. 1981. "Arquitectura y urbanismo durante la autarquía". In *Arte del Franquismo*. Madrid: Cátedra.

Dirección General de Regiones Devastadas y Reparaciones. June 1942. "La reconstrucción de España. Resumen de dos años de labor". Special issue of *Reconstrucción*, no. 24, June–July 1942. Madrid: Ministerio de la Gobernación.

Dirección General de Regiones Devastadas. 1941. "Las Obras de reconstrucción de Guernica [Vizcaya]" in *Reconstrucción*, no. 15, September, pp. 10–16. Madrid: Ministerio de la Gobernación, Dirección General de Regiones Devastadas.

Doménech Girbau, Luis. 1987. "Corrientes de la arquitectura española contemporánea". In *Arquitectura en Regiones Devastadas*, exh.cat., Madrid: MOPU.

Domènech, Lluís. 1978. *Arquitectura de Siempre: Los años 40*. Barcelona: Tusquets.

d'Ors, Victor. 1937. "Hacia la reconstrucción de las ciudades de España". *Vértice*, no. 3, 1937.

Du Greco à Goya. Chefs-d'oeuvre du Prado et des collections espagnoles. 50 ième anniversaire de la sauvgarde du patrimoine artistique espagnole 1939–1989. 1989 (exh.cat.). Geneva: Musée d'art et d'histoire.

Echegaray, Bonifacio de. 1937. Speech made on *Radio Euzkadi* on 4th May 1937. (Published in a booklet with other contributions made for a special radio programme organized by Socorro Rojo Internacional. *Emisión extraordinaria dedicada a los heróicos luchadores de Euzkadi, en la que participaron los jefes de la defensa de Madrid y representantes del pueblo Vasco*. Madrid: Ediciones S.R.I.)

Echegaray, Carmelo de. 1909. "El Árbol de Guernica". *Boletín de la Comisión de Monumentos de Vizcaya. Comisión de Monumentos de Vizcaya*, January 1909.

Echenique, Francisco. 1942. "Cuartel para Policía Armada en Oviedo". *Reconstrucción*, no. 20, February 1942: pp. 37–48.

Echenique, Francisco. 1942. "Plazas Mayores en la colonización del Nuevo Mundo". *Reconstrucción*, no. 21, March 1942.

Edkins, Jenny. 2003. *Trauma and the Memory of Politics*. Cambridge: Cambridge University Press.

Egido, José Antonio. 1997. "Mémoire, espace et société du bombardement de Guernica", unpublished thesis, University of Aix-en-Provence.

Elorza, Antonio. 1987. "Guerra y fueros en los orígenes del nacionalismo vasco". In Tuñon de Lara (ed.), *Gernika: 50 años después (1937–1987)*. San Sebastián: Universidad del País Vasco.

Elósegui, Joseba. 1977. "Guernica – 40 years later", *Time*, 2 May.

Erikson, Eric. 1972. *Young man Luther: A Study in Psychoanalysis and History*. London: Faber and Faber (reprint of 1959 ed.).

Escalera, Manuel de la. 1981. *Cuentos de nubes*. Madrid: Heliodoro.

Escalera, Manuel de la. 1994. *Ramas de un mismo tronco* (excerpt from *Muerte después de Reyes*. México: Editorial Ate). Santander: Caja Cantabria.

Esteban, José. 1998. "Las Brigadas Internacionales y la Guerra Civil en la Literatura", in Espadas Burgos and Requena Gallego (eds), *La Guerra Civil Española y las Brigadas Internacionales*. Cuenca: Universidad de Castilla y La Mancha.

Etxaniz Ortúñez, José Ángel (Txato). 2006/2007. E-mails, phone conversations and articles from *Aldaba*, no. 141, April–March 2006.

Etxaniz Ortúñez, José Ángel (Txato) and Vicente del Palacio Sánchez. 2003. "Presos Políticos: Mano De Obra Barata. El Hospital Penitenciario y el Batallón de

Trabajadores durante la reconstrucción de Gernika-Lumo (1938–1945)". In C. Molinero, M. Sala and J. Sobrequés (eds), *Los campos de concentración y el mundo penitenciario en España durante la guerra civil y el franquismo*. Barcelona: Crítica.

Farchakh Bajjaly, Joanne. 2006. "Can the media play a role in sensitizing or safeguarding archaeology in a post-conflict country?" Lecture given at the conference *Archaeology in Conflict*, 10–12 November, Centre for Applied Archaeology, University College London.

Fernández Cuenca, Carlos. 1967. *30 años de documental de arte en España*. Madrid: Esculea Oficial de Cinematografía.

Fernández Vallespín, Aristides. 1941. "Orientaciones sobre la reconstrucción de Toledo". *Reconstrucción*, no. 9: 9–15.

Fernández-Shaw, Casto. 1940. *Información para la reconstrucción del pueblo adoptado de Guernica*. Madrid: Dirección General de Regiones Devastadas y Reparaciones.

Forty, Adrian and Susanne Küchler (eds). 2001. *The Art of Forgetting*. Oxford: Berg Books.

Foucault, Michel. 1972. *The Archaeology of Knowledge*. London: Tavistok.

Foucault, Michel. 1974. "Anti-rétro: entretien avec Michel Foucault". *Cahiers du Cinéma*, 251–2, July–August.

Franco, Francisco. 1942. Speech given in La Coruña, 24 August cited by M.A. Criado "Auge y caída del 'cuñadísimo". In *El Franquismo año a año*, vol. 2, 1941–1942. Madrid: Biblioteca El Mundo.

Franco, Francisco. 1952. Speech given at the Alto de los Leones in the Sierra de Guadarrama on the occasion of the closing ceremony of the I Congreso Nacional de Excombatientes, 19 October 1952. http://www.filosofia.org/mon/tem/es0010.htm. (Most recent viewing: 3 April 2009).

Fusi, Juan Pablo. 1984. "The Basque Question 1931–7". In Preston (ed.), *Revolution and War in Spain, 1931–1939*. London and New York: Methuen.

Gallego Burín, Antonio (ed). 1938. *La destrucción del tesoro artístico de España: informe sobre la destrucción realizada por el marxismo en el patrimonio de arte español, de 1931 a 1937 según los datos aportados por las comisiones provinciales de monumentos*. Granada: Imp. Hª de Paulino Ventura.

Galtung, Johan. 1990. "Cultural Violence". *Journal of Peace Research*, vol. 27, no. 3, 291–305. London: Sage.

Galtung, Johan. 1996. *Peace by Peaceful Means*. London: Sage.

Gamboni, Dario. 1996. *The Destruction of Art: Iconoclasm and Vandalism since the French Revolution*. London: Reaktion.

García de Cortázar, Fernando. 2003. *Los mitos de la historia de España*. Barcelona: Planeta.

García de Cortázar, Fernando. 2005. *Atlas de Historia de España*. Barcelona: Planeta.

García Montero, Luis. 2006. "Setenta años de un crimen". *El País*, 18 August.

García-Gutiérrez Mosteiro, Javier. 2005. "Influencia de la pirámide en la arquitectura del primer tercio del siglo XIX". In *El arte foráneo en España: Presencia e influencia*. Madrid: Instituto de Historia, CSIC.

Garden, Mary-Catherine. 2004. "The Heritagescape: Exploring the Phenomenon of the Heritage Site". Unpublished PhD dissertation Department of Archaeology, University of Cambridge.

Garden, Mary-Catherine. 2006. "The Heritagescape: Looking at Landscapes of the Past". *International Journal of Heritage Studies*, vol. 12, issue 5, September 2006, pp. 394–411.

Gautreau, Marion. 2008. "La presse française face à Guernica: le traitement photographique d'un événement sans images". International Colloquium "Guernica ou l'image absente", Université Paris Est in collaboration with the University of Valencia and the Colegio de España (5 et 6 juin 2008).

Gaya Nuño, Antonio. 1964. *El arte europeo en peligro*. Barcelona: EDHASA.

Gaya Nuño, Juan Antonio. 1961. *La arquitectura española en sus monumentos desaparecidos*. Madrid: Espasa Calpe.

Geertz, Clifford. 1973. *The Interpretation of Cultures*. New York: Basic Books.

Gernikazarra Historia Taldea. 1991. *El Bombardeo de Gernika*. Catalogue of an exhibition organized in 1991 in Gernika by Gernikazarra Historia Taldea, Gernika-Lumo: Gernikazarra.

Gernikazarra Taldea. 1987. *Gernika Zaharra: Callejero, apuntes y anecdotas del Gernika anterior al 26–IV-37*. Gernikako Aldaba: Gernika.

Gervereau, Laurent. *Autopsie d'un Chef-d'oeuvre: Guernica*. Paris: Paris-Méditerranée, 1996.

Gibson, Ian. 2006. "Lorca: setenta años después". *El País*, 18 August.

Gillis, John R. (ed.). 1994. *Commemorations: The Politics of National Identity*. Princeton, NJ: Princeton University Press.

Giménez Caballero, Ernesto. 1935. *Arte y Estado*. Madrid: Talleres de Gráfica Universal.

Giménez Caballero, Ernesto. 1980. "La mística de la anticultura". In *La Guerra Ccivil Española*. exh.cat. Madrid: Ministerio de Cultura.

Gombrich, Ernst H. 1970. Aby *Warburg: An Intellectual Biography*. London: The Warburg Institute.

Gómez Aparicio, Pedro. 1940. "The Symbol of the Two Belchites". *Reconstrucción*, no. 1, April 1940: 6–9

Gonzalez Calleja, Eduardo and Fredes Limon Nevado. 1988. *La hispanidad como instrumento de combate: Raza e Imperio en la Prensa franquista durante la Guerra Civil española*. Madrid: Centro de Estudios Históricos, CSIC.

González Duro, Enrique. 2005. *La sombra del General. Qué queda del franquismo en España*. Barcelona: Arena Abierta, Debate, Random House Mondadori.

González, Felipe and Luis Cebrian. 2001. *El futuro no es lo que era*. Madrid: Aguilar.

Graham, Helen and Jo Labanyi (eds). 1995. *Spanish Cultural Studies: An Introduction*. Oxford: Oxford University Press.

Granja, José Luis de la and Carmelo Garitaonandia, (eds). 1987. *Gernika. 50 años después (1937–1987). Nacionalismo, República, Guerra Civil*. Cursos de Verano VI. San Sebastián: Universidad del País Vasco.

Granja, José Luis and José Ángel Echániz (eds). 1998. *Gernika y la Guerra Civil. Symposium: 60 aniversario del bombardeo de Gernika (1997)*. Gernika-Lumo: Gernikazarra bilduma.

Granja, José Luis de la. 1987. "El nacionalismo vasco ante la Guerra Civil". In M. Tuñón de Lara, J.P. Fusi, M. González Portilla, A. Reig Tapia et al. (eds), *La guerra civil en el País Vasco: 50 años después*. Bilbao: Universidad del País Vasco.

Grimau, Carmen. 1987. "La imagen en Euzkadi 1936–1937". In M. Tuñón de Lara, J.P. Fusi, M. González Portilla, A. Reig Tapia et al. (eds), *La guerra civil en el País Vasco: 50 años después*. Bilbao: Universidad del País Vasco.

Gutiérrez Valero, Ángel. 2005. "Postcards from Spain". In *Archive Cultures*, vol. 2. Barcelona: Fundació Antoni Tàpies.

Halbwachs, Maurice. 1925. *Les cadres sociaux de la mémoire*. Paris: Félix Alcan, 1925. Collection Les Travaux de l'Année sociologique.

Halbwachs, Maurice. 1992. *On Collective Memory*. Chicago: University of Chicago Press. New York; London: Harper & Row. (Translated by Francis J. Ditter, Jr. and Vida Yazdi Ditter)

Hall, Stuart. 1997. *Representation: Cultural Representations and Signifying Practices*. London: Sage.

Henare Amira, Martin Holbraad and Sari Wastell (eds). 2007. *Thinking through Things: Theorising Artefacts Ethnographically*. London: Routledge.

Hensbergen, Gijs van. 2004. *Guernica: The Biography of a Twentieth-Century Icon*. London: Bloomsbury.

Hermenegildo, Alfredo. 1994. Introduction and notes to Miguel de Cervantes *La destrucción de Numancia*. Madrid: Clásicos Castalia.

Hernández Hernández, Francisca. 2002. *El patrimonio cultural: la memoria recuperada*. Gijón: Ediciones Trea.

Hernández Martínez, Ascensión. 2008. "La restauración de monumentos en Aragón (1936 - 1958)". In Casar Pinazo and Esteban Chapapría (eds), *Bajo el signo de la victoria. La conservación del patrimonio durante el primer Franquismo (193601958)*. Valencia: Pentagraf Editorial.

Hernandez Rubio, Francisco. 1941. "Estudio de un pueblo adoptado Los Blázquez". *Reconstrucción*, no. 10, March, pp. 8–16.

Hladik, Jan. 2001. "The control system under the Hague Convention for the Protection of Cultural Property in the Event of Armed Conflict 1954 and its Second Protocol". *Yearbook of International Humanitarian Law*, vol. 4.

Hobsbawm, Eric and Terence Ranger (eds). 1983. *The Invention of Tradition*. Cambridge: Cambridge University Press.

Hodder, Ian (ed.). 1987. *The Archaeology of Contextual Meanings*. Cambridge: Cambridge University Press.

Hodder, Ian. 1981. *Pattern of the Past: Studies in Honour of David Clarke*. Cambridge: Cambridge University Press.

Hodder, Ian. 1989. *The Meanings of Things: Material Culture and Symbolic Expression*. London: Routledge.

Hodder, Ian. 2000. "The Interpretation of Documents and Material Culture". In Denzin and Lincoln (eds), *Handbook of Qualitative Research* (second edition). London: Sage Publications.

Hoffman, Susanna M. and Anthony Oliver-Smith. 1999. "Anthropology and the Angry Earth: An Overview". In S. Hoffman and A. Oliver-Smith (eds), *The Angry Earth: Disaster in Anthropological Perspective*. New York: Routledge.

Hollyman, John Llewelyn. 1976. "Basque Revolutionary Separatism: ETA". In Preston (ed.), *Spain in Crisis: The Evolution and Decline of the Franco Régime*. Hassocks: The Harvester Press.

Huntington, Samuel. 1991. *The Third Wave: Democratisation in the Late Twentieth Century*. Norman: University of Oklahoma Press.

Huyssen, Andreas. 1995. *Twilight Memories: Marking Time in a Culture of Amnesia*. New York & London: Routledge.

Huyssen, Andreas. 2003. *Present Pasts: Urban Palimpsests and the Politics of Memory*. Stanford, CA: Stanford University Press.

Inista Lopez, Andrés. 2006. *El niño de la prisión*. Madrid: Siddharth Mehta.

Iriondo, Luis. 1997. Speech made in Gernika on the 60th anniversary of the bombing, 26 April.

Isar, Yudhishthir Raj, and Helmut K. Anheier (eds). 2007. *Conflicts and Tensions*, The Cultures and Globalization Series, vol. 1. London: Sage.

Jackson, Gabriel. 1967. *La República Española y lu Guerra Civil*. México: Editora Americana.

Jelin, Elizabeth and Victoria Langland. 2003. *Monumentos, memoriales y marcas territoriales*. Madrid and Buenos Aires: Siglo XXI.

Jimenes, Guy. 2007. *L'enfant de Guernica*. Paris: Oskar jeunesse.

Jimeno, Alfredo and José Ignacio de la Torre. 1997. "Numancia y regeneración". In M. Díaz-Andreu and G. Mora (eds), *La cristalización del pasado: Génesis y desarrollo del marco institucional de la arqueología en España*. Málaga: Universidad de Málaga.

Johst, Hans. 1984. *Schlageter*. Translated with an introduction by Ford B. Parkes-

Perret. Stuttgart: Akdemischer Verlag Hans-Dieter Heinz. (First published 1933, Munich: A. Langen; G. Muller).

Jones, Andrew. 2007. *Memory and Material Culture*. Cambridge: Cambridge University Press.

Judt, Tony. 2000. "The Past is Another Country: Myth and Memory in Postwar Europe". In Deák, Gross and Judt (eds), *The Politics of Retribution*. Princeton, NJ; Chichester, UK: Princeton University Press.

Juliá, Santos. 2004. *Historias de las dos Españas*. Madrid: Taurus-Santillana.

Juliá, Santos. 2006. "Memorias en lugar de memoria". *El País*, 2 July 2006.

Keane, John. 1988. "More theses on the philosophy of history". In James Tully (ed.), *Meaning and Context: Quentin Skinner and his Critics*. Cambridge: Polity.

Keith, Michael and Steve Pile (eds). 1993. *Place and the Politics of Identity*. London: Routledge.

Kenyon, Frederic. 1937. "Treasures of Spain". *The Times*, 3 and 4 September.

Kenyon, Frederic. 1937. Letter. *The Times* of 20 July.

King, Alex. 2001. "Remembering and Forgetting in the Public Memorials of the Great War". In A. Forty and S. Küchler (eds), *The Art of Forgetting*. Oxford: Berg Publishers.

Kirschbaum, Julie and Desirée Sideroff. 2005. "A Delayed Healing: Understanding the Fragmented Resilience of Gernika". In Valle and Campanella (eds), *The Resilient City: How Modern Cities recover From Disaster*. Oxford: Oxford University Press.

Knightley, Phillip. 1975. *The First Casualty. From the Crimea to Vietnam: the war correspondent as hero, propagandist and myth maker*. New York and London: A Harvest Book, Harcourt Brace Jovanovich.

Kritzman, Lawrence D. 1996. "Foreword: In remembrance of things French". In *Realms of Memory: Rethinking the French Past, vol. 1: Conflicts and Divisions*. Kritzman (ed.). New York: Columbia University Press. pp. ix–xiv.

Küchler, Susanne and Walter Melion. 1991. *Images of Memory. On Remembering and Representation*. Washington and London: Smithsonian Institution Press.

Kurtz, Gerardo F. and Isabel Ortega. 1989. *150 Años de fotografía en la Biblioteca Nacional. Inventario de los fondos fotográficos de la Biblioteca nacional*. exh.cat. BNE. Madrid: Ministerio de Cultura. Dirección General del Libro y Bibliotecas. Ediciones El Viso.

Labari, Nuria. 2003 "La familia de Lorca rechaza la exhumación de los restos del poeta". *El Mundo*, 15 September.

Lamarca, Eva. 2007. "La memoria de Gernika". *El País Semanal*, 22 April 2007: 46–54.

Lambourne, Nicola. 2001. *War Damage in Western Europe: The Destruction of Historic Monuments During the Second World War*. Edinburgh: Edinburgh University Press.

Lammy, David. 2005. Speech at the "Where now for Black and Minority Ethnic heritage?" Heritage Lottery Fund event, British Museum, London, 24 October, 2005. www.culture.gov.uk/reference_library/minister_speeches/2038.aspx

Larrea, Juan. 1947. Gernika. Introduction by Alfred H. Barr Jr., translated by Dr. Alexander H. Krappe. New York: Curt Valentin.

Layton, Robert, Peter G. Stone, and Julian Thomas (eds). 2001. *Destruction and Conservation of Cultural Property*. London and New York: Routledge.

Lederach, John Paul and Janice Moomaw Jenner (eds). 2002. *A Handbook of International Peacebuilding: Into the Eye of the Storm*. San Francisco: Jossey-Bass.

Lederach, John Paul. 1997. *Building Peace: Sustainable Reconciliation in Divided Societies*. Washington D.C.: United States Institute of Peace Press.

Lefebvre, Henri. 1974. *La production de l'espace*. Paris: Éditions Anthropos. (Translated by Donald Nicholson-Smith, 1991, *The Production of Space*. Oxford: Basil Blackwell.)

Legarreta, Dorothy. 1984. *The Guernica Generation: Basque Refugee Children of the Spanish Civil War*. Nevada: University of Nevada Press.

Lévi-Strauss, Claude. 1966. *The Savage Mind*. Chicago: University of Chicago Press (translated by John Weightman and Doreen Weightman).

Lindqvist, Sven. 2001. *A History of Bombing*. London: Granta.

Lipe, William. 1984. "Value and meaning in cultural resources". In H. Cleere (ed.), *Approaches to the Archaeological Heritage*. Cambridge: Cambridge University Press, pp. 1–11.

Llorente Hernández, Ángel. 1992. *"Arte e ideología en la España de la postguerra (1939–1951)*. Unpublished doctoral thesis. Madrid: Universidad Complutense.

Llorente Hernández, Angel. 1993. "La Propaganda por la imagen y el arte en la postguerra. La Comisión de Estilo en las Conmemoraciones de la Patria y el Departamento de Plástica entre 1939–1945". In Tusell, Sueiro, Marín, and Casanova (eds), *El régimen de Franco (1936–1975). Política y Relaciones Exteriores*. Tomo I. Madrid: UNED.

Llorente Hernández, Ángel. 1995. *Arte e ideología en el franquismo (1936–1951)*. Madrid: Visor.

López Díaz, Jesús. 2003. "Vivienda social y Falange: ideario y construcciones en la década de los 40". *Scripta Nova: revista electrónica de geografía y ciencias sociales*, vol. VII, no. 146(024), 1 August. www.ub.es/geocrit/sn/sn-146(024).htm

López Gómez, J.M. 2006. "La actuación de la Dirección General de Regiones Devastadas en Aragón". In *Paisajes para después de una Guerra, 1936–1937*. Zaragoza: Diputación Provincial de Zaragoza.

López Mozo, Jerónimo. 2008. *El arquitecto y el relojero*. Alicante: Biblioteca Virtual Miguel de Cervantes.

Lorente-Fuentes, María. 2006. "Los 'escalvos' del régimen". In *El Franquismo año a año*, no. 20, 1960. Madrid: El Mundo.

Lyotard, Jean-François. 1984. *The Post-Modern Condition. A Report on Knowledge*. Manchester: Manchester University Press. Translation from the French by Geoff Bennington and Brian Massumi. (Original from c.1979, *La condition postmoderne : rapport sur le savoir*. Paris: De Minuit).

Madrazo, Mariano de. 1939. "El arte de la pintura. Realidad y orientaciones". *Domingo*, no. 105. Madrid, 19 February 1939.

Malraux, André. 1947. *Psychologie de l'art. Le musée imaginaire*. Geneva: Albert Skira Éditeur.

Mann, James G. 1937. "Spain's Art Treasures. Lost or Saved?" *The Listener*, 27 October.

Marín Muñoz, Antonio. 2007. *La reconstrucción de la provincia de Jaén bajo el Franquismo (1939–1957)*. Lopera: Marín Muñoz.

Marrero Cabrera, Juan Antonio. 2006. *Juegos de Guerra*. Madrid: Libro Hobby Club.

Marris, Peter. 1974. *Loss and Change*. Routledge and Kegan Paul: London.

Martín Gaite, Carmen. 1987. *Usos amorosos de la postguerra española*. Barcelona: Anagrama.

Martínez Cubells, José María. 1942. "Reconstrucción del pueblo de Guadarrama". *Reconstrucción*, no. 23 May, pp. 195–210.

Mazower, Mark. 2004. *Salonica, City of Ghosts: Christians, Muslims and Jews, 1430–1950*. London: HarperCollins.

McNally, Richard J. 2003. *Remembering Trauma*. Cambridge, MA; London: Belknap Press of Harvard University Press.

Mendelson, Jordana. 2005. *Documenting Spain: Artists Exhibition Culture and the Modern Nation 1929–1939*. Pennsylvania Park, PA: Pennsylvania State University Press.

Mendelson, Jordana. 2007. *Revistas y Guerra, 1936–1939*. Exh.cat., Madrid: Museo Nacional Centro Reina Sofía.

Menéndez Pidal, Luis. 1941. "Asturias : destrucciones habidas en sus monumentos durante el dominio marxista. Trabajos de protección y restauración efectuados o en proyecto". *Revista Nacional de Arquitectura*, no. 3; pp. 9–17, Madrid: Ministerio de la Gobernación, Dirección General de Arquitectura.

Menéndez Pidal, Luis. 1945. "Catedral de Oviedo: obras de restauración". *Reconstrucción*, no. 58 December, pp. 316–344.

Meskell, Lynn (ed). 1998. *Archaeology under Fire: Nationalism, Politics and Heritage in the Eastern Mediterranean and Middle East*. London: Routledge.

Miller, Daniel (ed.). 2005. *Materiality*. Durham, NC; London: Duke University Press.

Miller, Daniel, Mike Rowlands and Christopher Tilley. 1989. *Domination and Resistance*. London: Unwin Hyman.

Ministerio de Cultura. 1989. *Fuentes documentales para el estudio de la restauración de monumentos en España*. Madrid: Ministerio de Cultura.

Ministerio de Información y Turismo. 1939. "Ruta de Guerra del Norte", Archvio General de la Administración. AGA (03) 049.002 – 12028 – 22/44.

Moore, Niamh and Yvonne Whelan (eds*)*. 2007. *Heritage, Memory and the Politics of Identity*. Aldershot: Ashgate.

Mora, Pedro del la. 1938. "La destrucción del tesoro nacional por la revolución marxista". *Orientación Española*, Buenos Aires, no. 17, 15 May.

Moreno Torres, José. 1940. "Reconstrucción de España". *Reconstrucción*, no. 3, June–July 1940.

Moreno Torres, José. 1940. *Datos sobre la reconstrucción de España*. Madrid: Dirección General de Regiones Devastadas y Reparaciones.

Moreno Torres, José. 1944. *Speech made at the II Congreso de la Federación de Urbanismo y de la Vivienda*. Lisbon.

Moreno Torres, José. 1946. "El estado en la reconstrucción de las ciudades y pueblos de Españoles". Speech made at the Instituto de Estudios de Administración Local on 21 February. Madrid: Instituto de Estudios de Administración Local.

Morris, Benjamin. 2011. "'Not Just a Place': Cultural Heritage and the Environment". In Y.R. Isar, H.K. Anheier and D. Viejo-Rose (eds), *Heritage, Memory and Identity*, The Cultures and Globalization Series, vol. 4. London: Sage.

Müller, Jan-Werner (ed). 2002. *Memory and Power in Post-War Europe: Studies in the Presence of the Past*. Cambridge: Cambridge University Press.

Navarrete Martínez, Esperanza. 2001. *Comisiones provinciales y Comisión Central de Monumentos Histórico-Artísticos*. Parte 1. Madrid: Academia de Bellas Artes de San Fernando, Archivo.

Nicholas, Lynn H. 1994. *The Rape of Europa: The Fate of Europe's Treasures in the Third Reich and the Second World War*. London: Macmillan

Nietzsche, Friedrich. 1980. *On the Advantage and Disadvantage of History for Life*. Translated, with an introduction by Peter Preuss. Indianapolis; Cambridge: Hackett Publishing. Originally published in 1874 *Vom Nutzen und Nachteil der Historie für das Leben*.

Nora, Pierre (ed). 1984–1992. *Les Lieux de Mémoire*. (7 vols). Paris: Gallimard.

Nora, Pierre. 1989. "Between Memory and History: *Les Lieux de Mémoire*". *Representations*, no. 26, Special Issue: Memory and Counter-Memory. Spring, 1989: 7–24.

Nora, Pierre. 1996. *Realms of Memory: Rethinking the French Past. vol. 1: Conflicts and Divisions*. English-language edition with a foreword by Lawrence D. Kritzman, translated by Arthur Goldhammer. New York: Columbia University Press.

Nora, Pierre. 1997. *Realms of Memory: Rethinking the French Past. vol. 2: Traditions*. English-language edition with a foreword by Lawrence D. Kritzman, translated by Arthur Goldhammer. New York: Columbia University Press.

Nora, Pierre. 1998. *Realms of Memory: Rethinking the French Past. vol. 3: Symbols*. English-language edition with a foreword by Lawrence D. Kritzman, translated by Arthur Goldhammer. New York: Columbia University Press.

O'Keefe, Roger. 2006. *The Protection of Cultural Property in Armed Conflict*. New York; Cambridge: Cambridge University Press.

Oar-Arteta, Segundo. 2006. "La biografía de G.L. Steer de Nicholas Rankin". *Aldaba*, no. 140, March–April, pp. 20–24.

Onaindía, Alberto de. 1973. *Capítulos de mi vida. I: Hombre de paz en la guerra*. Buenos Aires: Ekin.

Onaindía, Santi. 1987. *Gernika*. Bilbao: Igarri. (poems by Telesforo Monzón and Mikel Zarate).

Ortega y Gasset, José. 2007. "En defensa de Unamuno". In *Obras Completas. Volume VII (1902–1925)* published by the Fundación José Ortega y Gasset in 2007: 388–392.

Ortega, Victor. 1976. *3,000 viejas fotos para la historia de Vizcaya. III, Guernica y el resto del señorío (desde 1850)*. Bilbao: La Gran Enciclopedia Vasca.

Ortego y Frias, Teogenes. 1975. *Guía de Numancia*. Madrid: Ministerio de Educación y Ciencia, Dirección General del Patrimonio Artístico y Cultural.

Ortíz, Carmen. 1999. "The Uses of Folklore by the Franco Regime". *Journal of American Folklore*, vol. 112, no. 446, Fall 1999.

Paliza Monduate, María Teresa. 1988. *Manuel María de Smith Ibarra: arquitecto 1879–1956*. Bilbao: Diputación Foral de Bizkaia.

Palmieri, Daniel. 2006. "When Neutrality Meets Ideology: The International Committee of the Red Cross, Franco and the Victims (1936–1965)". Paper given at the conference *War Without Limits: Spain 1936–1939 and Beyond*, University of Bristol, 17–19 July.

Paris, Roland. 2004. *At War's End: Building Peace after Civil Conflict*. Cambridge: Cambridge University Press.

Patterson, Ian. 2007. *Guernica and Total War*. Harvard, MA: Harvard University Press.

Payá López, Pedro. 2002. "Violencia, Legitimidad y poder local. La construcción simbólica de la dictadura Franquista en una comarca Alicantina. El Vinalopó Medio, 1939–1948". In *Pasado y Memoria, Revista de Historia Contemporánea*, no. 1. pp. 197–222.

Petrovic-Šteger, Maja. 2005. "Producing Bodies – Reproducing Persons: Thinking Human Remains in Postconflict Serbia". *Cambridge Anthropology*, 2005/2006, vol. XXV (3).

Pickering, William S.F. (ed.). 1975. *Durkheim on Religion: A Selection of Readings with Bibliographies*. London; Boston: Routledge & Kegan Paul.

Pollock, Griselda. 1988. *Vision and Difference. Femininity, Feminism and the Histories of Art*. London: Routledge

Pombo Angulo, Manuel. 1939. "De arte y de España" in *El Alcázar*, 14 February 1939.

Porlan, Albeto. 2004. *Las Cajas Españolas*. Spain: Drop a Star-Eurofícción-Iberautor. (Documentary film)

Powrie, Phil, Bruce Babington, Ann Davies, and Chris Perriam. 2007. *Carmen on Film: A Cultural History*. Bloomington: Indiana University Press.

Preston, Paul (ed.). 1976. *Spain in Crisis: The Evolution and Decline of the Franco Régime*. Sussex: Harvester Press.

Preston, Paul (ed.). 1984. *Revolution and War in Spain, 1931–1939*. London and New York: Methuen.

Preston, Paul. 1987. *The Triumph of Democracy in Spain*. New York: Methuen.

Preston, Paul. 1990. *The Politics of Revenge*. London: Unwin Hyman.

Preston, Paul. 2001. *El triunfo de la democracia en España*. Barcelona: Grijalbo.

Preston, Paul. 2003. *Las Tres Españas del 36*. Barcelona: Debolsillo.

Preston, Paul. 2007. "H. R. *Southworth*: una vida dedicada a la lucha". *Claves de razón práctica*, no. 173: 52–55.

Preston, Paul. 2008. *We Saw Spain Die: Foreign Correspondents in the Spanish Civil War*. London: Constable and Robinson.

Protected Art, 2005. Exh.cat., Geneva: Palais des Nations.

Przeworski, Adam. 1986. "Some problems in the study of the transition to democracy". In G. O'Donnell, P.C. Schmitter and L. Whitehead (eds), *Transitions from Authoritarian Rule: Comparative Perspectives*, vol. 3. Baltimore: Johns Hopkins University Press.

Quadra-Salcedo, Cayetana de la (ed.). 2001. *Villanueva de la Cañada. Historia de una reconstrucción*. Exh.cat., Centro Cultural La Despernada. 11 June–6 October 2001. Villanueva de la Cañada: Ayuntamiento de Villanueva de la Cañada, Concejalía de Cultura.

Raento, Paulina and Cameron J. Watson. 2000. "Gernika, Guernica, *Guernica*? Contested meanings of a Basque place". *Political Geography*, no. 19: 707–736.

Ramírez, Juan Antonio. 1981. "Imágenes para un pueblo. Connotaciones, arquetipos y concordancias en la iconografía de posguerra". In A. Bonet Correa (coord.), *Arte del franquismo*. Madrid: Ediciones Cátedra, Cuadernos Arte Cátedra.

Rankin, Nicholas. 2003. *Telegram From Guernica: The Extraordinary Life of George Steer, War Correspondent*. London: Faber and Faber.

Rankin, Nicholas. 2007. "A Case of Crusts: Fresh Memories of Guernica – Seventy years on". *Times Literary Supplement*, 6 July.

Reig Tapia, Alberto. 1987. "Guernica como símbolo". In M. Tuñón de Lara, J.P. Fusi, M. González Portilla, A. Reig Tapia et al. (eds), *La guerra civil en el País Vasco: 50 años después*. Bilbao: Universidad del País Vasco.

Reig Tapia, Alberto. 2006. *La cruzada de 1936: mito y memoria*. Madrid: Alianza.

Reina de la Muela, Diego.1944. *Ensayo sobre las directrices arquitectónicas de un estilo imperial*. Madrid: Ediciones Verdad.

Renau, Josep. 1937. "L'Organisation de la Défense du Patrimoine Artistique et Historique Espagnol Pendant la Guerre Civile". *Mousseion* (Office Internationale des Musées), vol. XI, nº 39–40, pp. 7–64. Paris: Institut International de Coopération Intellectuelle de la Société des Nations.

Renau, Josep. 1980. *Arte en peligro 1936–1939*. Valencia: Ayuntamiento de Valencia–Fernando Torres Editor.

Resina, Joan Ramón. 2000. *Dismembering the Dictatorship: The Politics of Memory in the Spanish Transition to Democracy*. Amsterdam: Rodopi.

Ricoeur, Paul. 1971. "The Model of the Text: Meaningful Action Considered as a Text". *Social Research*, vol. 38, no. 3, Autumn, pp. 529–562.

Ricouer, Paul. 2000. *La mémoire, l'histoire, l'oubli*. Paris: Seuil.

Ridao, José María. 1999. "La norma y el azar". *El País*, 19 November, p. 22.

Riegl, Alois. 1903. *Der moderne Denkmalkultus, sein Wesen, seine Entstehung* (Vienna). Translated by K. W. Forster and D. Ghirardo as "The Modern Cult of Monuments: Its Character and Its Origin". *Oppositions*, no. 25, Fall 1982: 21–51.

Rivera Blanco, Javier. 2008. "Consideración y fortuna del patrimonio tras la Guerra civil: destrucción y reconstrucción del patrimonio histórico (1936–1956). La restauración monumental". In Pinazo and Chapapría (eds), *Bajo el signo de la victoria. La conservación del patrimonio durante el primer Franquismo (1936–1958)*. Valencia: Pentagraf Editorial.

Rodríguez Fouz, Marta. 2004. *Los retos de la identidad: Jürgen Habermas y la memoria del Guernica*. Madrid: Centro de Investigaciones Sociológicas.

Rose, Gillian. 2001. *Visual Methodologies. An Introduction to the Interpretation of Visual Materials*. London: Sage.

Rose, Isadora. 1983. *Manuel Godoy Patrón de las Artes y Coleccionista*, 2 vols. Madrid: Universidad Complutense, vol. I, pp. 366–390.

Rose-de Viejo, Isadora. 2008. "El despojo de la colección de pinturas de Manuel Godoy durante la Guerra de la Independencia". In *Jornadas de Arte e Iconografía Sobre la Guerra de la Independencia*. Madrid: Fundación Universitaria Española.

Ross, Alex. 2008. *The Rest is Noise: Listening to the Twentieth Century*. London: Fourth Estate.

Rowlands, Michael. 1996. "Memory, Sacrifice and the Nation" in *New Formations*, no. 30, Winter 1996–97 dedicated to *Cultural Memory*. London: Lawrence & Wishart.

Rowlands, Michael. 2001. "Remembering to Forget: Sublimation as Sacrifice in War Memorials". In A. Forty and S. Küchler (eds), *The Art of Forgetting*. Oxford: Berg Publishers.

Ruiz Mantilla, Jesús. 2008. "Entrevista: La recuperación de la memoria histórica Laura García Lorca Sobrina del poeta y presidenta de la fundación". *El País*, 18 September.

Ruiz Mantilla, Jesús. 2008. "Los sobrinos de Lorca, divididos". *El País*, 18 October.

Ruíz Zapatero, Gonzalo and Jesús Álvarez-Sanchís. 1997. "El poder visual del pasado: prehistoria e imagen en los manuales escolares". In G. Mora and M. Díaz-Andreu (eds), *La Cristalización del Pasado: Génesis y desarrollo del marco institucional de la arqueología en España*. Málaga: Universidad de Málaga.

Ryle, Gilbert. 1968. "The Thinking of Thoughts: What is 'Le Penseur' Doing?" reprinted in 1971 (pp. 480–496) in *Collected Papers*, vol. 2, London: Hutchinson.

Salas Larrazabal, Jesús. 1987. *Guernica, Guernica*. Madrid: Ediciones Rialp SA.

Salgado-Araujo, Francisco Franco. 1976. *Mis conversaciones privadas con Franco*. Barcelona: Planeta.

Sambricio, Carlos. 1977. "'¡Que coman República!' Introducción a un estudio sobre la Reconstrucción en la España de la Postguerra" in *Cuadernos de arquitectura y urbanismo*. Special issue on the exhibition *Arquitectura para después de una guerra, 1939–1949*. Published by the Colegio Oficial de Arquitectos de Cataluña y Baleares. January 1977, pp. 21–32.

Sambricio, Carlos. 1987. "Madrid, 1941: Tercer año de la Victoria". In *Arquitectura en Regiones Devastadas*, exh.cat., Madrid: MOPU.

Sanchez Erauskin, Javier. 1994. *Por dios hacia el Imperio. Nacionalcatolicismo en las Vascongadas del primer franquismo (1936–1945)*. Donostia (San Sebastián): R&B Krisleu.

Sánchez Mazas, Rafael. 1939. "Herrera viviente". *Arriba*, 2 July.

Sánchez-Biosca, Vicente (ed). 2000. "La imagen del Alcázar en la mitología franquista". *Archivos de la Filmoteca*, no. 35, June 2000.

Sánchez-Biosca, Vicente. 2006. *Cine y Guerra Civil española: del mito a la memoria*. Madrid: Alianza.

Sánchez-Biosca, Vicente. 2008. "Arquitectura, lugar de memoria y mito. El Alcázar de Toledo o la imagen prendida". In Pinazo and Chapapría (eds), *Bajo el signo de la victoria*. Valencia: Pentagraf.

Sánchez-Silva, Carmen. 2007. "Toledo integra vida, trabajo y ocio". *El País,* Friday, 30 March 2007. 'Propiedades' Section, p. 3.

Sartre, Jean-Paul. 1963. "The Underprivileged Painter: Lapoujade". In *Essays in Aesthetics*. New York: Citadel Press. (Translated by Wade Baskin).

Saunders, Nicholas J. (ed). 2004. *Matters of Conflict: Material Culture, Memory and the First World War*. London: Routledge.

Schofield, John, William Johnson, and Colleen Beck (eds). 2002. *Matériel Culture: The Archaeology of Twentieth Century Conflict*, London: Routledge Press.

Schofield, John, Axel Klausmeier, and Louise Purbrick (eds). 2006. "Re-Mapping the Field: New Approaches in Conflict Archaeology". Berlin: West Kreuz Verlag.

Sebald, Winfried Georg. 2003. *On the natural history of destruction*. London: Hamish Hamilton. Translated from the German by Anthea Bell. (Originally published in 1999 as *Luftkreig und Literatur*. Munich: Hanser).

Sebastián García, Lorenzo. 1998. "Guernica, cuna del Gobierno Vasco. De símbolo foral a símbolo autonómico". In J.L. Granja and J.A. Etxaniz (eds), *Gernika y la*

Guerra Civil. Symposium: 60 aniversario del bombardeo de Gernika (1997). Gernika-Lumo: Gernikazarra bilduma.

Sección de Arquitectura, Servicios Técnicos de FET y de las JONS. 1939. *Ideas generales sobre el plan nacional de ordenación y reconstrucción*. Madrid: Servicios Técnicos de FET y de las JONS.

Semprún, Jorge. 1993. *Federico Sánchez se despide de ustedes*. Barcelona: Tusquets.

Shehadi, Nadeem. 2006. Lecture given at the conference *Archaeology in Conflict*, 10–12 November, Centre for Applied Archaeology, University College London.

Smirl, Lisa. 2008. "Building the Other, Constructing Ourselves: Spatial Dimensions of International Humanitarian Response". *International Political Sociology*, 2 (3): 236–53.

Southworth, Herbert Rutledge. 1977. *Guernica ! Guernica ! A Study of Journalism, Diplomacy, Propaganda and History*. Berkeley, California: California University Press. First published in French in 1975 as *La destruction de Guernica. Journalisme, diplomatie, propagande et histoire*. Paris: Ruedo Ibérico.

Stake, Robert. 1995. *The Art of Case Study Research: Perspectives on Practice*. Thousand Oaks; London: Sage.

Steer, George L. 1937. "The Tragedy of Guernica". *The London Times*, 27 April.

Steer, George L. 1938. *The Tree of Gernika: A Field Study in Modern War*. London: Hodder and Stoughton.

Stewart, Michael. 1939. "The destruction and preservation of works of art in Nationalist Spain". *The Burlington Magazine for Connoisseurs*, vol. 74, no. 431, February 1939: 72–76.

Stewart, Michael. 1939. Letter. *The Times* of 23 January.

Stig Sørensen, Marie Louise. 1987. "Material order and cultural classification". In Hodder (ed.), *The Archaeology of Contextual Meanings*. Cambridge: Cambridge University Press.

Stig Sørensen, Marie Louise. 1996. "The Fall of a nation. The birth of a subject: the national use of archaeology in nineteenth-century Denmark". In Diaz-Andreu and Champion (eds), *Nationalism and Archaeology in Europe*. London: UCL Press.

Storch de García, Jacobo. 2006. "La Dama de Elche regresa a casa". *Descubrir el arte*, no. 87, pp. 18–25.

Sturken, Marita. 2007. *Tourists of History: Memory, Kitsch, and Consumerism from Oklahoma City to Ground Zero*. Durham: Duke University Press.

Sueiro, Daniel and Bernardo Díaz Nosty. 1977. *Historia del Franquismo*. Madrid: Ediciones Sedemay.

Sueiro, Daniel. 1977. *La verdadera historia del Valle de los Caídos*. Madrid: Sedemay. (Republished in 1983 under the same title in Barcelona: Ed. Argos Vergara).

Sueiro, Daniel. 2006. *El Valle de los Caídos: Los secretos de la cripta franquista*. Madrid: La Esfera de los Libros.

Talón, Vicente. 1970. *Arde Guernica*. Madrid: San Martín.

Tarrats Bou, Francesc and Pilar Sada (eds). 2002. *Tàrraco en la fotografia del segle XX*. Tarragona: Generalitat de Catalunya.

Tesón, Nuria. 2006. "Esquelas de las dos Españas". *El País*, 10 September, p. 29.

Tilley, Christopher. 1994. *A Phenomenology of Landscape: Places, Paths and Monuments*. Oxford: Berg.

Toman, Jiri. 1994. *La protection des biens culturels en cas de conflit armé - Commentaire de la Convention de la Haye du 14 mai 1954*. Paris: UNESCO.

Toman, Jiri. 1996. *Protection of Cultural Property in the Event of Armed Conflict*. Ashgate: Dartmouth.

Tomás, Facundo. 2007. "*Guernica* according to Equipo Crónica". *Cuadernos del IVAM*, no. 10.

Tranche, Rafael and Vicente Sánchez-Biosca. 2005 (1993). *NO-DO: el tiempo y la memoria*. Madrid: Filmoteca Española, Instituto de la Cinematografía y de las Artes Audiovisuales, Ministerio de Cultura, 1993.

Treue, Wilhelm. 1960. *Art Plunder: The Fate of Works of Art in War, Revolution, and Peace*. London: Methuen. (Translated by Basil Creighton)

Tuñón de Lara, Manuel et al. (eds). 1986. *La Guerra Civil Española: 50 años después*. Barcelona: Labor.

Tuñón de Lara, Manuel et al. (eds). 1987. *La Guerra Civil en el País Vasco: 50 años después*. Bilbao: Servicio Editorial, Universidad del País Vasco.

Tuñón de Lara (ed.). 1987a. *Gernika: 50 años después (1937–1987). Nacionalismo, República, Guerra Civil*. Bilbao: Universidad del País Vasco.

Tusell, Javier. 2007. *Spain: From Dictatorship to Democracy, 1939 to the Present*. Oxford: Blackwell.

United Nations Development Programme. 2005. "Violent Conflict". *Human Development Report*, pp. 151–181.

Unsigned article. 1939. "En torno a la Biennale de Venecia". *Vértice,* no. 12.

Unsigned article. 1941. "Las obras de reconstrucción de Guernica", *Reconstrucción*, no. 15.

Unsigned article. 1943. "El director general de Regiones Devastadas entrega importantes obras al Gobernador civil y Jefe provincial". *El Correo Español*. 13 February.

Unsigned article. 1943. "Noticiario: Inauguración de edificios en Vizcaya". *Reconstrucción,* no. 31, March.

Unsigned. "Brunete: Reconstrucción del Hogar". *Reconstrucción*. no. 13 June.

Unsigned. 1937. "Guernica or the technique of lying". *Esprit*, June.

Unsigned. 1938. "El Martirio de las Obras de Arte". Special number of *L'Illustration* Paris, 5 February 1938.

Unsigned. 1943. "El director general de Regiones Devastadas entrega importantes obras al Gobernador civil y Jefe provincial". *El Correo Español*, 13 February.

Unsigned. 1978. "La comisión investigadora de Gernika solicitará al Gobierno español apertura de archivos, rectificación moral y una reparación simbólica". *Suplementos Deia*, Sunday 29 January, year 1, no. 201, Bilbao.

Unsigned. 1978. "La videncia del Gernika de Juan Larrea". *Suplementos Deia*, Sunday 29 January 1978, year 1, no. 201, Bilbao.

Unsigned. 1978. "Oteiza: la significación vasca del 'Guernica'". *Suplementos Deia*, Sunday 29 January, year 1, no. 201, Bilbao.

Unzueta, Patxo. 1981. "Culpan al Gobierno vasco de no apoyar la instalación del *Guernica* en Euskadi". *El País*, 22 November.

Ureña, Gabriel. 1979. *Arquitectura y urbanismo civil y militar en el periodo de la autarquía (1936–1945)*. Madrid: ISTMO.

Valverde, Fernando. 2007. "Los fusilados junto a García Lorca. Un libro recuerda al maestro y a los dos banderilleros fusilados junto al poeta". *El País*, 7 May.

Vázquez Astorga, Mónica. 2006. "Los monumentos a los caídos: ¿un patrimonio para la memoria o para el olvido?" *Anales de Historia del Arte*, vol. 16, pp. 285–314.

Vicent, Manuel. 2006. "Dueño del infierno". *El País Semanal*, no. 1.547, 21 May.

Viejo-Rose, Dacia. 2006. "Conflict and the Deliberate Destruction of Cultural Heritage". In R.Y. Isar and H.K. Anheier (eds.), *Conflicts and Tensions*, The Cultures and Globalization Series, vol. 1. London: Sage, pp. 102–116.

Vilar, Pierre. 1977. Foreword. In H.R. Southworth, *Guernica! Guernica! A Study of Journalism, Diplomacy, Propaganda, and History*. Berkeley: University of California Press, pp. ix–xvii.

Vizcaíno Casas, Fernando. 1996. *Los rojos no usaban sombrero: anecdotario menudo de la posguerra*. Barcelona: Editorial Planeta.

Winter, Jay and Emmanuel Sivan (eds). 1999. *War and Remembrance in the Twentieth Century*. Cambridge: Cambridge University Press.

Winter, Jay. 1995. *Sites of Memory, Sites of Mourning: Great War in European Cultural History*. Cambridge: Cambridge University Press.

World Bank. 1998. *The World Bank Annual Report*. The World Bank Group: the IBRD, IDA, IFC, ICSID and MIGA.

Young, James E. 1993. *The Texture of Memory: Holocaust Memorials and Meaning*. New Haven: Yale University Press.

Zabalgogeaskoa, Olga and Vincent von Jauregi. 1985. "La reconstrucción de Gernika. Entrevista con las cuatro personas de aquella época, que viven actualmente en Gernika". *Aldaba Gernikako Aldizkaria*, no. 13 January–February.

Zulaika, Joseba. 1998. "Tropics of Terror: From Guernica's 'Natives' to Global 'Terrorists'". *Social Identities*, vol. 4, no. 1.

Archival sources and official documents
(call numbers or dates for specific documents are referenced in the text)

Archive of Basque Nationalism, Sabino Arana Foundation, Artea

Archivo General de la Administración (AGA), Alcalá de Henares
  – Regiones Devastadas (RD) – (04) 081.001
  – Ministerio de Educación Nacional, Bellas Artes (BA) – (3) 055.003
  – Interior – (08)001.003

Archivo Histórico Nacional (AHN), Madrid
  – Causa General – 1332–2

Filmoteca Española, Madrid
  – No-Do newsreels

Centro Documental de la Memoria Histórica, Salamanca
  – Colección Carteles de la Guerra Civil

Centro de Investigaciones Sociológicas, Madrid
  – Encuestas
  – CIS. 2000. "25 años dspués". *Opiniones y Actitudes*, CIS, no. 36.

Consejería de Medio Ambiente y Ordenación del Territorio, Madrid
  – Planos

Biblioteca Nacional de España, Madrid
  – Cartografía

Gernika Peace Museum, Gernika
  – Archive of the Bombing

Gernika Gogoratuz, Gernika
  – Documentation Centre

Official documents:
Boletín Oficial del Estado (BOE)
Diario Oficial del País Vasco

Appendices

Appendix A
Key People in the Reconstruction of Spain, 1939–1959

Architects and art historians

Pedro Muguruza Otaño
1893–1952

Director General Directorate of Architecture.
Architect in charge of the *Valle de los Caídos* and *Ciudad Universitaria*.
Member of the *Comisión de Estilo en las Conmemoraciones de la Patria*.
General Commissioner of the *Servicio de Defensa del Patrimonio Artístico Nacional*.

Gonzalo de Cárdenas
1904–1954

Founder and editor of *Reconstrucción* and key figure in shaping the Directorate's projects as he was the Chief Architect of the Gabinete Técnico throughout the 10 years that Moreno Torres was Director General (1939–1951). Planner for Gernika's reconstruction.

Pedro Bidagor Lasarte
1906–1996

At the head of *Oficina técnica de la Junta de Reconstrucción de Madrid* (1939–1946); *Dirección técnica de la Comisaría de Ordenación de Madrid* (1945–1956); *Dirección General de Urbanismo y la Gerencia de Urbanización del Ministerio de la Vivienda* (1957–1969).

Fernando Chueca Goitia
1911–2004

Architect and art historian.
Catedrático of Art History of the Escuela Superior of Architecture of Madrid.
Chief architect conservator of Monuments Third Zone.
President of the *Instituto de España*, 1978–1986.
Dean of the *Colegio Oficial de Arquitectos de Madrid* 1999–2002.

Antonio Gallego Burín
1895–1961

Art Historian, Mayor of Granada.
Director, *Dirección General de Bellas Artes*, 1951–1961.
Commissioner of the *Servicio de Defensa del Patrimonio Artístico Nacional* (South).
Published in *Cuadernos del Arte*.

Luis Menéndez-Pidal
1896–1975

Architect, Commissioner of the *Servicio de Defensa del Patrimonio Artístico Nacional* (North).
Chief architect and conservator of Monuments First Zone (Leon, Oviedo, Zamora, Lugo, Pontevedra, Orense), 1941–75.
Published in *Revista Nacional de Arquitectura.*

Francisco Iñiguez
Almech
1901–1982

General Commissioner for *Patrimonio Artístico Nacional,* 1942–1962.
Chief architect, *Tesoro Artístico Nacional,* Second Zone (Burgos,Guipúzcoa, Vizcaya, Soria, Navarra, Zaragoza, Álava, Huesca, Logroño).

José Macián Pérez
1905–?

Director of *Regiones Devastadas,* 1951–1957.
Gobernador de Vizcaya, 1958–1961

Antonio Cámara Niño
1909–2007

Chief Architect in charge of projects of the *Dirección General de Regiones Devastadas.*
Director of the *Departamento de Reconstrucción de Edificios Oficiales* (from 1950).

Luis María de Gana
1911–1990

Chief Architect of *Regiones Devastadas* for the North.
Planner for Gernika's reconstruction.

Manuel María Smith
Ibarra
1879–1956

Prominent Basque architect, designed the project for the reconstruction of Gernika's main square.

Modesto López Otero
1885–1962

Head of the Madrid School of Architecture, 1923–1955, restorer.

Luis Gutiérrez-Soto
1896–1978

Architect (Key works of the period: *Ministerio del Aire*).

Luis Moya Blanco
1904–1990

Architect (Key works of the period: *Museo de América* and *Universidad Laboral de Gijón*).

Casto Fernández-Shaw
1896–1978

Architect, founded the architecture magazine *Cortijos y Rascacielos* and *Sociedad de Amigos de los Castillos.*

Jesús Rafael
Basterrechea
1908–2000

Architect, *Colegio de Arquitectos Vasco-Navarros,* designed Gernika's municipal market inaugurated 12 February 1943.

Key ideologues influencing the reconstruction

Ernesto Giménez
Caballero
1899–1988

Franco's speech writer, his *Arte y Estado* (1935) was influential in determining the policy towards the arts that the Franco regime would have.

Eugenio d'Ors
1881–1954

Philosopher, academic and influential Falangist ideologue. Director, *Dirección General de Bellas Artes*, 1938–39. Wrote an influential text *Teoría de los Estilos y Espejo de la Arquitectura* (1949).

Rafael Sánchez Mazas
1894–1966

Founding member of the Falange. Minister without Portfolio, 1939–1940 President of the *Patronato* of the Prado Museum (1951).

Agustín de Foxá
1903–1959

Diplomat and academic, co-founder of the Spanish Falange, "part of the cultural and literary offensive, dismantling the myths of the political opposition" (On-line dictionary of the Falange: www.plataforma2003.org/diccionario-falange/).

Víctor D'Ors
1909–1994

Architect. Wrote *Arquitectura y Humanismo* (Lábor, Madrid, 1967) as well as many articles on architecture in *Reconstrucción, Vértice,* and *RNA*. He designed the *Ciudad Azúl:* a model of the ideal Falangist city.

Diego Reina de la Muela
1910–1989

Architect, author of *Ensayo sobre las directrices arquitectónicas de un estilo imperial.*

Key political figures in the reconstruction

Ramon Serrano Súñer
1901–2003

Franco's brother-in-law. Minister of Interior, 1937–1940. Minister of the Press and Propaganda, 1939–40. Minister of Foreign Affairs, 1939–1942.

José Ibañez Martín
1896–1969

Minister of National Education, 1939–1951.

José Moreno Torres
1900–?

Dir DG *Regiones Devastadas,* 1939–1951. Mayor of Madrid, 1946–1952.

Joaquín Benjumea
Burín
1878–1963

Dir DG *Regiones Devastadas,* 1938–1939. Minister of Agriculture and Work, 1939–1941. Minister of Finance, 1941–1942.

Juan de Contreras y López de Ayala, Marqués de Lozoya 1893–1978

Historian and art critic, infuential in the world of heritage and the arts.
Director, *Dirección General de Bellas Artes*, 1939–1951.
Founder and first President of the *Asociación Española de Amigos de los Castillos* (1952–1953); Director of the *Academia Española de Bellas Artes de Roma*, 1952–57; President of the *Real Academia de Bellas Artes de San Fernando*, 1972–1978.

Rodrigo Vivar Téllez 1906–?

Gobernador Civil and *Jefe provincial del Movimiento* for Vizcaya, 1942–1944
Vice-secretary General of the *Movimiento*, 1944.

Appendix B
The Alcázar of Toledo: Building as Martyr

Even before the war of 1936–39, the history of the Alcázar of Toledo included several cycles of destruction and reconstruction. Toledo had been the capital of Spain under the Visigoths and El Alcázar was a fortress in Roman, Visigothic and Arab periods, undergoing cycles of destruction and repair. Charles V had it rebuilt in 1535 when he made Toledo the capital of Spain and of his Empire, living in it for a period. It was destroyed in 1710 during the War of Succession and subsequently rebuilt by Charles III of Spain to be used as a *Casa de Caridad*. It was burned down by Napoleonic troops in 1810 and rebuilt in 1882 when it became the General Military Academy (*Academia General Militar*). In 1887 it burned down again as the result of an accidental fire but was soon rebuilt, remaining a military academy. All of this history was soon overshadowed by the events of the civil war.

Toledo was already a propaganda hot spot of the civil war because of the high percentage of religious art and ecclesiastical buildings in the city, home to numerous treasures of built and movable heritage, including masterpieces by El Greco. This rich symbolic material was enhanced by the siege and destruction of the Alcázar. From 21 July to 28 September 1936 the Alcázar was the site of a fierce battle when the Nationalist General Moscardó, holed up inside with several hundred civilians and soldiers, fought off the Republican soldiers trying to seize it. As a result of this siege the building was almost entirely destroyed, and in February 1937 it was declared a ruin. There are two central elements to the symbolism of the Alcázar's destruction that reflect a major dynamic of the conflict: highlighting the heroism and self-sacrifice of one side versus the 'godless' barbarity of the other. At the heart of the legend is the story of how General Moscardó's son was taken prisoner by the Republican army. Father and son were put in touch in a telephone conversation during which, the legend says, upon hearing that his son would be shot if he did not surrender the father ordered his son to die proudly for Spain. This story was a recurrent theme in popular culture and inspired a movie *Sin novedad en el Alcázar* (Dir. Augusto Genina, 1941) which was filmed in the building's courtyard.

The *Alcázar de Toledo* has not stopped changing; in 2008 it was still undergoing construction work. A Decree of 1965 ordered the transfer of the Military Museum (*Museo del Ejército*) from Madrid to the Alcázar, where it was to be named *Museo del Asedio* – Museum of the Siege. However, only parts of the Military Museum's collections were actually transferred and the name was changed back in 1987. Only in recent years have definitive moves been made to send the rest of the collection to Toledo. In 2007 the Madrid site of the military museum was closed, its building to be refurbished for the Prado, and its collection was transferred to the Alcázar. The Franco reconstruction of the site was successful in turning it into an icon of the city. The architect Jean Nouvel revealed that his designs for a new neighbourhood outside the historic centre sought to "reproduce an icon of the city such as is the Alcázar" (Sánchez-Silva, *El País,* 30 March 2007).

Appendix C
The Sagrado Corazón de Jesús: The Monument's Symbolic Breakdown

Cerro de los Ángeles reconstructed, 1965 (AGA: 382F1418a).

Historical figures

Osius of Córdoba 258–357	Bishop of Cordoba, President of the first Council of Nicaea (325), author of the "Nicene Creed".
Don Pelayo 699–737	Ruler of Asturias, initiator of the *Reconquista*.
Isabel la Católica 1451–1504	Queen of Castile (of the Catholic Kings).
Columbus 1451–1506	Navigator, explorer.
Hernán Cortés 1485–1547	Conquistador of Mexico.
Diego Laínez 1512–1565	Jesuit priest, theologian of the Pope Paul III during the Council of Trent (1563–64).
Don Juan de Austria 1547–1578	Military commander (and illegitimate son of Charles I of Spain and Holy Roman Emperor Charles V) lead the naval victory at the Battle of Lepanto (1571).
Junípero Serra 1713–1784	Franciscan missionary.

Padre Polanco
1881–1939

Bishop, 'martyr' of the siege of Teruel after which he was made prisoner by the Republic in January 1938 and executed a year later.

Saints

Saint Agustine of Hippo
354–430

Saint Francis of Assisi
1181–1226

Saint Gertrude
1256–1302

Saint Theresa of Ávila
1515–1582

Santa Margarita María de Alacoque
1647–1690

Bernardo de Hoyos
1711–1735

Allegorical figures

Moral value
Charity

Allegorical representation in statuary, nun surrounded by children.

Virtue

Woman with flowers and girl in first communion robes.

Love

Peasant couple with a small child in their arms.

Penitence and
Repentance

Kneeling man in rags and shoeless.

Information taken from the official website of the *Cerro de los Ángeles*: www.cerrodelos-angeles.es The monument was built at the *Cerro de los Ángeles*, the geographic centre of the Iberian peninsula.

Appendix D
Re-codifying Space in Madrid : The Moncloa and the Ciudad Universitaria

The *Ciudad Universitaria*, or University City, was founded in 1927 through a royal decree from Alfonso XIII, who wanted Madrid to have university facilities on a par with the universities of other European capitals. (The first university of Madrid, dating from 1499, was located in Alcalá de Henares. When it was first moved to the city of Madrid proper, in 1836, it was housed in a variety of public buildings and in the private homes of wealthy families.) By the time the first faculty buildings were ready to be opened, the King had been deposed and they were inaugurated in 1933 by the President of the Second Republic, Manuel Azaña. The Republic continued construction on the University City, which became one of its crowning glories, not only for the innovation and modernity of the architecture, planning and design but also for the professors who taught there: José Ortega y Gasset, Julián Besteiro, and Santiago Ramón y Cajal, and the students and intellectuals that passed through it including many of the 'Generation of 27': Federico García Lorca, Luis Buñuel, Dámaso Alonso, Julián Marías. Proof that the renewed university and its campus were advanced for the time is that its first graduating class had over 40 percent female students.

During the war the University was one of the major Madrid frontlines, and was a key point in the siege of Madrid. There are many colourful accounts by the International Brigades that took part in this defence of Madrid, describing their use of books to build barricades and to keep themselves entertained between bouts of fighting. By the end of the war, however, over 40 percent of the University City had been entirely destroyed.

The importance and success of the *Ciudad Universitaria* during the Republic and its protagonism in the battle for Madrid meant that its reconstruction was of particular importance to the regime. On 12 October 1943, coinciding with the *Día de la Hispanidad* and the *Fiesta de la Raza*, the restored buildings of several faculties at the University were inaugurated. The symbolism of the date chosen, together with the grandiose display of ephemeral architecture put up for the occasion, indicate its importance. A provisional triumphal arch was erected at the Moncloa on the same location where the victory arch was later built. On the

Project developed in 1946 by Modesto López Otero; once built, the equestrian statue of Franco was never placed there. Built in 1953–56, a mausoleum was planned and built just behind the monument but was never used as such. Arco de la Victoria Moncloa, Madrid (photo Archivo Alfonso: AGA03-082-F1426 sobre 6). (© DACS 2010.)

esplanade in front of the Faculty of Medicine, a provisional 'Monument to the Fallen' was erected consisting of an altar and a cross 18 meters high. In front of it the tribune for Franco and other dignitaries was built, decorated with the *Victor* anagram (Bonet Correa 1996: 156). This rebuilding of the university, and the stamping on it of the new regime's symbols — aside from flags, anagrams, crosses and emblems the site was to be planted full of cypresses— was accompanied by a purge of the teaching staff and a restructuring of courses around the twin ideological pillars of Church and Falange. The reconstruction of buildings and pedagogical content was lead by José Ibáñez Martín (Minister of Education, 1939–1951).

Appendix E
Accounts, Reactions and Interpretations of the Bombing

First-hand accounts

*Guernica, town of 5000 inhabitants, literally razed to the
ground. (. . .) The 250 kgs knocked down a quantity of houses
and destroyed the water supply. So the incendiary bombs had
time to spread and work effectively. (. . .) As it was, just a
complete technical success for our 250s and the EC.B.Is.*
Wolfram von Richthofen, commander of the Condor
Legion (from his diary)

*For more than three hours wave after wave of bombers came,
and planes with incendiary bombs, and single machines that
came down to a height of about 200 meters to machine-gun the
poor people who were fleeing in terror.*
Basque priest Alberto Onaindía
(from his autobiography), 1973

Reactions

*Before God and History, which will eventually judge us all,
I hereby state that for three and a half hours German planes
bombed the defenceless civilian population of Gernika with
unprecedented viciousness.*
Lehendakari Aguirre,
27th April 1937, Radio Bilbao broadcast

*Aguirre is lying. We have respected Guernica as we respect
everything Spanish.*
Franco, *ABC-Edición de Andalucía,* 29th April 1937

*Guernica has now come under the control of the Ejército
Nacional. Better said, what is left of Guernica, the town that the
red hordes in sinister conspiracy with the separatists of Aguirre
have turned into ruins. (. . .) Guernica has been destroyed by the
reds at the service of the Basque separatists.*
ABC – Edición de Andalucía, 30th April 1937, p. 6

You have heard from incontrovertible sources how Guernica was destroyed by bombing and by fire. You have also heard what Guernica represents to the Basques and to the entire world. It is now the moment to declare with energy and decision who it was that destroyed Guernica.

Jesús María de Leizaola, Basque Minister of Justice and Education, 'Radio Euzkadi', 4 May 1937

First pictures from the Basque Republic of the Holy City of Guernica, scene of the most terrible air raid our modern history can yet boast.

Gaumont newsreel released on 6th May 1937 in British cinemas

Yesterday it was Durango, today it has been Guernica. Guernica! Our Guernica! The sanctuary of the Basque people, the sacred place where profoundly human laws were elaborated. Guernica has been razed. There is a desire to annihilate even the memory of our old liberties. Brothers of Navarre and of Euzkadi: a barbaric wave wants to drown all of our traditions, all the ancestral virtues of our great people.

Dolores Ibárruri, La Pasionaria, special radio programme of *Socorro Rojo*, 7 May 1937

Interpretations of why Gernika was bombed

Several people that I spoke with during my research trips to Gernika coincided in their conviction that the town was targeted because of its symbolic rather than strategic nature. Through these conversations I was able to begin identifying some of the myths and interpretations related to the bombing of Gernika and its subsequent reconstruction.

"For a psychological effect, the Tree, essence of Basqueness, of our being."
"They bombed to demoralize the Basques."
"They bombed it because it was the symbol of the Basques, because the Casa de Juntas was there."
"Since we have always been proud of what is Basque, to distance and punish us."

Interpretations of people who lived through the bombing (Cava Mesa 1996: 257–259)

As the Mayor of Guernica I affirm before the world as to the truth, the whole truth, and nothing but the truth of the tragedy of Guernica' (. . .) By fire Guernica has been razed to the ground

but Guernica lives on. Its sacred tree will blossom each springtime, it will call back its children; they will build their homes once more; the streets will be gay and happy and from their churches shall again rise the sound of their songs and prayers. Guernica, symbol of Basque liberty, symbol, too, henceforward of the ferocity of international fascism, lives on because Euzkadi lives on.
José de Labauria, mayor of Gernika,
'Radio Euzkadi', 4 May 1937

Guernica is not the only village that has disappeared under the destruction of fire and case shot; it is joined by a chain of misfortune to many other Basque villages. Nevertheless, it is the wanton destruction of Guernica and all that such destruction stands for, that has shaken with fright the whole world.
Bonifacio de Echegaray, member of the Academy
for Basque Studies, 'Radio Euzkadi', 4 May 1937

¡Guernica! Word that in only one day has crossed all the continents. You were a symbol and a horrendous crime had to be committed, this our great sacrifice, so that, like a phoenix, was reborn from your very ruins the sacred Tree, more vigorous than ever, and with it the conscience and being of a free nation: Euzkadi.
Sosa Barrenechea, Delegate of the Basque Government
to Madrid, radio programme of *Socorro Rojo*, 7 May 1937

The reasons for the study of Guernica lie in that it was the first city almost totally destroyed, and very importantly, Guernica is the cradle of the Basque Country.
La Construction Moderne, no. 27, 5 June 1938: 451

From the very first day Guernica became a symbolic event, owing to its unexpected repercussions (. . .) In a few days the very name of Guernica had become a more burning subject than the flames of its conflagration. And this is indeed the first distinctive aspect of a symbolic event.
Pierre Vilar's introduction to Southworth 1977: xi

It was in the Basque sacred city of Guernica, however, that the savagery of aerial bombardment of civilians was raised to its highest level, and the name of Guernica has become virtually synonymous with the atrocities of war since the attack.
Clark 1979: 70

For Basques, Guernica symbolised the historical legitimacy of their centuries-old popular democracy, the place where the Spanish monarchs had come since the early Middle Ages to swear under an oak tree a solemn oath to uphold Basque common law. Thus its bombardment represents a genocidal moment, the first in the Holocaust's 'architecture of atrocity' that would soon annihilate Jews, gypsies, homosexuals, and other marginal groups.

Zulaika 1998: 93

On Monday, 26 April 1937, a busy market day, the town became the experimental site of the second aerial bombardment of the Spanish Civil War targeted specifically against Basque civilians.(. . .) For many Basques, Gernika is the symbol of intervention and destruction caused by the Other.

Raento and Watson 2000: 714

Franco deliberately targeted Gernika because of its cultural significance to the Basque people, for whom the town symbolized democracy and autonomy. In attacking this town, which held no military or strategic significance, Franco aimed to destroy the symbolic centre of Basque self-rule and crush his enemy's morale.

Kirschbaum and Sideroff 2005: 159

Appendix F
Illustrative Selection of Works of Art Inspired by the Bombing of Gernika

Guernica, 1937, Spain, Socorro Rojo Internacional, film directed by José Fogués.

Guernika, 1937 film, Spain and France (Aux secours des enfants d'Euzkadi).

Guernica, 1937, Spain, film, Government of Euzkadi for Film Popular, Dir. José María Beltrán.

Guernica, 1937, Spain, film, production and Direction by Nemesio Manuel Sobrevilla.

Victoire de Guernica, 1938, poem by Paul Eluard.

Guernica, c. 1938, poem by A.S. Knowland.

From a Painting by Picasso, c. 1938, poem by Albert Brown.

Die Kinder von Gernika, 1939, novel by Herman Kestern (Amsterdam: Allert de Lange).

Picasso: for Guernica, 1939, poem by J.F. Hendry.

Sacrificio de Guernica, 1943, poem by León Felipe.

Guernica, 1949, USA, Museum of Modern Art NY, film directed by Robert J. Flaherty.

Guernica, 1950, film France, Dir. Alain Resnais and Robert Hessens, Pantheón Production.

Guernica: en Billedfantasi Inspireret af Picassos Billede, c. 1950, Denmark. Helge Ernst and Fritz Ostergren, Directors and Producers.

Victoire de Guernica, 1965, play by Luigi Nono based on Eluard's poem.

Gernika, 1966, cantata for txistu (Basque wind instrument) and voice by Pablo Sorozabal.

In Guernica, 1968, song by Joan Baez lyrics by Norman Roste.

El otro arbol de Guernica, 1969, Spain, Dir. Pedro Lazaga. Pedro Masó P.C./C.B. Films.

L'Arbre de Guernica, 1975. Babylone Films, Paris and CI.LE Roma, film Dir. Fernando Arrabal.

Guernika Arde, 1979, Spain, film Dir. Francesc Ribera.

Guernica – the Making of a Myth, 1980, BBC and Open University, film Dir. Anthony Aldgate.

Gernika, 1982, Hungary. Film directed by Ferenc Kosa.

A los cuatro vientos 'Lauxaeta', 1987, film directed by José A. Zorrilla.

Gernika, 1990, oratorio by Gorka Sierra.

1937, Apirilak 26, poem by Mikel Zarate.

Gernika, poem about the bombing by Telesforo Monzón (Basque Interior Minister).

En el aniversario de Gernika, poem by Oteiza.

In the titles of these works one can observe the use of the different spellings for Gernika. Two of these works, the 1949 film by the MOMA and the Danish film from 1950, are dedicated to Picasso's painting, and the Resnais film from 1950 uses illustrations from Picasso's sketches and painting as well as Eluard's poem to make an anti-war statement. Ian Patterson (2007: 32) identifies a number of plays, films and movies produced in the US that were influenced by the bombing: Barrie Stavis' 1939 play *Refuge*; Norman Corwin's 1939 *They Fly Through the Air With the Greatest Ease*; Archibald MacLeish's verse play of 1938 *Air Raid*; and Orson Welles' 1938 *War of the Worlds*.

Appendix G
Evolution of Gernika's Monument-scape

Monument to Peace *Gure Aitaren Etxea*	Eduardo Chillida, commissioned in 1987 on the occasion of the 50th anniversary and inaugurated on 27 April 1988.
Peace Research Centre *Gernika Gogoratuz*	In 1987 the Basque Government decided to create this research centre. Its name means 'Gernika remembers'.
Large Figure in a Shelter	This sculpture was created in 1986, and is one of Moore's last works. He had visited Gernika before the war. It was inaugurated on 7 July 1990.
Estela	By Jesús Aldama.
Gernika Peace Museum	Named as such in 2003.
Park of the Peoples of Europe	Created in October 1991 the park is landscaped to exemplify the four types of ecosystems of Euzkadi. The sculptures of Chillida and Moore are located in a specially designated part of the park.
Astelehena Jai	In 1991 Eduardo Gordo presented the winning entry of a contest run by the Town Hall of Gernika to render homage to the Basque agrarian sector; situated in the new market square.
Mausoleum	Built in the cemetery in 1994.
Ceramic tile mural of Picasso's *Guernica*	Created by *Cerámicas Queralt* in 1994 and includes the legend "*Guernica* Gernikara".

Monumento Homenaje al Batallón Gernika	This monument by Jesús Torre was installed in 1995 and is in homage to the *gudaris* who participated in the liberation of France in WWII. The dedication reads: *Gernika Gudarostean Gorazarrea* (Homage to the Gernika Battalion). The intention of the local government of Gernika-Lumo was to "honour a memory".
Marimeta	Monument by Jon Iturrarte Artola on Basque symbols – the deity 'Mari' and a haycock/hayrick – as well as the Tree, inaugurated in 1997.
Bust of George Lowther Steer	Inaugurated on the occasion of the anniversary of 2006.

Appendix H
Statement by German President Roman Herzog

Greeting on the occasion of a reception in the Centre for Peace Research Gernika Gogoratuz on 27th April 1997 offered to the surviving witnesses of the bombardment of Gernika

On the 26th of April 1937 Gernika was victim of an aerial attack by a squadron of the Condor Legion that converted the name of this city into an emblem of belligerence that took the undefended population by surprise, making it victim of the greatest atrocities. Since that day Gernika and the human suffering that this name symbolizes form part of the collective memory of our peoples.

Sixty years after the bombing new generations have grown up. But as victims of the bombing you still carry inscribed in your hearts the memory of that day and its consequences. For you is still present what to most of us is past though we should all feel saddened for the suffering that fell on Gernika.

I want to acknowledge that past and expressly recognize the culpability of the German planes involved. I address you as survivors of the attack and witnesses of the horror my message of condolence and mourning.

I evoke the memory of those persons for whom that day in Gernika shattered the joy of life, destroyed their families, destroyed their homes, and stole their community. I join you in mourning for the dead and wounded. I offer to you, who still carry the wounds of the past, my open hand in a plea for reconciliation.

(Reproduced in Michael Kesper, *Gernika y Alemania. Historia de una reconciliación*, 1998. Gernika: Gernika Gogoratuz. p. 85 and *Aldaba*, no. 87, May–June 1997: 29.)

Appendix I
Chronology of the Tree of Gernika

XIV	1742	1780	1811	1858	1892	1979	2004	2005
Father Tree planted		Father Tree dies (trunk conserved in a small temple)						
	Old Tree planted		Old Tree dies					
				Foral Tree planted	(survives the bombing, becomes infected with a fungus in 1991, stops growing new shoots)		Foral Tree dies	
						Young tree planted	(This tree feared infected, does not become replacement)	
								New Foral Tree planted

Index